Public Sociology

New Social Formations
Series Editor:
Charles Lemert, Wesleyan University

Public Sociology

From Social Facts to Literary Acts

Second Edition

BEN AGGER

ROWMAN & LITTLEFIELD PUBLISHERS, INC.
Lanham • Boulder • New York • Toronto • Plymouth, UK

ROWMAN & LITTLEFIELD PUBLISHERS, INC.

Published in the United States of America
by Rowman & Littlefield Publishers, Inc.
A wholly owned subsidiary of The Rowman & Littlefield Publishing Group, Inc.
4501 Forbes Boulevard, Suite 200, Lanham, Maryland 20706
www.rowmanlittlefield.com

Estover Road
Plymouth PL6 7PY
United Kingdom

British Library Cataloguing in Publication Information Available

Library of Congress Cataloging-in-Publication Data:
Agger, Ben.
  From social facts to literary acts / Ben Agger. — 2nd ed.
    p. cm. — (New social formations)
  Includes bibliographical references and index.
  ISBN-13: 978-0-7425-4105-4 (cloth : alk. paper)
  ISBN-10: 0-7425-4105-3 (cloth : alk. paper)
  ISBN-13: 978-0-7425-4106-1 (pbk. : alk. paper)
  ISBN-10: 0-7425-4106-1 (pbk. : alk. paper)
  1. Sociology—Methodology. 2. Sociology—Authorship. I. Title.
  HM511.A527 2007
  301.01—dc22   2006100814

Printed in the United States of America

♾ ™The paper used in this publication meets the minimum requirements of American
National Standard for Information Sciences—Permanence of Paper for Printed Library
Materials, ANSI/NISO Z39.48–1992.

For Sarah, Oliver, and Buddy the Cat

Contents

Series Editor's Foreword

The Necessary Truth-Telling
of a Public Sociology

Charles Lemert

Who was the first sociologist ever? This question is the basis for an entertaining, if endless, parlor game played by professional sociologists in their rare moments of leisure. The game is fun because there are no wrong answers. As a result, the question inspires original, even perverse competition.

Let me illustrate. One might begin the game with: The first real sociologist was Lycurgus of Sparta. He, after all, was the social legislator who laid down the laws and customs of Sparta in the seventh century B.C.E. Since Sparta has entered common language as the epitome of disciplined social order, the nomination makes sense. Someone else might counter with: Well, the problem with Lycurgus is that hardly anyone is convinced that he was really a he, a real person. Wasn't he more a mythic Spartan afterthought? Then another might add: Besides which, if Lycurgus, why not Hammurabi, the sixth king of Old Babylon? He ruled a good millennium before Sparta was organized. Hardly anyone doubts there was a real king of that name. Still another player can say: Listen, the eighteenth century B.C.E. was a long time ago, and the recent rulers of New Babylon (now Iraq) seem to have been a little too spartan in their discipline. And another: Well, come to think of it, if you prefer a candidate closer to cultural home (not a bad idea because it is hard to remember the names of the Ancient Chinese sages and legislators), why not Kleisthenes of Athens? Kleisthenes was, apparently, real enough and a very effective social thinker. It was he who in 508 B.C.E. laid down the principles of radical Athenian democracy, many of which survive in our time (though admittedly in less radical form). Then, again, someone adds: Why Kleisthenes, whose name is hard to pronounce, when Plato is better known and is just as good a candidate?

You see how the game is played. Start with Lycurgus, someone counters with Hammurabi, then Kleisthenes, or Plato, or one of the Sulla kings on the Korean peninsula—and you're off and running. From Plato of Athens to Ezekiel of Jerusalem (and involuntarily of Babylon), to Paul of Tarsus, to Tertullian of Carthage, to Augustine of Hippo. Ultimately one gets to Charles, the Baron of Montesquieu. But somewhere late in the sixteenth century, the game speeds up because, for reasons hard to figure out, the practice of naming people according to their hometowns disappears. The more modern names spring more easily to mind: Hobbes, Rousseau, Comte, Saint-Simon (as though the place name were a real name), even Kant, perhaps Hegel. Finally we are down to recent times. But still the list continues: If Marx, why not Hegel, or, of course, Spencer?

Then, somewhere around Spencer, the game slows to a walk. Up to that point the play is lively because, as I illustrate, any smart-ass can toss out a name in the well-founded hope that others wouldn't know for sure who he's talking about. It is a little like Scrabble without the blocks and extra points for Zs and Qs. But, as I say, the game changes once one gets to the late nineteenth century. All the tension dissipates. With Durkheim and Weber, or Park and Simmel, players fall away because it becomes foolish to argue. Obviously, after Durkheim in particular, the word "sociologist" comes to denote very specific characters. The shell game ends when the disciplinary cops turn the block. True, about that time there were a few marginal types like Simmel or Du Bois who weren't very good at getting "real" sociologists to recognize them as one of their own. Still, somewhere between 1892 and 1894, the Chicago men and Durkheim's did such a good job of making sociology an academic profession that the name-the-first-sociologist game gets really boring. As chess players can't get excited about checkers, so players of this game end up diffidently jumping each other's men with women and African-Americans and others—with, that is, names of those who are off the usual lists. Admittedly this is very much a guy's game. Women, in my experience, get far less excited by lists of people who came in first. Still, the game can be fun up to a point.

But what is the point illustrated by the game itself? Simply this: Up to Durkheim or so, all the names one might nominate for first-sociologist-ever are the names of the freelancers. Or, if not exactly freelancers, people who earned their keep by means having little, usually nothing, to do with the practice of sociology. They were not professional sociologists in any obvious way. Some were philosophers; others were kings or barons; a few were impoverished prophets; some, tentmakers. But none was paid expressly for doing sociology. Hence, an underlying conundrum:

Sociology is important business. It is the work by which people figure out what's going on in their relations with others. Since hardly anyone lives alone, there are few things more important to figure out. This is why one can always dredge up some name from any town or kingdom of a somebody who had a reasonably convincing idea of what was going on in that particular domain. Is there any reasonable way to disagree with this proposition? I suppose. Since, in the last century or so, sociologists have become more edgy and cantankerous than, say, Kleisthenes was, I am sure that someone out there is ready to complain about this statement. "That's just too simple-minded, Charles." Perhaps it is. I don't care if others have a different way to say it. But I am interested in the fact that, beginning with Durkheim and the Chicago people, being "too simple" became an ever more contemptuous way to describe one's definition of what sociology is.

Why is this? I think the answer may be that when sociologists started to get paid for practicing their craft they quite naturally wanted to establish standards. You can't have just anybody practicing sociology any more than anybody off the streets should do brain surgery. Sounds right, except that sociology requires fewer hard-to-acquire skills than brain surgery—or so it seems. I've never tried brain surgery. But I have done more or less reputable sociology for a long while. The longer I do it, the simpler it seems.

I'm in the minority on this. But I am not alone. I once heard Arthur Stinchcombe say that, on average, it took about six weeks to become an expert in any of the major subspecialties of sociology. Since no one I know is as smart as Stinchcombe, let's say it takes eight weeks. That's about it. And why not? Sociologists begin learning their trade with an enormous advantage over beginners at brain surgery. I actually once knew what the *medulla oblongata* was and where it is to be found. But I have long since forgotten the details, and that's all I ever really knew about brains. By contrast, let's take families. To date, like most people I know I have lived in several of them, observed many others at closer range than I wanted to, and heard from my friends about countless more. I knew about families before I even knew I had a brain.

So why then don't more people become sociologists of the family? Or, better yet, sociologists of law? Based on recent recruiting experience in my department, the latter are very hard to find and much in demand because nearly everyone is being sued these days (and, according to rumor, the rest are in jail, or soon will be). I think the answer may have less to do with "the standards of excellence" professionals of all kinds are always talking about than about standards of living.

Where I live there is an extraordinary excess of Episcopal priests. Why this is, I am not sure; but it is. As a result, it is very difficult for all those priests to find paid work. This is largely because the number of Episcopalians in need of priestly care is declining at a precipitous rate. There were 50 percent fewer Episcopalians in America in 1990 than there were in 1980. I realize that if the number halves every ten years there will always remain some faction of Episcopalians in need of ministry. Still, the decline is alarming to those already in the priesthood. As a result, the Episcopal church has wonderfully lofty "standards of excellence," and few of those who have been struck by the idea that they ought to be a priest get very far when they try to convince a local bishop. In Connecticut, those put off by the keepers of the keys end up spending their time hanging around Yale Divinity School, looking for an opening somewhere. Now, think about it. Is it not likely that the high standards attached to work as an Episcopal minister have less to do with "excellence" (which, even among Episcopalians, is thought to be God's business) than with the labor market for that kind of work? I am told, by contrast, that it is relatively easy to become a regular minister among Jehovah's Witnesses—a sect that is growing at a rate five times the rate at which Episcopalians are halving themselves.

You get my point. If just anybody who knew something about families wanted to become a sociologist of the family, pretty soon the labor market in that trade would be glutted. You just can't let everyone in. This is why it is a matter of ample economic significance for professionals to regulate their standards, which regulation always begins with polite dismissal of candidates whose view of their expertise is "too simple."

Don't get me wrong. We need professionals and they must meet standards. But somewhere along the scale of the professions currently being practiced—somewhere between brain surgeons, on the high end, and say undertakers, on the low end—there is a point at which the standards imposed have more to do with the job market for those already practicing than with the technical accomplishment of those seeking a job in it. I am not prepared to say that sociology ought not to be a profession. Nor do I believe that brain surgeons are beyond worry over about their economic well-being. But every one knows that professionals, whatever good they do, are much like any other income-earning occupation. Just look at what fluoride has done to orthodontia—once a very lucrative trade. Since fluoride began to put unspecialized dentists out of the business of filling cavities, many generalists of the trade have gone back to school to learn orthodontia. As a result, generalists in pediatric dentistry are able to charge a fancy fee for straightening the teeth of kids who only have to drink the local water to prevent decay. The orthodontists, hence, are left to scramble for a new niche like implant surgery. On it goes.

Actually, I should mention that much the same hamster wheel has already come in play in sociology. Sometime in the last few decades of the twentieth century, people who never bothered to get proper certification in sociology began practicing it. The most notorious of these professional pirates are members of local English departments. These days it is possible to look over the course lists of English teachers to find classes on culture, imperialism, race relations, gender politics, even social movements; and certainly the family. You can imagine how sociologists feel about this. They worked hard to become experts on these same subjects. (Okay, let's say fourteen weeks full-time, which surely exceeds the course and study hours required to pass a qualifying exam in almost any specialty in the field.) Then, along comes some joker who spent her graduate school days reading that other Spenser. She decides to teach, under another name, the sociology of family in a form only vaguely associated with the Renaissance literature that allows her courses to be lodged in English. This kind of thing is why so many sociologists go absolutely nuts over thinking they associate with English departments. Almost to a man, professional sociologists hate "cultural studies" or, worse yet, "poststructuralism"—not to mention "postmodernism." A good many "real" sociologists will use these names to attack people who dare to say something about social and cultural facts in the absence of a professional certificate.

There's the problem in a nutshell. A professional certificate is only worth what the market will bear. This being so, those already certified guard the gates carefully. There is nothing wrong with this—provided, that is, we can be certain that, on average, a brain surgeon knows her stuff well enough to ward off the undertakers, whose stuff is of little interest to any who fall before the knife of a bad surgeon. But there is a problem with *over-professionalizing* a practice that might do better left to nature. Undertaking, if it must be done, might as well be done according to some rules or another. But sociology is another matter.

If sociology is a matter of very considerable interest to almost everyone, then the masses who would like to know more about social things than their practical experience teaches them are fully justified to complain when the professionalizers of sociology overplay their hand. To a degree, all professions bluff. None wants the public to know their trade secrets. It's how they guard their gates and keep their jobs. But there is such a thing as too much. And this, in a word, is the subject of the book you have at hand.

Ben Agger's *Public Sociology* is a wonderful book, long needed. Agger has dared to tell the truth about the bluff currently being played by all too many professional sociologists; and he tells the truth with clear and unmistakable evidence. In one of the more memorable of his book's fine locutions, Agger describes professional, scientific sociology as "writing for career." Just so. Anyone who loves the field, and has been around it for any time whatsoever, knows that what Agger says is so. But, in my experience, only graduate students and other people new to the ways of the trade are willing to say it on a regular basis (though not, of course, in the immediate presence of those with authority over their careers).

It has taken someone of Agger's numerous and proven accomplishments to be able to speak truth to these odd scientific powers in his field. He was written very many excellent books, chaired a major department in the field, taught thousands of students, and administered a college at a very large and important university. He knows every angle of the professional game. Thus he writes about it with touching sympathy for those who suffer the abuse of having indecent colleagues look down upon excellent and prolific work because "it just wasn't sociological enough." I personally know of many thus mistreated, and many of them were not willing to endure or able to survive the mature blossom of an intellectual life, as has Ben Agger who, as he tells us, suffered just this sort of mistreatment. As I say, he knows every angle. He can be trusted.

Today we sociologists are enjoying a bit of a resurgence of public attention. More today than for a long while, sociologists want to write and speak for and to the general public. William Julius Wilson, Arlie Hochschild, Todd Gitlin, Elijah Anderson, Judith Stacey, Barry Glassner, and Alan Wolfe, among others, are the names of those who have done this very well and usefully. When you read this book of Agger's, you might at first be surprised by his claim that it is meant as a contribution to this movement. First of all, it is filled with tables and numbers. Second of all, it is largely preoccupied with sociological work published in the field's most professional journal, *The American Sociological Review.* And, third, it would seem to be a book that attends solely to a controversy of interest only to proper members of the professional field. But Ben Agger, in addition to doing these good works very well, does something else just as important. Again and again, he demonstrates the extent to which the high professional work in his discipline is founded on what he occasionally calls "secret writing." By courageously uncovering the tricks of his own field, Agger's book should be of general interest. Sociologists are not alone in their sneaky resort to ingenious mysteries to guard professional secrets and thus to protect themselves from public scrutiny.

The ideal of the public intellectual is fulfilled, I think, in two collective moves, only one of which is public in the sense of "appearing for all to see." When the work of a professional field is offered to a public, the professor of that field's wisdom turns to face the world—thus, necessarily, to expose his profession to a scrutiny it does not otherwise risk. Hence, the second move that must be made when a profession intends to serve a public. It must also tell the truth about itself. This is easier said than done. It is one thing to be the expert before an audience. It is another to assure that audience that what one says, in a sound bite or two, is competent truth on a par with that a patient demands of a brain surgeon. The surgeon, it turns out, never works in public. The sociologist can, and does. But when he does, the truths he offers for general consumption must be open for all to inspect. This, it is plain, will only be when members of the profession a public intellectual represents are willing to monitor those brief professions of their truth. But, of course, they will never do this if they, like surgeons and cops, are bound to a code of secrecy.

All professions keep secrets. But the dirty secrets of sociological practice can be awful in their effect because, when all is said and done, they keep the profession from truly giving the public what it wants—simple and clear explanations for what is going on in a complex world. No profession so devoted, as sociology has been, to the mumbo-jumbo Agger exposes will ever meet its promise to its public. The work of a public intellectual begins at home with honest and courageous housekeeping.

"Speak truth to power" has long been the proper slogan of honest public politics. But when the truth is told by those who are caught up in a profession, the slogan is double-edged. To speak truth to worldly powers, one must be certain he knows the truth of which he speaks—and this will never be without an open and collective debate about the truth of the truth told. I do not wish to say, and neither does Agger, that what sociologists do and say is utter nonsense. He loves the field to which, like others, he has devoted himself. He wants his profession to do more of what it has begun to do—to speak the civil truths people need to hear.

What Ben Agger has done for you and me, and for any one else who cares about the truth of social reality, is to turn his love of sociology back on those secret measures by which it keeps itself locked up in an ever narrowing cell in which the numbers count for naught.

Whoever might have been the first sociologist, he or she worked in and for a public. Hence, an irony: Not even the founders of the professional field of academic sociology wanted it to become what it has. Not Durkheim, nor Weber, nor the leaders of the famous Chicago and Columbia schools of sociology. Among the delicious treats and hopeful signs Agger offers us is evidence that professional sociology as a guild of secret keepers is a practice of relatively recent habits. It is not too late for this to change.

That the preciousness of academic sociology must yield its grip on the sociological imagination is so painfully clear that, for some of us, the pain is chronic. Ben Agger has shown us where the analgesic can be found: there, where it was in the beginning, whenever that was. We must begin to tell the truth to *and about* ourselves. If so, then our contributions to public life will grow and the world will in time hurt less. If not, as we have been warned for years now, sociology will slip silently off the screen of public regard.

Public Sociology is one of the first books in a new series, the very purpose of which is to keep sociology and the human sciences from losing their important place in the public regard. Judith Stacey and I are very pleased to edit this series under the general theme of *The New Social Formations*. We have commitments from authors, and plans to pursue others, who will write challenging books on the variety of new social formations just appearing at the beginning of the twenty-first century. For many complex reasons, social life is forming itself in ways that were inconceivable just a century ago when the social sciences came into being. Thus it is that Ben Agger's *Public Sociology* fits the purpose of this new series by uncovering the unexamined assumptions by which many study the social world. The books to follow in *The New Social Formations* series will examine the new formations themselves. Ethnicities, sexualities, masculinities, work and labor, housing, global ethics, and more are among the subjects upon which readers can expect to see books just as bracing and important as the one at hand.

Preface to Second Edition

I should have suspected, when I published the first edition of this book in 2000, that "public sociology" would become a brand, a convenient slogan or label endorsed by even mainstream sociologists! That is the way things work in fast capitalism. Call it cooptation or call it progress: Critical concepts are domesticated and even merchandised. We even find the American Sociological Association, a stable and cautious professional organization, to have endorsed the term, as have a number of prominent American sociology departments.

Call me skeptical. By public sociology, as will be clear from this second edition, I have in mind what Marx meant when he and Engels talked about the merger of theory and practice, of intellectual work and political action. Public sociology is activist in its orientation to the social world. That is why, in this edition, I take pains in my new concluding chapter to trace what I mean by public sociology to C. Wright Mills, Tom Hayden, SDS, and the New Left during the 1960s. I also discuss the more academic and less activist meanings of public sociology as I consider public sociology's mainstreaming.

Perhaps I am too skeptical! Perhaps it is good that sociologists are talking about the public implications of their intellectual work, whatever their political intent. One of the messages of this book is that political intentions are always buried within one's methodologies, however much one disguises those intentions. A public sociology will, among other things, explore these political agendas below the surface of what I characterize as positivism's secret writing.

Alan McClare is to be thanked for undertaking the publication of this second edition of Public Sociology. Thanks are also due Charles Lemert, who helped facilitate its publication. Joe Feagin, Charles Lemert, and Frances Fox Piven have offered valuable commentaries on the final chapter, helping me focus my argument.

Acknowledgments

I have benefited from readings of this manuscript by Joe Feagin, Charles Lemert, Tim Luke, Harland Prechel, and John O'Neill. Beth Anne Shelton, a nonpositivist empiricist, provided a window on the world of quantitative sociology, successfully explaining the ins and outs of journal writing and career building, but failing (through no fault of her own) to help me understand the term *heteroskedasticity*. I'm just dense! My children, Oliver and Sarah, occasionally allowed me to use the home computer when they weren't playing Batman or Haunted House. Thomas Rickert did indefatigable legwork to the Xerox machine and on the tennis court. Penny Barber helped prepare the graphic inserts and also "eighty-sixed" some glitches in the text. Dean Birkenkamp prodded me out of my doldrums as an administrator in order to write a book for Rowman & Littlefield. Although I was a year late with the manuscript, Dean has been a patient, imaginative, and encouraging editor, for whom I hope to write other books (hint, hint)! His example gives me hope about the future of academic publishing.

1

Sociology as Secret Writing: Lessons from Postmodernism

THE DISCOURSE OF A DISCIPLINE

Imagine a bright undergraduate student at a good liberal arts college. Her favorite professor is a sociologist who inspires her to seek a career as an academic sociologist. The student has taken the GREs and scored well. Her college grades are very strong. She is beginning to apply to graduate schools in sociology, based on her mentor's advice about goodness of fit between her interests and the strengths of various departments. The student has been told that the sociology job market is crowded and that she would do best to attend a graduate school at which she can acquire certain marketable skills, such as expertise in quantitative methods and statistics. However, the student, although she passed methods and stats in college, minored in English and loves writing. Math is not her strong suit, nor is she particularly interested in crunching numbers for a living. She wants to write and she wants to help improve the world, which, she feels, is what C. Wright Mills had in mind when he wrote (1959) *The Sociological Imagination,* a book she read in her freshman sociology course. Her favorite areas in sociology are theory and gender studies. She was active in her campus gay and lesbian alliance and worked at the town's women's shelter. She feels torn between wanting to pursue a prudent course of study in her sociology graduate education, a course of study that will give her skills and help her find a professorial job upon graduation, and answering to her inner voice, which is highly literary and activist. This book is written in order to help her think imaginatively about her chosen profession and its intellectual opportunities.

This is a story about writing stories, which is the gist of sociology. I want to convey the literary activities that underlie the sociology congealed on the journal page. By viewing sociology as storytelling, I do not rob it of rigor, method, high theory. All of these are stories in their own rights—versions, as I will call them, following the inspiration of Jacques Derrida, the Algerian-born founder of deconstruction, a perspective on knowledge as a necessarily incomplete written text. The protagonist in my story about stories is method, much as it was for Mills in *The Sociological Imagination.* I submit that method is argument, a text, that polemicizes quietly for

a certain view of the world. Watching me sitting at the computer entering changes
to this book, my young son Oliver asked me if I was writing a story. I said that I
was. He asked, "Who is the monster in the story? Is it Godzilla?" I said that there
is a monster, but it is called Method. Knowing that superheroes vanquish monsters,
Oliver said that I needed to get Batman in the story. I replied that Method is a
friendly monster, like one of the friendly and talkative dinosaurs in the video *The
Land Before Time*. For those of us who do not possess many quantitative skills (as
my colleagues call them), like the student I described above, method lies across a
great divide, inscrutable, vaguely hostile, to be left alone. But we need to befriend
method in order to understand it and engage it, perhaps changing its nature in the
process. I contend that we best view method as a literary style, not as representation or a machine, two possible metaphors for the forbidding method of my son's
storybook.

In addition to being addressed to the searching undergraduate described above,
this book is also written for working sociologists who are interested in sociology as
a "social text" governed by certain literary and editorial conventions and situated
in cultural institutions such as journals and publishing houses and in social and economic institutions such as universities. Sociology is writing for publication that
advances academic careers. My book explores the contemporary discipline of sociology from the perspective of its "discourse" as well as the disciplinary institutions
that house discourse. Exploring this discourse will introduce student-writers to
issues of apprenticeship and career building. My exploration will afford working
sociologists critical insights into the hegemony of positivist journal science,
methodology as a narrative, editorial gatekeeping, the management of academic
careers, and challenges to sociological writing posed by postmodernism. The social
movements of the 1960s taught us that sociology is political; the postmodern turn
in the social and cultural disciplines during the 1990s instructs us that sociology is
discourse. This social fact has not been systematically explored. In this book, I consider sociology as a social act that is above all literary—as writing.

This is a book about writing and reading in a discipline peculiarly resistant to
being viewed as literary, fearing that that would compromise its claim to be a science. By examining the writing and reading practices, the discourse, of a discipline,
we learn more about that discipline and about how to rethink its conventions,
where necessary. Sociology is writing, and, of course, not all writing is sociological. My intent is to foster a public sociology, which acknowledges that it is a literary version, confesses its animating assumptions and investments, and addresses crucial public issues. My project is unashamedly normative: I contend that sociology
should take the lead in building a democratic public sphere. My assessment is that
little sociology today is public; instead, much of it is dreary, conservative, unen-
livening, obsessed with method. How many of your favorite literary works are
works of sociology, especially the sort published in journals? What is distinctive
about much positivist sociological writing is that it suppresses the fact that it is writing at all. In the way of science, the author's fingerprints are erased from the fin-

ished text. It is, of course, possible to learn how to write silently, as if the words appearing on the page were not authored by a person with a certain sensibility, values, biases, and blind spots. Science erases evidence of authorial presence, of what certain French theorists call *ecriture*, because it wants to claim validity for itself. Science intends to be read a certain way, as if the words, numbers, and figures on the page reflected nature. In this sense, science is not a poem; it does not want us to worry about its literary style or guess at its meaning.

But we worry anyway, because the science page is no less in need of interpretation than those of Robert Frost or Yevgeny Yevtushenko. This is the important lesson of postmodernism: Reading writes. As Derrida has argued, reading is a version that, in its interpretive intervention in the text that is always somewhat opaque to itself, helps author the text. By the same token, science is not as different from poetry and philosophy as it supposes. Reading strongly intervenes in the sense and sentience of the science text, whether we call it sociology or physics. Postmodern theory enables us to view sociology as writing, and thus to write it differently, more publicly. This book is structured around six main concepts, all but one of which derive from postmodern perspectives on disciplinarity and discourse (e.g., see Linda Brodkey's [1987] *Academic Writing as Social Practice,* Julie Klein's [1990] *Interdisciplinarity* and Stanley Fish's [1995] *Professional Correctness*). The first concept is *authoriality*—the notion that writing in sociology requires deliberate authorial choices. The irony of positivism is that it teaches authors to conceal themselves, suppressing science's author in order to position itself as a mirror of social nature. Scientific sociology is secret writing. Once positivist sociology has been "authorized," read as a deliberately authored artifact, readers can contest its hidden assumptions.

The second concept I develop is sociological writing's *iterability.* As social practice, sociology's text is governed by certain conventions that are learned in graduate school and reinforced throughout one's academic career. Authorial choices are grounded in a given disciplinary culture, literary institutions, and an academic organization that constrain choice. However, because writers write science, like poets write poetry, and can write differently, these choices are subject to modification. Barthes's (1975) notions of the death of the author and pleasure of the text need to be resisted, even as we understand that scholarly writing takes place in a social context that threatens to replace author with figure and gesture—thus, thought with technique. The third concept, *undecidability,* is taken directly from Derrida. By undecidability, I mean that writing, no matter how science-like in its rhetorical conventions, does not solve intellectual problems with sheer technique, or method, because the sociological text does not perfectly mirror the world but rather is merely one version among possible versions. I develop Derrida's (1976, 1978) notions of *difference* and deferral in order to analyze the undecidability of scientific sociological writing. Fourth, I read sociological journal articles through the concept of their *narrativity,* referring to the way in which quantitative methodology is a rhetorical text that would convince readers of its peculiar, silent version of the social world. Method is rhetoric, argument, even polemic, in this view.

By developing the fifth concept of the book, *the ethnography and political economy of academic career building,* I examine how sociologists choose publication outlets in order to add value to their curriculum vitae and how they compose their articles and books in light of the "language games" (Wittgenstein 1976) characteristic of their particular subfields in the discipline. Here, the authorial choices sociologists make are examined in light of a literary political economy that stratifies publication outlets, both journals and publishing houses, in ways that have direct impact on scholars' careers.

The sixth animating concept of the book, *polyvocality,* is owed to the work of the theorist Bakhtin (1978, 1994). I argue that the recent postmodern turn in social and cultural theory and in ethnography requires members of a discipline such as sociology to view their academic practices discursively, in terms of deliberate authorial choices, literary conventions, and editorial practices that determine "what" gets published, and "where." Sociology is increasingly polyvocal, open to diverse voices, methods, theories, writing styles. The recognition of polyvocality does not reduce sociology's legitimacy but opens it to cross-fertilization from cultural and humanistic disciplines. It also legitimizes diverse intellectual styles. Hence, I argue that the discursive turn in sociology has begun to remake the discipline in fundamental ways.

READING SECRET WRITING

How disciplines write expresses their theoretical and normative frameworks. In their discourse, disciplines disclose themselves, the more so the more disciplines shun their narrativity—the fact that their busy professionals compose themselves and thus the world. In attempting to imitate the natural sciences in a "hard" objectivity and indubitability, sociologists replicate scientists' inattention to issues of discourse and narration that is characteristic of positivism. Positivists intend to copy the world, inscribing it in their texts. This is largely why the science page is larded with figural representations—graphs, charts, numbers, equations, scatterplots. These representations, as I explore in detail later, seek to mirror the world, silently but forcefully implying representation and thus validity. The less the science page deals in prose, the more it creates the impression that it has dispensed with authorial subjectivity—the whims of the writer, including her politics.

But authorial subjectivity is never entirely eliminated, allowing the science page to "deconstruct," Derrida's term for the way in which all writings, all versions, unravel into infinite regress once we strip away their pretense to be complete, comprehensive, without presupposition—solving all intellectual problems posed by their topic. Reading writes because reading strongly intervenes in texts that are forever fraying at the edges, begging questions, leaving clues, doubling back on themselves. The most deconstruction-prone texts are, like the science page, those that purport to eliminate authorial subjectivity, pretending perfect representation.

This book is not an argument against objectivity. Nor do I reject science. That science can be read, especially where it is "secret writing," strengthens objectivity, if anything. It can also strengthen science once science confesses its own narrativity. Although the argument advanced in this book borrows heavily from Derrida's deconstruction, it is not deconstruction*ist*. That is, I do not rest by demonstrating that the text of scientific sociology frays at the margins, dissolving into unspoken assumptions, ellipses, deferrals, values. Instead, I advance an argument for a better, more public sociology—one could even call it more scientific, if one takes liberties with what ordinarily passes for social science—that incorporates its own corrigibility (mistake-proneness) and narrativity (story-like quality) into its rhetorical method. This method is the way sociology writes, and thus writes the world. Although texts are both in and of the world, not enjoying privileged epistemological status claimed by the Enlightenment and then by the founder of sociology, Auguste Comte, texts do not exhaust the world. The text does have an "outside," against interpretations of Derrida's notion that there is nothing beyond the text.

Actually, I believe that Derrida meant only to say that texts such as science ooze out of their covers and off their pages in such a way as to make the text/world distinction rather problematic and the search for certainty futile. Certainty is a version, like any other, that is inherently uncertain, fallible. By addressing the textuality of science, inspired by Derrida but moving his argument in the direction of the sociology of science via the Frankfurt School's critical theory, we treat the science text as belonging to the world and indeed contributing to the world, albeit silently. Science argues. It argues for a state of affairs, an ontology (theory of being). This may not seem immediately clear, especially where scientific method appears far removed from argument, instead busying itself with figural means of presentation. The science page, as I call it, removes narrativity to footnotes, endnotes, the abstract beginning the article. The text is larded with the rhetoric of scientific presentation, notably including quantification. As I indicated above, these contribute to the impression of science's representational relationship to the world, producing a *science aura* (Agger 1989b). This aura, created by the narrative features of science's literary method, stakes science's claim to objectivity.

I said above that we can read method two ways, either as *mirror* or *machine.* As a representation mirroring nature, method demonstrates its worth and wares by freezing the world on the journal page, using all of the figural paraphernalia that we ordinarily take to be the essence of science. This representational strategy is crucial to positivism's discourse. Sociological authors lard the journal page with the representational figures of science in order to claim scientific status for sociology, implying that we should regard science as a mirror of nature. I call this discursive strategy the "gesturing" of method, talking the way method is thought to talk in physics or chemistry. One can also profitably read method as a machine: Data flow into the machine of method, and, through a kind of industrial conversion, knowledge flows out the other end. According to this metaphor, sociological authors clutter the science page with figure, gesture, and the technical details of method in order to let readers "see the technology"—method—that converts data into knowledge. Either way, whether method is mirror or machine, a methods-driven sociology seeks to convey the impression of its authorless objectivity.

In saying that objectivity is an impression fostered by a certain literary technique displayed on the science page, we do not deny or degrade the goal of objectivity. Instead, we distinguish between objectivity's aura—what makes science seem scientific—and a more substantial objectivity that resides in truth claims. Almost inevitably, the Derridean turn in interpretive studies is taken to mean opposition not only to science but specifically to sociology, which, as a study of the social, is seen by some to be even more perspectival than work in the natural sciences. Although sociology is in its nature reflexive, in that sociologists are social actors who inhabit the same world as their research subjects, there is nothing about postmodern theory that disqualifies sociology as a disciplinary project. While I have qualms about the "disciplining" tendencies of disciplinarity, especially in light of Foucault's (1977) work on social control, there is nothing irreconcilable about being a sociologist and a postmodernist. Postmodernism teaches valuable lessons about the contribution of discourse, including science, to society, enriching both the sociology of science and what Friedrichs (1970) called the sociology of sociology.

This book is fundamentally a decoding and enriching of method far beyond the purview of most research methodology textbooks and courses. Method includes not only the systematic ways in which we study people, organizations, and institutions, but also the ways in which we *narrate* our findings and theories. Not only are research methods imbedded with values, constructions, theories of being that, in effect, constitute arguments. The literary strategies of sociology are subject to being deconstructed in order to be understood—and engaged—as the arguments for one or another states of social being they really are. Method does not resolve arguments with reference to claims outside of argumentation. Recognizing this need not disqualify the deployment of "data" as buttresses of argument but only acknowledges that data are themselves frozen bits of social history that can be thawed into the molten arguments they are.

The quantitative and qualitative methods students of sociology learn are valuable if we are to conduct empirical sociology in disciplined, methodical ways. But method is not a royal road to truth as much as it is secret writing, encoding one or another values, theories, programs, ontologies. The narrativity of science must become part of the canon of research methodology inasmuch as *journal science* is governed by literary habits that are quite arbitrary, deriving from the history of narrativity in the natural sciences. These habits involve certain means of literary presentation that are thought to make science science. Sociologists learn these habits through apprenticeship in graduate school and early in their academic careers, as they begin to submit papers for publication. Later, I will discuss the process of editorial gatekeeping that requires authors who are learning discipline to "revise and resubmit" their work in gestation. There is nothing inherently wrong with acquiring professionalism in these ways if by professionalism we mean learning how to script one's work for other professionals in the field.

As budding sociologists learn how to craft term papers and dissertation chapters into refereed journal articles, they also learn how to read published articles. In reading, they acquire both valuable career capital and literary skills that are translated into *citation,* the process by which one establishes a toehold for one's work in an established canon to which one seeks to make modest revision. This is how what Kuhn (1970) called normal science proceeds. But emergent sociologists do not learn how to read what I am calling the secret writing of the discipline encoded in mathematical and figural presentations, representing an ordered world, as argument. Rather, they read the writing uncritically for what it purports to be—manipulations of data that cumulate into the "literature" of a discipline or subdiscipline. They "cite" articles they read within their fields as they translate their reading into their own writing, which they submit for publication. In this process, they ignore the literariness of their research literatures, the fact that science is an authored practice that proceeds according to certain de-authorizing habits and techniques that needlessly silence the authorial pulse and constrain literary imagination.

There is nothing wrong with reading science in this way. After all, findings, although grounded in literary activities that use method as a rhetoric of representation, take on lives of their own outside of the text. It is nontrivial that eating asparagus may retard the onset of cancer. However, the text of cancer research matters because it helps frame and even constitute findings that are, in Derrida's terms, undecidable—unfree from their contexts, circumstances, methods, glossaries, and sponsoring agencies. More interesting, though, for me here is not the nontrivial nature of sociological findings elaborately tabled, graphed, and plotted in the pages of *American Sociological Review (ASR)* and *Social Forces.* One can learn from demography and criminology about American society and social problems. One cannot address these problems except through "findings," as I have called them. I am more interested in the way in which "findings" constitute, and are constituted by, the text of sociological journal science that typically goes unaddressed in research methods classes and in the everyday discourse of the discipline.

This "text," as I am calling it, is the way in which journal science conceals authorship—the literary choices writers make—in order to portray science as objective. Although objectivity is to be prized, the text belongs to the realms of subjectivity and objectivity. Journals reproduce disciplines in their own images, setting standards of discourse for junior and senior practitioners. At the same time, the findings reported in journals constitute objectivity in that they become part of the canonical literatures defining what can be known within the subfields of social psychology, criminology, family, social movements. Not only are what Durkheim (1950) called "social facts" constituted through choices made by methodologists—questionnaire construction, measurement, etc. Authors make deliberate literary choices when they present their findings, even—especially—where they conceal their own busy artifice from view. My argument here is simply that the secret writing of science is a textual accomplishment governed by certain literary norms. As such, science could be crafted differently, acknowledging, even embracing, its authoriality. There is nothing decisive about the presentation of findings in socio-logical journal articles, which imitate articles from the natural sciences. We are not compelled to abstract the article in about 100 words, followed by sections present-ing a literature review, methodology, discussion of findings, and brief conclusion. Journal articles *narrate their worlds,* even—especially—where they appear de-authored, uninformed by literary, ontological, political perspective. Far from value-free, method argues; it is rhetoric.

Methodologists well understand the ontological nature of their approaches. They recognize that survey instruments (questionnaires), sampling techniques, and inferential statistics make large assumptions that influence "findings." It is a very short step from recognizing the values imbedded in method to treating the literari-ness of journal science as a sociological topic—something to be investigated. This does not render science illegitimate but acknowledges the rhetorical nature of sci-ence, opening science's scripts to multiple possibilities. In this, I follow closely the Frankfurt School's argument for enlightenment. They contend that the Enlighten-ment, which enthroned positivist method as the transcendence of myth, was the more mythic for all that: "Enlightenment behaves towards things like a dictator towards men" (Horkheimer and Adorno 1972: 9). In denying ontology, values, and politics, positivism only reproduces the frozen world it depicts as unalterable "fact."

A critique of the sociological discipline was mounted by Alvin Gouldner (1970) in *The Coming Crisis of Western Sociology.* The critique of sociological positivism was initially a critique of sociology's preference for the status quo, prefigured in the Frankfurt School's analysis of scientism. In the 1960s, as I noted, we recognized that sociology is political. Now, with the postmodern turn in the humanities and social sciences, we recognize that sociology is discourse, even where positivists pos-ture a representational version of the text. In this book, I join these two critiques by examining the literary conventions of sociology, demonstrating their artifice and even arbitrariness and auguring an approach to disciplinary discourse that celebrates the author's presence in the text as science's ineradicable humanity.

THE PROJECT OF SOCIAL PHYSICS

Auguste Comte characterized sociology, his new discipline, as "social physics," trading on the intended resemblance of sociology to the natural sciences. He wanted sociology to enjoy the unchallenged objectivity of physics, depicting social laws that characterize all forms of human association. His law of the "three stages" was, in fact, a framework for understanding social progress and not a description of societal invariance. Comte, like his early sociological brethren such as Durkheim and Weber, linked sociology to social progress in the sense that the "laws" they describe would, in being reproduced by citizens in everyday life, acquire perma-nence. Sociologists would inculcate the supposed laws' inevitability, hence bring-ing them into being. The sociological founders depicted the inevitability of capi-talist industrialization, suggesting that all societies evolve from simple to complex stages where complexity is equated to industrial capitalism of the late nineteenth and early twentieth centuries. This suggestion that history unfolds according to a certain preordained purpose is conveyed by a scientific sociology. Sociologists, in disclosing capitalism's teleology framed in terms of binding social laws, brought about "progress" by inducing people's compliance with laws of private property, nuclear family, Judeo-Christianity, and the nation-state. Thus, the text of science freezes social facts into social fate, ironically concealing its own role in converting text into practice.

The science text, as I am calling it, intends to reproduce the existing social world by portraying it as inevitable and necessary. It does so by appearing to be simply a mirror of nature, not a deliberate human version replete with ontology, theory, values, politics. Comte's social physics—sociology—did not use the elaborately figured, tabled, and numbered journal page to produce the appearance of social laws' intractability and inevitability. Instead, he, like Durkheim, Weber, and later Parsons, narrated their concepts of social laws using old-fashioned prose; they postulated laws of capitalism and patriarchy, exposing their theoretical formulations to opposing arguments. Marx spent most of his adult life attempting to refute those claims, which, he argued, protected the status quo by cloaking it in the illusion of permanence. Following Hegel, Marx stressed the *historicity* of capitalism, emphasizing its susceptibility to change, especially given what he took to be its self-contradictory tendencies such as the tendency for the accumulation of immense private capital to lead to widespread impoverishment.

Debates between the intellectual protégés and descendants of Comte, Durkheim, Weber, and Marx were conducted with full awareness that the positivist postulate of social laws was arguable, open to dispute. These protagonists created the classical tradition of social theorizing that survived until Parsons. Although some of us believe that that tradition can be revived, since the 1970s the mathematization of American sociology has driven out concerns of grand social theorizing, instead returning to Comte's notion that sociology is virtually a natural science. Unlike Comte, though, the mathematical sociologists do not engage in what they regard as speculative sociological theorizing but instead attempt to advance sociology by way of method and its figural representation on the journal page, squeezing out not only theory but virtually all reasoned prose.

Where sociological theory in the tradition of Durkheim, Weber, and Marx was unashamed of its narrativity—it was argument—today scientific sociology is secret writing. Authorial artifice is concealed (as subtext) underneath the representational pyrotechnics of the journal page. As we shall see, this is a very thick page in its dizzying array of gestures, symbols, annotations, technical addenda. It appears to extirpate narrative but in so doing narrates all the more forcefully, substituting what I call *representationality,* and thus the implication that science mirrors social nature, for old-fashioned argument. The journal page attempts to capture the world in its nature-like depiction of it, thus reinforcing Comte's original quest for social laws. This deauthorized version of social physics is more impregnable than narrative positivist social theorizing in its substitution of technique for text, concealing argument underneath dense layers of figure virtually impenetrable by deconstructive reading.

This thick text of method can be read once we deploy the techniques of deconstruction, owed largely to Derrida. He identified the tendencies of all texts to "deconstruct," once read strongly enough. Their assumptions, omissions, ellipses, glosses, and deferrals draw attention to themselves, suggesting the incompleteness of their versions. Derrida did not intend to produce a perfect or clean text that would somehow counter these self-deconstructing tendencies. If anything, he celebrated the indeterminacy of texts as an opening for new texts, new versions of the world. Although some versions are better or worse than others, according to whatever criteria the reader deploys, such as objectivity, creativity, scholarliness, all are versions; they unravel once we probe deeply into their structures and styles. This unraveling need not scandalize those who pursue objectivity; understanding the deconstructing tendencies of science texts restores the author to science and helps one start good arguments (between versions) that can enhance objectivity. Derrida's main point is that there is no last word, nothing "outside the text," as he said, that enables one to anchor texts in certainty. No amount of defining and refining of one's terms—no amount of method, differently put—will solve all intellectual problems. Definitions must be defined, clarified, argued, to the point of infinity. As I said earlier, this helps us see that method itself is a text, a version, an argument, that could be phrased differently. Neither method nor theoretical slogan can do our thinking for us, enabling us to avoid grappling with the deconstructive tendencies of all literary versions, including deconstruction itself, I should hasten to add.

Comte's sociology has been methodologized into the phrases of the journal article, monograph, grant proposal. Restoring the author to social physics advances the Derridean program, which could be called simply *authorization*. Authorization introduces discourse and argument where before only figure had stood. As deconstruction demonstrates, figure is itself argument—in journal science, an argument for a world frozen into the peaks and valleys of graphed intelligence and thus not susceptible to social change. Comte's social physics not only provided for the possibility of social change; his law of the three stages, as he called it, attempted to bring about social change by portraying capitalist modernization as inevitable. Durkheim and Weber followed up on this, describing the industrial division of labor and bureaucracy as concomitants of social and economic progress. Although neither was completely sanguine about this vector of historical unfolding—anomie and alienation abound in industrial capitalism—they felt that a nuanced, empathetic sociology could be a gadfly of sorts, correcting some of the excesses of otherwise exuberant progress. Grand sociological theory in this tradition was teleological, portraying higher societal purposes in terms of large-scale social laws. This teleology allowed for incremental social reform, but not fundamental social change—revolution. Yet even the original reformist teleology of social physics has been dropped out of post-1970 scientific sociology as sociology has canonized its theoretical origins and moved beyond both theory and reform, into rarefied methodology and career building.

It is my argument here that preoccupation with methodological refinement and strategic career building within a discipline dominated by quantitative methods spelled the end of grand theorizing. This is an argument made in different ways by C. Wright Mills and Gouldner. I move beyond their analyses by looking closely at the rhetorical strategies of positivist journal science using the conceptual and analytical tools of postmodern theory. Mills and Gouldner were certainly on the right track in understanding how mainstream U.S. sociology had become a potent political force. What I add to their framework is a literary and institutional analysis of how methodologically oriented journal sociology advances academic careers and reinforces a peculiarly static worldview by dropping out *narrativity* from founding sociological theorizing. Social physics has become more physics-like and less social over the past hundred years, especially since 1970, as method has eclipsed theory.

SOCIOLOGY AND THE CULTURAL TURN

All of this is quite ironic: as sociology has become more science-like, other social sciences such as anthropology and history and humanities disciplines such as English have been turned upside down by theoretical developments imported from Germany and France. The growing cultural studies movement has changed the face of many interpretive disciplines and even begun to make inroads in sociology (e.g., Denzin 1992). Cultural studies or the cultural turn has transformed our thinking about the relationship between writing and reading as well as between the text and society. It is no longer possible to pretend that texts lack authors or authorial perspective. This has abundant implications for what used to be called the sociology of science and science studies.

My approach here is to turn the theoretical orientation and techniques of cultural studies upon sociology. This is not meant to undermine sociology, for I am a sociologist of a sort and proud of it! (The sort I am is a student of the social who treats science as a version. Many mainstream colleagues would view me as an imposter.) It is rather intended to deconstruct sociology as a text that can be read for what it conceals about its fundamental values. I thaw the page of journal science into the molten, muddy, sometimes muddled discourse it is. This does not abandon journal argumentation but suggests ways to reformulate journal discourse and in fact the whole institution of "cultural production"—e.g., publishing and editing—in sociology. My approach also suggests ways for students to learn to read and write journal sociology not as a static, presuppositionless text but as argument. I seek a public sociology that confesses its undecidable literariness without abandoning the aim of objectivity.

This cultural studies approach to sociology as discourse need not undermine sociology. Sociology is a vital and defensible project that has shed a great deal of light on societal dynamics since Comte. Both fine-grained empirical studies and broad-gauged conceptual work have illuminated many issues in social psychology, criminology, social change, population studies, gender, family, race, and socioeconomic stratification. Durkheim's original study of the religious correlates of suicide inspired this tradition. His concept of "social facts"—determined behavior—also moved social physics into its second, law-seeking, stage. I defend and even celebrate a version of sociology—the version that views itself *as* a version, as argument. I advocate attention to disciplinary discourse that "reads" sociology qua social physics as a *disciplining* discourse and also points the way toward de-disciplining sociological discourse that does not suppress the author but goes public with its animating assumptions and broad-based social concerns.

Ideally, then, we would retain sociology's keen attention to the rapidly transforming empirical world—I (Agger 1989a) have called this fast capitalism—while suggesting problems with existing disciplinary discourse and proposing new discourse. The cultural turn in interpretive theories has prefigured this work. Cultural studies is not opposed to empiricism; it is empirical itself, if we accept that discourses are themselves social data. Cultural studies makes possible an interrogation of disciplinarity that furthers the overall projects of improving disciplinary discourse and making possible interdisciplinary projects such as cultural studies itself. The cultural turn, as I am calling it, draws attention to *authoriality*—the fact that culture, including disciplinary academic work, can be traced to authorial artifice and, as such, can be crafted differently.

This is decidedly not an argument for plain language or against technical argot. Technical terms are essential to the taxonomic and conceptual work of mature disciplines, of all serious intellectual work. Neither method nor theory can do without complexity. Both could be less obscurantist, though. Charles Lemert, a professor of social theory at Wesleyan, writes more elegantly and openly than does Habermas, without sacrificing complexity on the altar of the quotidian. What concerns me about the latter-day version of social physics displayed in the journals and monographs and taught in graduate school is the way in which narrativity—evidence of authorial argument—is suppressed in the interest of sheer representation. Method is good and necessary, as long as we acknowledge that method argues. Method's argument can be argued, and argued with. There are many ways to study stratification, gender, the nation-state. The ways in which we conduct and compose these studies express basic theoretical assumptions; method constitutes results.

Research methodologists know this about sociological conventionalism. Lacking a cultural studies perspective on disciplinary discourse, they quickly fall into the habit of scripting their science as if it merely reflected a given social world and did not also help constitute that world. Once we accept the artifice of method, we realize that method can be narrated in a host of different ways, some of which give full vent to authorial perspective. Today, journal methodologists relegate method to a singular section of their articles, reporting on the methods in use as if they were the technical codes found in small type on drug containers indicating the chemistry of the drug and potential side effects.

The cultural turn can issue in a fruitful sociology of science and sociology of sociology that need not abandon quantitative method. For unfortunate reasons, the critique of the Enlightenment has been conflated with a rejection of mathematics. The "mathematization" of the social world, a central feature of what the Frankfurt School called domination in late capitalism, is not to be confused with mathematics and especially with inferential statistics. These statistics allow sociologists to generalize from samples to populations, the stock in trade of generalization. Mathematics becomes mathematization—ideology—when we take the leap from the statistical analysis of the correlation of "variables" (suicide and religion, in Durkheim's famous example) to inference of physics-like laws of societal motion. Most quantitative sociologists do not trouble themselves about this leap from correlation—the simultaneous occurrence of events—to causality because, they argue, their research methods are as yet immature, permitting relatively low correlations. But the conflation of correlation and causality, mathematics and mathematization, subtly reinforces the physics-like model of a sociology that pursues incontrovertible social laws, hence reproducing the existing society by reproducing/reflecting it discursively, mirroring it on the journal page.

Methodology becomes ontology where we assume that the brush strokes of research method such as social statistics are, in fact, the nature of disciplinary work. But if method is artifice and artifact—text—we render method's outcomes ("research findings") corrigible and deconstructible, not essential. This is not to say that the crime rate or average family income do not exist, for they do. It is only to say that they do not exist "outside the text," as Derrida put it, without reference to the ways we theorize, study, and sometimes count them. Crime and income deconstruct into the myriad ways in which people transact these things and sociologists decide to study them, "operationalizing" them. By *operationalizing a variable* we produce an account of social things that allows others to see them, too. We can agree upon a way of measuring family income that takes account of messy events such as single-parent households that rely on child support payments. But we cannot conclude that family income can be addressed without what are essentially theoretical exercises in operationalizing them, defining their terms of study.

Cultural studies helps us prevent method from coalescing into ontology somehow beyond social and political theorizing. Social physics seeks to confuse method and ontology precisely because sociologists who follow the science model originally proposed by Comte want their findings to do political work, reproducing the present society. Although they may personally oppose certain social problems and vote for candidates from the Democratic Party, their sociologies replicate physics in order to bring about a certain order of societal being preordained in social laws of progress, industrialization, capitalism, patriarchy, racial supremacy, and the domination of nature. In furthering their science, these sociologists further a world in which science pretends to have no author, and hence cannot intervene politically. Political partisanship is disdained as a sullying of sociological professionalism that has allowed sociology to be marginalized in universities since the contested 1960s.

SOCIOLOGICAL PROFESSIONALISM
AND INSTITUTIONAL CREDIBILITY

Sociology's science-like text is thought to legitimize sociology in academic life at a time when administrators doubt that sociology pays its way in the fashion of electrical engineering and economics. As I explore later, sociology's institutional crisis was precipitated after about 1970, as undergraduate majors and graduate students declined, professorial jobs became scarce, and grants dried up. After the Sociology Department at Washington University in St. Louis, a good department by most sociologists' standards, was abolished in the late 1980s, sociologists began to worry acutely that the sociological project had to be sanitized, scientized, and professionalized in order to demonstrate its societal applicability and grantworthiness. Social physics was not and is not formulated in a sociopolitical vacuum. Comte founded the discipline of scientific sociology in order to guide industrial-era progress. Methodologically oriented sociologists since World War II and especially since the episode at Washington University have worked to shore up sociology's legitimacy in the contemporary research university, putting to rest the tired alliteration of sociology with socialism, social work, and the sixties.

Many mainstream quantitative sociologists believe that this legitimation is best achieved by *professionalizing* sociology, making it appear like the natural sciences in its methodology and the professional disciplines in its utilitarian contribution to society. These moves, especially after Washington University, are thought to give sociology institutional credibility that it risked losing during the 1960s, when sociology was unashamedly activist and social-problem oriented, and again during the 1970s and 1980s, when a good deal of applied sociology was dispersed or decentered into applied social science disciplines such as social work and criminology.

Although much can be said for legitimizing academic sociology, especially as university budgets erode and faculty time use comes under increasing scrutiny by suspicious administrators, professionalism risks becoming a monolithic discourse that squeezes out marginal discourses such as critical theory, feminist studies, and qualitative approaches to sociological method. Professionalism, as Foucault understood, appears to require an Otherness by comparison to which it is judged to be superior. For sociology, this Otherness is non-science, whether unabashed political advocacy, a holdover from the 1960s, or obscurantist theory that does not purvey its wares in the mainstream professional journals. For some, Otherness is simply non-disciplinary/undisciplined work—not "real sociology," as some of my former mainstream colleagues used to say.

Real sociology defies Otherness by engaging in quantitative analysis, building on established journal literatures compiled over the past five to ten years, engaging vouchsafed sociological topics, and publishing in legitimated journals and monograph houses. Although one can defend professionalism for its universalism and commitment to merit-based reward, professionalism needs to be ecumenical enough to accommodate a variety of intellectual and methodological styles. The problem here is that sociological professionalism, as conceived by proponents of latter-day social physics, positions itself against the varieties of non-sociology that, it argues, have led to sociology's eclipse in the university. In particular, sociological professionalism/social physics counterposes itself to the activist sociology of the 1960s, which endures as critical theory, feminist studies, and cultural studies. These outlaw versions scandalize those who believe that sociology must compete for institutional resources by enthroning scientific objectivity and method, thus hoping to duplicate the successes of electrical engineering and economics in acquiring research grants, a service role in guiding the state apparatus and institutional cachet.

If professionalism could be won without requiring Otherness as counterpoint, especially the politicized, perspectival, authorial, engaged Otherness of cultural studies and critical theory—non-sociology—textual politics might be less intense. It makes good sense to defend the relevance and sophistication of sociological theories and methods in order to lay claim to both institutional resources and societal credibility. However, it is essential that we preserve the possibility of *plural* theories and methods, thus allowing for a multiplicity of textualities and approaches to authoriality. In de-authorizing its version of science, social physics thwarts the possibility of other versions that may be just as credible, thoughtful, rigorous, such as critical theory.

The argument from sociology's need for institutional credibility needs to be rejected if it is driven by a singular social physics model of disciplinary discourse. Alternative discourses can also win credibility for sociology, even where they stray outside traditional disciplinary boundaries, as much good work does today, given the explosion of interdisciplinarity, especially in cultural studies and feminist studies. It is not obvious that the only model of social research that will win friends and influence people is grant-driven and quantitative. Although that may be an appropriate strategy for mainstream sociologists at Wisconsin and Michigan, alternative sociological discourses might be more credible at Oberlin and Wesleyan, where privileged students are intent to learn more about their highly stratified society in which elite education is available only to the lucky few.

Throughout this book, I draw on Bakhtin's concept of polyvocality, arguing that there be no master discourse but only plural, local, perspectival discourses, given the tendency of master discourses to deconstruct into a babble of tongues. The issue of polyvocality is highly relevant to the question of a discipline's institutional credibility in that it would seem to disallow master disciplinary discourses from disqualifying alternative discourses. Foucault, in *Discipline and Punish,* takes this issue further, arguing persuasively that certain social science disciplines exist *to discipline,* in their language games predetermining their responses to certain social issues, such as crime and homosexuality. He argues that master disciplinary discourses are, in effect, forms and forces of social control that answer to society's need for solutions to various problems attendant on industrialization and the rise of capitalism.

Polyvocality and professionalism need not contradict each other where we acknowledge that there are different legitimate discursive strategies available to disciplinary academics. This book seeks to explore the mainstream discursive strategy—I call it journal science—as well as alternative strategies. These alternative strategies also pursue institutional credibility for sociology. The strategists of ethnography, qualitative sociology, and critical theory all believe that sociology can be defended, especially at a time when the social problems of late capitalism abound. We do not necessarily abandon professionalism by rendering professional discourse polyvocal, both within and across disciplinary lines. We could be said to reinforce professionalism where we ask hard questions about the literary conventions of a discipline such as sociology, which, unlike physics and chemistry, is passionately bound up with its subject matter—people in groups in history. This is precisely what Gouldner and O'Neill (1972) mean by *reflexivity*, the capacity of sociologists to view themselves sociologically.

A SOCIAL THEORY OF THE TEXT AND THE PUBLIC SPHERE

In much of my work on critical social and cultural theory, I have begun to articulate a social theory of the text, arguing that books—here, disciplinary discourse—"write" authors. This is not to deny literary intentionality and purpose but rather to argue that our language games, as Wittgenstein called them, send powerful messages and encode significant meanings about the nature of the social world. To stipulate concepts, relate those concepts to an existing social-scientific literature, measure them, and portray and discuss findings require strong authorial commitments to a certain version of theory and method. The less self-conscious authors are about the theory-drivenness of these literary conventions, the more their work will "write" them—that is, the less able they will be to examine critically the methods of their research and its literary presentation. Without authorial self-consciousness of this type, sociologists reproduce whole worldviews unwittingly, especially the social physics worldview that freezes what Durkheim called social facts, notably our determination by putative social laws, into our social fate.

A social theory of the text treats the text, here a disciplinary one, as a social topic. It wants authors to take charge of their and our social fate by denying sheer representation—the positivist pretension that writing, especially scientific writing, mirrors the world. A social theory of the text has two elements: It views the text as a deliberate authorial product; it also views the text as having an internal logic—language game—that imposes its own meaning on the text. Thus, texts can be viewed as an interplay between authorial intent and the structuring logic of the language game in use. In the case of journal sociology, there is an interplay between the conventions of journal writing, publishing, and editing and the ways in which authors narrate their arguments and findings. It is inadequate to view journal science as a necessary mode of presentation that cannot be modified, lest disciplinary institutional legitimacy erode. It is equally inadequate to view narrativity as unbounded by convention, extant literature, method, theory, and the nature of one's data. My argument here is not that "anything goes." Neither is this an argument for simply replicating existing convention in the ways in which main-stream empirical sociologists script their research.

Although there has been attention to how sociologists write (e.g., Howard Becker's 1986 book on the subject), for the most part this has not been theoretical attention. Such attention—a social theory of the text—would suggest ways of reading secret writing and of making sociological writing less secretive, more narrative, more accessible to critical readings, more public. I pull insights from post-modern theory and critical theory to assemble a social theory of journal sociology that can serve these two purposes. Although much of what I have to say will be critical in the sense that research methodologists typically do not view their work as either textual or theoretical and resent the probings of nonquantitative outsiders, a social theory of sociological writing is meant to be constructive, "narrativizing" dense work in order to make it available to readings and other writings.

In reading secret writing, a social theory of the text renders public what hereto-fore has been the private domain of disciplinary professionals. The customs of disciplinary writing are now to be viewed as sociological topics in their own right. These customs teach the discipline and discipline in turn. I do not decide against or in favor of disciplinarity because scholars can have either strong, singular disciplinary identities, plowing well-established fields, or, like me and my ilk, they can have diffuse, plural identities, working both within and across disciplines at once. My own degrees cover three fields, sociology, political science, and economics. Much of my theoretical work since graduate school has taken me deeply into the humanities, where these questions of discourse and theory are more frequently asked than in my home discipline of sociology. Many of my sociological colleagues have stuck with sociology since the beginning; they are comfortable reading and writing for the *ASR* and *Social Forces* as well as for the half-dozen leading specialty journals in sociology.

None of us is wrong in the way we approach narrative conventions. We read competently in our various fields, and we teach our students how to do so. As a critical theorist, I am interested in the social theory of the text because I believe that disciplinarity affects and is affected by society, much in the way that Foucault argued. Unlike Foucault, who was not by affiliation a sociologist, I direct my attention to what has become my home discipline, even as I stray outside of it for intellectual resources. I came to sociology during the 1960s, when sociology best addressed the rapid social changes and social movements of the moment. Although in my view sociology has closed off too many alternative discourses, I remain sociologically oriented because sociology is the discipline best positioned to address subsequent social and cultural changes and chart alternative futures. I remain committed to a version of sociology because no other discipline so directly takes up the question of social change.

During the 1960s sociologists Gouldner and O'Neill began to turn sociology's lens upon sociology itself. My own mentor, John O'Neill, explicitly developed what he and Gouldner, albeit somewhat differently, called reflexive sociology. This book is an exercise in reflexivity, equipped with tools of postmodern theory, critical theory, and cultural studies, all of which began to be translated into English during the 1970s. To Gouldner and O'Neill are added Horkheimer and Adorno's *Dialectic of Enlightenment,* Lyotard's (1984) *Postmodern Condition,* Culler's (1982) *On Deconstruction,* and Eagleton's (1983) *Literary Theory: An Introduction.* Out of this German and French melange comes a version of disciplinary self-critique that I have called disciplinary reading (see my 1989c *Socio(onto)logy*). A disciplinary reading uses theoretical tools, such as a social theory of the text, to prise out of disciplines their hidden wisdom, conventions, tropes, and blind spots. This does not unravel disciplines as much as displace them, taking their omissions and deferrals as signs of their true natures, thus strengthening them from the outside by asking the question of their answer. (Durkheim [1950] did much the same thing in *Rules of Sociological Method,* the first book about sociological method ever written, when he mapped sociology as a region unoccupied by psychology.)

This calls into question the stable disciplinary identities I spoke of before. A deconstruction of sociology reveals its weaknesses that are then made good with intellectual tools from other disciplines. Inherently, disciplinary reading calls disciplines into question, inviting transdisciplinarity or pandisciplinarity as a reasonable response. I am pandisciplinary, more by virtue of the unplanned contingencies of my intellectual formation—who I studied with, what I read, the twists and turns of my career—than by design. Pandisciplinarity is a natural outcome of disciplinary deconstructions that inherently threaten the stable, singular identities of disciplined scholars. And yet one can hold to discipline, as many of my colleagues do, because their reading and writing serve them well, resolving their intellectual problems in their own terms, notably by way of method.

It is troubling for positivist sociologists to view method as text, as argument. Social physics is grounded in the Durkheimian notion that we can treat method as a neutral tool for conducting social research. Unlike Feyerabend (1975), I am not against method, only against method that pretends to be something other than what it is—rhetoric. This is not to say that method proceeds arbitrarily. Sampling, questionnaire design, inferential statistics are all rigorous language games that solve problems, albeit within their own frames of reference. We can learn a great deal about people's attitudes and behavior from large-scale survey research. A recent study of American sexuality by University of Chicago social researchers (Michael et al. 1994) gives the lie to extravagant claims about promiscuity and rapidly changing sexual mores. This study is not only well-grounded methodologically but reflexive in its own right: it carefully differentiates itself from other studies with less rigorous methodologies.

I have used Wittgenstein's term *language game* above, and I will continue to use it throughout this book. It is at the center of my argument that method is a rhetorical practice that does not solve problems definitively but asks us to suspend our questioning about its deepest assumptions and to defer our skepticism about its absolute objectivity. Wittgenstein (1986) first used the term "language game" in the mid-1930s, and he elaborated it in his 1976 book *Philosophical Investigations*. By language game he meant a context of usage within which speakers use language to get things done (ideas transacted, buildings built, problems solved) and thus defer discussion about language's inconsistencies, gaps of meaning, definitions until the future. This notion of a language game became central for social phenomenologists and ethnomethodologists, who stress people's abilities to reason practically, within the everyday situations in which they find themselves. Ethnomethodologists counterpose this practical reasoning to theoretical reasoning, which reflects on assumptions and transcends everyday particulars in order to look down on the world from above. Wittgenstein stressed that it is impossible for philosophers and scientists to look down on the world, transcending the everyday transactions of meaning that defer deep discussions about first and final things to another day. My contention here is that methodology is a language game, with its own internal rules and rituals and its own suppressions of certain deep animating assumptions, such as about the possibility of social physics. It is a very productive language game, producing, like the machine I mentioned earlier, all sorts of new knowledge about the world. But as a language game, method does not escape the vicious circle of definitions undefined, assumptions concealed, ultimate meaning deferred. It is, in Derrida's terms, a version and must compete with other versions that do not necessarily view themselves as mirrors or machines.

Recognizing the truth about method as a language game, methodologists debate vigorously amongst themselves. There is no lack of reflexivity here. However, this is debate that proceeds within a single language game and not beyond the boundaries of methodological discourse. Once we demonstrate the rhetorical nature of methodologies, we open its text to many readers and writers, demystifying it but never replacing its rigor. The Chicago study was not published in a specialist sociology journal but rather as a relatively accessible research monograph with a trade house. Although the prose style was dispassionately third person, in the fashion of the journals, there were relatively few representational obstructions of the kind that litter the journal page, granting access to the ordinary literate reader. Methodology here was not the main text but a subordinate one, to be plumbed by interested professionals. In the journals, method is frequently the main text, subordinating conceptual and theoretical issues to technique and thus thwarting public readings. Interestingly, the authors chose to issue an accessible monograph with Little, Brown and, simultaneously, a more technical and methodologically oriented version for professionals (Laumann et al. 1994) with the University of Chicago Press. The authors demonstrate that research can be presented effectively for a general trade audience. They also demonstrate that one can write multiple versions of the same work, suggesting polyvocal approaches to the text of science, which admits of diverse presentations, some more public than others.

The overarching political and social value expressed in this book is that the public sphere of open discussion among enlightened citizens has been imperiled with the rise of what theorists variously call late capitalism, mass society, and the culture industry. Academics espouse the specialized technical discourses of their fields, amassing citations by other academics and thus building careers. Meanwhile, citizens inhabit a cybersociety in which news and culture blur with entertainment, available from television, blockbuster movies, the World Wide Web. In fast capitalism, as I term it, *instantaneity* prevails, where people do not conduct considered readings of others' reasoned arguments but rather are immersed in a cyberspace in which the boundary between text and world blurs to the point of indistinguishability. This was precisely the direction of the argument made by the Frankfurt School theorists after World War II, as mass culture thwarted what they call enlightenment by exhausting critical insights, integrating them smoothly into the dominant, everyday ideology of adjustment and acquiescence. Today, in the era of CNN and the Internet, instantaneity (what Marcuse [1964] called one-dimensionality) overtakes reason, leaving only professional academics as custodians of considered judgment.

For this reason, academic professionalism is not to be abandoned but rather transformed into a vehicle of public discourse. This is not to eschew specialization and technical language; the educated public can learn to crack the code of journal discourse that does not conceal its authoriality but rather provides road maps into the thick sense and sentience of its text. It is rather to follow on the arguments of Habermas (1975), Sennett (1977), Lasch (1979), and Jacoby (1987) for a reinvigoration of the public sphere, reversing both what Lasch called the "culture of narcissism" and what Jacoby (1987) called "the age of academe," with its practiced obscurantism. Journal writing can be a voice of reason, a venue for reasonable voices, a site of public culture, as long as journal discourse acknowledges that it was authored intentionally, has blind spots, does not solve all problems (with method), and can be revised by other voices. Disciplinarity deconstructs into public culture without losing its purchase on professionalism, and thus on the prospect of the advancement of knowledge.

READING CONVERTS INTO WRITING

For the secret writing of sociology to be revealed, readers must learn to read differently and writers to write differently. Reading must be aggressive, probing the subtext of figural discourse for its textual sense. Method can be read if approached properly, with an eye toward its theoretical underpinnings. Writing must acknowledge the author's presence and perspective, intending dialogue and even dispute. This acknowledgment of authoriality is not intended as a royal road to objectivity, revealing the author only in order to bracket authorial subjectivity through rigorous cleansing procedures. The acknowledgment of authoriality invites readers into the thickets of the text, provoking them to respond. The author's self-disclosure demonstrates that the text has been written from the perspective of authorial subjectivity *and can be rewritten.* Every reading is already a writing, a strong version.

It has been said often that much sociological writing, indeed scientific and social-scientific writing generally, is turgid and leaden. Although I favor good writing that pays attention to grammar and syntax and is graceful, not presuming too much on readers who should not have to abide authorial arrogance, my aim is not to teach good writing. I leave that to teachers of composition. Most good writers probably teach themselves by imitating good writing. Rather, my interest here is in cracking the code of highly figural, methods-driven sociology that substitutes mathematics for argument and thus has virtually nothing interesting to say about our contemporary predicaments—poverty, global warming, runaway population growth in nonindustrialized countries, nuclear proliferation and terrorism, sexism and racism, the ruination of the environment, soulless suburbanization, the loss of meaning, adolescent alienation, the uneven development of democracy in politically developing nations and regions, the disorganization and unplanned character of domestic and global capitalism (that is but a short list).

Although *ASR* articles have been written, reviewed, and edited by highly intelligent and well-trained professionals, most of whom know much more about social statistics and research methods than I ever will, very few *ASR* articles, or articles published in other leading American sociology journals, have much to say about these pressing social concerns. Instead, most sociological journal articles are written in order to persuade the reader, deans, and funding agencies that sociology has attained the status of a real science, thus recouping sociology's loss of institutional clout that began to occur during the 1970s, as sociology departments lost both undergraduate and graduate enrollment, grant opportunities dried up, and the sociology job market virtually disappeared. Although I strongly believe that universities and societies require sociology in order for us to understand ourselves and our social institutions, which frequently run amok, I do not believe that sociologists make a persuasive case for themselves by writing mathematized, highly figural discourse that, in effect, freezes the social world on the journal page in much the fashion of Auguste Comte's original "social physics." This positivist journal discourse replaces theoretical argument and conceptual thinking with the techniques of methodology, preventing sociology from engaging the surrounding social world, and virtually ensuring that sociology will be incomprehensible to people who lack advanced training in methods and statistics. Sociology risks talking only to itself, lacking a public dimension that was clearly present in the work of the European founders, who wrote quite narrative, often polemical essays and books. It was also present in the engaged sociologies of the 1960s, such as the work of C. Wright Mills, who, in *The Sociological Imagination,* made much the same argument I am making here, albeit without resorting to words such as *discourse* and *narrativity.*

Mills launched what one might call a pre-postmodern critique of the lack of sociological relevance. He even used the term *postmodern* to describe our emerging capitalism (Mills 1959: 166). He lamented the fact that what he called "The Scientific Method" was replacing reasoned prose with technique, guaranteeing an "abstracted empiricism" that fails to say much, clearly, about important issues. My critique of sociology comes after postmodernism, which furnishes insights about how to read sociological discourse, and after mainstream sociologists in the 1970s began to regain lost sociological legitimacy by positioning sociology as a science. I take Mills's critique of sociology a step further, incorporating insights from critical theory and postmodernism that shed further light on how what he called The Scientific Method plays itself out as a literary strategy, within its peculiarly impenetrable language game. The interpretive challenge is to crack the ironclad code of methodological sociology, revealing it to be argument—for a world gestured in the journal pages. French theorists such as Derrida call this decoding "deconstruction," suggesting that if the elusive thread of science's meaning is pulled hard, the text of science begins to unravel into postures, passions, perspectives, polemic. No amount of scientific discursive work can protect science from being read this way, as narrative and not only as a technical procedure larded with figure and methodological gesture.

In looking at sociology this way, we gain insights into how we might compose, review, edit, and teach sociology differently, returning sociology to the passions and polemics of the new social movements of the 1960s, when sociology had much to say about a world that was fragmenting as students and citizens agitated to end the war in Vietnam and win civil rights for black people in the American South. As positivist discourse, sociology plays a powerfully ideological role, purporting to represent the frozen social world without introducing theoretical perspective or politics and thus, by way of its "de-authorization," hardening that world into our seeming social fate, captured in statements of law. Although the Frankfurt School theorists, Marx, and Mills all favor science and enlightenment over myth and ideology, they contend that positivism is an inadequate theory of knowledge, inaccurately reflecting how knowing and science really work—or write. In particular, positivism reduces science to technique, to method, where science requires imagination, flights of fancy, intellectual risk-taking. In pretending to be free of values, science becomes dogmatic in its own right, disqualifying modes of knowledge that do not pretend an absolute objectivity.

In the chapters that follow, I trace sociological positivism as a literary strategy, a way of writing. I examine its typical gestures, particularly its reliance on method, which is portrayed as sheer technique, not also a mode of argumentation, which I contend it really is. I also examine the literary work of reviewers and editors, who condition the sort of writing that is done. I then examine the last sixty years of American sociological writing. It is striking that sociologists did not always write this way, that a methods-driven sociological discourse only came to dominate the journals after about 1970, in response to American sociology's deepening institutional crisis. I then offer examples and suggest principles of a different kind of writing, which I call public sociology. In developing this notion of a non-positivist public sociology, I do not reject quantitative method but argue that a more public version of method requires self-translation into its animating assumptions, viewing it essentially as theorizing. I want the bright student, with whom I began this chapter, to feel that she can continue her education as a new sociologist without sacrificing her interests in writing and in social change.

2

Learning Discipline Discursively

READING BEFORE WRITING!

Reading interpolates, interrogates, interprets. No version, no matter how methodical, can do without such literary interventions, for writing does not read itself. This is precisely what Derrida meant by "deferral," referring to the ways in which quandaries of meaning are forever pushed ahead (deferred) into the future, when they will be reengaged by new textual acts. Writing cannot solve itself, even the most methodical, science-like writing. Only reading responds to writing with missing sense. Reading does not so much correct writing as help writing understand its omissions, slips, aporias, tropes in terms that are not immediately apparent to the author. No author can fully anticipate her reception, less because one does not fully know one's audience than that language is opaque to itself, especially where authorial subjectivity has been buried underneath the dense conventions of the methodical text.

A guide to writing, and writing differently, is also necessarily a guide to reading, and reading differently. We cannot write strongly, unafraid of authoriality, unless we read strongly, deep into the text's animating assumptions. Much of students' time spent in graduate school is devoted to reading and then converting their reading into literature reviews that drive dissertations, monographs, and journal articles. Reading converts into writing where it draws students into literatures, canons, and subfields from which academics derive their singular identities as disciplinary scholars. This conversion happens earlier and earlier, as doctoral students recognize that they must publish even before their dissertations are complete in order to hope to compete in crowded disciplinary labor markets. A social theory of the text must attend carefully to the boundary between reading (graduate training) and writing (for publication) in order to understand the ways in which disciplines reproduce themselves. If we understand this boundary well, we can understand how to transform disciplinary discourse by changing not only editing and publishing practices but also how we teach, write, and read in graduate school.

Of course, reading never ceases. The more voluminous one's curriculum vita, the more one reads in order to stay current and stay ahead. I have a friend who publishes prodigiously; he owns 10,000 books! This is nothing less than an investment in career capital—his own. These 10,000 books have enabled him to write nearly ten of his own. He reads and publishes across disciplines, having staked out a career in critical theory. Reading not only acquaints one with the existing field or fields, it also helps one find one's voice, developed in counterpoint to the voices and views of others. The more one reads, the more one is ready to write, knowing how sentences are crafted, paragraphs strung together, chapters framed. This is not to say that reading automatically becomes writing. Some readers only read, and others write occasionally. It sometimes seems that a few people, driven and talented, have written all the books.

One is first disciplined by what one reads, beginning in one's undergraduate major and extending to graduate work. Disciplinary identity allows one to situate one's reading in an established literature and one's writing in an established profession. Discipline becomes a problem only if it obstructs thought, preventing it from straying far from the beaten path. Yet the reading required to learn a discipline is necessarily liberating in that it requires the reader secretly to rewrite what one reads, filling in gaps with missing sense and correcting errors. Reading affords what Habermas calls dialogue chances, empowering readers to stand on the shoulders of giants and sometimes engage these giants in intellectual contest. I took a first-year undergraduate seminar at York University from John O'Neill, whose work I explore in chapter 8. We struggled through Hegel's (1967) *Phenomenology of Mind* and Marx's (1964) *Economic and Philosophical Manuscripts.* More than any other experience as a student reader, this seminar set me on my course to write social theory, acquainting me with Hegel and Marx, an awesome experience, and giving me a real-life role model—a professor who publishes his own ideas. I will never forget how, after class one day, O'Neill gave me the page proofs of a colleague's forthcoming social theory book—the late-breaking news of a profession in which I was apprenticing! He also showed me the stacks of pages of a manuscript he was writing in longhand. Today, I regularly cite his eventually published book, as it has become a part of my standard literature of orientation—O'Neill 1972!

Reading, then, opens the way to writing. One learns style; referents; a canon; and, above all, a certain intelligence from the pages of others. As a graduate student I imagined what it would be like to be "published." I fantasized about sending a chapter of my dissertation-in-progress to a journal for its editorial consideration. Eventually, I sent it, and, after revision, it was published (Agger 1976). It was called "Marcuse and Habermas on New Science." I rewrote it a dozen times, believing that I was polishing toward perfection. Little did I realize that this was impossible, given Derrida's strictures on undecidability. (I was just beginning to read the Tel Quel group in the original French. Most of Derrida had yet to be translated.) The paper, like the dissertation as a whole, did not stray far from the cited works. I was still far too novice to add significantly to the theories of the Frankfurt School; it was enough to work closely within their ambit and comment on various themes that engaged them. It occurred to me even then that publishing my first article might well initiate my professional career. Although I was unclear about the norms surrounding academic tenure, I knew that one needed to publish.

After all, my mentor did, and I knew that he had earned tenure. Today, graduate students in the best sociology departments learn early how to build their vitae, converting their reading into term papers, chapters, and then published articles. Unlike me, most of them do empirical work that is frequently authored with their professorial mentors. These mentors teach them where to publish—*American Sociological Review (ASR)* is the most-valued outlet, with others close behind. By now, with the very tight sociology labor market, it is necessary to publish before one completes the dissertation, entering the job market with two or more solid refereed articles in the best journals and the promise of more to come.

Converting reading into writing is a career-building strategy. Graduate students are advised to polish term papers, which are larded with citations of the existing literatures, for eventual publication. In this way, graduate education prepares students for transforming their reading into writing, helping them establish careers. Although there is much to be said for this strategy (as I just stated, I employed it myself), it could be argued that reading done in graduate school—indeed, reading generally—needs to be serendipitous, aimless, playful, and undirected if the reader is to be saturated with the published intelligence of others. This is not a generalist argument for a well-rounded readership but an observation about the frequently unpredictable nature of reading's relationship to writing. Although graduate students need to learn how to cite literature as a way of framing their own disciplinary contributions—this is the very positive sense of the term "becoming disciplined"—I would hesitate to endorse reading's conversion into writing *as method* that can be taught even to beginning graduate students. If reading is driven simply by the motivation to build a career, we risk premature specialization that closes off other intellectual avenues and also reduces the scope of one's own disciplinary work.

The most luminous sociologists have read widely, both within and beyond their disciplines. The professionalization of the discipline, especially during the past twenty years, has turned graduate education ("training") into routine—method—especially as reading converts into publishable, career-building writing. Although one should hesitate to eschew professionalization, especially its norm of merit-based reward in the research university, this professionalization has reduced the scope and nature of many students' reading, which now converts merely into the assemblage of a "literature" to be cited ritualistically. Learning the rich and varied history of the discipline has been reduced to a semester in graduate-level sociological theory, during which students quickly read the classics (or a textbook surveying the classics) and then push onward into their "real" training in research methods, statistics, and the various "substantive" fields of the discipline. This forgets that Durkheim, Weber, Marx, and Parsons had encyclopedic knowledge of a whole range of social science and humanities disciplines. They were not only theorists but well-versed in a host of what sociologists now call empirical literatures. All read voluminously. This reading did not convert mechanically into their writing but informed it. They were not reading toward their first academic job or for tenure; they were not amassing citations, although they did cite others in their writing, engaging other authors in dialogue. They read in order to be worldly intellectuals conversant with others' scholarship and style.

At one level, this is to state the obvious: Marx and Weber were not "trained" in graduate school to be budding professional academics. As Jacoby observes, the public intellectual has gone the way of other cultural anachronisms such as urban bohemia and good bookstores. Public intellectuals have narrowed into professional academics. This troubles Jacoby because, as a former New Leftist, he wants to revivify the collapsing public sphere and galvanize progressive social change. He writes to change minds and even the world, not for tenure. At another level, Marx and Weber's conversion of their reading into writing reflects an undisciplined approach to textuality that revels in the text as a literary experience. Although readers learn to write by reading, reading is done for its own sake. The reason that reading turns into writing is because, with Derrida, readers complete what they read, filling in authorial gaps and silences. The more one reads, and reads aggressively, the greater the likelihood that one will write in counterpoint, contest, even collusion. Marx was not staking out a career while reading for years in the British Museum. He was drinking deeply of an important public discourse—bourgeois economic theory—in order to add his own voice of protest to the workings of a capitalist market economy. Marx read critically, to understand and thus oppose.

This is not the style of reading taught in sociology graduate programs. Although disciplined reading is done with an eye toward staking out a slender research niche within an established literature such as criminology or demography, this reading is not done against the grain, questioning the very right of disciplines and whole social orders to exist. There is a place for both styles of reading. One can read within a discipline in order to build a career. One can read a discipline in order to understand its place in society. Busy sociological empiricists do the first kind of reading; sociological theorists like me do the second kind. Neither is privileged; both require reading to become writing. The purpose of this book is to identify the locales and habits of both approaches to reading, using insights from outside of sociology proper to understand sociological discourse, not to debunk or dismiss it but to compose better sociology. For me, this public sociology springs from an understanding of sociology as a literary accomplishment that can be crafted in a variety of different ways, some more reflexive, open, and engaged than others.

Sociological writing is *iterable;* although performed by particular writers, it could be accomplished by any writer, given its disciplinary nature. At least, it would like us to believe this about itself. (I will contest this later on, as I envisage new ways of scripting science.) Sociological writing is best viewed as social practice, governed by certain literary conventions learned in graduate school and then reinforced throughout one's academic career. Authorial choices are grounded in a given disciplinary culture, literary institutions such as refereed journals, and universities that constrain choice. And all of these are situated in the political economy of early twenty-first–century American and global capitalism that frames academic pedagogy and research. However, because writers write science and can write differently, these choices are subject to modification. Barthes's notion of the "death of the author" is premature, even as we understand that scholarly writing takes place in a social context. In this chapter, I am interested in how students and young professionals are positioned as literary apprentices who have the peculiar goal of learning how to write professional prose that conceals its own authorship underneath the conventions of method. To initiate and advance one's academic career, one must publish. But how does one write for publication while denying one's role as an author?

To become a working academic—to get one's first job in the university world and to keep it—one must write an original dissertation and publish subsequent research. But that already gets ahead of the story. In order to publish, one must learn to write like others who publish, even as one carves out a niche for oneself. And before one writes for publication, one must learn how to read professional writing. Indeed, I advance the argument here that learning how to read involves nothing less than acquiring a certain professional identity. Although there are other aspects of professional identity (a particular graduate school, mentors, methodology), I maintain that identity is largely a discursive outcome: it involves learning how to read and write. I go further in this book: sociological identity involves learning a particular kind of discourse that conceals the fact that published sociology, whether articles or books, has been authored, from the perspective of literary, personal, political agency. Peculiarly, becoming a sociologist requires that one learn certain styles of reading and writing and then forget or deny that one's professional identity is discursively grounded. Most sociologists do not view themselves as writers, even though they spend much of their time engaged in literary craft.

To become a working academic requires one to have learned how to read professionally—the journals, monographs in the field, conference proceedings, reviews of one's own work, letters from editors requesting revisions. One must learn how to read professional discourse before—and as—one writes it. Typically, advanced graduate students have already published before they leave graduate school. In very crowded labor markets, it is necessary to build a vita before one graduates. In disciplines such as English and history, 400 or 500 applicants may apply for a single tenure-track job. When I was a dean at the University of Texas at Arlington, the chair of the history department showed me a list of the ten best applicants for a tenure-track position in women's history. Virtually all of the ten had published books, or had books in press, *before* graduation. But all of this writing for publication occurs near the end of a doctoral student's career. Much unpublished writing precedes this, and, before that, much reading must be done.

Although a good deal of this preparatory reading consumes content, learning what Parsons said, how demographers construct population pyramids, and the names and contributions of the leading social psychologists, I am interested in reading writing as an exemplar, a model of would-be professionals' writing. This is what it means to learn discourse: one imitates the writing of other sociologists, mimicking their articles' structure, sequence, use of methods and literature reviews, approaches to summarizing and analyzing data, and conclusions, suggesting new lines of research. One learns how to cite the work of others, a topic discussed below. One learns style, tone, a certain posture toward what I would call authoriality—the apparent role played in a text by the writer. This last issue will prove to be key throughout this book: Writing sociology frequently involves concealing the fact that a text has been written by an author with perspective, politics, passion. This is the essence of a positivist approach to social science, which I prefer to view as a discursive posture of the writer toward her own role in the production of a text. Let us define positivism as the efforts of the sociologist-author to create the impression that her written work reflects a world out there and is not a literary product. Writing is seen by positivists to stand outside of the world, whereas Wittgenstein and Derrida ground writing squarely in the world, from which there is no exit, even—no, especially—by science.

All of these activities of literary craftsmanship and authorial suppression are habits, learned from the writings of others who have qualified as professional sociologists. None of this comes naturally. It must be acquired through professional apprenticeship. Learning how to read professionally enables one to write, and to write in a way characteristic of scientific sociologists, who present findings and offer interpretations that advance their disciplinary fields. Learning how to write sociology is different than learning how to write literary criticism or journalism in the sense that many sociologists purposely suppress the fact that their articles and monographs are, in fact, texts—corrigible, perspective-ridden literary outcomes inevitably smudged with authorial fingerprints. In the humanistic disciplines, including history and non-positivist anthropology, the literariness of writing is openly acknowledged. Literary style is prized, especially where writing is judged elegant, felicitous, well-crafted. In mainstream sociology, as in the natural science disciplines such as physics, chemistry, and biology, style is not an issue, especially where "research" is not confused with "writing," which is disdained or simply viewed as unproblematic by most working sociologists, who churn out journal articles rooted in data and method while denying that they are writers, busily engaged in literary craft.

Although editing for style occurs in graduate school, by one's teachers, and in journal and monograph editing, this is usually cursory and technical in nature. Punctuation and spelling are corrected, syntax improved, usage rendered consistent. Also, the first-person presence of the author is expunged, if it still exists as a trace, imparting a tone of objectivity to the final draft. The author is trained to edit out her own subjectivity, personality, values. In this sense, I contend that positivism, a theory of knowledge, is grounded in discursive practices that attempt to purge science writing of literariness, the appearance of having-been-written. A positivist approach to textuality dispenses with the concept of the text altogether, instead reducing science and social science articles to a formulaic pattern of presentation. Science writing is mechanical, ritualistic, constrained, dispassionate, composed in passive voice. It is susceptible to being abstracted, cited, swallowed by the canon.

In this context, learning to write is not made thematic in graduate education. Indeed, it is denied, as science authors are taught to de-authorize their literary activities, which are instead framed as piecemeal, productivist research driven by data and method, not by literary imagination. Few instructors of graduate research methodology classes treat method as a text, or the text of methodologically oriented journal articles as discursive. Textuality is invisible, hidden. Scientific sociology is counterposed to speculative human studies such as philosophy and literary studies, from which sociology is said to have broken since Comte, Durkheim, and Weber. Speculative work is writing, whereas science is driven by method, which necessarily, it is thought, bests writing by being hard, definite, lawful. Nevertheless, no matter how much sociology may believe itself to have broken with the literary fields and approaches, all of which acknowledge unashamedly the central role played by the author, sociology is a discourse and, as such, it must be learned. My point here is that students begin this acculturation process as they learn to convert their reading into writing, albeit secret writing ashamed of its own authoriality, which eventually they submit for publication. This secret writing is called *research*.

This conversion, as we shall see in the following section on the practice of citation, launches professional careers. Until one publishes, or at least completes a dissertation, one cannot claim to have mastered the discipline, to be disciplined. Although one need not publish to sustain a successful, tenured professional career at teaching-oriented universities (and today even research universities pay lip service to the importance of undergraduate teaching), at the very least one must convert one's reading into a dissertation. The doctorate of philosophy remains the union card for most would-be academics outside of performance-oriented disciplines such as music, theater, and art. And the dissertation demonstrates one's mastery of professional discourse, especially where it rests so heavily on the mastery of the relevant literature of one's chosen subfield. The dissertation allows the junior author to situate a narrow research subject within a larger field, demonstrating that the author has learned how to communicate within the language games of the field. One cites what needs to be cited—all relevant work published on, or near, the same topic over the last decade; one shows conversancy with the dominant theories and methods in the field; one claims mastery of a topic within the field that does not disrupt the evolutionary momentum of prevailing research and simultaneously avoids the charge of irrelevance.

In graduate school and beyond, one learns to master disciplinary discourse. In American sociology, especially among quantitative empiricists, the process of learning to master this discourse is fraught with irony, given what I just said about how the discourse of positivist sociology and social sciences obscures the role of authoriality—of a text having-been-written by a perspective-ridden author. This is not to say that every sociologist is a positivist in this sense—a literary positivist; many are not. However, the discipline is controlled by major departments in large state universities, especially in the Midwest, in which the discursive style of de-authorized quantitative empiricism holds sway. I have called this approach to writing, which conceals the author and her strong intervention in the text, *Mid-western empiricism*. I have made the argument that it is best to view positivism as a discursive approach to writing science rather than as explicit doctrine. Although positivism certainly has epistemological elements, such as its view of knowledge as a passive representation of an external world that intends to achieve the status of lawfulness, positivism is most powerful as discourse, not doctrine, a way of figuring the science page in order to produce the impression of objectivity. This discourse decenters the author and suggests in its discursive protocols that social science is not a literary product or process but simply an extension of the nature-like world itself. Science in this sense is treated not as a human artifact but as a part of nature, here social nature, that simply records the phenomenal world but does not constitute it. By "constitute" I am using a philosophical term to indicate the strong role that idealists, especially German idealists, feel that knowledge plays in constructing, contextualizing, framing knowledge. When one says that science plays a certain constitutional role, one is not saying, with solipsism, that science simply imagines the world and can alter it willfully. One is saying that knowledge, here including its text, plays a significant role in framing its findings such that one cannot say that science is value-free or theory-free. Methodologies, glossaries, theoretical apparatuses, even the literary presentation of science, help constitute the findings. One cannot remove science from literary inspection, treating it as a blank slate on which data are imprinted.

POSITIVISM AS A DISCURSIVE STRATEGY

Graduate students learn to write like their professorial mentors, who generally believe that sociology is not text but science, not act but fact. Although many ethnomethodologists, symbolic interactionists, and practitioners of cultural studies and critical theory would demur, mainstream quantitative empiricists view learning the discipline as a process of ingesting the substance of methods, grounded theory, and the various empirical findings and frameworks of subdisciplines such as demography and criminology.

Mainstream quantitative empiricists do not view this process as discursive, even though a great deal of time in graduate training is spent reading, writing, and revising writing. It is my contention that the ability to write (and speak) sociology is taught and learned in graduate school, in spite of the contradictory claim of many positivists that sociology as science is not discourse but method, thus securing for it a certain institutional legitimacy at a time when sociology is on the defensive. In the major graduate programs in American sociology, mentorship consists largely of teaching one's dissertation supervisees how to convert their term papers and dissertation chapters into career capital—refereed articles and grants. Once pregraduation publications are secured, time is also devoted to helping one's students find their first tenure-track jobs, which is a discursive process in that one needs to compose a credible vita and a convincing letter of application. In my former department at SUNY-Buffalo, regular workshops were held on vita construction, the application process, and even on "how" to interview at the American Sociological Association annual meetings.

At Buffalo, we would encourage our students to submit papers for journal publication. We and the student would pore over the reviews, which we hoped were not too devastating. We would read them as situated texts, as reflections of the readers' perspectives on their small corner of the discipline. We would help the student think through the revision-and-resubmission process, which of course involves writing, editing, polishing. We would assist them in writing letters to the editor covering the submission of their revised papers, defending their revision strategies and addressing the readers' various concerns. Much as we held workshops on vita construction, we conducted workshops on the job talk, where students would present research in the interview setting, fielding mock questions and comments from a pesky audience. These job colloquia involved the presentation of sole-authored papers prepared by the student reflecting her own, or perhaps collaborative, research to date. My quantitative colleagues frequently included their students on their research projects, resulting in coauthored and multiauthored papers that would be put through the submission, review, and revision processes. Frequently, before submission, these joint projects would receive dry runs as presentations at regional and national conferences.

Graduate school is also a discursive site in that doctoral students who teach learn to prepare—to write—course syllabi, producing discourse (syllabi) about discourse (teaching). In preparing these course outlines, they situate themselves by claiming "areas" of specialization for themselves—social psychology, demography, social movements, methods, and statistics. Thus, the sociological self is discursively constituted in one's account of what one teaches; by the same token, one's courses produce sociological identities in one's students, filling them with "content"— assigned reading, homework, term papers.

Similarly, doctoral preliminary examinations are an important disciplinary site as advanced graduate students write answers to questions designed to assess their degree of professionalization, based on demonstrated mastery of various substantive "literatures" of their chosen fields of expertise. Preliminary examinations are usually focused on reading lists, literatures, that the student reviews in the written answers—a crucial literary ability, as we will see, enabling one to publish journal articles that ground a slender research topic in a presumably broad-gauged literature on advancing knowledge. Preliminary examinations are gatekeeping rituals that bridge graduate coursework and the first stirrings of one's research career in the dissertation to be undertaken once the prelims have been passed. The mastery of literature begets the production of literature as students begin to acquire new identities as publishing professionals.

Once we acknowledge that writing sociology is a discursive practice taught and learned in various venues at the beginning of junior faculty members' careers, we deprivilege sociology's claim to be free of perspective, passion, and polemic. As I shall demonstrate throughout this book, this claim to be value-free hinges on methodology's capability to resolve disputes and advance science. But far from being an Archimedean arbiter of disputes, methodology is already argument, a way of making a case, and not a neutral observer or umpire, as positivists contend. Method is, in a Derridean word, undecidable, incapable of resolving all of its own quandaries without stepping outside itself for alien intellectual resources—such as theory. As we unpack the pages of journal science, we discover that method is rhetoric, a way of persuading people, that rests heavily on its ability to figure its argument, thus giving it the appearance of hard science. In other words, method is a text and, as a text, can be read for what it is really recommending, which is a frozen social world described by social laws, ever the aim of scientific sociology since Comte. Even if individual sociologists may not endorse the inert world gestured by method, they participate in the chilling language game of social physics by repeating its gestures and thus its world.

Graduate training, then, is talkative; students learn to read, write, and present themselves. If they attend positivist graduate programs, they peculiarly learn a mode of writing that pretends to be method, not literature. This is peculiar because method, as I have said, is simply a way of writing about the world that claims exemption from the notion that writers are creatures of perspective and position. Positivist method eschews position because it accepts the Enlightenment notion that a disinterested science affords power over nature and society. But as Horkheimer and Adorno argued in *Dialectic of Enlightenment,* the pretense of disinterestedness, of value-freedom, is the most impregnable value position of all.

Mine is an argument against neither method nor interest. One can study the social world methodically, carefully creating survey-research instruments that allow one to generalize from samples to whole populations. One cannot necessarily learn the world by talking to the next-door neighbor. And the acknowledgment that writers inevitably take positions in composing themselves does not court relativism or nihilism if we recognize, with Habermas, that we can adjudicate truth claims by appealing to reason, which he formulates as the power of the strongest argument. Many of the findings of empiricist sociology are nontrivial and help us better understand society in order to change it. Much work on social stratification illuminates racism, poverty, and sexism. Criminology frequently indicts the flawed criminal justice system. Gender studies reveal insidious patterns of patriarchy. However, once we go beyond using method as a way of talking persuasively about data, positioning it somehow outside of language and thus interest, we imbue it with qualities it does not possess, such as the ability to resolve all intellectual disputes without disputing, as it were. Methodologists recognize that there are no certainties about method, no royal road to truth, but only indeterminacy. Although some methods are better than others for particular purposes, more appropriate to the data and research context at hand, this is circumstantial and not essential. For example, the best way to generalize from appropriately selected samples of 1,500 people to the population of the United States about political party preference in the next general election is to submit a closed-ended questionnaire to members of the sample. On the other hand, in order to understand the meanings that women attach to domestic violence, it may be more effective to interview them at length, building insight out of unstructured narratives.

Not only is method text; debates about method are necessarily conducted in discourses that do not clinch arguments without resorting to persuasion and even polemic. Method solves nothing; its technique does not end debates. Method is simply a means of figuring arguments that draw on deeper arguments and assumptions about the nature of the social world. Positivism is a discursive strategy that attempts to end discourse with the certainties afforded by technique. Positivism fails because method is argument, and can be argued. This avoids relativism because some arguments are better than others, embodying reason. We know this, as Habermas has argued, because the most rational arguments build consensus among speakers, who intend universal understandings. If we were to collect the twenty most esteemed research methodologists in American sociology in a seminar room, there is no doubt that they could construct a study of public opinion about President Clinton's alleged sexual transgressions that would leave little to chance. These twenty methodologists would construct a study that would likely be both valid and reliable; that is, it would reflect popular opinion accurately and admit of replication by other researchers. However, these twenty wise men and women would not exhaust possible approaches to studying Clinton's philandering, nor would they produce a survey instrument that avoids ambiguity. Their questionnaire would not ask all of the most interesting questions, nor would their statistical inferences about the population as a whole be unassailable, utterly avoiding the possibility of error.

Positivism is a textual strategy, a way of presenting data that intends to convey the impression that the data are somehow frozen in time and not molten; indeterminate; in Derrida's terms, undecidable. This would seem unproblematic when we are talking about family income in the year 1998 as an index of wealth or social class. However, even in this example, we need to be clear about what constitutes a family as well as income. Does the income generated by a cousin who lives in the family domicile count? Do winnings from a scratch-off lottery ticket count? Our operational definitions of family and of income must be argued; other definitions are possible. The interesting philosophical issue here is whether data about "family income in 1998" exist apart from our measures of them. On one level, it would seem obvious that families earned income last year. On another level, though, one might better conceptualize individual-level earnings as an indicator of wealth or social class, especially considering that many families are fragmented and live apart and in nonnuclear combinations of adults and children. Method helps simplify the world in order to study it. Although this affords ample insight and makes generalization possible, it is not clear that positivism as a discursive strategy is appropriate to sociology in the same way that it is appropriate to physics or biology.

The reason for this has to do with the impression created by positivist sociology that the world is relatively transparent, fixed and finite, thus eliminating chaos and change, which tend to thwart science. In other words, one has to decide whether sociology ought to aspire to be a science in the same sense that physics is a science. Even physicists since Heisenberg and Einstein have had doubts about this issue of physics as a science that pursues time-invariant laws. The revolution in relativity theory suggests that even laws are relative to time and place—context. Positivist sociologists want to freeze the world into invariant patterns—laws. They accept Comte's original program for what he called positive philosophy—sociology— which was to enhance modernization by recognizing modernity's inevitable unfolding. Comte expressed the teleology (purpose) of an unfolding history in his law of the three stages, which describes the evolution of Western societies from simple to complex, tradition-bound to rational.

Comte, Durkheim, and Parsons felt that sociology, Comte's social physics, could recognize the "necessity" imbedded in modernity's history and facilitate it by providing on-course corrections. This is the main contention of Parsons' functionalism contained in books such as (1951) *The Social System*. This doctrinal positivism is defended in wordy tomes, not methodological gestures. From this functionalism we derive the notion that sociology and social policy are to address "social problems," conceptualized as episodes of the social system's dysfunction but not as fundamental "contradictions," in Marx's sense, at the bedrock of society. In grasping social laws of capitalism, patriarchy, Judaeo-Christianity and the domination of nature, sociology would reproduce their inevitability by depicting them as fate, necessity. As ideology, then, sociology depicts the unalterability of the present social order while acknowledging that various social problems—untoward poverty, urban blight, bad schools, premodern discrimination against women and minorities, the decline of community—actually retard progress.

Sociology has always engaged with social problems. Durkheim worried about suicide caused by alienation in a secular era; Weber discussed the "iron cage" of excessive bureaucracy, shackling individual creativity. Even sociological journal articles routinely conclude with passing discussions of policy implications, although these are afterthoughts, appendages to the main text of the articles, which is usually highly figural. The main text of positivist sociological discourse is not prose at all but the methodological gestures dominating the standard journal page—the compulsive methodological meanderings that have overtaken the discursive reason of Parsons-era sociology. Custodianship of sociology's fundamental system-preserving role has shifted from theory (Durkheim, Weber, Parsons) to method, which merely gestures what before used to be postulated explicitly in the sweeping claims of grand theory. The notion that these were "grand" claims is, of course, method's, by contrast to which it presents itself as matter-of-fact, the materiel of sociological civil engineering concerned to build a bridge, not a paradigm (see Turner 1998, 1999 for a discussion of sociology as an engineering discipline).

As sociology closed the door of radical social change, which would upset supposed societal evolution, it opens the door of personal betterment—upward mobility. This is precisely what Mannheim (1936) in *Ideology and Utopia* meant by ideology, a "worldview" that does not upset modernity but augments it. The founding sociologists recognized, with Marx, that the development of capitalism would have numerous rough spots, even backsliding, that imperil the social system by failing to take care of unfortunate individuals who fall by the way. In a society and economy based on competition, there are losers for every winner. Where Marx theorized that competition would lead to system-wrenching contradictions that could not be contained even with statist fine-tuning, such as the fiscal and welfare interventions recommended by Keynesian economic theory, the founding sociologists contended that capitalism could contain these irruptions by utilizing ideologies, such as sociology, that urge people to work within the system to better themselves and overcome what they are urged to conceptualize as personal troubles, not public issues. In particular, with Weber, people are advised to seek meaning in their private lives now that what Weber called the disenchantment of the world makes it difficult to derive meaning from the public sphere.

Positivist sociology conjures the impression of oppression's inescapability, even if many sociologists are card-carrying progressives. As a discipline, sociology imitates the discursive posture of the natural sciences, which views its own text as a mirror of nature. Although advanced physicists and other natural scientists have come to acknowledge the historicity of their own disciplines, sociologists who believe they mirror social nature imitate a version of the natural sciences from before relativity. Although they defend this as an institutional survival strategy and nothing more, especially given their progressive politics, they are positioned by disciplinary discourse to write conservative sociology—conservative in the sense of using positivist literary strategies in order to suggest a lawful social universe. No matter how politically minded graduate students may be, and few were more politically minded than those of us who came to sociology during the 1960s when it was a vocabulary of protest, scientism gets the better of those who adopt and reproduce the literary conventions of positivism.

Although it is certainly true that findings can be used to support radical causes, my point here is that positivist journal sociology sits on the page inertly, choking off its own potentially critical insights by virtue of its participation in the lifeless discourse of positivism. Thus, its findings are lost to critical reason and public discussion. Journal science overwhelms critical intention and turns it back on itself, where the conventions of positivism are repeated thoughtlessly in order to get one's work published and advance one's career. This is not to suggest or endorse a conspiracy theory whereby latter-day Comteans, armed with sophisticated social statistics, gathered in a back room at the American Sociological Association annual meetings and plotted the positivist takeover of the *ASR*, the most prestigious U.S. sociology journal. That meeting in a smoke-filled room never took place. Instead, literary norms emerged over time that informed and were informed by the institutional positioning of sociology, including the shifting sites of influence from Ivy League departments and Chicago to what I have characterized as Midwestern empiricist departments at Michigan, Ohio State, Wisconsin, Penn State, Minnesota, and Texas.

APPRENTICESHIP TO SCIENTISM I:
DE-AUTHORIZING ONE'S WRITING

Graduate students begin to learn four aspects of the literary strategy of positivism. First, they are taught to write without acknowledging that they are doing so. They learn to suppress the literariness of their work, even though many hours are consumed in reading, writing, and revising. Second, they ground their own work in a cluster of citations of canonical articles and monographs that helps frame their research problem and method. Third, they replace prose with the figural gestures of method as sociology subtly shifts its locus of meaning from considered argumentation to the appearance of nature's mirror via methodology. Finally, they learn to revise in response to readers' concerns, questions, and cavils.

These literary skills are often acquired in sequence; the third skill, replacing prose with figure in order to create what I call the science aura, arrives just as the student is ready to submit work for publication. All four of these aptitudes will be discussed at length. Here, I want to indicate the sort of "unlearning" that has to occur before the student-apprentice can compose herself professionally and sustain a successful career by publishing. The first skill is the ability to view one's writing not as writing at all but rather as the busy activities of science as these are translated from methodology to text. At a time when many people now compose at the desktop or laptop computer, there is less leap than there used to be from method to written product. After all, one might well perform statistical analyses of data using SPSS on one's microcomputer, after which one writes them up. There is a virtually seamless transition between data analysis and writing now that people can use Windows-like programs in order to move back and forth between computer tasks without much friction. Before microcomputing, there was a more evident mediation between data analysis and the drafting of one's articles and monographs, which was often conducted in longhand.

As one apprentices to scientism—positivist sociological writing—one relearns one's attitude toward one's literary creations. Although at a certain level one can never forget that one is writing while crafting the various sections of a journal article or the chapters of a dissertation, as one becomes professionalized the drafting and crafting process becomes second nature. Articles are not written, they are prepared in the authorial assemblage of their constituent segments—literature review, discussion of method, discussion of findings, policy analysis, conclusion. As one learns how to write science, writing becomes formulaic; one does not have to remind oneself to expunge the first person, cite work published in the last ten years, prepare and then insert tables and graphs at the appropriate places in the text, and abstract the article before submission. All of these activities become routine as one comes to believe that what is being produced is not a literary outcome but a chunk of science produced by a team of collaborators engaged in the *bricolage* of bench science.

One learns how to compose articles without seeming to have written them, with an efflorescent authorial subjectivity running wild and dictating untoward, unprofessional outcomes. Articles are prepared, produced, assembled, put together, revised, polished. It is rarely said that they are written, except by qualitative sociologists prone to ethnography who recognize that both their work and data are narrative (e.g., Richardson 1990). The "real" work of scientific sociology is viewed as methodological, involving the choice of appropriate research instruments and strategies, data collection, and statistical analysis. Although reviewers for journals read for style as well as substance, editing for style typically involves the disciplining of an exuberant literary subjectivity, who may overindulge in first-person prose, political polemic, or untoward generalization ("going beyond one's data"). Positivist writing corrals literary subjectivity precisely in order to create the impression that science is objective and hence to be trusted. In my final chapter, I will suggest alternative ways of reading and writing science that do not compromise objectivity but allow for more accessible and democratic discourses of science.

To go beyond one's data is a serious indictment by reviewers. One may well appear to offer overreaching interpretations because findings are trivial and do not advance the literature sufficiently to warrant publication. If tenure rests on the publication of ten to fifteen refereed journal articles, as well as the preparation of grant proposals, effective teaching, and service on departmental and university committees, by the end of the fifth year in academic rank, one must not have too many articles rejected. It is also imperative to have a number of papers out for review at any time in order to maximize the probability that at least some of them will be accepted before the tenure decision. (Most accepted articles have to undergo revision before they are finally accepted.) In this context, one is sorely tempted to move speculatively "beyond" what the data may, within the language game of method, allow one to conclude about the topic under investigation. The ability to balance the significance of one's work with the constraints supposedly imposed by data and method is crucial for a successful career. If one does trivial work and takes no intellectual risks, one will meet the same fate—rejection after rejection—as if one's interpretations of data run wild, going far beyond what data and method, within their own logics and language games, will support.

APPRENTICESHIP TO SCIENTISM II: CITATION AND THE CANON

This avoidance of rejection leads to the second skill that must be acquired by disciplinary initiates. One must learn to ground one's work in an existing literature or canon and then defend the claim that one's work adds to this canon, moving it gradually forward. Trivial findings do not justify publication. Similarly, findings that move too far beyond the established boundary of the existing research literature do not constitute normal science, the bread and butter of mainstream empiricists. One must learn how to cite the canon, situating one's own work within it and then warranting one's marginal contributions of knowledge. The literary device used in this context-setting work is *citation,* the parenthetical acknowledgments of the work of other contemporary scholars who have already published in one's subfield of choice. Citations occur most frequently in the *literature review* sections of papers and monographs, which introduce the work, situating the author's own foray in an established context or literature.

Citation not only grounds one's work in like-minded scholarship. It also gives one's own work legitimacy, the citation of authority affording authority. Interestingly, citation has the potential to undercut the de-authorization process described in the section above in the sense that authors are cited, suggesting that science proceeds through, not around, Blau and Duncan (1967), Davis and Moore (1945), Hochschild (1989), England and Farkas (1986). Authorization and de-authorization exist in tension, the one providing counterpoint to the other. Although what Kuhn called normal science is machine-like in the sense that it makes progress over the heads of mere individuals (unless those individuals do path-breaking work that constitutes a paradigm shift, as he termed it), this gradual progress occurs with respect to an existing body of knowledge, to which names and the dates of their relevant publications—citations—are attached. Although citation is merely parenthetical work, it is work that is so important in authorizing one's own work that it begins articles, monographs, and dissertations.

Citation is a literary skill, in spite of its scientific appearance as a natural outcome of disciplinary accumulation. Davis and Moore's 1945 article and England and Farkas's 1986 book do not typically understand themselves in terms of a made-to-order canon, tradition, or literature to which one can assign a name, in particular the name constituting the title of the article that cites them. Let's pretend that the *ASR* has just published an article that cites both Davis/Moore and England/Farkas in the literature review section that opens the article. The article happens to be titled "Gendered Principles of Inequality: Stratification in the U.S. before and after the Women's Movement." Such an article could legitimately cite "classics" such as Davis/Moore and England/Farkas. However, neither Davis, Moore, England, nor Farkas necessarily understands their work in that way. Although they might well consent to the usage of their work in the context of the aforementioned *ASR* article, the author has taken license in subsuming their work under the rubric of "Gendered Principles of Inequality."

This is especially true where the citation stops with the date of the publication cited but does not provide information about a particular passage or page, let alone why they are relevant. Typically, such discussions are confined to footnotes or endnotes, which editors and reviewers increasingly regard as wordy and uneconomic. I view notes as essential sites of self-reflection and further argumentation in which one makes a case for one's citations, both in agreement and disagreement with them. However, authors increasingly dispense not only with notes, except highly technical methodological asides, but with the reference to particular page numbers that could at least guide further reading and better establish one's claim to use the authority of others' work as authorization for one's own. And England and Farkas are probably not cited alone but in parenthetic strings, with authors and their dates of publications separated by semicolons, their relevance to the author's argument remaining unexplicated.

This is perspectival, self-conscious authorship at its best: the writer is not dead but splendidly alive, assembling an argument, buttressed with reference to others, in the bricolage of citation. Poetic license is taken as England/Farkas echo Davis/Moore in support of an argument none of them would have made as such. Citation constitutes, argues, grounds, founds, rebuts. It is busy work that reflects a lively literary sensibility, not the soulless machine of science. In establishing a literature, sociological writers write literature, acknowledging the literary in their field and in their own work. Even though citation usually ceases or peters out after the opening literature review, in which the author claims authority (author-ity!) for her own contribution to the advancement of science, citations can still be found in the methodological sections of the paper, especially inasmuch as method is not machine but poetry, subject to multiple meanings and usages. Wherever one finds citation, one finds authoriality bursting out of the straitjacket of science—making arguments, appropriating others for one's own position, engaging with interlocutors, creating whole fields out of difference.

Citation can be cynical, too. Students are taught to cite those who may review their work inasmuch as editors often send papers to reviewers whose work is listed in the paper's bibliography. Editors do this not because they want softball reviews but because they understand that fields are founded in literature review sections of articles, with the important names on one's own topic sausaged together in the lengthy parenthetical citations collecting numerous and sometimes heterogeneous authorities under one roof, in defense of one's argument. In this, editors intuitively appreciate Wittgenstein's argument that sense is made and reason advanced within what he called language games, which litter the fields of scientific disciplines. It could be said that papers are most fairly reviewed within their own language games, frames of reference, theoretical and methodological traditions, communities of authority. To send the paper on gendered principles of inequality to scholars in social movements or criminology would necessarily produce poisoned reviews, especially if we take seriously the claim that sociology has become a highly differentiated field grounded in narrow specialization.

The disciplinary initiate cites those who may review her work because in doing so she canonizes their work, subsuming them under the parenthetical umbrellas of accumulated wisdom that mark the field. Not only is this flattering. Citation is productive activity in the sense that it produces the field—here, gendered principles of inequality—that, as "literature," takes on a life of its own, susceptible to others who work within, or near, it. Paula England cited once leads to second, third, fourth citations by others. Citation, then, not only produces fields. It also produces and reproduces reputation, influencing where England is hired, her salary, her publication and editorial opportunities, her life chances overall. In England's case, some well-placed articles on what one might call economic sociology with a feminist intent early in her career allowed her to move (upward) from the University of

Texas at Dallas to premier sociology departments at the University of Arizona, Penn, Northwestern, and Stanford, greatly accelerating her career. Not long after moving to Arizona, England was invited to edit the *ASR*.

Let me render this analysis of citation somewhat quantitative. I compared the number of times that England and I have been cited in a given year, as reported in the *Social Sciences Citation Index*. (I subtracted self-citations from each annual count.) The counts are a bit unreliable in that my new bifocals made it difficult to keep England's many citations straight; I could as well have measured her long lists of counts. In the year 1981, when we were both nobodies, I recorded one citation of my work, while England recorded nine. In 1989, I recorded no citations, and England recorded sixty-two. Clearly, her career, by mainstream standards, had gathered substantial momentum during the intervening years. By 1995, my count had swollen to twenty-seven, while England's was ninety-four. For purposes of historical accuracy, I should add that my counts throughout the 1990s were helped by an article I published in the *Annual Review of Sociology* on postmodernism and critical theory, which was cited by several mainstream sociologists; England suggested my name to the *Annual Review*'s editor. In 1998, the last year for which I have data, my count had fallen to twenty-one, and England's count continued to expand to 113. As I indicated, she now works at Stanford, while I work at Texas-Arlington. Her bid to become editor of *ASR* was successful; I applied twice, unsuccessfully, to be editor of the American Sociological Association journal *Sociological Theory*.

Citations produce careers not only by virtue of their reproduction, as those within the field come to repeat the citations done by others, England and Farkas reproducing themselves throughout the field by scholars who keep up to date with the current journals. They also produce careers through the directly economic currency of citation indexes, such as the *Social Sciences Citation Index*. These indexes list the occasions on which published papers are cited. Thus, as I showed, one can count the number of times that England is cited between 1992 and 1996 and compare her citation count to the counts of others. Departments sometimes use these counts to measure a scholar's "visibility." In my former department at Buffalo, we conducted an outside chair search. Members of the positivist faction in the department amassed citation counts of the leading candidates, in aid of its argument that a "mainstream" sociologist, as indicated by the number of a chair candidate's citations, would benefit the department in its struggle for internal resources and external recognition in the field. Universities often require that candidates for tenure and promotion include a list of their citations in their promotion dossier.

Citations are a measure of something: simply inasmuch as they are taken seriously in hiring and promotion decisions, they matter. And they do afford an interesting glimpse of the ways in which both literatures and careers are produced (see Cronin 1984). Flaws with the citation method of assessing a scholar's visibility have been noted often. Citation indexes usually do not include citations found in books. For scholars who work in the book mode, such as most people in social theory, citation counts may be nearly meaningless. As well, not all journals are surveyed in citation indexes. Journals off the beaten path may be omitted, skewing the results of a comprehensive analysis of a work's centrality to the field. Finally, the citation methodology itself tends to add value to existing citations in the sense that people who read citation indexes for an indication of the prevailing literature in the field reproduce citations simply because they have been cited before. Thus, literatures, as well as reputations, enter into a cycle of self-inflation.

There is nothing wrong with any of this if we are cautious about the methodology of citation. Fields revolve around established literatures, which are advanced by scholarship within them. Literatures by their nature reproduce themselves through scholars who cite them. In this sense, citation is a strong literary act. Fields depend on citation for their very existence. Without having available a literature to be referenced in the particular researches done by disciplinary practitioners, fields would disintegrate into chaos. If there was little or no continuity in citation practices, there would be no disciplinary or subdisciplinary stock of knowledge that moves forward glacially with each published and cited contribution to it. Fields would deconstruct into disarray as articles and books did not appear to build on the ones before them. However, we must not lose sight of the fact that citation is perspectival, requiring authors to assert connections between works that, others might argue, do not cohere into scholarly consensus. Citation, then, is a literary artifice sustaining authors' warrants of the contribution of their work to an existing body of knowledge. Upon deconstructive scrutiny, citations of cumulative knowledge decenter into myriad voices that could as well be cobbled into very different pastiches of invisible fields.

In graduate school, one learns how to cite, and thus how to be disciplined. There is a lot of reading to be done, both of current literature routinely cited and of the prehistory of one's field—what was published in the 1940s, 1950s, 1960s. Generations are connected by the filial relations among mentors and their students. Parsons had progenitors as well as students. His students have students. To understand neo-Parsonian sociology, for example in the oeuvre of Jeffrey Alexander (1982), the UCLA sociological theorist, one needs to understand where Parsons was coming from as he attempted to move sociological theory forward. Parsons is important because he and his students trained many subsequent sociological theorists, who cited in his name. Citation prevents disciplinary amnesia, reminding us that sociology is a sociohistorical project in the service of the Enlightenment—the dominance of social nature, the advance of capitalism. Citation extends back only far enough to ground one's paper on the gendered principles of inequality in pregiven authority—here, the latter-day fields of social stratification and gender inequality.

Although science's past is punctuated by its break with myth, here the notion that gender inequalities in society stem simply from men's physical superiority, science moves forward quickly, requiring one to discard last decade's authorities for new ones. Fast academic capitalism replaces authority quickly in order to produce career surplus value—publications and citations. One must stay current, reading around in the journals, in order to cite the most contemporary sources. If there is a dearth of such sources, perhaps one's field has become moribund or metamorphosed into another field. Social-exchange theory has given way to rational-choice theory, including scholars such as Hechter (1987); the human-capital perspective is now the social-capital perspective, with the work of Coleman (1990). In graduate school, one learns something of the intergenerational inheritance of accumulated authority, only to leave behind the 1960s and even 1970s as one begins to publish. Beginning to publish affords one the luxury of discarding the past, even the relatively recent past, in favor of last year's or last issue's cites. The more one's research is focused, the less one has to know (or the more one can forget) about a field's prehistory. In this sense, theorists tend "the classics," not only the Europeans such as Comte, Durkheim, and Weber, who founded the discipline, but even the Americans who worked the field in the 1930s such as the Chicago School sociologists or the Parsonians who worked in the 1950s. Theory becomes the history of the discipline and not an overarching attempt at social explanation, as it was for Weber and Marx. Theory is the field in which dead and forgotten cites are buried.

This approach to the establishment of fields has advantages and disadvantages. If science moves quickly, building on the shoulders of giants and creating new expertise decade by decade, one can be sure that research is advancing, both methodologically and substantively. Current articles from the *ASR* are more sophisticated, denser, more amnesiac than *ASR* articles from the 1960s, let alone the 1930s. They are at once more "like science" and more sophisticated in their grasp of their fields' literatures and methods. They are "more professional" and less broad-gauged than their counterparts fifty years ago. But they are also less likely to knit together different fields in pursuit of total social understanding, less likely to produce general theory, less likely to paint with a broad brush without ignoring particulars. Classic articles such as Davis and Moore's 1945 paper on social inequality are less likely to appear today, in which narrow specialization, figural display, and instant authority hold sway. It may also be true that article publications in the leading sociological journals have more impact on one's career fortunes than they did previously, both as rejection rates rise and as the currency of professionalism, measured by where one publishes, increases in value. In the leading mainstream sociology departments, for example, it is no secret that people who write articles must publish frequently in the "big three"—*American Sociological Review, American Journal of Sociology, Social Forces*—to earn tenure and promotion. This was less true even two decades ago, when more journals "counted" and when published books were considered more widely to be a legitimate mode of scholarship.

Although citation establishes fields and in this sense establishes connections between researches, it promotes amnesia with respect to the prehistory of problems. The currency of citation is recency, except where "classics" are concerned— articles and books judged timeless by disciplinary scholars. Check the number of such classics cited in the leading sociological journals. The European founders are rarely cited, except in the occasional theoretical article, which is likely to be an article on the history of theory and the discipline. Work from the 1930s, 1940s, 1950s,

1960s, even 1970s is rarely cited, even though graduate students are taught that every empirical field contains classic statements that must be read or at least engaged in abstract form. The *Annual Review of Sociology* publishes high-level literature reviews that prepare students for doctoral comprehensive examinations. These reviews cover the field, but rarely extend back more than five or ten years. It is generally agreed that working professionals who seek to integrate literature reviews into their papers rarely need to delve further back into the prehistories of fields' literatures but only to know what is current. Although it does not hurt to know the prehistory of one's field—most would argue that this is indispensable—prehistory can be dispensed with once one begins to publish, if only in the interest of journals' economy.

APPRENTICESHIP TO SCIENTISM III:
FIGURING THE WORLD

One learns how to write sociology not mainly as prose but rather as figure. This conveys the impression that sociology is a science, much like the hard natural sciences, in its dependence on method. The discursive use of figure promotes the science aura, the science-likeness or scientificity of journal sociology. In this sense, graduate students are taught to write the journal page, not simply the prose that they have traditionally associated with the craft of authorial artifice. As one is professionalized in graduate school and beyond, one learns how to figure one's work so that it resembles what is taken to be science, clogging the journal page with the busy hieroglyphics of method. In the next three chapters, I read this dense figural landscape for what it silently says about the discipline and world. As method is figured, the reader is left with the impression that sociological technique resolves arguments and moves the literature forward. It matters little "what" method argues but simply that the research in question is being driven by research methods and statistical manipulations that comprise what people ordinarily regard as science.

I am not saying simply that these methods are imbedded with values, theories, frameworks that tend to determine their outcomes—for example, how one studies inequality—but that the dominance of the journal page by the busyness of method *is argument itself,* especially in what it excludes. Method's gestures argue for the resemblance of sociology to the law-seeking natural sciences, which has the tendency of freezing the data being presented into what members of the Frankfurt School called "social nature." Method argues for a social world that is essentially static, even if dynamic patterns are being described. It argues for a world mirrored by the sociologist on the journal page in support of the project of science, depicting the frozen world in statements of law.

Method's "text" involves its displacement of prose—reasoned argument—with figure: graphs, charts, equations, scatterplots, and other technical gestures. Figure comes to be the main text of quantitative journal sociology as prose is squeezed out and reduced to notes, which themselves have been truncated or turned into

figure. Positivism is a discursive strategy where figure replaces old-fashioned argument, thus arguing—for a frozen, changeless world—all the more effectively. Even
if sociologists report less-than-perfect correlations between variables, say crime and
poverty, the displacement of prose with figure suggests an ordered, law-governed
society that can eventually be reduced to cause-and-effect relationships given
enough normal science supported by research grants and reported in mainstream
journals. Figure presages causality, even if methodologists add numerous marginal
disclaimers about confidence levels, sampling problems, the lack of theoretical
sophistication that would knit the data together.

   That hesitancy is the stuff of science, which promises nothing more than incremental progress through piecemeal research. As a discursive strategy in U.S. sociology, positivism is less doctrine than literary gesture. Those who figure their *ASR*
articles may even disdain positivism, or dismiss such rarefied talk as unproductive
metatheory. The lawfulness of the social world is only implied on the journal page
by its intention to represent the world in all its overt busyness and thickness. The
particular text of positivism's literary agenda is its mathematization of the social, its
postured resemblance to mathematics. Positivist journal articles are clogged with
sections describing methodology and then data analysis that could have been lifted
from mathematics journal pages. This is defended as the rigor and technical sophistication required by advanced social science. By the time graduate students have
completed their coursework in quantitatively oriented sociology departments, they
have usually taken at least two advanced social statistics classes and perhaps classes in
matrix algebra and calculus. Students are encouraged to attend workshops such as
the ICPSR (Inter-university Consortium of Political and Social Research) summer
school at the University of Michigan in order to refine their methodological and
statistical expertise. Imitating their faculty mentors, they purchase the thin green
paperback Sage primers on research methods and statistics, periodically consulting
them for methodological troubleshooting as they write papers and journal articles.
Conversations around watercoolers in mainstream sociology departments are as
likely to be about methods as they are the pennant race or presidential politics.

   This is precisely the source of positivism's dominion: it appears not to be metaphysics, literature, poetry, philosophy. Instead, it is a protocol, as analytic philosophers have contended, a way of doing research that appears to have put issues of
metaphysics to rest. Derrida would disagree: metaphysics haunts physics because both
are discourse, and hence undecidable—unable to rest with a final truth because truths
are always expressed in indefinite, slippery, ambiguous language, hence requiring
clarifications (which invite further clarifications). Physics—methodological gestures—drives out prose on the journal page because physics appears to end arguments, getting on with the business of science. It is not so much that workaday positivist sociologists invest in a physics-like model of the social universe but rather that
they have been taught that method gets us beyond metaphysics and metatheory.

   Even this model of physics as value-free method no longer persuades physicists,
who accept relativity and have done so since Einstein and Heisenberg. The revo-

lution in the philosophy of science brought about by relativity recasts physics as laden with philosophy and perspective. Workaday social science positivists who seek to produce the science aura with sheer method, thus eliminating myth and metaphysics, are decades behind philosophers of natural science who, since Einstein, understand their own work as corrigible, undecidable, perspectival. Thus, sociologists who accept Comte's image of sociology as social physics imitate an out-of-date physics, creating the irony that natural scientists are more comfortable with metaphysics than social scientists who clamor for greater institutional prestige by imitating physicists' journal pages. This is possible because latter-day sociological positivism is not doctrine but rather convention, reliant on method to figure the journal page, thus reducing the claim of prose, philosophy, literature, theory. Few read Comte anymore, let alone Heisenberg and Derrida. Sociological positivism is taught much in the way that elementary students learn how to write, through practice not theory.

My empirical colleagues at Buffalo not only did not read Derrida; they viewed him as a non-sociologist, a nonperson, in the sense that he did not contribute to the recent empirical literatures of their various fields. Reading him was viewed as a waste of time, which would be better spent on professional socialization. Graduate students were taught to learn the "skills"—writing the journal page—that would get them published, and hence jobs. Although one cannot argue with such survival strategies in an era of crowded academic labor markets, the aversion to philosophy of science and discourse analysis of science is ironic at a time when philosophers of science are intensely concerned with issues of both metaphysics and method, for example the discussions of chaos theory.

Mine is not an argument against method. Method is always necessary in empirical research, especially if we are to generalize from samples to whole populations. But one can learn methods, even sophisticated ones, while viewing them as literary gestures, which they always are. The science page can be approached as literature, both by writers who craft it and readers who decipher it. This does not deprivilege method but rather democratizes it, allowing it episodes of self-consciousness and self-clarification that open up science to outsiders. Method is not the antithesis of literature, except to positivists who claim that their methods allow them to break with literature and philosophy. Method is discourse, even though not all discourse is method. That is, one can study the social world rigorously, using sophisticated techniques of sampling, questionnaire construction, and inferential statistics allowing one to generalize from samples to populations, without stepping out of the realm of discourse: in writing up one's methods, one engages in an act of literary artifice, making deliberate authorial choices that influence how one's science gets read. Method is especially discursive and literary where its author pretends that method escapes the realm of textuality, attaining a higher, less subjective truth. In this respect, one could say that positivist method's discourse conceals its own discursiveness through elaborate literary gestures. One must write hard and well in order to conceal that one is writing. Or, as I said in *Socio(onto)logy,* positivist sociology is secret writing.

Secret writing can always be read as such, once we locate the author's voice within it. This voice is ineradicable. No amount of methodological muting can silence it. Methodologists especially understand the artifice-like nature of their work, being the first to recognize how many deliberate and often nonobvious choices must be made as one goes to study and then compose the social world. Graduate training that is methods-intensive involves a great deal of attention to the indeterminacy—Derrida's undecidability—of research methods. There are vast and growing literatures on how to construct survey instruments (questionnaires), how to do face-to-face interviews, how to sample, how to analyze one's data, how to write up one's methods and results in convincing ways. Many more empirical sociologists are engaged in this training and research on methods than are engaged in my sort of deconstructive analysis of science's text! Method is nearly a discipline in itself not only because would-be sociologists and even practicing sociologists have much to learn before they publish, but because methodology does not lie beyond the literary or philosophical. Methodology requires deep theoretical decisions that lie at the heart of the artifice-like nature of science, in fact that guarantee its humanity. Again, one need not choose between method and literature if one accepts that research methods require deliberate discursive choices and do not admit of singular approaches to problems.

Would-be sociologists must learn both how to read and write methods. Readers of methods must penetrate the surface appearance of methods and statistics as nonliterary, even antiliterary. Writers of method must learn to conceal their own artifice, presenting methods as sheer technique. During the course of one's apprenticeship as a professional sociologist it is difficult to shift from one discursive stance to the other. The more deeply one gets into methods, the more one understands how methodology does not solve intellectual problems or resolve disputes but merely points the way toward better, if incomplete, understandings. The more technically proficient one is, the further removed one becomes from methods as the apotheosis of literature. The literariness of method simply becomes a nonissue. At the same time, training refines the discursive presentation of methods as nonwriting. I suggest that this irony is instructive; it helps us understand the contradiction between depth and discourse, demonstrating that the further one penetrates methodology as a text so dense no light can penetrate, the closer one gets to literature, philosophy, metaphysics, theory.

To be sure, this depends on the sociologist recognizing the irony of training and erudition. Recognizing this irony requires an approach to the journal page as discourse, not machine or mirror. For a practitioner of empirical sociology to problematize the journal page, subjecting it to thoughtful analysis and reflection, probably requires that practitioner to have read beyond her special field, into the realm of cultural studies, postmodernism, the sociology of science. It is only in these intellectual worlds that one could come to see one's own discursive practices as deliberate authorial choices learned in graduate school and then reproduced throughout one's professional career. It is only in these realms that one could imagine alternative literary practices of science that do not rest on the concealment of authorial artifice. One of my interests in this book is to explore non-positivist literary approaches to the crafting of science prose that do not sacrifice empirical rigor to the acknowledgment that science writes. I am convinced that training and depth need not contradict each other if we reformulate training as a self-consciously discursive experience, opening scientific sociologists to their own literary interventions in the sense and sentience of the journal and monograph page.

APPRENTICESHIP TO SCIENTISM IV: REVISION AND RESUBMISSION

In graduate school one learns how to read not only the journals but reviews of one's own work, in particular the reviews written by anonymous article referees approached by the journal editor as arbiters of a work's publishability. Typically, empirical sociology journals will send submitted papers to at least two or three established scholars in one's field. These reviewers are asked whether the manuscript in question warrants publication, either as such or after revisions. It is commonplace for papers that are eventually accepted for publication to undergo at least one revision and frequently two or more in response to reviews and to the editor's attempt to arbitrate such reviews. This is called the "revision and resubmission" process.

I have already noted how citation produces careers by anticipating that cited authorities will be the anonymous reviewers of one's submitted work. This assumes that reviewers are flattered by reference to their own work! Editors will often send one's submitted work to the scholars cited most frequently within it, especially where these scholars already command respect. Editors may also send one's work to people who are not cited but are considered knowledgeable about the field, including junior scholars who have published and perhaps even advanced graduate students at the editor's own institution or otherwise known to her through conferencing and other networks. Just as citation produces careers, so does one's reading of and response to prepublication article and monograph reviews. If it is the case that revision almost always precedes eventual publication, it is clear that the ability to read and respond to reviews is central to the establishment and advancement of one's career.

John Stuart Mill first wrote about the "marketplace of ideas," arguing that the community of science is essentially democratic in the sense that good ideas, through discussion, dialogue, and debate, will survive critical scrutiny, regardless of the station (rank, age, class, gender) of their proponent. Following Weber, Robert Merton (1996) has written extensively about the process of "univeralism" in science, involving a rigorous process for appraising written research before publication. In a mature discipline, the worth of scholarship is established through the *peer-review process,* a double-blind submission and evaluation process whereby the author does not know the identity of reviewers and reviewers do not know the identity

of the author. The leading sociology journals even ask authors to remove identifying references to themselves, such as citations of their own work and evidence
of their institutional affiliation. The assumption here is that science is best advanced
by anonymous scrutiny of anonymous submitted work.

Stanley Fish (1989), the noted literary theorist from Duke, has argued convinc-
ingly that authorial anonymity is problematic for at least two reasons. First, savvy
readers can often detect the identity of the author anyway, recognizing both style
and substance in her ineradicable fingerprints. Second, Fish argues that knowing
the identity of the author helps readers understand the broader literary context
within which one works. Fish is not particularly troubled that the suspension of
anonymity might give well-established authors an unfair advantage. Interestingly,
monograph publishers routinely disclose the identity of manuscripts' authors to
readers, but not the other way around. Perhaps they feel that Fish is correct that
readers produce more objective evaluations if they know the identity of the author.
Increasingly, social science journals invite reviewers to sign their reviews, disclosing their identities to the authors whose work they have reviewed.

In any case, the review process is designed to provide both editor and author with
dispassionate appraisal of a work's value. Inasmuch as journal editors make publication decisions based on reviews that they solicit, authors, especially junior ones, cannot afford to be cavalier about the reviews that their submitted work receives. Typically, if the reviews of the first-generation manuscript are strong enough, the editor
will invite the author to submit a revised version of the paper for editorial consideration or perhaps even accept the paper outright. The editor will usually offer her own
reading of the reviews, suggesting what is most important in them. In addition, the
editor will invite, indeed require, the author to provide a statement about how she
did the revisions and why she ignored certain advice proferred by readers. In this context, it is crucial for would-be practitioners to learn how to read and respond to
reviews, especially contradictory ones, and then how to undertake revisions.

Graduate students already benefit from the responses of faculty mentors to their
term papers and dissertation chapters. Perhaps the best advice that graduate students
will receive is about how to construct a dissertation supervisory committee that will
be maximally helpful to the student, facilitating eventual publication of one's work
and introducing one to professional networks through which the student lands her
first tenure-track job. The relationship of student to faculty mentor is a paradigm
of the relationship between author and reviewers: in both cases, there is a politics
of advice-giving and receiving that the student and junior author cannot afford to
ignore. This is not to deny that important intellectual substance is transacted
between the parties to these relationships. Dissertations and submitted articles are
definitely improved by expert readings that lead to substantive revisions. However,
it is important to view the student/mentor and author/reviewer relationship as
involving discursive politics—a politics of reading and writing.

Later, I will examine examples of reviewers' comments about submitted papers,
the editor's interpretation of these reviews as the basis for guidance given to the

author as she revises, and authors' responses to these comments. It is clear that reviewers' comments, like faculty comments on student work, have a certain contingent quality: they are borne of perspective and need to be read as such. This is not to ignore potential validity or utility in the production of science but only to understand papers as texts, even countertexts, that need to be read for their own blind spots and biases. This is especially important when readers disagree about a piece of work. Students have to juggle the responses of dissertation committee members to their drafts when there is disagreement among committee members. In order to earn their doctorates—union cards!—students must reconcile their committee members' disagreements, enabling them to do a final draft acceptable to all members. This is thoroughly discursive work, involving both rewriting and discussions that seek to produce consensus among committee members and between committee and student. Similarly, the author confronted with diverging responses to her submitted paper needs to address this divergence in her revision as well as in the letter she writes to the editor describing why she made certain changes but not others.

Professional sociologists learn how to "revise and resubmit," which always involves the politics of discourse—understanding criticisms, revising in their light, balancing opposing evaluations of one's work, and providing accounts of why one proceeded the way one did. These are career-making (or breaking) activities: it is nearly impossible to land a first tenure-track job even at a teaching-oriented institution without having completed and successfully defended a dissertation. It is impossible to negotiate the tenure track at research universities without publishing. And, as I noted above, little submitted work is accepted outright, without the call for revisions driven by readers' reports. One's reading of these reports immediately involves one in deconstructive work, making sense of frequently conflicting evaluations that reflect the readers' own perspectives and passions and then negotiating revisions that satisfy the readers without totally rewriting the paper. I return to these issues in chapter 6.

To make life even more harrowing for the tenure aspirant, most editors send revised papers to a subset of the original reviewers. For example, if one receives three initial reviews, the editor may well send the revised paper to two of these original reviewers and to a new reviewer. Of course, the new reviewer is unpredictable. The discursive politics of evaluation and revision may well shift in response to a reading by a person who has not evaluated the original draft. Authors are bedeviled by this possibility of new readings after they have labored on revisions. Editors cover themselves carefully by indicating to authors that, should they be willing to undertake revisions in response to the first round of reviews, publication cannot be guaranteed. Many journals disclose data on the rate at which revised drafts are published, allowing the author to calculate the reasonableness of investing time in revisions. Sometimes, instead of putting a paper through a second round of revisions, an editor will give the author a conditional acceptance, which essentially says that a once-revised paper will be accepted for publication if the author agrees to make certain changes specified by the editor (via her reading of the second round of reviews).

Learning how to deal with discursive politics is an important part of professional socialization. Exacerbating the anxieties involved in review-driven revisions is the fact that the author's "tenure clock" (the years, frequently five or six, between one's first hiring and the timing of the tenure decision) ticks loudly. It may take three months for a journal editor to secure three first-generation reviews. The author can spend another few months turning around revisions and preparing a statement about why she accepted some, but not all, advice from reviewers. It may take another three months for the editor to secure re-reviews from some of the first-generation reviewers and a new review or two in response to the revised draft. Even if the paper is accepted, the author may do final revisions, either dictated by the editor or conceived by the author. The journal may have a backlog of accepted papers that delays eventual publication for a year or more. It is not uncommon for the author to invest two years moving a first "final" draft of a paper through to publication. Although many tenure and promotion committees view work "in press" as the equivalent of actual publications, the tenure candidate cannot afford to be viewed as having hurriedly begun to publish just before the tenure decision, resulting in a disproportionate number of papers that have been accepted but not yet published. When the long gestation process of refereed journal articles is coupled with the high rejection rates of the best sociology journals—as high as 90 percent—it becomes clear that the ability to read and respond to reviews is a matter of survival.

My former mainstream colleagues at SUNY-Buffalo would often have as many as half a dozen papers out for review at any time. Some of these would necessarily be revised papers. In an institution that expected ten or more published journal articles in high-quality outlets, with a six-year tenure clock, this was necessary as a hedge against rejection and delays. For sociologists who work in the book and monograph mode, the gestation process might be much longer, with reviews taking half a year to trickle in and with the revision and re-rereview process taking longer than for journals. Typically, sociology departments that "count" books as valid publications also expect a handful or even half a dozen published journal articles for tenure, raising the bar for sociologists considerably higher than for scholars in humanistic disciplines such as English and history, in which it is commonplace to expect a published dissertation, plans for a second book, and perhaps a small handful of articles for tenure at the leading research universities.

Although mentorship involves a degree of intellectual subordination, if not sycophancy, the peer-review system used by journal and monograph editors puts special pressure on apprenticing scholars to respond to reviews constructively and expeditiously. Even if the author may disagree with what is recommended by the reviewers and editor, getting one's work in print is essential for the establishment and advancement of academic careers. Compromises are made, and corners cut. This is not an argument for a more ascriptive system of publishing, in which what gets published is purely a function of who one knows and one's reputation. And yet, in a sense, what gets published under the peer-review system also depends on who one knows as well as on what one cites. Studies (e.g., Lewis 1998) of publishing and higher education indicate clearly that work submitted by authors from prestigious universities, with well-known mentors, are more likely to receive favorable readings (and, I might add, editorial handling) than is work submitted by unknowns, from nowhere (see Caesar 1992). Again, this is why both choice of graduate school and mentor and dissertation committee matter so much.

This is tantamount to suggesting that the peer-review system is not thoroughly objective. It is not, if we consider that readings done by reviewers are themselves invested in certain versions of legitimate scholarship, certain versions of the discipline and field, certain methodologies and theories. This is not an argument for utter relativism; it is possible to identify incompetent work within the frame of reference of the author's language game or discourse community. Epigones may flatter by imitating, but that is not necessarily enough to get one's work accepted. One must still do good work, that is, work deemed good by a few reviewers and an editor. If one crafts one's writing by putting it through multiple iterations composed with an ear toward how it will sound to readers, one will get one's work published—somewhere, eventually! (Maybe not in time for tenure, or in the right places. . . .) However, once we open the door to the possibility that readings may be jaundiced by one or another factor all the way from theoretical and methodological disagreements with the author to the list of authorities cited, the process of evaluation becomes murky—undecidable. I will return to the quandaries of writing for publication when, in chapter 6, I consider how authors respond to journal article reviews in pursuit of publication.

3

Beginning Science

OBSTRUCTED WRITING AND THE SCIENCE AURA

Journal articles are written for publication, in order to move both careers and science forward. They can be read by studious readers, but their reading is purposely obstructed, as I argue here. It is obstructed because that is how positivists create what I have called the science aura, erasing signs of a text's literariness and replacing it with science's busy figural work and postured mirror-like representation. For science to gesture method and mirror social nature does not require literal photographs of the world; in the case of sociology, unlike biology, that would be difficult. Sociology's representational quality lies in its creation of a journal page that appears to be part of social nature itself, a piece of facticity that bespeaks objectivity, representation, value-freedom, the abandonment of the literary.

In figure 3.1, we have an illustrative three-dimensional representation of earnings distributions from 1967 to 1987. More than a two-dimensional graph, plotting income along y and x axes, this figure suggests, subtly, that income is virtually a natural phenomenon, resembling a geological formation. The figure nicely captures the balance between the impression of severe inequality, which a two-dimensional representation might have suggested, and only mild inequality. The authors probably did not intend to suggest such a balance. They are merely using contemporary techniques to introduce a third variable—data relative to the 1967 earnings decile–into what is ordinarily a two-dimensional analysis. This figure is an example of more to come that, taken together, replace reasoned prose with the gestures, especially figural in nature, of science.

Inexperienced readers have a difficult time making initial sense of this geological representation of social data. This is because science obstructs its own reading in order to position itself outside of textuality. The figure suggests a formation found in nature, not social facts constructed by sociological writers. The pages of science are collected in monochromatic journals that accumulate on one's shelf as a canon, literature, body of knowledge that do not belong next to the vivid literature of detective fiction or one's collection of music CDs but can best be viewed as the sedimentation of disciplinary advancement. Nonetheless, science can be read, its code cracked, and hence it can be written differently, more publicly. In this chapter and the following two chapters, overcoming literary roadblocks erected by

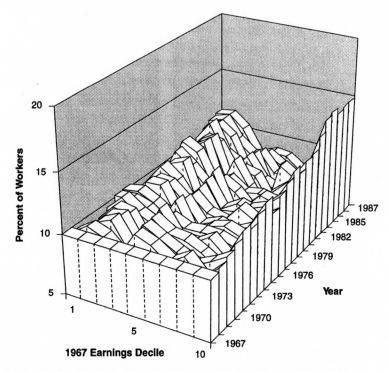

Figure 2. Relative Earnings Distribution Series for Full-Time, Full-Year Workers, 1967 to 1987

Figure 3.1

science for itself, I read sociological journal pages as deftly concealed products of literary artifice.

At the beginning is the abstract, noted earlier. The individual articles are summarized in a hundred or more words above the body of the published journal articles. Abstracts render superfluous a more literary reading that samples the text and texture of the various sections of the article, what humanists call its narrative. Indeed, these abstracts are now to be found on-line, in various disciplinary indexes. Although the inert collected issues of sociology journals may occasionally get read, for example by an author seeking a citation for her own writing, these journals defy leisurely, inquisitive reading by virtue of their apparent elimination of the author. They do not beckon the reader to explore further, much beyond title and abstract. Authors who cite may not have read the whole text, or any of it. This text is not to be read in the same way one reads a biography, newsmagazine, or work of grand social theory, with formulations assimilated slowly, turned over in one's mind in a way that may cause daydreaming or unbridled imagination. Journal articles exist as traces of science's busy work, to be consulted occasionally by specialist readers.

They exist mainly as vehicles of career advancement, prime real estate for sociologists who seek tenure and promotion.

Who compels narrow sociological specialization? Who is to discourage science's use of the passive voice? Who is to tell editors and publishers not to encase their words in monochrome journal covers that line one's professional bookshelf in chronological order, signifying the inexorable progress of science? Who is to disqualify the use of technical symbols and figures on the journal page? Outside of context, ignorant of positivism, science's obstructed reading might not matter. But positivism helps reproduce the given social world by representing it as lawful, hence necessary. The mute representation of the positivist journal page suggests a lawful, nature-like, ordered world in which capitalism, patriarchy, and the domination of nature eternally hold sway, representing the end of history prophesied by Comte. How science composes itself matters because texts are nucleic language games through which power is transacted. Although the world is not all text, as certain postmodernists sometimes imply, the text is a world, a way of representing relationships and hence a relationship itself. Science does not beckon to lively readers because it does not want to be engaged in dialogue by readers who probe its logic, question its grounds, argue its assumptions—who do more than simply add to an evolving literature that disciplines the imagination.

Disciplined professionals would probably defend thick journal discourse that is less inviting than a Steinbeck novel, most Web pages, or even an introductory sociology textbook on grounds of parsimony as well as specialist language: the pages of science are scarce and need to be spent wisely, with as much shorthand as possible, including hieroglyphic figures connoting the gestures of method. As well, professionals would defend technical usage as the code of specialization, without which taxonomists could not advance knowledge much beyond the commonsense and commonplace. I defend a certain version of sociology vigorously because sociology helps us grapple with questions of human misery, justice, community, and democracy. As one who came to sociology during the 1960s and learned answers to my questions about social injustice and budding social movements from sociology and sociological theory, I am not mounting a humanist critique of social science generalization, which abstracts from unique individuals in order to understand people in groups and in the context of larger structures. However, I believe that the tools of sociology, including newfound insights from cultural studies and critical theory, can be turned back upon sociology itself, in this case its discourse, exploring why articles in the *American Sociological Review* (*ASR*) read the way they do and how we might compose our research differently, in a more public way, restoring the author to view as a way of signifying that we can author our lives, not just our scholarly papers.

The issue, then, is not simply technical language—terms such as demographic transition theory, heteroskedasticity, LISREL. After all, discourse theorists have their own terms—narrativity, undecidability, deferral! None of these terms is privileged in the sense that it can be used without reference to a context of usage within which it solves some problems but creates others. This book on writing sociology may help certain readers and writers think differently about the sociological text, but, at the same time, I may beg more questions than I answer. There is no "outside" to language, no Archimedean point of epistemological privilege from which we can be granted access to perfect lucidity through certain protocol statements, such as those of mathematics. Since the Enlightenment, mathematics was seen as the harbinger of such unsullied truths, somehow taking us to a plane of understanding above ordinary language as well as speculative philosophy. The obstructions to reading that litter the positivist journal page in sociology primarily involve the replacement of prose by the protocols of mathematical method, which are taken by positivist sociologists to epitomize science as they understand it. Technical usage obstructs reading if it is not situated within a context of usage that is reflexive about basic assumptions and solicits dialogue about those assumptions, necessarily broadening its discourse community to include nonparticipants in its field.

In these chapters on method I noticed that positivist technical usage suppresses dialogue about its root assumptions both by concealing them, perhaps pretending that it makes no assumptions, and by discouraging outsiders from entering its particular discourse community. Technical usage can be probed for its aporias, contradictions, lapses—what it necessarily excludes—and it can be explained economically to nonusers. Only by writing accessible, reflexive prose can we create a democratic community of science that becomes a model for democratic community generally, embodying what Habermas calls the ideal speech situation.

Ideal speech, in this view, is discourse that is reflexive, acknowledging assumptions, accessible and solicitous. It eschews brow-beating and dogma. It avoids obscurantism. It militates against its own canonization. Democratic speech augurs democratic community without courting a Luddite, antiscience posture. In my imagined better world, sociologists could still publish sophisticated, in-depth research in journals such as the *ASR* without obstructing readings, hence reinforcing a representational concept of its own text that, I contend, is inimical to social freedom. A representational text freezes the world into what Durkheim called social facts, instances of people's determination by impinging laws. Literary obstructionism abets sociological positivism where it intends to portray a frozen, nature-like society, suggesting itself as method. Although one can legitimately write methodology, method needs to be understood as argument, laying itself bare to other versions, and hence other worlds.

Positivists might respond by pointing to the peer-review system as democratic and dialogical, opening science to the best efforts. Peer review facilitates discursive democracy where it is understood that the dialogue between author and reviewers is grounded in their respective language games, requiring us to read readings as versions in their own right. Even the reviewer needs to be reviewed, where reading is understood to be fraught with perspective and position. I am not persuaded that, on the evidence of how articles are really processed and evaluated by journals, the referee system genuinely constitutes John Stuart Mill's marketplace of ideas inasmuch as there are rampant discursive politics involved in the selection of referees and in the adjudication of reviews. Articles may not stray far from conventional canonical wisdom if they are to stand a chance of being accepted. The peer-review system tends to reproduce what was published last year, and the years before that. Writers are disciplined by virtue of the powerful momentum of the discipline's literary and substantive norms, which tend to exclude certain types of research—qualitative, theoretical, political, non-positivist. Journal editors maintain that they publish the best of what is submitted. I would respond that nonmainstream sociologists do not submit to journals such as the *ASR* because they know that such work will be rejected, either outright or after hostile reviewers are chosen, leaving the scarce pages of these elite journals to hard-core empiricists. I have read *ASR* editors' rejection letters to authors that attempt to soften rejection by saying that, in effect, "pages of *ASR* are scarce and only the best work will be accepted. Don't feel too bad and good luck placing it elsewhere, in lesser outlets."

For these reasons, the peer-review system, especially under positivism, is not a particularly viable metaphor for communicative democracy. A better metaphor is Habermas's notion of ideal speech, which is anchored by his critique of the legitimation crisis of the public sphere in late capitalism. Habermas links the eclipse of democracy to the absence of democratic public discourse. The "system," as he (1984, 1987) terms it, borrowing Parsonian language here, excludes the civic rationalities of people's everyday lifeworlds in which speech actors are motivated by the intent to create consensus and make judgments based on the power of the strongest argument. An inveterate rationalist, Habermas grounds critical theory in people's abilities to make sense together and to ground democracy in a civic discourse based on that emergent consensus.

To Habermas I add insights from critical discourse theory in order to understand how sociology is written and published, and how it could be written and published differently. Journal discourse that produces the science aura inhibits democratic speech and a viable public sphere, keeping outsiders out and portraying an intractable social order. Although the findings of positivist sociology can be used for progressive purposes, especially where inequalities are exposed, the representationality and gestural quality of most such research discourages social change. Journal articles' lack of reflexivity not only obstructs alternative readings; it also acquiesces to the physics-like portrayal of the social world promulgated by Comte. These go hand in hand: the death of the author kills off the subject—all subjects. Lifeless prose reflects, and thus guarantees, a lifeless world. As Foucault (1977: 215) wrote, "discipline is a physics."

This account may seem overdetermining, ascribing more world-historical efficacy to positivist sociology than it deserves. The Frankfurt School's (1972) *Aspects of Sociology* suggests otherwise. Sociology is ideology, or, for them (see Horkheimer and Adorno, *Dialectic of Enlightenment* 1972), positivism: Comte's "positive philosophy." In postulating social laws, sociology thwarts rebellion and transformation.

As the door of personal betterment is opened, with the rise of consumer-oriented capitalism or what non-Marxists termed mass society, the door of radical social change closes. This is vouchsafed by a scientific sociology that, with Parsons in his *Social System,* renders capitalism, patriarchy, Judaeo-Christianity, and the domination of nature our unavoidable destinies. Although sociology is not the only ideology, its positivist version is a modal example of a discourse that reproduces the given social order by reproducing/representing it in static, unalterable terms. Durkheim's discourse of social facts' determination of our behavior subtly informs conventional wisdom as we acquiesce to Kant's duality of the realms of freedom and necessity. Bourgeois ideology has always portrayed alienated labor, or Durkheim's heteronomy, as our social fate, thus reproducing it as social texts become lives (that are then refrozen into social facts).

For Comte, Durkheim, Weber, and Parsons this representation involved explicit statements of laws—the three stages (Comte), collective consciousness through secularization (Durkheim), the rationalization of the world (Weber), social-systemic pattern maintenance (Parsons). Alienation was doctrine. For latter-day positivists, figure mirrors social nature—the present—through representation that is pasted directly into sociology's social text as the snippets of figure and figured prose displayed here. Sociology gestures laws but no longer discloses them explicitly in the discourse of lawfulness, the project of bourgeois grand theory. Stepping back from the founders' ironclad discourse of causality, positivists are hesitant about imputing causality, preferring to describe mere correlations, the simultaneous occurrence of events. This is not a reasoned skepticism, as it was for the Scottish philosopher David Hume, but an implicit skepticism that holds out for the eventual cumulation of correlations, through piecemeal research, into total understanding.

There are three differences, then, between the doctrinal positivism of the discipline's founders and the merely discursive positivism of the journal scribes: The founders gave us explicit statements of laws, summarizing what they claimed to be the inexorability of capitalist modernization; they produced grand theories that did not hesitate to generalize from limited evidence about large-scale social structures and their purposes; Durkheim, Weber, and Parsons recognized that lawful capitalist progress bore human costs, for Durkheim anomie, for Weber the bureaucratic iron cage and the disenchantment of the world, for Parsons deficits of pattern maintenance. As ideology, sociology was to cheerlead for social laws, to which people then adjusted their behavior, hoping not for social change but merely for personal betterment. For latter-day positivists, though, sociology drops out this explicitly normative dimension and contents itself with the busy figural world of physics-like journal science, which contributes not to grand theorizing and its worldview of overall progress, albeit mixed with irony and skepticism about the human costs of progress, but merely to the advancement of particular disciplinary fields under the sign of quantitative methods, which are gestured and not narrated in old-fashioned prose. Weber's lamentable iron cage of industrial progress has become the journals' mirror of social nature as reason is reduced to method. *ASR* authors do not purvey social criticism, even within an overarching framework of capitalism's inevitability.

One might say that the founding sociologists argued that sociology was science because it broke with metaphysics and became a version of what Comte called positive philosophy or social physics, which represented the highest or third stage of societal evolution. For Durkheim, sociology's resemblance to science rested in method (see his [1950: 1–13] *Rules of Sociological Method* for a discussion of social facts), which explains the impact of "independent variables" (e.g., religion) on "dependent" ones (e.g., suicide). Weber argued that scientific sociology was a moment in overall societal rationalization, although he was ambivalent about whether the "loss of meaning" brought about by secularization was justified by rationalization. For journal positivists, though, scientificity lies not in explicit statements about the relationship between sociology and the world but resides implicitly in a representational discourse that replaces prose with method. Gone are grand theorizing; speculative reason; normative statements about progress; and, importantly, social criticism, when society falls short of predicted progress. Latter-day sociology has become merely gesture, abandoning speculative reason to the undisciplined.

For Comte, as for the Enlightenment generally, science foretold, and thus helped bring about, progress. Sociology was ideological in the sense that it demarcated the possible and necessary, private betterment and capitalism, respectively. Sociology became social criticism for Durkheim and Weber, who in their critique of empty instrumental rationality set the stage for the Frankfurt School's critical theory, where they argued that capitalism created unintended social problems of personal meaninglessness and social disintegration. Although ideological (social physics), sociology also provided a normative critique of industrializing capitalism that began to disappear as the themes of the founding European sociologists were Americanized by Parsons in his (1937) *Structure of Social Action* and later in *The Social System* (1951). Parsons dropped out normative critique and instead restored sociology's purely ideological function where he used Durkheim and Weber to support his model of pattern maintenance, which seamlessly integrated personal and institutional-level rationalities, goals, and meanings. With the conservative retrenchment of the 1970s and after, even in academia, normative critique was utterly eliminated from the agendas of post-Parsonian positivists more interested in producing the science aura than in issues of grand theory and social policy. For these journal scribes, the issue of sociology's relationship to the polity and society has become purely a question of legitimizing sociology in the university by demonstrating its resemblance to the hard physical sciences. And where policy is considered, it is relegated to concluding remarks in journal articles and not made central to the main agenda of sociological research.

In the rest of this chapter, I disassemble standard empirical journal articles into constituent components. Narrativity is expunged as these articles increasingly come to resemble physics and mathematics in which prose takes a back seat to figure and number. Although most such articles do not mean to tell a good story, or even to be read as literature, they can be reconstructed as the stories and arguments they really are, as secret writing. In the following chapter, I read method rhetorically. I examine the assumptions sociological writers make when they abstract their articles, begin with a stage-setting literature, describe methods and findings (usually in highly mathematical ways), conclude with a glance at policy, and construct brief notes and bibliography as well as acknowledgments. I contend that in "marginalia"—what article authors render marginal by comparison to the main methodological discussion—some of the most interesting traces of authorial sensibility are to be found, making such marginal components of the article and monograph worth serious attention from a deconstructive point of view.

ABSTRACT

The opening discursive gesture of journal science, an article abstract is a condensed version of the argument. Consisting of a hundred or so words distilling the article into bare-bones problem, method, and results, the abstract is usually printed above the article for ready reference, and differentiated from the body of the article by being set in italics. Published first, these are usually written last by authors who hurriedly prepare them for editors. In its nature, the abstract renders the article superfluous, summarizing tersely what is to follow. One writes the abstract by surveying key points, the direction of one's argument, one's method, and a terse discussion of findings. First-person language is often eliminated. Abstracts are usually written in the passive voice: "It was found that. . . ." An abstract may be all that many readers read, even though it is the last part of the paper written by the author. Interestingly, abstracts are not refereed; they are sometimes revised or prepared after the articles have been accepted. And even if they are prepared before the papers have been submitted, reviewers rarely comment on them.

The figures (excerpts from journal articles) presented here and throughout the book are to be viewed as figures and as facts before they can be read as the literary artifacts they really are. In their dense, almost impenetrable presentation, they seem to defy reading and, as such, make it imperative that they be read. The abstract contained in figure 3.2 consists of five sentences and 126 words. The article's title, "Remarriage of Women and Men after Divorce: The Role of Socioeconomic Prospects," contains twelve words. Including the "author's note," acknowledging the granting agency that supported the research and various academic helpers and readers, the first page of the article contains more abstract, title, author's name and affiliation, and acknowledgment than actual prose.

That sociology views itself as susceptible to being summarized says something about its self-conception as a science that reports findings. Although one can probably summarize any text, reducing its length, complexity of gestures, meandering, and equivocation, it is notable that journal writers and editors believe that articles can, in fact, be abstracted. This is an especially interesting assumption in light of the fact that journal science is already tight, disciplined, thick, with literary extrava-

Figure 3.2. This analysis of remarriage among the Wisconsin Longitudinal Study's cohort of high school graduates investigates the relationship between socioeconomic prospects and remarriage after divorce. This article expands on previous efforts by including multiple measures of socioeconomic prospects and considering their importance over an extended time frame. In addition, a comparative approach is taken in this analysis, with the importance of socioeconomic prospects considered for the remarriage of both women and men. Several competing hypotheses are tested, with results indicating that, for women, the appropriate model of remarriage varies with age of separation from the first husband. With few exceptions, socioeconomic prospects are not found to be related to the remarriage of men. The implications of these findings for patterns of poverty among divorced women are considered.

gances carefully eliminated, including traces of the author's subjectivity. By the time papers submitted to sociology journals with 10 percent acceptance rates have gone through two or more stringent revisions, the article is as tight as a drum—and becomes tighter still once the copyeditor has applied blue pencil to the last revision. In this light, the abstract might as well consist of two or three key sentences culled from each of the sections of the article, omitting extravagant detail and the elaborate figural work of method. In effect, by the time editorial work and copyediting have tightened the submitted final draft of the paper, there is little left for the abstract to omit or ignore in the way of prose. The article is already an abstract of the looser, probably more literary draft, which, in the process of revision and editorial work, has not only lost length but also has had the traces of authorial sensibility squeezed out of it. It is commonplace for leading social science journals to refuse to consider papers longer than thirty or forty manuscript pages, already requiring authors to do abstracting work even before they write the official hundred-word abstract, at the end of the drafting process.

Abstracts abound because it is assumed that science can be abstracted in the sense that one can summarize the findings of a paper in physics, medicine, or kinesiology. Abstracting supposes that one can separate argument and method from findings, the stuff of normal science or bench science. Articles are engines of piecemeal empirical research, which add to existing knowledge by improving and sometimes modifying prior understandings of the reasons why adolescents commit murder, newly democratic nation-states undergo counterrevolutions, childless couples have higher family incomes than couples with children but also higher rates of mental illness. Findings are separated from both theory and method, even though findings are not only framed but constituted by the approaches, both technical and conceptual, used in the research. Authors do not think twice about preparing abstracts, either for purposes of publication or perhaps in order to have their full-length papers considered for presentation at a conference. Abstracts are intended and read as technical summaries of the work that follows, not authorial embellishments that need to be theorized.

I theorize abstracts because I contend that they reveal a good deal about science's conception of itself as susceptible to being abstracted. I also theorize abstracts because it is notable that articles already abstract from authorial subjectivity; abstracts are, in effect, meta-abstracts—abstracts of abstracts, which the de-authorized science text has become. As such, they further reduce authorial presence, both enhancing the article's science aura and further removing readers from the realm of the literary that might otherwise engage their critical judgment and propensity for dialogue. Not only do abstracts summarize lifelessly; by speaking in passive voice, they suggest their own summarizing intent, removing focus from abstracts as possible deconstructive topics in their own right. Of course, students are taught to write abstracts beginning in elementary school, where they compose book reports and summarize stories. Frequently, graduate seminars teach abstracting by having students summarize the findings of papers and monographs. Although this is certainly a way of teaching reading, skimming full-length works for their most useful constructions, it is also a way of teaching writing, which directly comes into play when graduate students begin to publish. It could be argued that it is useful to be able to read one's thirty-page manuscript before one submits it to a journal and summarize it briefly. This enforces a critical circumspection that both helps one reduce extraneous length in the paper and regard the work from the outside, as it were, viewing it the way that other professional readers might. Even non-journal writers learn how to abstract where they propose book projects to publishers in a prospectus. (I proposed this book to Rowman & Littlefield in just such a prospectus.) A book proposal or prospectus summarizes the book's argument, breaking it out into chapters and perhaps even subchapter units; identifies a market for the book; discusses competing titles; projects a certain length; and stipulates a probable delivery date. For non-journal writers like me, abstracting is as much a part of my everyday professional life as it is for journal sociologists.

There is a difference, however. Book prospectuses are rarely written in the passive voice. Nor do they simply discuss findings and locate the work in a given literature. There is little premium placed on expunging authorial presence from book proposals. In fact, editors benefit from seeing the literary sensibility of the author. Can she write? Does she understand the field? Is the prospectus polished? Is she likely to have follow-through? Does she understand professional norms, such as how-to-write-a-prospectus? *Is* this a good investment for the house?

The book proposal, although an abstract of sorts, makes a case for the full-length project, which has not yet been written. The article abstract does

Figure 3.3. The long-term effects of parental divorce on individuals' mental health after the transition to adulthood are examined using data from a British birth cohort that has been followed from birth to age 33. Growth-curve models and fixed-effects models are estimated. The results suggest that part of the negative effect of parental divorce on adults is a result of factors that were present before the parents' marriages dissolved. The results also suggest, however, a negative effect of divorce and its aftermath on adult mental health. Moreover, a parental divorce during childhood or adolescence continues to have a negative effect when a person is in his or her twenties and early thirties.

not propose that the full-length article be read but rather substitutes for that reading, reducing an already tight presentation into an airtight mass. The proposal expands into argument; the abstract intends to substitute description for argument, when, in fact, method argues. In explaining, translating, summarizing, defining, and abstracting, one is not moving closer to truth but merely substituting sense for sense, sentience for sentience. The explanation, translation, summary, definition, and abstract do not avoid their own undecidability, their own need to be explained and explored. Explanation cries out for further explanation, circularly, because even definitions need to be defined. There is no positivist ur-text, such as method or mathematics, that ends such circularity. Abstracting may move us further from a context in which assumptions are probed openly and reflexively, preempting the type of authorial self-consciousness that characterizes book proposals, among many other non-positivist documents. This is not to equate self-consciousness and truth but only to suggest that abstracting is peculiarly deaf to its own subtext of position, passion, perspective that underlies every version.

The diligent student must learn how to abstract, reducing an argument to bare essentials and further concealing busy authorial artifice in the name of science. The savvy student will recognize that the body of the journal article is itself a kind of abstract and that abstracting is an argument in its own right—in this case, for a version of science that reduces itself to findings and attempts to silence metaphysics altogether. Seen this way, one can subject abstracts to deconstructive reading, learning from their studied silences and suppressions. And one can write them with an eye toward disclosing not only "findings" but the authorizing theoretical apparatus that underlies the full-blown article, in this resisting the notion that abstracting necessarily conceals its own metaphysic. Inasmuch as abstracting is relatively unsupervised by editors and reviewers—but read carefully by many readers before they plunge into the full-blown article—authors have leeway in how they approach the task of abstracting, which, I contend, involves more than meets the eye.

LITERATURE REVIEW

Much more appears to be at stake in the literature review section of articles than in the abstract. The literature review begins and grounds the particular research to be reported later. Literature reviews have a number of purposes: 1. They connect one's research to an existing tradition of scholarship. 2. They constitute a field, to which they claim filiation. 3. They differentiate themselves from that existing tradition in order to claim their own validity and relevance. 4. They suggest a cumulative model of scholarship. 5. They help one establish networks that advance one's career. 6. They propose testable hypotheses, the hallmark of bench science. As I noted earlier, one spends much of one's graduate career ingesting the literature of the field or fields. One is led to the literature by faculty mentors, first in organized classes and then through the initial work on the dissertation. As well, if the student works with her mentor on a research project, it is often the task of the student to draft the literature review. The student's development of a sense of the literature begins to constitute her professional identity, anchoring dissertation writing and work on articles before graduation in an established tradition of scholarship. If one has a productive and well-networked mentor, the mentor will introduce the student to the scholars she cites at conferences, opening the way for further research collaborations, invitations to conferences, and employment opportunities.

Connection

The first function of the literature review is to ground one's work in a preestablished tradition of scholarship. This tradition is perpetuated through "the literature," articles and monographs published on the topic during the course of the last decade or so. The article writer cites existing scholarship in the opening section of the paper, making parenthetical reference to other scholars' publications, with the date of publication given and sometimes including page numbers, where the author is quoting directly from that publication or targeting a particular section of it. Using American Psychological Association style, the dates of the cited work correspond to an alphabetized list of authors cited in the article's bibliography or "references," in *ASR* terms, where full publication references are provided, including the title of the work and the journal in which the article has appeared, along with page numbers of the article: "It has been established that living in small towns is correlated positively with mental health (Jones 1989; Smith 1995a, 1995b)."

In this sense, citation canonizes—one's argument, one's work, the field to which one claims reference. (I will touch upon the constitution of fields directly below.) Citation suggests that one's work is not path-breaking but belongs to what Kuhn calls normal science; it advances existing scholarship slowly and painstakingly. By citing others who, one claims, have done similar work—work on the same topic, from within the same field, using similar methods and theories—one claims validity for one's approach. By grounding one's work in an existing literature, one immediately defends oneself against the charge of eccentricity. This is not to suggest that citation is merely the acknowledgment of others' work. In saying that one must cite the canon or literature, I am not saying that one may cite just anything. In an article on the crime rate in Wyoming one may not cite Plato or Freud. Although both Plato and Freud belong to important literatures, civilizational ones, neither can be cited in an article on crime in Wyoming inasmuch as neither has published recently, and both are "off topic." While it is conceivable that one could cite an epigram from a classical thinker in one's opening or concluding sections in order to provide a measure of high seriousness, it is likely that reviewers and editors would recommend or require expunging this arabesque in the interest of parsimony. Although one may cite canonical scholars, they must belong to the field's contemporary canon—scholarship within one's narrow tradition of investigation.

However, one may canonize one's argument by appealing to classical theorists and earlier sociologists of unimpeachable reputation who have contributed to, or

Figure 3.4. Why do some couples live by the common pot and others by separate purses? Why do some couples see themselves as an integral economic unit with inseparable fates and fortunes rather than as two free agents joined expediently for the exchange of goods and services? These are fundamental questions about social organization. On a domestic scale, these questions recall Tönnies's (1957) concern with Gemeinschaft and Gesellschaft, Durkheim's (1933) preoccupation with organic and mechanical solidarity, and Homans's (1974) and Blau's (1964) interest in social exchange.

Figure 3.5. *Educational expansion* is another popular explanation of long-term inequality trends. As early as the middle of the nineteenth century, John Stuart Mill (1848) predicted that the diffusion of education would lead to a decrease in inequality (Lindert and Williamson 1985:356). The standard economic argument was made well by Lecaillon et al. (1984), who explained that, *ceteris paribus* (i.e., ignoring fluctuations in demand for educational skills). . . .

Figure 3.6. Explaining the emergence of social differentiation has been a major goal of sociologists since efforts by Spencer ([1874–1896] 1898) and Durkheim ([1893] 1984) founded this tradition a century ago. I attempt to further this line of research by developing a theory of information and social structure that provides one formal explanation for the emergence of social differentiation. An important characteristic of this theory is that it does not require an assumption of initial differences in the natural endowments or structural positions of individuals to explain social differentiation. Amplifying and adding precision to the arguments of Spencer ([1874–1896]

even initiated, scholarship in one's claimed tradition. Thus, one might find Durkheim cited in a paper on crime or Weber in a paper on bureaucracy. Frequently, methodologically driven articles are given the imprimatur of derivation from a long sociological tradition when the author traces the genesis of her problem in the opening paragraphs of the article, thus warranting the legitimacy that tradition bestows. The more specialized one's topic, the more one needs to ground one's work in a tradition that can be traced further back than the last few years of publication on the topic. The authors in figures 3.4, 3.5, and 3.6 appeal to Tönnies, Durkheim, Homans, Blau, John Stuart Mill, Spencer, Rousseau, Simmel, Weber, and Park for intellectual legitimation, claiming that their topics—the economic organization of marriage, income inequality and development, social differentiation, and status characteristics—can be derived from seminal sociology. The author of figure 3.7 also cites more contemporary "classics" such as work by Dahrendorf, Garfinkel, and Goffman. None of these citations refers to empirical work that could be said to constitute normal science.

How does one decide who belongs to the canon? This is what one learns in graduate school and beyond! One learns who has made major and minor impact on the field, especially recently. A chairperson once told me that his department was not interested in hiring me because they wanted to hire people who were at least "small stars." One should cite small stars, medium ones, and luminaries! This chairperson measured the extent of one's stardom by the number of citations of one's work listed in the *Social Sciences Citation Index,* a topic addressed ear-

1898), Durkheim ([1893] 1984), and Rousseau ([1755] 1992), I demonstrate that a tendency toward social differentiation can be an inherent characteristic of a social system, regardless of whether the system is originally differentiated or undifferentiated.

Figure 3.7. Status characteristics are essential constituents of social life. People differ by gender, race, wealth, beauty, age, reading ability, dialect, and other characteristics, and those distinctions may carry great social significance. Not surprisingly, interest in status can be traced to the earliest days of sociology. As Simmel ([1908] 1950) observed, "The first condition of having to deal with somebody . . . is to know with *whom* one has to deal" (p. 307). Weber ([1922] 1968) viewed status characteristics as connoting social worth and therefore as part of a society's stratification system, along with wealth and power. Park's (1928) conception of interaction began with individuals' classifying each other in terms of age, sex, and race; the resulting inferences organized conduct.

lier. This is a good example of how citation constitutes reputation, and thus has important career outcomes. And it reproduces itself, where journal authors cite those who have been cited before, creating a multiplier effect. Citation by an author in a leading journal breeds further citations, both in leading and lesser journals, canonizing one's work. One need not have published extensively, either within a single field or in multiple fields, for one's work to have been canonized, especially if one publishes one article or a few articles in the leading journals, whose abstracts, and perhaps even articles, are read/cited by many. A single citation may mushroom into hundreds of citations, creating surplus citation value.

By and large, the more one publishes (in journals), the more frequently one is cited and has one's citations compiled by citation indexes. Although one can become deservedly visible, even famous, for a single pathbreaking article, the literature in the sociology of higher education finds a positive relationship between the quantity and quality (here, visibility) of one's work. I am assuming that visibility correlates positively with quality. (It is unlikely that bad research would be often-cited, except as an exemplar of bad research.) Even very productive scholars have vitae of uneven quality, that is, with a mix of visible (and well-cited) and less-visible (and more obscure) pieces, especially if one has crossed a threshold of visibility somewhere, as one's career gathers momentum. For a career to gather momentum may mean either that one has suddenly become productive, having learned how to publish quickly, or that one publishes a highly visible article or book that greatly accelerates one's rate and quality/visibility of citation. Visibility and productivity may be strongly correlated where a well-regarded and oft-cited publication produces many invitations to publish, either book chapters or articles in special numbers of journals.

Returning to the question of who one should cite, let me offer this rough rule of thumb: One should cite everyone who has published on one's topic in the last five or ten years. This assumes that one can determine readily how many people have published on the topic, not necessarily an easy call, as we shall see below. To put this another way, one should cite everyone cited by everyone else who publishes on one's topic, including not only the leading opinion makers in the field but arrivistes, for example, their students and their students' students.

Let me offer three examples of citations that demonstrate the connection of one's work to an existing body of scholarship.

The author of figure 3.8 collects twenty examples of recent publications on her topic, how states regulate gender relations in the labor market. Although insiders familiar with the actual publications immediately recognize that the cited work is diverse and ranges far beyond the topic claimed for it, the author, a Wisconsin sociologist, has not taken untoward liberty by encasing these many citations in her parenthetical citation sausage. These citations *could be said* to belong together as examples of recent work relevant to the author's topic. It is also notable that the author cites herself as belonging to this emergent literature, suggesting that the reader curious about the reasonableness of lumping these people together could well begin with a reading of Orloff 1991 in order to ascertain the sense of the author's own earlier constitution of this canon.

The authors of figure 3.9 claim nine citations as evidence of what they contend is a growing trend in how scholars conceptualize the meanings attached to housework. They do not cite themselves. In the same paragraph, the authors sausage together two other groups of three authors each who contribute to related work. This all takes place in the second paragraph of the article, doing the work of stage setting that is one of the usual tasks of the literature review. In the paragraph immediately following, the authors warrant the inclusion of their own work in this emergent literature: "Our study contributes to the small but growing literature. . . ." In the following sentence, they begin to differentiate their work from the material just cited, a topic to follow in this chapter: "We address a broader range of potential sources of such perceptions than do previous studies. . . ."

In figure 3.10, the authors cite four studies that demonstrate that "the conditions mothers experience at work are related to their parenting."

Figure 3.8. No one who has listened to debates about the welfare state[1] in the United States or in other advanced capitalist and democratic countries—about "welfare mothers" or childcare support—could doubt the importance of gender relations to social provision by the state. Many recent analyses have recognized that states regulate gender relations in the labor market, polity, family, and elsewhere (Wilson, 1977; Peattie and Rein, 1983; Shaver, 1983; Ruggie, 1984; Piven, 1985; Pascall, 1986; Sapiro, 1986; Connell, 1987; Sassoon, 1987; Gordon, 1988a, 1988b, 1990; Pateman, 1988a; Abromovitz, 1988; Laslett and Brenner, 1989; Mink, 1990; Walby, 1990; Orloff, 1991; Lewis, 1992; Skocpol, 1992).

Figure 3.9. Therefore, there has been a recent theoretical and empirical move toward reincorporating research that considers housework as not only a rational resource-determined or gender role attitude-determined activity, but an activity filled with wider symbolic, interactional, and relational meanings (Bernard, 1972; Coltrane, 1989; DeVault, 1991; Erickson, 1993; Hochschild, 1989; Ishii-Kuntz & Coltrane, 1992a; Shaw, 1988; West & Fenstermaker, 1993; West & Zimmerman, 1987).

Figure 3.10. Although research shows that mothers' employment status has few reliable implications for their parenting (Bronfenbrenner & Crouter, 1982; Gottfried & Gottfried, 1988), the conditions mothers experience at work are related to their parenting (Crouter & McHale, 1993; Menaghan & Parcel, 1991; Piotrkowski, Rapoport, & Rapoport, 1987; Voydanoff, 1987). · Earlier research finds links between family life and work conditions related to demands, compensation, content, and the social context of work.

As they explain directly below, "[e]arlier research finds links between family life and work conditions related to demands, compensation, content, and the social context of work." What is curious about this parenthetical citation of four authors in figure 3.10 is how what might be viewed as a commonplace—work conditions constrain parenting in important ways—is thought to require sociological buttress in the form of citations. In a textbook survey of work and family issues, this might be unnecessary. In a specialized article on housework, the authors feel compelled to cite support for their contention that working conditions influence parenting. Thus, what gets cited depends partly on literary context.

Although one can track published output in one's field simply by reading journals, abstracts, monographs, conference proceedings, meeting programs, and citation indexes, one also needs to know what is in the publication pipeline, especially work authored by junior faculty and graduate students. This is work in press, under review, or in preparation. Although a good deal of such work will usually surface in the programs of national and regional sociology meetings as conference papers, some of it will slip through the cracks. One of the most reliable ways to stay abreast of late-breaking developments in one's field, allowing one to cite reliably, is to do a lot of reviewing for journals and monograph publishers. That way, one will see many manuscripts in one's field as they are in process, either first submitted or perhaps in later stages of the revise-and-resubmit process. One is likely to review work if one is viewed as a scholar with standing in the field. Reputation, thus, reproduces itself! People asked to review are often those with high visibility. They are visible because they publish and have their work noticed (cited). Having access to work-in-process by virtue of receiving invitations to review is not only an index of one's standing in the field but, circularly, it produces even higher standing because it gives one access to late-breaking developments that one can cite in one's own work and that instruct in where the field is going.

Sociologists of higher education have shown that the majority of all published work is produced by a minority of the discipline's faculty. Of course, this does not account for variations in institutional type, preventing us from recognizing that faculty at junior colleges and four-year schools have heavy teaching loads and are not expected to publish or publish much. Nor does it account for variations in productivity within institutional type and even within given departments. Most publishing occurs in research universities, where faculty have light teaching loads and ample institutional support for research. However, within the top twenty sociology departments in the United States, one is likely to find considerable variation in both the quantity and quality/visibility of research output for reasons that have nothing to do with institutional type and much more to do with variations in faculty members' work styles, energy, career stage, creativity, and networks.

In constructing the literature review section of the paper, it is tempting to overcite as a hedge against omitting people one should have cited—perhaps the reviewers themselves! The economies of publishing militate against overcitation, as do other norms governing inclusion. In the first place, one duplicates what others in the same field, working on the same topic, cite. There are probably certain canonical sources on crime in Wyoming that find their way into every paper on the subject. The smaller the field and the narrower the topic, the more limited the canon will be. Although one can make a case for additional, unusual citations, especially if one's perspective on Wyoming crime is somewhat unusual, these must be credible, bearing on the particular argument in question. It makes little sense to cite Durkheim on crime because "everyone" who works in the field of criminology recognizes Durkheim's original influence on the genesis of the field, unless, of course, one is offering an explicitly Durkheimian perspective on crime in Wyoming. By the same token, one need not—should not—cite C. Wright Mills's *Sociological Imagination* where he talks about private troubles and public issues. "Everyone" knows this cite; it would be hackneyed to resurrect it in a specialized paper to be submitted to the premier journal *Criminology,* let alone the *ASR.* One must not cite too much, things too far afield, or things that "everyone" already knows.

Beginning authors may be tempted to add parenthetical authority to every single sentence or construction, fearing censure for unsupported claims. Seasoned authors understand where arguments need buttress from higher authorities. One of the tricks of reviewing literature is to get one's cited authorities to do work they may well not have intended, taking literary license in claiming them for one's own argument and, in this respect, not descending to particular passages, with identifying page numbers, that clearly support one's argument (but see Kiser and Schneider 1994; figure 3.14, below).

In figure 3.11, the author sausages together quite diverse work—Tilly, DiMaggio and Powell, Polanyi, and others—in order to provide examples of what she calls a "relational/network and institutional analysis," her guiding framework and theoretical auspices. Certainly, the nature of "relational/network and institutional analysis" is not clear to most sociologists. The author is attempting to buttress her analysis of citizenship and the public sphere with this sort of perspective, which she defines as "presuppos[ing] that institutional relationships and relational networks consistently 'outrun' social categories." Although her article on citizenship is ingenious and breaks new ground, I draw attention to her rhetorical approach to claiming diverse high-visibility authors for a theoretical and analytical perspective that she has, in effect, created out of whole cloth, without detailed argumentation about why Polanyi and Tilly are involved in an overlapping endeavor. In the next paragraphs of her article, the author clarifies what she means by relational/network and institutional analysis,

Figure 3.11. My argument rests on a relational/network and institutional analysis (Polanyi 1957a, 1957b, 1977; White, Boorman, and Breiger 1976; White 1992; Tilly 1984, 1988; DiMaggio and Powell 1991; Bearman 1985; Lachmann 1987). This approach presupposes that institutional relationships and relational networks consistently "outrun" social categories. I define institutions as organizational and symbolic practices that operate within networks of rules, structural ties, public narratives, and binding relationships that are embedded in time and space (Polanyi 1957b; March and Olsen 1984; Meyer and Rowan [1977] 1991; Jepperson 1991; Friedland and Alford 1991).[10]

Figure 3.12. Much of the research conducted by sociologists of mental health begins with the long established associations between mental health problems and socioeconomic status (Dohrenwend and Dohrenwend 1969; Faris and Dunham 1939; Hollingshead and Redlich 1958), marital status (Gove 1972; Gurin, Veroff, and Feld 1960; Turner, Dopkeen, and Labreche 1970) and, more recently, gender (Alissa 1982; Nolen-Hocksema 1987; Weissman and Klerman 1977).

Figure 3.13. Legitimation has long been recognized as a fundamental social process that mediates the relationship between power and authority and affects the establishment, persistence, and change of social organizational forms (Habermas 1975; Scott 1995; Walker and Zelditch 1993; Weber [1918] 1968).

Figure 3.14. There is wide agreement among historians that the Prussian tax system between 1640 and 1806 was among the most efficient in Europe (Schmoller 1921:142, 159; Carsten [1964] 1981:276; Finer 1949:724; Rosenberg 1958:104; Behrens 1985:86; Vierhaus 1988:111).

employing the malapropism "agential" in her phrase "an institutional and relational approach rethinks the agential relationship between citizenship and the activities of social classes." In a loose way, the author counterposes her approach, for which she claims the authority of Polanyi, Tilly, and others, to Marxism. This is the real subtext of her claim to derive from a unified theoretical perspective: she is seeking intellectual leverage against Marxist class analysis.

In figure 3.12, the authors begin their article about the epidemiology of social stress, an imaginative treatment, with a comment that many diverse researchers, from the 1930s to the 1980s, "[begin] . . . with the long established associations between mental health problems and socioeconomic status." They frame their examination of the social distribution of exposure to stress within this larger empirical tradition, which was initiated, they tell us in the next paragraph, by Faris and Dunham in 1939. I do not doubt that the three authors know their literature well. What is notable is that they do not delve into their citations at all but simply use the citations as markers of a "long established association" between mental health and social class. In the next sentence, the authors admit that "[i]t has usually been assumed that there are important etiological messages to be found within these established links, but the exact nature of these messages has been the subject of considerable debate." The authors propose their research as a partial resolution of this debate. Their paper is twenty-one printed pages long, not short by *ASR* standards. Presumably, they do not elaborate on the framework of their research, stretching back to 1939, in the interest of literary economy and instead get on with the real business at hand—their empirical research on stress exposure.

In figure 3.13, the authors begin with a similar framing, drawing together quite diverse authors such as Weber, Habermas (his book *Legitimation Crisis*), and Scott in support of their particular approach to the problem. Like many article authors, this team does not delve into the particulars of the canonical Weber; his 1968 cite is his lengthy *Economy and Society*. This is much the same unexplicated Weber one finds in introductory sociology textbooks, pictured as a bearded disciplinary founder who passed down many of the preoccupations of contemporary sociologists. He is merely a signifier of the disciplinary legitimacy of the topic of legitimation and not someone whose particular arguments are taken seriously, at least for the purposes of this article. Similarly, the critical theorist Habermas is lumped together with scholars who might well oppose the letter of his analysis of the legitimation problems of late capitalism. Habermas would probably oppose the theory and method of Ridgeway's micro-level research on group processes. But where the first sentence beginning the article from which I have taken figure 3.12 presents support for a rather substantive finding (the relationship between mental health and class), the first sentence of this article suggests only that "[l]egitimation has long been recognized as a fundamental social process. . . ." This important sentence does little more than warrant the importance of the topic that is treated in the subsequent article. In the next sentence, the authors refer to the "acknowledged importance" of legitimation as a sociological topic, building on the authority of Weber, Habermas, and others. Many sociological articles begin with similar sentences that warrant the importance of the topic to be treated with parenthetical reference to diverse work demonstrating the topic's storied importance. It would not take much to subject such first sentences to caricature or to dispense with them altogether.

This is perhaps the key artifice involved in assimilating others' research to one's own, and one that could be remedied by requiring all citations to include page numbers that refer to actual quoted material in the body of one's argument (or, at worst, in notes, which are themselves changing into thick figures, as we shall see later). If I claim the authority of England and Farkas (1986), am I deploying them illustratively, as a guide to further reading, or as authors who made a particularly strong argument for a certain claim that I am advancing (or opposing)? Too often, I fear, authorities are cited iteratively simply because others who work in the same field have cited them already. It is often unclear exactly what work citations are doing in one's text, raising the question about why they are there in the first place except as talismans, placeholders, signifiers. As with many of the patterns discussed in this book, this one is not seamless. Kiser and Schneider, in their dense and well-supported article on taxation in early modern Prussia, begin with a sentence (figure 3.14) that supports a sweeping statement with detailed citations of chapter and verse. They cite no fewer than six authorities, with page references provided, to support their claim that the Prussian tax system between the years 1640 and 1806 was remarkably efficient!

I am not convinced that it matters whether the author assimilates scholarship to her argument that does not neatly fit because I am not convinced that literature reviews are read more closely than abstracts, with every nuance carefully considered by the reader. Although literature reviews are replete with broad claims, such as assimilations of others' work, most readings rush by, lingering only long enough to identify the article as belonging to this or that set of citations, which tend to swallow whatever theoretical identity the article may possess. Sociological citations signify; they do not build an intellectual lineage carefully. What they signify is topographical location within the flexible, shifting boundaries of the discipline (England and Farkas . . .), having quite different meaning for one author than another, depending on the uses to which England and Farkas are quietly being put. Rarely is there enough explication of citations for readers to judge how they are being read by the author and whether that reading is a valid one. As I will explain shortly, the eclipse of the discursive footnote and endnote has much to do with the declining standards of citation.

In figure 3.15, the author signals the "rediscovery" of the influences of politics and the law on socioeconomic matters by citing five diverse sociologists who are characterized as "economic" sociologists and three scholars in related fields who do similar work. There is little reason (and probably no space) for further discussion of these works, especially inasmuch as her point is that these works complement Marshall's "inclusion of social rights in the definition of . . . citizenship," which is the author's main concern. In figure 3.16, the author begins a paper on the economic organization of marriage with a reference to two sets of authors, Bellah et al., the authors of (1985) *Habits of the Heart,* and Aldous, in support of the contention that "families are supposed to be buffers against self-interested individualism. . . ." She goes on to cite Bumpass as an example of a sociologist who discovers a tension between individualism and commitment to groups, and hence her paper unfolds as an attempt to explore how couples deal with the efficiencies and inefficiencies of pooled resources. Although Bellah et al. could be read to defend the family as an institution, they do not polemicize or prescribe. It is hard to imagine that either Bellah and his coauthors or Aldous do not agree with Bumpass and the author Treas that tensions exist within families between individualism and collectivism. The author's whole first paragraph, devoted to stage setting, hinges on the supposed counterpoint between Bellah and Bumpass, between idealism and realism. A realist reading of Bellah et al. would probably insist that this counterpoint is merely a literary device designed to introduce a data-based article on transaction costs in marriage.

For scholars in interpretive and document-driven disciplines such as history and English, topographical citations that signify but do not explain violate disciplinary norms regarding painstaking, prudent scholarship. Empirical sociologists might well defend their rough-and-ready approach to scholarship, freighting the

Figure 3.15. Marshall's inclusion of social rights in the definition of modern citizenship is a major contribution to theories of citizenship. His definition provides insight into the political and legal constitution of socioeconomic life, a theme recently "rediscovered" in economic sociology (Bell 1981; Block 1990; Granovetter 1985; Stinchcombe 1983; Swedberg 1987) and other fields (Sahlins 1976; Hirschman 1984; Joyce 1987, 1991).

Figure 3.16. Families are supposed to be buffers against self-interested individualism because they emphasize love rather than the divisive monetary preoccupations of the marketplace (Bellah, Madsen, Sullivan, Swidler, and Tipton 1985; Aldous 1987).

methodology section of articles and monographs with greater significance than the stage-setting prolegomena found in literature reviews. This defense of the centrality of method peculiarly converges with certain deconstructive strictures about the rights of readers to read strongly, bending texts into surprising meanings without a great deal of close fidelity to actual texts. Derrida's reading of Hegel comes quickly to mind here. A Derridean might well defend the sausage-like parenthetical string of citations of many authors, without page numbers indicated, that buttress one's sense of the field in the opening literature reviews. The Derridean might view this approach to citation as strong reading that dispenses with the precious mechanisms of scholarship found in tradition-bound disciplines such as English and history. As a sometime-Derridean, I can see the sense in this, although what bothers me about the literary convention of sociological literature reviews is the way in which texts are used only as signifiers of topographical locale and not also as substantive engagements in their own right. What England and Farkas said in 1986 matters, even though it matters in different ways to different authors, and justifiably so, given the interdisciplinarity of England/Farkas. A different approach to reviewing literature might allow the author strongly to engage England/Farkas without becoming mired in scholarship so minute that the larger context within which they have significance becomes swamped by excruciating detail. I will return to the notion of alternative modes of sociological writing in chapter 8.

Constituting the Field

I have just introduced the notion of a work's or works' topographical location in the field. I use the term *field* frequently in this book, without yet defining it. Where a discipline is the organized institutions, practices, norms, methods, and theories constituting an intellectual component of the contemporary university (e.g., sociology, physics, philosophy), a field is a subset of a discipline within which specialized intellectual activities take place. Fields occupy topographical locations on the surface of disciplines, and sometimes they cut across disciplines (such as topics in cognitive science and cultural studies, two rapidly growing interdisciplinary fields). Fields are smaller and more specialized than whole disciplines and, unlike disciplines, they are not as clearly defined or mapped, and their definitions and locales may shift over time. By and large, disciplines are organized and differentiated units in the university setting, for example, by department, and they have national and regional voluntary associations, to which dues-paying faculty members belong. These associations sponsor journals and conferences. Fields are much more informally organized, although one can find conferences and even journals identified by field. A field may be no wider than a topic treated in a journal article—that is, issues of work and family, household demography, neofunctionalism.

Authors establish fields simply by asserting them, as we see below. For the authors of figure 3.17, research on "welfare states and labor markets" and "studies of the effects of ideology on political structures and policies" constitute a field, including the two publications listed in the first citation, the four publications listed in the second cite, and an additional three publications listed in the third cite (with three repeated from the second citation). One of the coauthors includes himself in the first set of cites, suggesting (accurately) that he has helped constitute the field. Although most sociologists outside of this particular area of research will recognize many of the names cited—Skocpol, for instance—the particular field itself, as drawn by the authors, is quite narrow and specialized.

The authors of figure 3.18 cite a whole bevy of publications—fourteen—that are said to characterize "the search for dependence effects . . . [in] development studies" during the past and present decades. This is a well-crafted and noncontroversial list of authors, and their common position is reasonably stated. Interestingly, the authors challenge dependency theory's contention that a nation's dependence on a "core" state wrecks havoc with its own economic well-being, an argument they hinge on methodology. In figure 3.19, the relevant field is characterized as "the literature on inequality and development," and in particular the authors focus on the "effect of *political democracy* on inequality" within that larger literature. The authors trace this literature all the way back to Lenski's influential 1966 book, *Power and Privilege,* although they do not neglect more contemporary citations.

Figure 3.20 represents a special case of a field-constituting citation. Here, the field is the literature on doctor–patient interactions, exemplified by "numerous" empirical studies that are cited. Yet in the same paragraph the authors indicate a gap in the literature that they attempt to fill, concerning interaction among physicians themselves. First, they cite Freidson (1989), followed by six additional cites that apparently differ with Freidson's position. Did Freidson study doctor–doctor interactions, constituting the exception to the rule? Or did he

Figure 3.17. Further, studies of the effects of ideology on political structures and policies have become increasingly common (Sewell 1985; Skocpol 1985; Steinmetz 1990; Stephens 1979). Cultural values and resources can have surprisingly strong effects on such varied political and economic phenomena as party formation, revolutions, policy processes and outcomes, and unionization (Wuthnow 1989; Skocpol 1985; Orloff and Skocpol 1984; Steinmetz 1990; Stephens 1979).

Figure 3.18. The search for dependence effects dominated development studies in sociology during the 1980s and into the 1990s (Bornschier and Chase-Dunn 1985; Boswell and Dixon 1990; Evans and Timberlake 1980; Jaffee 1985; London 1987, 1988; London and Robinson 1989; London and Smith 1988; London and Williams 1988, 1990; Stokes and Jaffee 1982; Wimberley 1990, 1991; Wimberley and Bello 1992). The basic premise of this research is that "dependence" is the major impediment to development in poor countries (Chase-Dunn 1975).

Figure 3.19. The effect of *political democracy* on inequality has been a major theme in the literature on inequality and development and the occasion for much disagreement concerning the nature and direction of causal effects (Lenski 1966; Cutright 1967; Jackman 1974, 1975; Bollen and Jackman 1985a; E. Muller 1988, 1989; Simpson 1990; Crenshaw 1992; Hughes 1994).

Figure 3.20. The content and structure of doctor-patient interactions have been the subject of numerous empirical studies (e.g., see Anspach 1993; Fisher and Todd 1983; Frankel 1984; Heath 1986; Maynard 1991; Mishler 1984; Silverman 1987; Strong 1979; Waitzkin 1991; West 1984), but the processes of *interaction among physicians* have not been investigated (Freidson 1989; but see Anspach 1993; Atkinson 1995; Bosk 1979; Cassell 1991; Good 1995; Millman 1976). As Atkinson (1995) observed, there is little sociological understanding of the "interactions—some fleeting and informal, others more formally contrived—through which medical practitioners consult one another" (p. 34).

Figure 3.21. Some years ago, Ridgeway (1991) presented a theory of the social construction of status value. The theory has been extended and stated formally (Ridgeway 1997b; Ridgeway and Balkwell 1997), and parts of it have been confirmed experimentally

fail to do so, remedied by other scholars' work? Only a medical sociologist could figure this out, given the pattern of citations here. Finally, in figure 3.21, the authors derive a field from the work of a single scholar, which, they argue, constitutes the field's foundation. Cecilia Ridgeway, a sociologist at Stanford, is cited no fewer than six times in this paragraph. Later, I will touch on the way in which grand theory has been reduced to middle-range theory, as Merton called it, such that the authors could characterize Ridgeway's contribution as "status construction theory." In this case, the authors frame the field to which they contribute as devolving from the work of a single scholar, whose work has been elaborated and even tested experimentally by others.

Where disciplines house human beings who organize themselves in order to work within them, fields are held together by literatures, canons, research studies. My claim here is that literature reviews help establish and reinforce fields by bringing together published works in relations of intellectual convenience. The claims made in literature reviews about interrelationships among these works constitute fields, at least in the eyes of the beholders. This is not to deny that authors can be claimed by different fields, for different purposes, even cross-purposes. For example, the work of Habermas might be claimed by critical social theorists, by post-Marxists, and by juridical scholars. Someone as intellectually diverse and wide-ranging as Habermas makes himself available to be cited heterogeneously. More narrow scholarship, say on crime in

(Ridgeway et al. 1998; Ridgeway and Glasgow 1996). Status construction theory solves some important and difficult theoretical puzzles; in particular, it explains how *gender* can acquire status value. Ridgeway (1997a) demonstrates applied usefulness of the work, showing how status construction processes figure in organizations and elsewhere to reproduce gender inequality.

Wyoming, makes itself available for fewer citations, within fewer fields.

Where disciplines have organizational as well as discursive dimensions, given their institutional loci in the university and professional associations, fields are mainly discursive, involving writing and publishing. They are discursively constituted by authors who derive authority—author-ity!—from those whom they cite in the name of their project, their field. This authority is rarely present on the surface of texts inasmuch as writers do not compose themselves in terms of their reception by disciplinary fields. They recognize that their work is iterable, available to many versions. In this light, abstracts can be read as attempts to exercise a degree of control over how one is received by those who would use one's work to constitute fields. Abstracting helps position one's work for others who will cite it in the self-constitution of their own authority. If I write a paper on social movements that claims to use a symbolic-interactionist perspective, I am making it available to those who work in the fields touched by symbolic interactionism as well as social movements. Authors influence their own reception, especially when they position their work topographically, both in the literature review section of their paper and in the abstract.

Literature reviews both constitute fields—the authorities cited, for whom one claims a certain intellectual homogeneity—and authors, who hope to have readers view them in light of those who they have cited. If I cite Habermas authoritatively, I seek a Habermasian imprimatur; I situate myself topographically in, or near, Habermas-land. Citation is thoroughly constitutional; it is a strong version, especially where works do not sort neatly themselves into nonoverlapping fields but must be sorted, through argument or at least inclusion. One of my criticisms of this sort of constitutional activity is that citation rarely involves sustained argument about why particular authors are seen to constitute a field, apart from their parenthetical naming as buttresses of one's argument. I raised this above where I noticed that most authorities named in literature reviews are not distinguished by specific citations of particular formulations that are quoted and discussed, with page numbers given. The many discursive fields constituted by journal articles are so discrete, ephemeral, unexplicated, and rapidly changing that authors do not pause to consider carefully whether the boundaries drawn around fields—literatures—make sense, given the sense and sentience of the arguments for which identity is claimed.

In figure 3.22, the author argues that the focus of a field—"issues of class and state formation"—has returned to an earlier focus (T. H. Marshall 1949!) of "citizenship and democratization." This "resurgence of sociological interest" is ascribed to world events. It is not clear whether citizenship and democratization are a subset of issues of class and state formation or whether this moves the erstwhile field of class and state formation in a somewhat new direction. As in all of the earlier approaches to citation discussed in this section on fields, figure 3.22 exhibits a rather ad hoc approach to field-constitutive citation, collecting authors who are said to share a common topic and approach to a set of intellectual problems. As in all of the cases examined here, the author's constitution of the field enables her to situate her work in a discourse community to which she claims connection and from which she claims differentiation.

In figure 3.23, the authors cite no fewer than twenty articles that are said to constitute a particular perspective on the sociology of household labor. These are characterized as "theories" and they are divided into various "models," all of which view household labor mechanistically and instrumentally. In the following paragraph, the authors discuss a different, less mechanistic perspective on household labor, citing four scholars. The authors situate themselves within this emerging tradition. This is an extraordinarily comprehensive, well-researched paper that leaves no stone unturned. Here, the authors carefully constitute a field comprising twelve authors and then self-consciously affiliate themselves to an emerging, if neighboring, tradition. They clearly stipulate what assumptions (about housework) unite the twelve authors and then take pains to identify their points of disagreement with that approach.

Think about it this way: academic authors scramble to finish their dissertations and publish before leaving graduate school in order to find their first tenure-track jobs. Once on the tenure track, especially at research universities, they must publish quickly and well in order to earn tenure. To publish ten to fifteen refereed articles by the end of one's fifth year as a faculty member (the sixth year being the up-or-out year, during which the tenure decision is made) requires one to write a lot and be willing to undertake numerous revisions. For their part, journal editors are deluged with manuscripts, most of which are eventually rejected. Sociological discourse takes place in fast capitalism, as I have termed it. People write hurriedly, for publication. They read quickly, if at all. Literatures are like quicksilver, subsisting as pixels on the computer screen that, once editorially vetted, are typeset from disk. The faster the rate of literary production in the fast metabolism of academic capitalism, where only the strong survive,

Figure 3.22. Citizenship and democratization are back on the sociological agenda after a prolonged focus on issues of class and state formation (Brubaker 1989, 1992; Orloff 1992; Tilly 1990a, 1990b; Alexander 1991, 1992; Wolfe 1989, 1992; Zaret 1989; Mann 1987).

Figure 3.23. The most visible group of theories in the literature on household labor begins with a mechanistic, instrumental view of housework. These theories include exchange models (Becker, 1981, 1985; Blair, 1994; England & Farkas, 1986; Ross, 1987), resource models (Blair, 1994; Brayfield, 1992; Chafetz, 1988; Coltrane & Ishii-Kuntz, 1992; Hiller, 1984; Ishii-Kuntz & Coltrane, 1992a, 1992b), time availability models (Blair, 1994; Coltrane & Ishii-Kuntz, 1992; Hiller, 1984; Ishii-Kuntz & Coltrane, 1992a, 1992b), and economic-based power models (Blumberg & Coleman, 1989; Coleman, 1988; Hiller, 1984).

the less likely it is that authors make considered arguments for the ways in which they have constituted their fields, examining carefully the intellectual lineages of their problems.

The rapid metabolism of academics' literary lives causes amnesia about the prehistory of one's intellectual problems. Writers do not have time (or space) to reconstitute their fields in ways that open their topographies to critical examination. They simply array their citations, without page numbers, into the sausage-like parenthetically encased strings that do silent work in the opening literature review sections of their dissertations, monographs, and articles. I have never seen, or received, a review that took issue with the selectivity of citations in the literature review. Occasionally, glaring omissions will be noticed by reviewers and editors. This essentially leaves the constitution of fields up to authors, who produce and reproduce fields through their mechanical citations of others' citations. A citation rapidly gathers momentum when it suggests itself as a model for others, who cite the same sources/fields in order to get published, and when citations are codified in citation indexes that influence not only the constitution of fields but people's careers.

Differentiation

Just as the literature review places boundaries around citations that cohere into fields within which normal science is conducted, so the literature review provides an occasion for authors to differentiate their work from the work of others in the field.

Figure 3.24. In contrast, a recent theoretic analysis (Heckathorn 1992) argued that under certain circumstances, heterogeneity of interests can impede collective action, polarizing a group into opposing camps rather than coalescing members toward a unified collective action. Through a similar process, variation in the costs of contributing to the public good (i.e., cost heterogeneity) can also hamper collective action. Earlier theoretic analysis had noted the potentially divisive effects of group heterogeneity. For example, Durkehim ([1893] 1947) viewed social solidarity in traditional societies as based on similarities among actors (i.e., mechanical solidarity) rather than differences. To be sure, he also claimed that solidarity *could* be based on differences among actors (i.e., organic solidarity), but in his view this potential had yet to be fully realized in industrialized societies.

Comparing these two lines of research is difficult because the models differ in explanatory scope. First, Oliver et al. (1985) and Marwell et

It is not enough for a paper to cite extant scholarship in making the case that one's research topic is legitimately situated within the scope and method of the field in question. One must also differentiate one's work from that of others within the same field in order to produce an account of why one's research is needed. Although every article and monograph changes the field, the differentiation of one's research from that of others in the field is done not in order to redirect what Kuhn called normal science but rather to sanction one's own attempt to publish. If one's citations provide the basis of the claim that one's topic is situated in a conventional field staked out by others who one cites, one must also provide a rationale for one's claim to add value to the exist-

al. (1988) modeled only the "first order" collective action problem faced by a group, thereby assuming that provision of the public good was strictly voluntary. Their model did not consider the possibility that a group might resolve its collective action problem through "secondary sanctions," e.g., norms or laws prescribing cooperation or proscribing defection. In contrast, Heckathorn (1992) assumed that collective action is organized through secondary sanctions and ignored voluntary provision of the public good. Of course, both means of organizing collective action are common. Second, the studies examined somewhat different forms of heterogeneity. Although both groups analyzed heterogeneity of interests, Oliver et al. (1985) and Marwell et al. (1988) also considered resource heterogeneity, while Heckathorn considered cost heterogeneity. Finally, Oliver et al. (1985) and Marwell et al. (1988) studied collective action systems with a range of production functions, while Heckathorn (1992) considered a single class of accelerating production functions. Because of these differences in scope, further analysis is required to assess the robustness of these studies' conclusions.

I analyze the effects of group heterogeneity using a somewhat more elaborate model than previous studies.

Figure 3.25. For our purpose, an examination of marriages that have occurred—a traditional sociological approach to studying assortative mating—is not adequate (Johnson 1980; Atkinson and Glass 1985). Such an approach omits any analysis of the population at risk of marriage and hence cannot estimate marriage rates or describe the availability of eligible partners—factors that influence the marriage behavior of particular groups.

Figure 3.26. Our model of Marx's theory differs from those of Hobsbawm (1973), Friedland (1982), Goldstone (1982), Jessop (1990), and other secondary sources whose studies depict only the essence of Marx's theory. We disaggregate Marx's theory in order to identify an array of causal factors and to make explicit the often

ing literature, moving the field forward incrementally.

All of these authors build on the previous literature of their field and thus advance it. After having grounded his analysis in Durkheim, the author of figure 3.24 not only improves on Marwell and Oliver but on *himself*!—Heckathorn 1992. Intriguingly, this Heckathorn cites the 1992 Heckathorn without identifying himself as that Heckathorn. Heckathorn the author de-authorizes his previous 1992 authorship by characterizing his earlier paper as "a recent theoretic analysis" instead of as "my earlier paper." This is a frequent literary device of normal scientists. What this Heckathorn does to best his 1992 embodiment is to "analyze the effects of group heterogeneity using a somewhat more elaborate model than previous studies." This is not construed as a major advance, a shift in perspective or paradigm, but a cautious elaboration, precisely the nature of normal science. In figure 3.25, the author is more audacious, dismissing the "traditional sociological approach to studying assortative mating" in favor of a new and improved version. This is an unusually strong statement for a normal scientist to make.

In figure 3.26, the authors put distance between themselves and four other authors, who are dismissively characterized as "secondary sources" that treat only of the "essence of Marx's theory." The empiricist coauthors "disaggregate Marx's theory" into "causal factors," a stock in trade of positivist sociology. Although there is much to admire about their imagina-

assumed causes, relationships, and scope conditions. The initial important relationship is
between economic development and class
exploitation.

Figure 3.27. Past research on academic promotion is incomplete. With substantial evidence indicating that research productivity
affects the rate of promotion, previous studies
have not included measures of both the quantity and the quality of publications. Most studies have shown that women advance in rank
more slowly than do men, but relevant variables like productivity are often uncontrolled.
Moreover, no study has dealt satisfactorily with
the unique problems associated with duration
data. Our analyses offer a more complete
specification of the processes of advancement
in academic rank using event history analysis,
a method that is designed for this type of data.

Figure 3.28. Although many of Weber's insights
are valid, we argue that limitations of his analysis
are responsible for the incorrect argument that
the efficiency of Prussia's tax system was due to
bureaucratization. The main limitation in both
Weber's discussion and in contemporary analyses is a failure to specify the general conditions
under which bureaucratic organization is more
efficient than other organizational forms.[4] This
gap in the argument, coupled with the emphasis
on the efficiency of bureaucracy, has resulted in
a tendency to overestimate the number and type
of structural conditions within which bureaucracy
will be more efficient than other mechanisms for
controlling officials.

In this paper, we attempt to develop Weber's
insights further by using contemporary theoretical tools to specify the general conditions
under which bureaucracy will be more efficient
than nonbureaucratic forms of recruiting, mon-
itoring, and sanctioning tax collection agents.
Stinchcombe (1959), Chandler (1977),
Williamson (1975, 1985), and Coleman (1990)
argue that in many conditions bureaucracies
are not the most efficient organizational forms
and suggest very different causal mechanisms
affecting bureaucratic efficiency.

tive analysis of Marx's theory of
rebellion, which they find timely in
light of their data, it is interesting that
they are claiming an original reading
of Marx that breaks out his theory
into falsifiable claims, an unusual
approach to Marxian theory and
analysis. In figure 3.27, the authors
characterize past research on rank
advancement in academic careers as
methodologically wanting, failing to
control for "relevant variables like
productivity." They fault past work
for failing to deal adequately with
duration data, which, in this case, are
best addressed using event-history
analysis. And, finally, "previous studies have not included measures of
both the quantity and quality of publications." The paper that unfolds is
methodologically sophisticated and
shows real conversancy with data,
method, and substantive sociology.
Finally, in figure 3.28, the authors
warrant their contribution by pointing
to "limitations" in Weber's original
analysis of Prussian taxation, in particular his argument that bureaucratization rendered Prussian taxation efficient. In the next paragraph they
promise to improve on Weber "by
using contemporary theoretical tools
to specify the general conditions
under which bureaucracy will be
more efficient than nonbureaucratic
forms. . . ." And, exemplifying the
tendency of authors to cite cumulative advances in scholarship, a topic of
the next section, they cite ten studies
(including one of the coauthor's own)
to demonstrate that "in many conditions bureaucracies are not the most
efficient organizational forms. . . ."

Inasmuch as this is an historical paper, it is reasonable for the authors to lay the blame for misunderstanding Prussian taxation at Weber's feet.

This differentiation of bench science from its enveloping literature is a problematic literary accomplishment inasmuch as journal sociology has become highly specialized, as I discussed above with reference to the constitution of ever-narrower fields. Specialization, which often emerges most clearly in the methods section of articles and monographs, must rely heavily on literature reviews in order to justify the meager gains achieved by the research in question. Crime in a Wyoming county between 1967 and 1973 must be defended as a topic of interest to others in the field constituted by the literature review. The literature review anchors the research in an established field, from which one then claims differentiation in order to sanction one's own slender topic, the publication of which only arguably contributes to the cumulation of knowledge. The piecemeal research reported in most empirical sociology journals must derive from tradition—the recent canon—and yet advance tradition by making marginal innovations. The claim that articles innovate deconstructs where it is recognized that the research rests heavily on citation in order to sanction its topic, which otherwise has little generalizability. And citation is an undecidable, deferring, question-begging authorial act, a veritable work of fiction sausaging disparate sources together into seamless science. For science to admit that it is science fiction in this sense would open it to enriching public debate, including new fictions and truths.

In fact, most innovations are methodological, involving measurement, data collection, the statistics used. The more specialized journal sociology becomes, the less impressive are its findings, which may not advance the field. In fact, when literature reviews are inspected, as I have been arguing, they often reveal no closely knit field of theory, method, and findings that could be advanced by like-minded research but merely contingent claims for a field's coherence that are neither argued nor explicated. Differentiation, usually technical in nature, is claimed for particular research that has little in common with the cites listed parenthetically in the opening literature review. Not only is the research trivial; it does not follow from, or further, the ersatz tradition upon which it claims to build.

Thomas Kuhn's work is important here. He argued that scientists usually engage in "normal" science, the everyday research that builds insight upon insight without real illumination. Science only advances significantly when paradigms "shift," such as the move from Ptolemy's to Copernicus's conceptions of the universe or the leap from Newton's physics to Einstein's. Journal sociology disqualifies paradigm shifts by its very nature as narrow, cumulative, methods-driven, and obeisant to a literature reflecting scholarly consensus within a field. Although individual articles have influence in that they are frequently cited and somehow enter the general vernacular of sociologists, the likelihood that individual articles published in the *ASR* or *American Journal of Sociology* shift fields or create or combine into new ones has declined greatly since the 1970s, when methodology began to drive the claims authors made about differentiation. The methodologically driven discipline today all but makes impossible the broad-gauged paradigm shifts that clearly characterized empirical sociology before the turn of the century, when founders such as Durkheim and Weber unashamedly painted with a broad brush as they struggled to comprehend the large and necessarily interdisciplinary themes of an emergent capitalism.

Thus, authors must work hard to differentiate their work from the literature that, they claim, constitutes the field in which they work. Innovations are frequently methods-driven, as the following figures indicate. In figure 3.29, the authors seek to "[improve] . . . upon current methods." In figure 3.30, the authors "attempt to sort out causal paths" between their chosen variables, "using a longitudinal sample." In figure 3.31, the authors lament the fact that past researchers have "rarely incorporated the careful measurement of economic deprivation." In figure 3.32, the authors best past research by using a "prospective longitudinal database on a heterogeneous sample. . . ." Past studies on their topic "rely heavily on case study designs, small convenience samples, and cross-sectional or short time periods." In figure 3.33, the authors promise a bit more than a mere technical advance, although they use the discourse of "testing" to situate their quite theoretically oriented article squarely within the domain of science.

These innovations may be trivial because work has become highly specialized in the interest of building careers, not the discipline. Articles are written to be published; authors view their main readers not as specialists in the field but as the reviewers of their manuscripts and the journal editor. Writing written to be published, not read, is more likely to be infelicitous, larded with technical constructions and arcane methodological gestures. It is also more likely to be insubstantial, hewing so close to the prevailing literature claimed in the opening section that one cannot be accused of "going beyond one's data," a methodological sin. Risks are not taken as authors worry about getting published en route to tenure and promotion. Where innovation occurs, it occurs at

Figure 3.29. In this paper, we propose an approach to measuring distributional inequality that improves upon current methods. This approach provides a descriptive method rich enough in detail to identify where distributional changes have occurred, a flexible set of summary measures, and a framework for statistical inference. The measures have been designed specifically to distinguish between the competing explanations of the shifts in inequality. When applied carefully and in the context of other research (e.g., case studies of the reorganization of work and wage hierarchies within firms), this approach provides considerable information about the relative accuracy of the mismatch and polarization theories.

Figure 3.30. In this study, we attempt to sort out the causal paths between gender role attitudes and reports of marital quality using a longitudinal sample of married people.

Figure 3.31. First and foremost, past research linking economic disadvantage and child development has rarely incorporated the careful measurement of economic deprivation.

Figure 3.32. In this study we make several contributions to the emergent literature on state-owned enterprises in socialist economies

undergoing transformation. First, we introduce a new prospective longitudinal database on a heterogeneous sample of manufacturing establishments from Bulgaria. Extant studies of restructuring enterprises rely heavily on case study designs, small convenience samples, and cross-sectional or short time periods. Few designs include multiple years of organizational data before and after the imposition of macroeconomic reforms.

Figure 3.33. Our study contributes to the small but growing literature on perceptions of housework fairness by offering a more comprehensive exploration of the factors shaping perceptions of fairness. We address a broader range of potential sources of such perceptions than do previous studies, testing the effects both of factors highlighted in the established literature and of more symbolic factors that have received attention recently. Moreover, whereas previous studies of perceptions of housework fairness have tended to focus exclusively on women, we consider the effects of this broad array of factors on a sample of both men and women. In addition, we consider not only married couples but heterosexual couples of varying relationship statuses. Using data from the National Survey of Families and Households (NSFH), we investigate how men's and women's perceptions of the fairness of their household division of labor are affected by (a) time availability and the division of labor, (b) individual resources and interdependence within the couple, (c) attitudes toward gender roles and family, (d) perceptions of the qualities of household labor, and (e) social interaction between partners within the couple.

the margin, in measurement and method, topics that are not without interest but that fail to advance paradigms in the way that earlier speculative sociologists attempted to do.

Differentiation fails, thus, to be very different at all. Articles have an ever-the-same quality, reproducing canonical literature that does not cohere, failing to rethink that literature substantially or innovate at the methodological margin. Differentiation is claimed, but seldom demonstrated, except in the methods section. But even more crucial than the methodological orientation of most empirical research is the fact that the literature one cites as constitutive of a field does not cohere intellectually, vitiating one's intention to move it forward gradually through one's own self-differentiating but cumulative research. The sociological works packed into citation sausages rarely constitute normal science as understood in the natural sciences, where paradigms are based on deep theoretical consensus about the nature of fields and disciplines. Although introductory sociology textbooks portray a well-integrated discipline based on substantial intellectual consensus, there is rarely general agreement about a common body of findings, theory, and method that help orient bench science in sociological fields.

In a discipline such as sociology, it does not make much sense to pursue a dubious natural science model of intellectual advancement. I contend that the most interesting sociology (and probably the most interesting physics) necessarily breaks the boundaries of paradigms, helping illuminate the social in new ways and continually redefining the topographical map of the discipline, and neighboring disciplines, as fields burst through the fences artificially surrounding them. The best science is not normal. As well, I am not persuaded that it makes sense to view previously published work as belonging to literatures that constitute fields, especially where work that crosses over and between fields and disciplines is increasingly the norm in both the social sciences and humanities. The notion of a field suggests more intellectual stability and greater intellectual consensus than actually exist in sociology. We would be better off abandoning the notion of literatures that ground fields and of incremental work from which particular reseach claims minor differentiation. Of course, the abandonment of this model of science would cause us radically to rethink the ways that journal sociology is written, structured, and published, and the way that sociologists organize themselves in the university and relate to the public sphere. Here, I want to suggest only that the concept of differentiation, when examined closely, implies a model of intellectual cumulation and consensus within fields that bears little relationship to what is actually taking place in sociology today.

Figure 3.34 suggests that "[c]ross-national research has thus far failed to provide consistent support for either position. Studies on modernization theory have yielded contradictory results." The author attempts to remedy this with his own research. Figure 3.35 cites contradictory evidence on sex differences in promotion, concluding the paragraph with an attribution to another author to the effect that further research is needed to clarify this important issue. After having suggested that the Prussian tax system between 1640 and 1806 was efficient, the authors of figure 3.36 acknowledge lack of consensus about the reasons for this. Hence, their contribution. In figure 3.37, the author of an unusually non-positivist article on corporate restructuring in an era of neo-Fordism acknowledges that scholars in the area "often have diametrically opposing views." In figure 3.38, the authors cite eight articles whose research shows that men's attitudes predict who does what in the realm of household labor; they also cite two other articles whose research disagrees. (They seek to resolve this disagreement.) Later, I will address the ways in which journal authors acknowledge what Derrida calls undecidability, particularly in their discussions of methods, where they address contradictory evidence, insufficient method, or underdeveloped theory, confessing, in effect, that their work defers the ultimate truth and, in the meantime, must content itself with versions. If read symptomatically, these occasional

Figure 3.34. Cross-national research has thus far failed to provide consistent support for either position. Studies on modernization theory have yielded contradictory results. Russett and associates (Russett, Alker, Deutch, and Laswell 1964:306), Feierabend et al. (1969) and Hibbs (1973) reported the expected curvilinear relationship between the level of economic development and the incidence of political conflict. Other investigations, however, revealed the relationship to be linear and negative (Flanigan and Fogelman 1970) or nonexistent (Hudson 1970).

Figure 3.35. A variety of studies based on different samples, fields, and years have found that women are underrepresented in high academic ranks and that they are promoted more slowly than men (Bayer and Astin 1975, p. 801; Bernard 1964, pp. 120–126; Committee on the Education and Employment of Women in Science and Engineering 1979, p. 60; Cole and Cole 1973; Hurlbert and Rosenfeld 1992; Rosenfeld and Jones 1986; Szafran 1984). However, Bayer and Astin's (1968) study found no sex difference in the initial ranks of science doctorates in 1964. Summarizing research in this area, Rosenfeld (1991) concluded: "The persistent effect of sex even after controls for a number of supposedly relevant variables suggests there is still more to learn about the promotion process" (p. 20).

Figure 3.36. There is no consensus among historians on why the Prussian tax system between 1640 and 1806 was so efficient. In this paper, we use agency theory to analyze the causes of this efficiency. We derive general propositions about the determinants of efficiency in tax collection, focusing primarily on the conditions under which bureaucratic forms of agency increase or decrease efficiency.

Figure 3.37. Researchers who have addressed changes in the managerial process often have diametrically opposing views. Some have suggested that corporations are establishing decentralized cooperative work teams, extending managerial freedom, weakening the boundaries between managers and the managed, emphasizing informal networks, and increasing autonomy and participation (Piore and Sabel 1984; Peters and Waterman 1984; Kanter 1989; Chandler 1990). Others have argued that the managerial process is becoming more centralized: Managers are further removed from decision-making centers, autonomy is declining, and middle-managerial work is being degraded (Shaiken 1984; Carter 1985; Heydebrand 1985; Smith 1990; Burris 1993). Some argue that the ideology of managerial decentralization obscures this degradation (Smith 1990).

Figure 3.38. *Gender-role attitudes.* Studies of housework behavior have often addressed gender ideology as a predictor of household division of labor (Hochschild, 1989; Huber & Spitze, 1983), with many concluding that men's attitudes are especially important pre-

acknowledgments undermine the positivist project.

Cumulation

I have already begun to address the cumulative model of science that governs the ways in which sociologists craft their literature reviews, suggesting intellectual consensus and stable and continuous field boundaries. Given consensus and stable field boundaries, it might make sense for sociologists to view their work as cumulative, with each article building on the ones before it in their given field. Work does not cumulate, however, because there is little intellectual consensus, even within fields, and because field boundaries are far from stable or continuous. Instead, work is all over the place, chaotically located on the terrain of (and even beyond) the discipline—"beyond" in the cases of those of us who have not been trained in sociology at the doctoral level, do not write standard sociology, and do not publish in the mainstream outlets.

The literature review promises cumulation; consensus; and stable, continuous field boundaries by linking citations of supposedly homogeneous work in unexplicated parenthetical strings. Literature reviews must bring readers to the present, where the article in question improves on prior studies without abandoning the notions of consensus and stable field boundaries. Articles are written as if all members of the field's discourse community—all the people one cites—would recognize the

dictors (Baxter, 1992; Bird, Bird & Scruggs, 1984; Ross, 1987; Huber & Spitze, 1983; Perry-Jenkins & Crouter, 1990; Kamo, 1988; Pleck, 1985; Perrucci, Potter, & Rhoads, 1978)—though some research contradicts these findings by concluding that women's attitudes matter more for certain household tasks (Hardesty & Bokemeier, 1989; Ishii-Kuntz & Coltrane, 1992a).

progress promised by the article in question. The literature review is written in such a way as to conventionalize scientific progress, which becomes an unproblematic outcome of marginal innovations accomplished by the research in question. In this, the author destines her own work for parenthetical citation by the journal's readers and reviewers, who readily integrate the research in question into the field's literature, regardless of the actual contributions made by the article. It is enough to presage one's own canonization by producing claims of originality and innovation.

In figure 3.39, the author indicates that four other publications have demonstrated that "the presence of actors with diverse characteristics facilitates collective action." It is notable that this is stated in the first sentence of his article, suggesting that the field into which he enters is governed by consensus about this basic proposition. In figure 3.40, the author indicates "[t]hree points of agreement [in] the sociology of citizenship." Interestingly, deeper in her paragraph, she acknowledges that there is some disagreement over the role of war for state formation. "Despite" this line of argumentation, "most scholars" disagree, strengthening her presentation of the field's consensus. In figure 3.41, a notably nonfigural paper on racial politics in 1960s Birmingham, the author indicates that a particular explanation of "the civil rights movement's victories . . . is entrenched in the sociological . . . [literature]," following this with seven cites. Interestingly, the author takes issues with this explanation, presenting a very different account of what happened in Birmingham that has virtually no buttress in the established literature. Here, the cumulative model is debunked by the striking efforts of a solo scholar, who assays a different interpretation of events based on his archival research into the matter. In figure 3.42, we return to form, where the authors cite approvingly an emergent consensus about the greater propensity of young married couples with children than childless couples to attend church. This is the point of departure for their own line of research, which attempts to clarify whether it is marriage with children that explains this variance or whether it is simply the aging process, which they examine from a lifecycle perspective. They do not overturn the consensus but dig deeper into what causes the finding. In figure 3.43, examined above in the discussion of fields, "long established associations" between mental health and socioeconomic status are acknowledged, supported by nine cites. Again, as in fig-

Figure 3.39. Research on the impact of group heterogeneity on collective action has found that the presence of actors with diverse characteristics facilitates collective action because it increases the likelihood that a "critical mass" of highly motivated contributors will emerge to initiate action (Olson 1965; Hardin 1982; Oliver, Marwell, and Teixeira 1985; Marwell, Oliver, and Prahl 1988).

Figure 3.40. Three points of agreement dominate the sociology of citizenship. First, the basic definition of citizenship provokes little controversy. Usually modern citizenship is defined as a personal status consisting of a body of universal rights (i.e., legal claims on the state) and duties held equally by all legal members of a nation-state (Marshall 1964; Brubaker 1992).[2] Second, sociologists tend to agree on the historical development of citizenship. Despite contributions that stress the importance of war for formation of the state (Tilly 1990a, 1990b; Giddens 1982, 1987; Therborn 1977; Turner 1986), most scholars assume that the legal requirements of an emergent capitalist society were chiefly responsible for the birth of modern citizenship rights (Bendix [1964] 1977; Moore 1966; Giddens 1982, 1987; Barbalet 1989).

Figure 3.41. This explanation of the civil rights movement's victories during these years is entrenched in the sociological and political science literatures (Howard 1966; Hubbard 1968; Watters 1971; Garrow 1978; McAdam 1982, 1983; Barkan 1984).

Figure 3.42. Young married couples with children are more likely to join religious organizations and attend religious services than are young adults who are childless and unmarried (Carroll and Roozen 1975; Mueller and Cooper 1986; Roozen, McKinney, and Thompson 1990).

Figure 3.43. Much of the research conducted by sociologists of mental health begins with the long established associations between mental health problems and socioeconomic status (Dohrenwend and Dohrenwend 1969; Faris and Dunham 1939; Hollingshead and Redlich 1958), marital status (Gove 1972; Gurin, Veroff, and Feld 1960; Turner, Dopkeen, and Labreche 1970) and, more recently, gender (Al-Issa 1982; Nolen-Hocksema 1987; Weissman and Klerman 1977).

ure 3.39, this is stated in the first sentence of the article, providing a point of departure for the authors' contribution to normal science. These authors, with the prominent exception of the author of figure 3.42, who flies in the face of his field's consensus, are bidding to have their published work included in the forward-moving literature of their fields.

The fact alone that one has published in a refereed organ destines one for inclusion in the process of cumulation. One will be cited by others who read and review. One's published article will appear in the *Social Sciences Citation Index* under one's own name, a kind of self-citation that already produces career capital by virtue of having been referenced. Publication produces value quite apart from the intrinsic merits of articles and monographs. Publications occupy space in the field, pushing its boundaries ever outward. Although purists will maintain that one can distinguish between "good" and "bad" articles, even in an elite journal with a very high rejection rate such as the *ASR,* for the purposes of both one's inclusion in the canon and the production of career capital it matters only that one's work appears in such highly selective outlets. Simply for an article to be published in a refereed outlet requires it to have undergone numerous reviews and revisions, suggesting that a threshold of "quality" has already been met. This is a tense issue in promotion and tenure deliberations: Productivist faculty and administrators believe that there is a strong positive correlation between quantity and quality of research, while nonproductivist evaluators argue that it is not enough to be published in selective outlets but rather one's work must be further evaluated by committees for evidence of quality and originality.

Although it could be argued that only "good" research should be included in the evolving canon of one's field, I am suggesting here that simply having published is enough to warrant one's inclusion in future literature reviews, especially given the increasingly "panoptical" (Foucault) nature of the academic world, in which virtually everything in the way of faculty performance gets noticed and evaluated. This panoptical trend may well be accelerated by on-line "publishing," which is already requiring faculty and administrators to consider seriously how one weights publication in electronic journals. While I defend quality, whatever that might mean, I am only observing the tendency for publication as such to earn an article's or monograph's way into the literature of fields, quite apart from the substance of theory, method, and findings presented. Cumulation, like an avalanche, swallows everything in its path—good, bad, and indifferent research—as long as it is noticed by citation indexes, readers, reviewers, faculty and administrative tenure committees. At a time when faculty have Web pages displaying their vitae and photograph, the estimation of intellectual visibility becomes as simple as Internet surfing.

Citations, incremental intellectual advance, career capital all accumulate with publication. They add value to themselves, again reminding us that what one publishes is less important than that, and how much, one publishes. If the quality and quantity of research are strongly correlated, as I believe they are, this is less a problem than meets the eye. The fact that publication in itself is more important than an external judgment of a publication's quality, beyond the judgments already rendered in the review and editorial processes, is not problematic if one recognizes that quality and quantity are positively related and if one appreciates the extraordinary vetting that accepted articles have already undergone. It has always struck me as strange that published reviews of books count heavily in the tenure, promotion, and hiring processes even though most reputable publishers rigorously review books and, initially, even book proposals before investing tens of thousands of dollars in their production, much as journals subject prepublication manuscripts to rigorous reviews. This is not an argument against critically evaluating published work but only an acknowledgment that published work has already been scrutinized by readers and editors, and probably revised at least once, and usually a few times, in response to that scrutiny. After all, the review process is a contingent literary practice replete with blind spots, bias, perspective, position. Papers of dubious value can find their way into print, especially if the author commands undue respect and receives softball reviews and gentle handling by the editor. Although the journal review process is double-blind, manuscript reviewers can often infer the author's identity. And the editor can decide not to subject a paper to stringent revisions, especially if she believes that a busy, famous author would view that as an infringement.

Ultimately, the issue of whether articles within fields cumulate into an ever-evolving, ever-advancing totality is empirical. One would need to read the vast volume of articles by topic and field in order to evaluate whether they add value to the literatures they cite. I suspect that we would find little agreement about how the boundaries of fields should be drawn, and we would find little evidence of the genuine advancement of knowledge within the framework of consensual paradigms. We would not find sheer chaos, though, because literatures, theories, and methods reproduce themselves across generations, cohorts, and even articles. Reviewers, who presumably know their fields well, reduce chaos by reading carefully, expunging eccentricity and wild claims, nudging articles toward a measure of standardization and epistemological good citizenship. Discursive analysis would reveal remarkable homogeneity of style and structure in articles published in the major journals; that homogeneity is what makes this book possible. Standardization is both imposed on authors and self-imposed by writers who also read and review.

Articles evaluating the extent of cumulation within fields are few and far between. Thirty years ago (see Friedrichs [1970] and Gouldner [1970]), the sociology of sociology was an intellectual program intended to decide issues such as this. However, this remained largely a programmatic agenda, with little journal space (although a few monographs) devoted to checking systematically the extent of fields' homogeneity and gradual evolution. This is partly because pages are scarce and partly because most sociologists have been too busy building careers via piecemeal empirical research to subject sociological bench science to a kind of meta-analysis. For the most part, sociological reflexivity (see O'Neill 1972; Agger 1989c) has come from outside of the empirical mainstream, in fact from outside of sociology proper (see Klein). Although students in research methodology seminars are still taught that sociology is a science that seeks cumulation, toward the end of discovering hard-and-fast social laws, virtually no one actually checks to see whether cumulation is taking place. "Cumulation" is merely a rhetorical strategy that legitimizes the frequently aimless meanderings of methods-driven empirical sociologists who publish disciplined articles and work in universities situated in the capitalist state.

How, then, are the research agendas of sociologists established, if not by a purposeful attempt to test hypotheses systematically proposed to advance disciplinary knowledge in pursuit of social laws? Opportunism reigns, especially as federal funding of pure and applied research has declined precipitously during and since the Reagan presidency. Research agendas reflect what gets funded, which is a result of shifting policy priorities at the national and state levels. This is why we see federal and foundation funds spent on criminology and gerontology but not on the study of poverty and racism. Research agendas reflect the availability of large data sets, such as those provided by the Inter-university Consortium of Political and Social Research (ICPSR) at the University of Michigan. Research agendas represent what is current in the discipline, which may or may not reflect these external priorities. Finally, research agendas mirror patterns of intergenerational mentorship and coauthorship, where productive and job-worthy graduate students tend to work in areas occupied by their productive and well-connected mentors. These mentor/mentee relations may not be purposely planned by the student but are often the result of choices about where to attend graduate school influenced by contingent factors such as spouse or partner's career.

Networks

This takes us to the final function of literature reviews, which is to establish as well as reproduce networks of influence in the wider profession. I have already indicated that people cite prospective reviewers as a hedge against their ire about being omitted. My four years spent as an academic administrator slowed my rate of research productivity and thus, in a few years, I will begin to notice my declining influence on the work of others. (An iron law: Grayness of hair caused by administrative stress varies inversely with publication rate!) People cite instrumentally for other reasons: they reproduce others' literature reviews in order to pass muster with reviewers who put a price on being current. It is fatal to submit a paper on a topic that has been treated recently by another author who is not cited. Reviewers will suspect the author's credibility. Authors also cite in order to make contacts who may become professional friends and bestow invitations to conference and publish as well as become future colleagues. The 1980s term for this, "networking," describes the variety of ways in which the people one cites become friends and colleagues or at least bestow favors, proving beneficial to one's career.

Fields are not only bounded by cited literature. Within fields, people read and comment on each others' work, publish together, recruit each other, and offer one another jobs. There is a great deal of discursive and social activity within fields, which, for many, are more significant lifeworlds than the discipline as a whole. I know most of the leading scholars in my field, even though I may have met some of them only once, if at all. We correspond, trade manuscripts, write letters of reference on each others' behalf, engage in professional gossip. We cite each other not simply to scratch each others' backs but to signify our membership in a small community that we nurture—U.S. critical theory. Not all of us who work this field have secure senior faculty positions at leading universities, positions that belong to opinion makers. My world is stratified rather differently than mainstream Midwestern empiricism. The leading theorists may work at small liberal arts colleges, second- and third-tier state universities, and even hold positions outside of sociology. By and large, we do not obtain grants or do pragmatically policy-relevant work. Although people in my small field do not commit professional incest knowingly, there is a good deal of attention to the fragility of each others' careers, especially given our outsider status in the discipline. Many of us came to our work in the 1970s, when academic jobs were extremely scarce, and our careers have been neither predictable nor charmed by comparison to the careers of our cohorts who studied at Michigan or Princeton, obtain NIH grants, and publish in the *ASR*.

Fields matter more for many of us than do disciplines because disciplines such

Figure 3.44. Direct all correspondence to Noah Mark, Department of Sociology, University of Arizona, Tucson, AZ 85721 (nmark@U.Arizona.edu). The central ideas in this paper developed out of conversations between the author and Miller McPherson. I have also benefited from comments by Paula England, Linda Molm, an *ASR* Deputy Editor, and three anonymous *ASR* reviewers. This work was supported under a National Science Foundation Graduate Fellowship.

Figure 3.45. Authors' Note: This article was prepared for a symposium at the November 1993 annual meeting of the National Council on Family Relations, Baltimore, MD. . . . Address correspondence to 1267 CDFS Building, Department of Child Development and Family Studies, Purdue University, West Lafayette, IN, 47907-1267. E-mail: Shelly@vm.cc.purdue.edu.

as sociology have become sprawling and heterogeneous. I have less in common with a social psychologist at Florida State than a critical theorist at Dayton. My field, critical theory, extends beyond sociology's traditional disciplinary boundaries to include colleagues in philosophy (e.g., Doug Kellner at UCLA), English (Fred Jameson at Duke), history (Martin Jay at Berkeley), and political science (Tim Luke at Virginia Tech). Our daily professional world is a busy one, involving writing, reading, reviewing, conferencing, and lecturing. Few of these activities are sited at the core of U.S. sociology, including the American Sociological Association annual meetings. We work on the periphery, or in different disciplines altogether. Few of us have departmental colleagues who read the same books we do or who read books at all, except on vacation. Our empirical colleagues may view us with disdain or at best incomprehension. One of my erstwhile empirical colleagues at Buffalo denounced my kind of work as "speculative bullshit" because I did not employ what he called "quantitative indicators" in my research, forcing me to look elsewhere for collegiality and intellectual sustenance. For this reason, field-based activities—working and networking—acquire a great deal of importance. (When I accepted a job in Texas, the Buffalo colleague offered to help me pack my boxes!)

Electronic communication facilitates the constitution of fields. The authors of figures 3.44, 3.45, and 3.46, like many other sociology journal authors today, include their e-mail addresses in acknowledgments at the foot of their first pages. Just as e-mail has changed the ways that firms and government agencies do business, so it has changed the face of academia by dramatically reducing transaction costs involved in communicating and greatly accelerating the rate of transmission and reception. Whether this is wholly good is a more complicated question, involving issues of community and individuality. Here, I notice how the publication of an e-mail address at the foot of an article facilitates the constitution of fields, which are now joined not only by publication and conferencing but electronically, through feedback from readers to authors. I have even taken the liberty of contacting a number of authors in my sample here for their assistance in this project, requesting their file of reviews and reviews of their paper as well as their corre-

Figure 3.46. Direct correspondence to Karin A. Martin, Department of Sociology, 3012 LSA Building, University of Michigan, Ann Arbor, MI 48109-1382 (kamartin@umich.edu). I am grateful for comments, insights, and assistance from Howard Kimeldorf, Laurie Morgan, Adam Smargon, Emily Stenzel, and three anonymous *ASR* reviewers, and for support from a Rackham Faculty Fellowship at the University of Michigan.

spondence with the journal editor, including their statements of how they responded to reviews. In one case, the author quickly agreed to provide this material. In another case, an untenured author in a prestigious mainstream department asked how I would handle this information in my chapter on reviewing, below. Although I could have found their e-mail addresses through other sources, such as the American Sociological Association's *Guide to Graduate Departments* or an Internet e-mail address search engine, the fact that I could locate them simply by reading their acknowledgments simplified matters all the way around.

Much academic activity transpires over the internet. Using e-mail, academics do the talkative work of constituting fields. Disciplinarity fades where fields—people—are connected electronically. Not only does this forge and maintain connections; it also speeds up the rate of discourse, which has both negative and positive implications. People may write too fast and too much; on the other hand, their isolation is readily overcome when they can communicate effortlessly and quickly with their colleagues in Lincoln, Blacksburg, Appleton. In my forthcoming book *Self and Cybersociety*, I examine the implications of electronically mediated discourse for the public sphere, including academic life. Suffice it to say here that electronic communication, a central component of fast capitalism, needs to be considered in any analysis and critique of disciplinarity, and particularly of disciplinary discourse, given the major implications of the Internet and Web for the ways in which academics talk to each other, conference, and publish. It may well be that e-communication will make fields, as opposed to disciplines, even more significant for academics as people increasingly conduct their work and relate to their colleagues outside of the formal framework of department and discipline, instead "connecting" electronically and conducting their intellectual business that way.

Social relations are less formalized in field than discipline, and hence field-based discourse is more dialogical and democratic. Although the formalized relations of disciplines do not absolutely require that journal writing be formulaic and foreswear authoriality, the informal relations of fields make it easier to do discourse differently, including the ways in which writers write and publishers publish. The sheer narrativity of word processing could well be viewed as "author-friendly," encouraging revision and hence leading to a view of writing that stresses its inherent iterability. Although word processing and e-mail can encourage cavalier authorship, triggering volumes of unedited, thoughtless prose, the fact that one can revise with minimum friction by manipulating pixels, as opposed to letters carefully traced using a fountain pen, suggests that electronically mediated communication is more amenable to rethinking, discouraging premature literary closure. Fields are more democratic for all this, incorporating revision as a cardinal principle of what Habermas calls the ideal speech situation in which dialogue chances are roughly equal, people refrain from browbeating, and speech intends to produce consensus.

Hypotheses

A sixth function of the literature review section is to produce testable hypotheses, a hallmark of positivist sociology. This may occur in the literature review or later in the methods section. In the full text of the article from which figure 3.48 is taken, fully twenty-three hypotheses were derived! Hypotheses emerge from the act of an author's differentiation of her work from the cumulating consensus of the field, on which she builds. A rigorous methodological protocol is designed to test these hypotheses, the results of which provide the basis of further exploration. In figure 3.47, the authors draw "several hypotheses . . . from [their] overview of the effects of Catholic opinion. . . ." Here, the literature review makes way for hypotheses, which are labeled H, with a numerical subscript, followed by a colon, in indented text. This is a typically formal way to tease out and display hypotheses derived from the literature review. In figure 3.48, hypotheses are outlined in a separate section of the article with that name; twenty-three are presented! In figure 3.49, hypotheses are discussed in the section of the paper on "the model," which is said to rest on four assumptions. A signature of positivism, it is said that a precise model "permits . . . clear predictions," with a footnote indicating that the reader may obtain a detailed description of the formal model and attendant computer programs directly from the author (perhaps using e-mail).

In the following two chapters, I look further into the journal article, examining methodology, conclusions, and what I call marginalia such as bibliographies, notes, and titles. As in this chapter, I examine the ways in which certain positivist journal conventions have serious implications for both writers and readers, suppressing authorial sensibility in the name of a model of science that is, at best, out of date. My critique will set the stage for an alternative conception of sociological writing that does not suppress the literariness of science in the name of science, refusing the dichotomy of

Figure 3.47. Several hypotheses can be drawn from this overview of the effects of Catholic opinion and structures on union strength.

Figure 3.48. Our main thesis is that the dynamics of market relationships are driven by competition, power, and institutional forces. We now describe the specific effects of each force, which are developed primarily from the perspective of a client obtaining advertising services. Each hypothesis assumes that all other factors are held constant (ceteris paribus). Concepts, measures, and hypotheses are summarized later in Table 3 (see p. 168).[8]

Figure 3.49. The precision of a formal model based on the four assumptions presented above permits generation of clear predictions.[7]

objectivity and literary subjectivity or sensibility. That science writes should be an occasion for celebrating science and rephrasing it in civic discourse, not announcing the death of the author, as certain antiscience postmodernists have done.

4

Method as the Main Text

FIGURING METHODS AND MODELS

Here, I closely examine the journal's methodological world—a quite Derridean one! I examine the methods sections of recently published sociological journal articles in order to understand how they narrate method. After the literature review section has been completed, the author presents her own research, first in the section on methods and next in the section that discusses findings. In the following chapter, I examine the way papers conclude, sometimes with a glance at policy implications and usually with a discussion of how the research's shortcomings require future research—a programmatic agenda. I also consider the paper's "marginalia": notes, bibliography, acknowledgments, titles. These are all texts in their own right, important statements about the research, the author, and the world. That they have been relegated to marginalia, like all prose in the article that tends to be under sway of method, says a good deal about the direction of sociological writing these days. I wonder whether marginalia are, in fact, quite central to the article's argument and whether these are the places where we should begin in developing a version of sociological writing that celebrates the author and makes way for dialogue, the linchpin of a democratic community of scholarship.

Methodologically inclined readers, indeed most empiricists, regard the abstract and literature review as marginalia; they may not even bother with notes, bibliography, acknowledgments, title, which have virtually no standing as topics of interest. They do not view sociology as discourse but only as a means of communication that does not warrant metasociological treatments, such as this one. The gist of articles is the discussion of method and findings—what the paper is "really about." Although I recognize that mainstream empirical sociology journals publish nonquantitative work, even the occasional article in theory, the format I am describing applies to virtually every published article, especially those that present data. Even the authors of qualitative and theoretical articles who otherwise experience *science envy* can produce the science aura through careful literary strategies designed to making something—figure—out of nothing, sheer prose.

Figure 4.1 appears in a qualitative article—an article without quantitative data. The author is a junior sociologist from a prestigious department. Her *American Sociological Review* (*ASR*) article is lengthy and substantive, treating conceptual

Figure 4.1

and theoretical issues regarding citizenship and the public sphere. By almost any account, this is a worthy topic, treated imaginatively by this author. Figure 4.1 appears early in the article; it is a map of English counties between about 1600 and 1850. There is no evident need for this figure in the text. It appears in order to relieve the article's prosefulness. Six pages later we find figure 4.2, a pictorial representation of the legal infrastructures of France and England in the seventeenth and eighteenth centuries. This summarizes information presented in the article nicely and, again, gives the article a figural appearance. In figure 4.3, taken

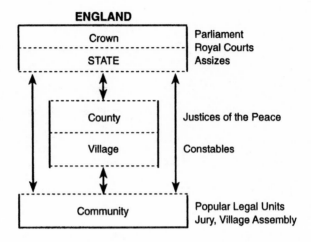

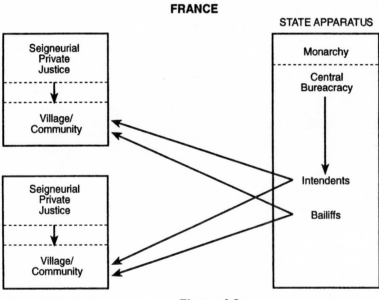

Figure 4.2

from an ethnographic article in medical sociology, we find two "extracts" of transcripts of conversations between doctors and reviewers about patient needs. Although the interweaving of text and such transcripts has been a standard feature of ethnomethodology since Garfinkel's (1967) *Studies in Ethnomethodology,* the repeated use of this literary device in this *ASR* article adds virtually nothing to the reader's comprehension. Instead, it is used merely to "figure" an otherwise

Extract 1

```
 1   R:    The information I have is he's six an'-=with a
 2         history of recurrent uh otitis and (0.1) uh
 3      -> I think 'e had previous tubes, (0.5) but according
 4      -> to the information we got from a Doctor (Katz),
 5      -> (.) the pediatrician's o[ffice,
 6   D:                            [Uh huh.
 7         (.)
 8   R: -> He has uh- (0.2) they i- I don't get any
 9      -> documentation of any problems at all in the last
10      -> year.
11         (.)
12   R:    And I- from their office
13         [so I wanted to check with you.
14   D:    [Uh huh.
15   D:    'et's see uh. (0.4) I saw 'im on thirty May
16         ninety one,....                    (6190: August 7, 1991)
```

Extract 2

```
 1   R:    I'm Doctor Grayson and I'm
 2         reviewing Michelle Ravine for tubes?
 3   D:    Mmhm.=
 4   R:    =You may hear a beep=We record our calls.
 5      -> (0.2) And (.) actually I don't have too much
 6      -> information here=this uh=I have- I know she's four,
 7      -> (0.1) and she's had uh history of an effusion,
 8      -> (0.2) but the information I have is that she's
 9      -> recently had a hearing test which was normal.
10         (0.2)
11      -> R:And uh- and I know she's had an effusion but
12      -> I don't know how long it's been documented for.
13   D:    Wh- what- (.) when did she have a normal
14         hearing test?
15   R:    I don't have the date,=it just says here hearing
16         test within normal limits. [hh An' I don't know if
17   D:                               [(M-)
18   R:    that was ju[st-
19   D:               ['Cause we did an audiogram on th' hh
20         ninth of April which was .hhh abnormal.
21   R:    Oh. Okay, (0.3) uh what di- could you tell me what
22         the-=how much-=uh loss there was?
23         (0.2)
24   D:    Well she hh .hh (.) is uh twenty an' twenty-five
25         decibel levels in the low tones.   h
26   R:    Okay. Alright.=Yeah I'm- I'm (.) glad you corrected
27         that. .hh Do you know how long she's had this
28         effusion?=                         (2222: April 22, 1991)
```

Figure 4.3

unrelievedly nonquantitative article composed entirely of prose. In these fashions, even qualitative sociology published in mainstream journals finds a way to interrupt the flow of their text with figural work. In chapter 7, on changes in *ASR* discourse since the 1930s, I compare this figural tendency to earlier modes of presentation.

The more that the methods sections exclude prose in favor of technical gestures such as formulae, tables, equations, charts, scatterplots, regressions, the more it is attended to as text by knowing, technically skilled readers. Here, I examine closely these particular figural gestures, notably mathematization, representation, and the inversion of text and figure. The ensemble of these gestures creates surplus sign value—the science aura. The less discursive the methods section is, the more method matters as discourse. Papers may have two methods sections, the first presenting the approach taken in the actual research and the second discussing findings. Both are of great interest to practitioners because it is here that differentiation from the literature usually occurs. Technical innovations are claimed at the margin—sophistication of survey instruments, imaginative use of inferential statistics, amount of variance explained. Equations (models) relating variables to each other are proposed—"specified." Sociology becomes an exercise in mathematics once the literature review has been left behind. Although articles conclude with a retrospection on the relationship of findings to widen the field, along with a programmatic call for future research and attention to policy implications, in effect the methods sections move the research out of the conceptual discourse of one's field, in which theories of the middle range (Merton) are proposed in order to explore topical issues in criminology, demography, social psychology. Method promises truth.

In figure 4.4, a trenchant critique of dependency theory is advanced on purely methodological grounds—"[i]n a word, modeling." By modeling the authors refer to the equations used by sociologists to relate dependent and independent variables. The authors contend that they can best dependency theory by using "a difference model in place of the semi-difference model . . . that is standard in dependency research." Method, in this view, mediates intellectual arguments, this side of absolute truth, which awaits fully mature methods. In the meantime, sociologists are satisfied with correlations, statements about the simultaneous occurrence of events. Although Hume argued persuasively that we cannot infer causality from correlations, social scientists make the case that the stronger the correlations calculated, the closer we come to a physics-like indubitability, which, after all, was precisely Auguste Comte's program for sociology as "social physics." Empirical sociologists busy themselves with the explanation of variance, as it is called—the account of how much

Figure 4.4. Our data and measures are the same as, or similar to, those used by dependency researchers, yet our conclusions diverge sharply. Why? In a word, modeling. We use a difference model in place of the semi-difference model (including the stock-and-flow model) that is standard in dependency research.

impact independent variables have on dependent ones. For example, we may find that people's income levels vary positively with years of formal education. A complicated sociological model might include education as one independent variable among others, such as race, gender, whether one lives in a city or rural area, religion, that theoretically may have impact on variations in people's annual incomes. It may be that education explains some, but not all, of the variance in income, depending on how these variables are measured (operationalized). A sociologist of stratification may spend a career developing models of income determination that move closer and closer to a full understanding of socioeconomic inequality, gauged in terms of how much variance models explain. Although no one has yet come up with laws that operate in each and every circumstance, positivists hope that sociological findings will cumulate into a big picture—perfect causality.

One of the basic differences between positivists and non-positivists is that positivists believe that sociology is not yet ready to stipulate hard-and-fast laws because its methods are as yet immature. Non-positivists argue that sociology will never arrive at laws because people, who are defined by their "historicity" as well as free will, are not like pieces of matter in the physical world in that people can organize together in order to change their social and economic circumstances, as they have throughout human history. This is the fundamental issue in the philosophy of social science: Are there social laws? Or, somewhat differently, can we understand social behavior as having been caused by impinging social forces? People of my political and intellectual bent strongly oppose the concept of social laws because we believe that such representations actually dampen people's efforts to bring about fundamental social change. As Marx argued, these representations become ideological, promoting the view—false consciousness—that society cannot be changed in far-reaching structural ways. This is not to view individual positivist sociologists as ideologists who oppose social welfare, the rights of women and people of color, and nurturance of the environment. Most sociologists are at least a little bit left of center. Rather, positivism is a theory of knowledge and approach to producing discourse that positions the author, even in spite of her good political intentions, in a representation of the world that freezes it, reducing the role of writing, and thus political and social action, to mere reflection or mimesis. In fact, according to non-positivists like me, writing is never fully reduced to mimesis or copy because writing as ideology provokes people's inaction, creating a self-fulfilling prophecy: if society is frozen into lawfulness, then the most individuals can do is accommodate themselves to its program, which, in the case of late capitalism, involves individual betterment, mobility, embourgeoisement, even helping others in piecemeal ways—giving to charity, recycling newspapers, opposing cruelty to animals. Sociology provokes adjustment by representing the present as a plenitude of social being. But we learn something by realizing that, as postured representation, sociology strongly, if secretly, writes and thus acts, suggesting that different versions of the world are in fact possible.

The first theorists to view positivism this way were Horkheimer and Adorno in *Dialectic of Enlightenment,* where they lamented the truncation of enlightenment into positivism, a false idol of modernity. Especially pernicious to them was the mathematization of the world, which is exactly what I am criticizing about the discourse of journal sociology. In their view, mathematical method solves no intellectual problems, substituting figure and gesture for thought. In post–World War II capitalism, we increasingly dispense with old-fashioned theoretical statements that defend and justify capitalism, such as Adam Smith's (1937 [1776]) *Wealth of Nations* or Talcott Parsons's (1951) *The Social System.* Under sway of mathematization, such grand narratives give way to quantitative social science that utterly dispenses with normative theory in favor of a preoccupation with method. But Horkheimer and Adorno argue that the apparent "eclipse of reason" by method is, in fact, a substantive value position in its own right, appearing to abdicate philosophical argument for the secret argument of positivist method, which denies the possibility of social change and embraces a deceptive view of itself as sheer representation, instead embracing what Weberians term instrumental rationality.

Habermas represents the second generation of the Frankfurt School. In books such as (1971) *Knowledge and Human Interests* and (1984/1987) *Theory of Communicative Action,* Habermas suggested that instrumental reason or sheer operationism needs to be supplemented by a communicative approach to rationality that locates dialogue about values in a normative community of equal speakers—critical theory's version of democracy. I happen to disagree with Habermas's essentially Kantian approach to the two rationalities, instrumental and communicative. (Kant argued that it is possible to separate the world into realms of necessity—lawful determination—and freedom.) Habermas concedes the realms of "necessity," of technology and science, to positivists, who argue that one can interact with nature and deal with scientific concepts and data without interjecting philosophy, metaphysics, values, theories. He abandons technology and science to positivists, instead arguing that we should concentrate our intellectual and political efforts on creating a public culture in which people engage in rational discussion about the uses to which technology and science should be put. Characterizing Horkheimer's, Adorno's, and Marcuse's work as a "heritage of mysticism," Habermas (1971: 32–33) rejects their contention that one can fundamentally reconstruct science and technology in accord with what Marcuse calls the "life instincts" such that science and technology become fully humanized and dis-alienated.

This is a critical issue in that it helps us better understand what is at stake in reading journal sociology. If Habermas is correct that method can be viewed as value-free, then it may be possible to defend the methodological preoccupations of empirical sociology, instead contextualizing empirical findings so that they illuminate issues in theory and help us make better public policy through democratic dialogue. I suspect that Habermas would view most of the findings reported in U.S. empirical sociology journals as quite trivial, although perhaps his own encyclopedic erudition would enable him to learn something from them. Yet I side with his predecessors Horkheimer, Adorno, and Marcuse where they contend that it is not enough to enlarge the sphere of communicative democracy without also thinking through new discursive practices of science that fundamentally acknowledge the undecidability, humanity, ambiguity, and sheer literariness of science, not only opening science to outsiders but changing the ways we do and write science and interact with nature using technology.

This was the goal expressed by a twenty-five-year old Marx, in his *Economic and Philosophical Manuscripts,* which became the basis of his critique of capitalist alienation, culminating twenty-four years later in Volume One (1967) of *Capital.* Following the Hegel of *The Phenomenology of Mind,* early Marx argued that people become truly human through work—*praxis,* the Greek word for self-creative activities. This work involves interactions with nature, other people, and concepts. In this sense, Marx disputed Kant's claim that work is inevitably toil, occupying the supposed realm of necessity. Marx also disputed Hegel's contention that work necessarily becomes alienated (self-estranged) from the person, preventing the person from becoming truly human except through rational thought and transcendence, the core claim of Hegel's idealism. Marx even in his philosophical adolescence recognized that work can be organized in such a way that people do not experience "loss of the object," the products of their labor, but can realize their true humanity in self-creative activities and provide for their basic material needs. This, of course, was the essence of his vision of communism, which, in his early writings, he grounded in the notion of nonalienated self-creative activity—labor.

I contend that Marx, like the first-generation Frankfurt School theorists, would have viewed science as praxis, self-creative activity involving imagination, discourse, and community. In this respect, as well as in his conception of the relationship of theory and practice, Marx opposed positivism, in spite of the latter-day reading of Marxism as a secret positivism, determinism, and economism, a reading initiated by his collaborator Engels and later embellished by the Bolsheviks, Stalin, and various other European Leftists such as Althusser (1970) and Colletti (1973). Far from being a socialist version of social physics, as Engels essentially characterized it, Marxism is a humanist philosophy that stresses the role of the person, imagination, free will, and consciousness—today, one might add, writing. This is an interpretation that emerged in the tradition of Western Marxism, begun by the Hungarian theorist Georg Lukacs in his 1923 (1971) book *History and Class Consciousness* and furthered by the Frankfurt School theorists and the French existential Marxists Jean-Paul Sartre and Maurice Merleau-Ponty (see Poster 1975; Agger 1979; Lichtheim 1961).

It is not an untoward segue from journal sociology to early Marx. Journal sociology is positivist where it compartmentalizes theory and method, although what passes for theory in the literature review section is a pale imitation of theorizing. Early Marx and the first-generation Frankfurt School thinkers theorized the possibility of a *new science* (see Marcuse 1969; Agger 1976) that plays with ideas, concepts, and methods in ways that are at once intellectually productive and self-creative. A central thesis of Marcuse's *An Essay on Liberation* is that we can fundamentally transform our relationship to nature and to ideas, hence revolutionizing the "mode of production," as Marx called it, and also, as Poster (1990) later termed it, the "mode of information," and not only the social "relations of production," that involves class warfare between labor and capital. Only in this way do we really overcome Kant's bifurcation of the realms of necessity and freedom, refusing to abandon the realm of necessity to alienated labor alleged by Adam Smith, David Ricardo, Comte, Durkheim, Weber, and Parsons to be an inevitable concomitant of rationalization. With early Marx, Marcuse, Adorno, and Horkheimer want to bring about a regime of reason, of rationality, that extends beyond civil society to include our very metabolism with nature and knowledge. In books ranging from (1960) *Reason and Revolution*, a treatment of Hegel, to (1955) *Eros and Civilization*, his important attempt to lay critical theory on a Freudian foundation, to, in the 1960s, (1964) *One-Dimensional Man* and (1969) *Essay on Liberation*, Marcuse has consistently called for a mode of "erotized" rationality so thoroughgoing that the liberated "life instincts," a Freudian term reinterpreted for the purposes of critical theory, issue not only in new socialist relations of work, involving ownership and control of the labor process, but in a new mode of production that fundamentally blurs the boundary between Kant's necessity and freedom so that people engage in precisely the sort of self-creating praxis Marx proposed as the essence of communism in the manuscripts of 1843–44.

Although Marcuse and his Frankfurt cohorts did not discuss disciplinarity and disciplinary discourse explicitly, the postmodern turn in social and cultural theory, beginning with the Derridean writings of the Tel Quel group in France during the 1960s and extending through Foucault, Lyotard, Baudrillard, French feminists such as Kristeva and Irigaray, and proponents of British cultural studies, allows critical theorists to focus on the politics of discourse, including disciplinary writing. There is convergence here with the work of Pierre Bourdieu, a French sociologist and social theorist, who examines disciplinarity as a discursive site and practice in (1988) *Homo Academicus*, and with the writing of Russell Jacoby. Marcuse's student at Brandeis, Jacoby, in his (1987) *The Last Intellectuals* and then in (1999) *The End of Utopia*, examines the academization of critical theory from the perspective not of postmodern discourse theory but of a critical sociology and social history of university life, pondering how activist New Leftists such as himself became obscurantist academics in their midforties once they decamped to the university and pursued tenure. This caused them to lose touch with a wider public formerly enjoyed by scholars such as Irving Howe, John Kenneth Galbraith, and sociology's own C. Wright Mills, who wrote not for tenure but in order to edify and irritate. From within literary theory, scholars such as Linda Brodkey, Julie Klein, and Stanley Fish (1995) examine academic discourse as socially situated practices that both reflect and transform the public sphere by thinking critically about how academics compose themselves, both in their narrow discourse communities and for the public at large.

Bourdieu, a theoretically oriented observer of contemporary social life, has trained his scholarly eye on the cultural terrain of academic life, bringing to *Homo Academicus* the same intellectual apparatus he has developed in earlier work, such as his impressive book (1984) *Distinction*. Blending Weber, Marx, and French postmodern theory, Bourdieu examines intellectual life as an ensemble of practices that are to be understood as both structural and subjective, involving both constraint and voluntary agency. Of particular interest in *Homo Academicus* is Bourdieu's discussion in his chapter "The Critical Moment" of the intellectual underpinnings and consequences—such as postmodern theory itself—of the 1968 May movement in France, joining insurgent students and workers in a mobilization against bureaucratized, administered aspects of French university life, political institutions, and issues of class. Bourdieu makes the point that the postmodern theorists such as Derrida and Foucault who were actively involved in May 1968 and whose antiauthoritarian philosophical politics energized the attack on French Communist Party orthodoxy, such as the work of Althusser, never became established superstar academics in France, remaining somewhat marginalized in spite of their huge influence abroad.

Although there is overlap between my approach to discursive practices of discipline and Bourdieu's study of academic practice, the difference is that Bourdieu tries to legitimize his work as science, resorting to many of the same figural and gestural strategies, such as technical language and dense graphical representations, deployed by sociological bench scientists. In *Homo Academicus* as in much of his other work, Bourdieu reinforces scientism in order to legitimize his cultural sociology, often burying his ample substantive insights deep within his taxonomic, terminological, tabled approach to writing the social text. For example, his representation on p. 80 of *Homo Academicus* is ponderously titled "The space of the arts and social science faculties: analysis of correspondences: plane of the first and second axes of inertia—properties." Although not a doctrinal positivist, Bourdieu drinks deeply of discursive positivism, deploying many of its authorial signatures. Unlike mainstream American sociologists, he does not confine his voluminous writings to the academic journals, instead, on the strength of his visibility in French intellectual life, finding publishers willing to issue his work in book-length form.

All of these critical traditions focus on academic writing as a contingent literary, social, and political activity that needs to be examined from outside, or above, the discipline in question. Although there are possible defenses of technical language, a critical perspective on disciplinarity suggests that the conventions we follow when we compose journal articles and books have profound sociopolitical implications for our conception of public life, and can be changed. In compartmentalizing the methods sections—real science—from literature review, pro forma concluding discussion of future research and other marginalia such as abstracts, titles, notes, and acknowledgments, journal sociology suggests a conception of society reminiscent of Comte's notion of sociology as social physics, yet without even Comte's normative intent, which was to smooth out capitalist progress. The notion of sociology as a hard science such as physics that merely reflects a static world is played out in the highly figural work of articles' methods sections, leaving broad-gauged social theory and social criticism to people who work outside of the sociological mainstream. Sociologists are no longer gadflies, muckrakers, polemicists, but rather disciplinary, disciplined professionals who pursue careers within the language games and discourse communities of the prevailing positivism, which subordinates theory and critique to method, scientific journal publication, and grants.

Discourse-oblivious sociologists do not exhibit much patience for the postmodern turn in social and cultural theory. Nor do they purvey the sociology of sociology, even in pre-postmodern terms. Thus, they maintain that "how" they write has little or no bearing on "what" they write. The conventions governing journal and monograph writing are simply that—mores, in Sumner's language, that should not be overinterpreted. These same sociologists would probably view method as value-free, not freighted with theoretical and philosophical constructs. Contradictorily, they defend their own technical languages—method—but also reject much theory, especially the kind that examines disciplinarity and disciplinary discourse, as useless, a marginal practice of those who cannot count (and thus don't count). These scholars simply have little interest in discourse or discourse theory. They maintain that this kind of work, focusing literary attention on how disciplined professionals write, and how their style affects the meaning of their work, is much ado about nothing, diverting us from the busy work of publishing bench science and preparing grant proposals. Although they do not approve of the sociology of sociology, they cynically practice it: they reject postmodernism as wordplay engaged in by weird colleagues down the hall and across the campus who obsess about the niceties of literary presentation—theory—because they cannot do real sociology, driven by method.

Is method a text? By text I mean a vehicle for meaning that does not necessarily appear on its surface. A regression equation, relating dependent and independent variables and estimating their respective weights, discloses not only specific meanings about the way in which social facts, Durkheim's term for instances of social determination, are interrelated, say suicide and social class, but suggests regression as a theoretical means for understanding social behavior as having-been-caused. In figure 4.5, the authors move beyond "simple descriptive statistics" to a more complex multivariate model relating the dependent variable, what they call "force of attraction," to independent variables such as age, sex, and education. As they describe, "The dependent variable is the log of the ratio of the force of attraction in the later year to that in the earlier year." (I should add that this article is about to invert the ratio of text to figure, a topic below, where on the next page high mathematics is followed by a whole page devoted to a table [figure 4.6] indicating "weighted least-square coefficients" in the authors' regression analysis.) The prose of figure 4.5 is exceedingly dense; technical terms clog the text, testing readers' comprehension of

MULTIVARIATE ANALYSIS OF MARITAL TRENDS

The above analysis uses simple descriptive statistics to examine changes in the availability of potential spouses and the force of attraction. We now introduce a multivariate model to identify more precisely the age, sex, and education groups for which changes in the force of attraction (i.e., changes in marriage rates net of availability) have been greatest. The dependent variable is the log of the ratio of the force of attraction in the later year to that in the earlier year. To identify the influence of various characteristics on the force of attraction, we first estimate a main effects model:

$$\log\left(\frac{\alpha_{ijkl}'^2}{\alpha_{ijkl}'^1}\right) = a + \Sigma b_i X_i + \Sigma b_j X_j + \Sigma b_k X_k + \Sigma b_l X_l,$$

where α_{ijkl}^t is the force of attraction between males aged i with education k and females aged j with education l in year t; X_i, b_i is a dummy variable representing membership in ith age category for males and the coefficient of that category, respectively; X_j, b_j is the equivalent variable and coefficient for females aged j; X_k, b_k is the equivalent variable and coefficient for males with education k; and X_l, b_l is the equivalent variable and coefficient for females with education l. We use weighted least-squares regression. Weighting is used in order to correct for heteroscedasticity, i.e., unequal variances that are a result of varying population sizes in each cell (Pindyck and Rubinfeld 1991). The proper weight is the inverse of the variance of the dependent variable. In accordance with Agresti (1990, p. 55), the variance of the log of the ratio of the forces of marriage attraction (forces have been transformed into proportions) is

$$\sigma^2 = \left\{\frac{1-\tilde{a}_{ijkl}'^1}{N_{ijkl}'^1}\right\} + \left\{\frac{1-\tilde{a}_{ijkl}'^2}{N_{ijkl}'^2}\right\}.$$

Figure 4.5

the language game of statistics: multivariate, dummy variable, log, main effects model, coefficient, weighted least-squares regression, heteroscedasticity.

Advanced graduate students in high-powered quantitative programs who have taken their second statistics course should be familiar with this language, which is otherwise daunting to initiates and outsiders. The method section does not unpack or reflect on its social assumptions; method *does*. There is nothing wrong with deferring such discussions about assumptions, especially in the interest of parsimony. However, I contend that positivist method intends to end or preempt such discussions in the interest of diverting social research from metanarrative, reflexive considerations that tend to whittle away the scientific imprimatur of empirical sociology, further jeopardizing sociology's status in the academy and society. For method to defer discussion of theories and assumptions that underlie it suggests that method lies somehow outside the realm of discourse or the textual. Recall Derrida's famous claim that "there is nothing outside the text," by which he meant that there is no vehicle of meaning that can dispense with considerations of perspective, passion, politics. What he calls logocentrism I am calling method.

The methods section includes an opening discussion of the instruments (e.g., questionnaires) used in the study, the nature of the sample, and perhaps the statistical techniques used in analyzing the data. Models—equations—are also specified (a term of

Table 2. Weighted Least–Squares Coefficients For Regression of Change in the Force of Attraction to Marriage on Selected Independent Variables: United States, 1972–1979 and 1979–1987

Independent Variable	1972–1979 Model 1	1972–1979 Model 2	1979–1987 Model 1	1979–1987 Model 2	1972–1987 Model 1	1972–1987 Model 2
Intercept	$-.29^{**}$ (.09)	$-.27^{**}$ (.10)	$.28^{**}$ (.08)	$.38^{**}$ (.08)	$-.06$ (.09)	$.07$ (.10)
Male						
14–19	$-.14$ (.09)	$-.37^{*}$ (.17)	$-.04$ (.11)	$-.01$ (.17)	$-.18$ (.12)	$-.45^{*}$ (.19)
20–24	$-.07$ (.06)	$-.18^{*}$ (.09)	$-.08$ (.06)	$-.10$ (.09)	$-.15^{*}$ (.07)	$-.32^{**}$ (.10)
30–34	$.06$ (.11)	$.11$ (.11)	$-.19^{*}$ (.09)	$-.18^{*}$ (.09)	$-.16$ (.12)	$-.08$ (.12)
35–44	$-.31^{*}$ (.14)	$-.25$ (.14)	$-.07$ (.12)	$-.09$ (.13)	$-.42^{**}$ (.14)	$-.35^{*}$ (.15)
45+	$.04$ (.18)	$.12$ (.19)	$-.17$ (.17)	$-.18$ (.18)	$-.09$ (.20)	$.02$ (.21)
Female						
17–19	$-.08$ (.09)	$.13$ (.15)	$-.80^{**}$ (.09)	$-.80^{**}$ (.15)	$-.87^{**}$ (.10)	$-.62^{**}$ (.17)
20–24	$-.10$ (.08)	$-.02$ (.10)	$-.33^{**}$ (.07)	$-.34^{**}$ (.09)	$-.42^{**}$ (.09)	$-.32^{**}$ (.11)
30–34	$.16$ (.17)	$.13$ (.17)	$.05$ (.13)	$.12$ (.13)	$.16$ (.17)	$.19$ (.17)
35–43	$-.10$ (.17)	$-.17$ (.18)	$-.11$ (.16)	$-.00$ (.18)	$-.19$ (.17)	$-.23$ (.19)
Male						
Less than high school	$-.02$ (.07)	$-.01$ (.15)	$-.05$ (.08)	$-.06$ (.15)	$-.08$ (.09)	$-.09$ (.17)
Some college	$-.23^{**}$ (.06)	$-.27$ (.15)	$-.06$ (.06)	$-.03$ (.16)	$-.21^{**}$ (.07)	$-.19$ (.17)
Female						
Less than high school	$-.00$ (.07)	$-.03$ (.14)	$-.07$ (.09)	$-.02$ (.15)	$-.03$ (.09)	$-.00$ (.17)
Some college	$.21^{**}$ (.06)	$.25$ (.15)	$.03$ (.06)	$-.04$ (.15)	$.22^{**}$ (.07)	$.18$ (.17)
Homogamy						
Male older than female	—	$-.17$ (.09)	—	$-.06$ (.09)	—	$-.27^{**}$ (.11)
Male younger than female	—	$.09$ (.13)	—	$-.24$ (.13)	—	$-.07$ (.15)
Male better educated than female	—	$.10$ (.16)	—	$-.18$ (.17)	—	$-.08$ (.19)
Male less educated than female	—	$.03$ (.16)	—	$-.07$ (.17)	—	$-.01$ (.19)
R^2	.116	.133	.332	.360	.370	.392
Adjusted R^2	.072	.075	.299	.317	.337	.351
Number of cases	270	270	270	270	270	270

$^{*}p < .05$ $^{**}p < .01$

Note: Numbers in parentheses are standard errors.

Figure 4.6

art), relating dependent variable (e.g., church attendance) to independent variables (e.g., age, gender, marital status, number of children, social class). Regression analyses assessing the correlations between variables, with appropriate controls for the intermediate effects of other variables, are performed, and data typically summarized in tabular form as hypotheses derived from the literature review are tested. As we see below, the models are almost always expressed in mathematical notation, including Greek letters and subscript. Here, I examine the overt text of these models, with a discussion in the next section of the elaborate use of figure in these gestures.

In figure 4.7, which is taken from the article, discussed above, about gender differences in academic rank advancement, the discussion of methods occupies nearly three pages. It should be noted that the issues of measurement and modeling are crucial to this article; thus, what might be viewed as methodological fetishism should probably be forgiven, in light of the complexity of the measurement issues involved. The discussion of the data and sample are not difficult and require no math background. In figure 4.8, the authors introduce a lengthy discussion of methods and modeling used in their test of modernization and world-systems perspectives. As in the article on promotability in science, this comparison of the two global perspectives requires careful methodological discussion and adjudication. This is not to say that the methods are value-neutral or theory-neutral; they encode deep assumptions about society and change. In figure 4.9, we find a typical discussion of methods: the authors describe their data—a database of questionnaire responses from 19,001 high-school seniors. (The article is about church attendance in early adulthood.) The dependent variable "is the probability that person j is a member of a religious organization at year t . . ." and so on. The description of method continues on the next page of the article. In addition to the ample methodological detail contained in the body of the text, describing data source, variables, and the model itself, two lengthy footnotes are printed at the bottom of the page, trailing over onto the next page, providing further detail about the surveys used and the questionnaire items themselves. Again, this is typical detail found in such articles, split between the body of the text and the notes. Although I will argue later that discursive footnotes and endnotes have declined in journal sociology, and even

---

METHODS

The dependent variable in our analysis is whether or not a scientist was promoted to the next academic rank and, if promoted, how many years elapsed before promotion. If a scientist was promoted, we know exactly how many years it took to advance in rank. If a scientist was not promoted, perhaps because the scientist took a job outside of academia or because data collection ended before promotion occurred, the time of promotion is undefined or unknown. If promotion occurred in conjunction with a move to an unrated department, the time of promotion is undefined because we do not know how long promotion would have taken if the scientist had remained in a rated department.

All cases in which the time of promotion is undefined or unknown are referred to as *censored*. If censored cases are ignored, estimates of the effects of independent variables are bi-

Figure 4.7   continues

ased (Yamaguchi 1991, pp. 3–9). The most natural approach to this problem is the methodology known variously as event history analysis, survival analysis, or duration analysis. Within this class of methods, we use the discrete-time logit method discussed by Brown (1975), Allison (1982, 1984), and Yamaguchi (1991). A discrete-time approach is particularly apt for this application because academic promotions usually take effect between the end of one academic year and the beginning of the next.

Let $t = 1,2,3...$ represent the successive years in a given academic rank. The discrete-time hazard function, denoted by P_t, is the conditional probability that an event (e.g., promotion to associate professor) occurs in year t, given that it has not occurred prior to t. The dependence of P_t on explanatory variables is assumed to follow a logit model,

$$\log\left[\frac{P_{it}}{1-P_{it}}\right] = \alpha_t + \beta_1 x_{it1} + ... + \beta_k x_{itk}, \quad (1)$$

where the subscript i indicates the individual and the subscript t indicates the year in a given rank.

Explanatory variables may be constant over time or they may vary over time. For example, characteristics of the scientist's mentor do not change as the scientist ages, whereas a scientist's publication count or marital status may change with time. Explanatory variables that can take on different values in each year are referred to as *time-varying* variables. The possibility that values of independent variables will change over time is reflected in the time subscript to the x's in equation 1.

We expect a scientist's probability of promotion to change over time, independent of changes in variables like productivity. For example, all else being equal, the probability of promotion from assistant professor to associate professor should be near 0 at year 1, should peak at around year 6, and then decline and level off in later years. We refer to the change in the expected probability of promotion over time as the *time structure* for promotion. In equation 1, the time structure is indicated by the subscript t on α, which allows the intercept to differ for each year. We simplify this structure by restricting the α_t's to be a fourth-order polynomial in time:

$$\alpha_t = \alpha_0 + \alpha_1 t + \alpha_2 t^2 + \alpha_3 t^3 + \alpha_4 t^4. \quad (2)$$

Equation 2 allows α_t to change over time without requiring a separate parameter for each year. Although a second-order polynomial might seem sufficient to allow a pattern of increasing probabilities followed by decreasing probabilities, keep in mind that the dependent variable in equation 1 is the logit or log-odds of promotion, not the probability. Because probabilities are a nonlinear transformation of the logit, the fourth-order polynomial is necessary to allow the expected change in probabilities over time.

To explain how our results are presented, we develop the model further here. Let

$$\alpha' = \left[\alpha_0\,\alpha_1\,\alpha_2\,\alpha_3\,\alpha_4\right], t' = \left[1\,t\,t^2\,t^3\,t^4\right],$$
$$\beta' = \left[\beta_1 ... \beta_k\right],$$

and

$$x'_{it} = \left[x_{it1} ... x_{itk}\right].$$

The model to be estimated can be written as:

$$\log\left[\frac{P_{it}}{1-P_{it}}\right] = \alpha't + \beta'x_{it}. \quad (3)$$

Taking the exponential of equation 3 and solving for P_{it} yields:

$$P_{it} = \frac{1}{1+\exp\{-\alpha't - \beta'x_{it}\}}. \quad (4)$$

The expected probability of promotion is a function of time and the independent variables at a given time. The α's allow the expected probability of promotion to vary over time for any given values of the x's, and thus represent the *time structure* for promotion.

The β's indicate the effects of the explanatory variables. A simple transformation of the β's has a direct interpretation: $100\left(e^{\beta_j}-1\right)$ is the percentage change in the odds of promotion for a one unit increase in x_j, holding other variables constant. The standardized effect is computed as $100\left(e^{\beta_j s_j}-1\right)$, where s_j is the standard deviation of x_j. This indicates the percentage change in the odds of promotion for a standard deviation change in x_j, holding other variables constant.

To compare the processes of promotion for men and women, the α's and β's are allowed to differ by sex. The equality of corresponding coefficients can be tested with t-tests, and the equality of groups of coefficients can be tested with likelihood-ratio tests.

Figure 4.7   continues

The processes of promotion for men and women are summarized by plotting the expected probabilities of promotion over time. As shown in equation 4, expected probabilities must be computed at specific values of the explanatory variables. Two sets of values for the explanatory variables are used. First, means are computed separately for men and women. These are referred to as *group means*. Second, *pooled means* are computed by combining the men and women. Plots using group means — sex specific means — reflect differences in the time structure, in the effects of explanatory variables, and in the sex-specific values of the explanatory variables. In plots using pooled means, differences in the expected probabilities reflect only differences in the time structure and in the effects of the explanatory variables.

The event history model can be estimated by a maximum likelihood method using the following computational strategy.[3] First, break each individual's event history into a set of discrete person-years. There will be one record for each year in rank, and one record for the year of promotion if the scientist was promoted. Second, create a dependent variable that has a value of 1 for person-years in which promotions occurred, otherwise 0. Explanatory variables are assigned whatever values they had at the beginning of the year. Finally, pool all these person-years and estimate a logistic regression model using a standard maximum-likelihood logit program.

Figure 4.7

in the monograph world, the lengthiest notes are reserved for discussions of method, as we see in these cases.

MATHEMATICS AS AURATIC DISCOURSE

Discussions of data sources are almost immediately followed by a description of the "models"—equations—used in the analysis. We have already seen examples of such models, which occur in mathematical notation, with an accompanying prose discussion. I read these models, and the subsequent description of findings, as figures that clog the methods sections of quantitative journal articles. These figures occur both in the midst of prose, for example the presentation of models relating dependent and independent variables, and outside of the text proper, in the ur-text of hard science, with entire pages devoted to tables, graphs, and other figures representing science's world. The science aura is produced, thus, by both highly detailed and mathematically inflected discussions of method and model and the elaborate figuring of method and model, which dominates the journal page. There is interplay between these science-enhancing strategies that should be seen as adding value (units of science aura!) to each other. Perhaps surprisingly, the discussion of models that occurs in prose does not often simplify or translate the figural presentation, as prose itself becomes a kind of figure, thick with technical detail.

Scott Long's sophisticated discussion of method and model in his account of how he and his coauthors went about studying sex differences in promotability in science is no less "auratic," for instance his use of the word "polynomial," than is the use of mathematical symbolism, which dominates the journal presentation of high social science. By auratic I mean the signification of meaning by the form of discourse

MODELS AND ANALYSIS

To formally evaluate the modernization and world-system perspectives, I use structural equation models to specify the causal connections among the latent variables. Using LISREL VII (Joreskog and Sorbom 1989), which is based on the maximum-likelihood procedure, I estimate the measurement and causal parameters from the correlation matrices and standard deviations for each indicator (using listwise deletion). I report the measures of goodness-of-fit between the models and the observed data as the ratio of chi-square to degrees of freedom (χ^2/df) and goodness-of-fit index (GFI). Standardized parameter estimates and t-values are presented to assess more accurately differences in causal structures between the various models. Since the sample size is fairly small and all the available cases are used, the significance level was set at .05 (one-tailed-test); the corresponding t-value for 72 cases equals 1.67.

Figure 4.8

itself—the original Declaration of Independence signed in ink on roughhewn paper, the painting *Mona Lisa* housed in the Louvre behind glass, the distinctive Nike ads that end with the words "Just Do It," the thick math of science and social science. A work's aura suggests its authoriality as a version of what it purports to be—a document framing a nation, a famous painting, an advertising campaign that blurs the boundary between the commodity and hip/athletic lifestyles, real science. Aura is authorial signature, the fingerprints of creative artifice. Where the literature review, at least until the section on hypotheses, is composed for readers who may not have taken two graduate statistics courses (and perhaps also attended the Michigan ICPSR [Inter-University Consortium of Political and Social Research] or University of Essex summer schools on advanced data analysis), prose and figure found in the methods sections blur to the point of indistinguishability, given the highly technical nature of each. The auratic function of quantitative method in sociology lies precisely in the dense difficulty of the math-like, math-looking discussions and representations that dominate the middle sections of sociological journal articles. Prose becomes figure, and figure functions as a kind of text or ur-text, gesturing, if not arguing for, the work's scientific legitimacy.

This ur-text includes tables, graphs, charts, scatterplots, statistics, equations, and other accouterments of mathematical modeling. In the discipline of political science, what is called formal modeling, based on game theory, is an important trend in the discipline, especially in the field of international relations. This produces papers that could as well be published in mathematics journals. Unlike Long's paper, many such forays, such as Heckathorn's or Mark's, do not analyze empirical data but are purely formal exercises. The mathematization of American sociology (see Turner and Turner 1990) can be traced to the work of the first Comteans such as Ward, Sumner, Park, and Giddings. In the 1930s Lundberg continued this trend, as a mathematical positivism made further inroads in the discipline. However, as we shall see in chapter 7 on changes in sociological journal discourse, sociologists primarily used descriptive statistics until the 1970s, when more sophisticated and math-like multivariate analysis became commonplace. And formal modeling had no place in the dis-

---

ANALYTIC STRATEGY

We use panel data on a single cohort of respondents to examine the effects of age, family formation, and other characteristics on
religious participation. Religious participation is represented by a dummy variable that
equals 1 if the respondent is a church member and 0 otherwise. We fit a probit regression model of church membership at each of
three ages that span the period when family
formation is most likely to occur, at about
ages 22, 25, and 32. By comparing the coefficients obtained at these different ages, we
observe how aging changes the impact of personal characteristics on the probability of religious participation. By using regression
standardization techniques, we distinguish
the effects of age-related changes in means
of independent variables from effects of age-
related changes in coefficients of these variables. Independent variables in our model include a measure of religious participation at
about age 20, so that the coefficients for other
variables indicate their effects on changes in
church membership since that age.

An appropriate model for this strategy is

$$P_{tj} = \Phi(b_{0t} + Sb_{it}X_{itj} + e_{tj}),$$

where P_{tj} is the probability that person j is a
member of a religious organization at year t,
X_{itj} is the value of the ith variable that is hypothesized to affect church membership of
person j at year t; b_{0t} is a constant term at
year t; b_{it} is the coefficient at year t of the ith
variable that is hypothesized to affect reli-
gious participation; e_{tj} is the residual at year
t for person j; Φ is the normal cumulative
distribution function (the area under the normal curve).

Figure 4.9

cipline much before the last decade. Thus, only in the past twenty years, at the outside, did sociology journals come to resemble mathematics journals, both figurally
and in the level of sophistication and detail of their methodological prose. For most
of U.S. sociology's first century, a relatively unencumbered prose was in the saddle.

In figure 4.10, taken from a paper on the formal modeling of group behavior, the
page is littered with mathematical notation. The only parenthetical citation on the
page is to the author's own 1990 paper. Although this is not private language, there
are few sociologists who can read this page with benefit. Here, the interweaving of
technical prose and mathematical figure is so complete as to convert the article almost
entirely into gesture, with content becoming form. In figure 4.11, a common representation, we take a giant step backward in the level of technical proficiency
required of readers. We are presented with a three-dimensional figure summarizing
what the authors call mean force of marital attraction, with variation by sex and age
between 1972 and 1987. This is followed on the next page by a similar-looking
figure representing mean force of attraction by sex and education in the United States
between the same years. These graphs support the ample prose of the text, which
describes the study in detail.

In the next figure, discussion of the model and methods occurs in two separate
sections. Figure 4.12 presents the authors model of unionization, "expressed in
simple linear-additive functional form (no interactions expressed . . .)." In their
second set of analyses, the authors provide a second model relating unionization
to Catholic population size and a measure of Christian Democratic party rule.
Again, as with earlier articles, it is difficult to distinguish between text and figure

inasmuch as both are larded with technical detail—characteristic of most mathematically oriented discussions of models and methods. On the next page of the figure, the top half of the page is taken up with a table of variables' definitions, presented in rows. By now, the paper has trailed off into technical matters of method, leaving conceptual and theoretical discussion behind for the time being.

In figure 4.13, a data-based paper, a case is made for "difference models." This is a case based on mathematics; the two pages in question are full of mathematical notation, including difference models. This is the paper on whether modernization benefits the masses, and, as I said earlier, method and models are crucial to the authors' argument that dependency theory has overstated the deleterious effects of modernization on peripheral nations. Inasmuch as the authors hinge their argument to method, it is no surprise that we find sentences such as "Because $\log(Y2)$ − $\log(Y1) = \log(Y2/Y1)$, and $\log(Y2/Y1)$ measures the growth rate of Y (Jackman 1980; Firebaugh 1992: equation 3), the difference-of-logs model is a growth-rate model." A footnote follows, in which "rate" is technically defined.

Mathematics in sociology will be defended as both economical and powerful, enhancing robustness, a favorite word of quantitative methodologists. There is no doubt that math can do important intellectual work, as physicists have known for years. Mine is not an argument against mathematization but an observation that the auratizing function of math's figural gestures, from equations with Greek coefficients to tables of weighted least-squares coefficients, is an important part of the positivist project, which has long since abandoned Comte's goal of attaining laws of social motion. Absent hard-and-fast certainties about social life, the sort of general-theoretic understanding sought by scientific sociologists from Comte to Parsons, positivism has become *gestural,* an auratic literary protocol that thwarts access and critique. Reading the methods sections of *ASR* articles makes it very difficult to avoid the conclusion that a great deal of this gestural work involves a mathematizing fetishism. Although the sociologists who gesture in these ways are competent professionals who understand the meaning of *second-order polynomial,* surely sociology of this sort could be written more accessibly, with less technical detail that squeezes out reasoned prose and a greater attempt to explain technical terms to outsiders and disclose their assumptions about knowledge and society.

The argument will be made that technique and technical discourse drive scientific advance. Popularization is decried as the stuff of textbooks. I am not calling for textbook-level journal sociology; technical language certainly has its place, both in theory and method. But the extent of mathematization, serving a largely auratic function as the gestures thought to make would-be science science, is daunting, not only pushing aside prose but insinuating its way into prose itself as the boundary between text and gesture fades to nothing. Although the author of figure 4.13 tackles an important issue—the debate between modernization theory and dependency theory, the outcome of which has bearing on foreign policy—I do not accept the authors' claim that the debate will be resolved by modeling, involving issues of measurement. The debate will only be resolved by theoretically driven empirical research and argu-

Computing the number of defectors when ego chooses compliant control is somewhat more complex because it requires specifying the model of intragroup control (see Heckathorn 1990). Let E_{c2i} be the *efficacy of ego's compliant control over actor j*, and let O_{c2i} be ego's opportunity to exercise that compliant control. Thus, if O_{d1j} is j's opportunity to defect (not contribute) prior to ego's exercise of compliant control, then j's opportunity to defect (not contribute) *after* control, O'_{d1j}, is

$$O'_{d1j} = O_{d1j}\left(1 - O_{c2i}E_{c2i}\right). \tag{8}$$

Furthermore, ego's opportunity to defect is assumed to remain unchanged, i.e., I assume that *ego does not control ego*.

Other actors may also exercise compliant control. For example, if actor j is controlled by S_{c2}, (the set of actors other than ego who initially choose compliant control), and if that is the only control on j's opportunity to defect, it follows from recursive application of equation 8 that the first actor who exercises control reduces the opportunity to defect to $(1 - O_{c2a} \times E_{c2a})$; the second actor further reduces it to $(1 - O_{c2a} \times E_{c2a}) \times (1 - O_{c2b} \times E_{c2b})$; and the set of S_{c2} controlling actors reduces it to

$$O_{d1j} = \prod_{k=1}^{N}\left(1 - O_{c2k}E_{c2k}\right) \text{ for } k \in S_{c2}, k \neq i, j,$$
$$= 1 \qquad \text{if } S_{c2} = \varnothing. \tag{9}$$

Note that if the set of actors choosing compliant control is empty (i.e., $S_{c2} = \varnothing$), opportunities to defect (not contribute) are assumed to be unlimited (i.e., $O_{d1} = 1$). Thus, in this model, opportunities to defect are limited only by the actions of others. To simplify the equations that follow, this latter condition will not be restated.

Ego's opportunity to not contribute can be computed if the above expression is modified to acknowledge that ego is potentially controlled by all members of the set of actors (excluding ego) choosing compliant control, S_{c2}:

$$O_{d1i} = \prod_{j=1}^{N}\left(1 - O_{c2j}E_{c2j}\right) \text{ for } j \in S_{c2}, j \neq i. \tag{10}$$

If ego chooses to exercise compliant control, ego increases by one the number of compliant controllers targeting other actors in the system. Any other actor j's opportunities to not contribute after ego's exercise of control, O'_{d1j}, is given by substituting equation 9 into equation 8:

$$O'_{d1j} = \left(1 - O_{c2i}E_{c2i}\right) \prod_{k=1}^{N}\left(1 - O_{c2k}E_{c2k}\right) \tag{11}$$
$$\text{for } k \in S_{c2}, k \neq i, j.$$

The number of defectors if ego chooses a strategy of *full cooperation*, i.e., contributes to public goods production and encourages others to do the same, D_{cc}, is given by substituting the post-control violation opportunity O'_{d1j} into the expression for D_{cd} in equation 6:

$$D_{cc} = \sum_{j=1}^{N} O'_{d1j} \quad \text{for } j \in S_{d1}, j \neq i. \tag{12}$$

This, in turn, yields a public goods production level of

$$L_{cc} = 1 - \left(D_{cc}/N\right)^{F}. \tag{13}$$

The number of defectors if ego chooses a strategy of *hypocritical cooperation*, i.e., does not contribute but encourages others to contribute, D_{dc}, can be derived by substituting O'_{d1j} for O_{d1j} in the expression for D_{dd} in equation 4. Thus, the number of defectors, D_{dc}, is

$$D_{dc} = O_{d1i} + \sum_{j=1}^{N} O'_{d1j} \quad \text{for } j \in S_{d1}, j \neq i. \tag{14}$$

This yields a level of public goods production of

$$L_{dc} = 1 - \left(D_{dc}/N\right)^{F}. \tag{15}$$

Oppositional control can be modeled in a manner similar to compliant control (Heckathorn 1990). First, the opportunity of other group members, j, to exercise compliant control, O_{c2j}, can be represented as a function of the efficacy of oppositional control of the controlling actor(s) k, E_{o2k}, and the set of actors exercising oppositional control, S_{o2}:

$$O_{c2j} = \prod_{k=1}^{N}\left(1 - E_{o2k}\right) \text{ for } k \in S_{o2}, k \neq i,$$
$$= 1 \qquad \text{if } S_{o2} = \varnothing. \tag{16}$$

This expression summarizes the total effect of oppositional control exercised by actors other than ego on opportunities for each other group member j to support compliance. If no actors exercise oppositional control (i.e., $S_{o2} = \varnothing$), opportunities to exercise compliant control are assumed to be unlimited (i.e., $O_{c2j} = 1$). To simplify the equations that follow, this condition will not be restated.

Figure 4.10

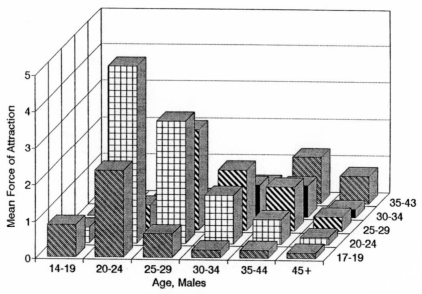

Figure 1. Mean Force of Attraction by Sex and Age: United States, 1972–1987

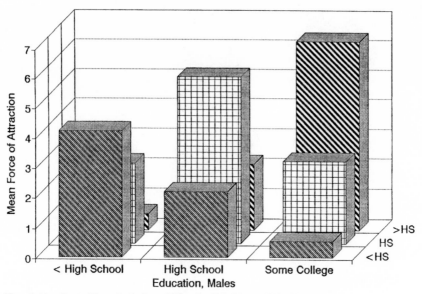

Figure 2. Mean Force of Attraction by Sex and Education: United States, 1972–1987

Figure 4.11

An Integrated Model of Unionization: Structure and Culture

By integrating business cycle and rational choice models of unionization (Griffin et al. 1990; Wallerstein 1989) and indicators of Catholicism suggested by Stephens (1979), we develop a model of union strength that incorporates both structural and cultural elements. Although we have simplified these models to fit them into our analysis, key features of the original theories have been retained. Again, in our model we do not expect our cultural measures to outshine the structural factors in explaining unionization, but we do expect them to better inform the model.

_____

[13] Alternatively, patrimonial heritages may carry such strong legacies of social solidarity and integration as to promote union integration and prevalence, once unions have exceeded some threshold of irrepressible social power. However, this hypothesis is more tentatively offered than that highlighted above in our text.

Our basic model of unionization, expressed in simple linear-additive functional form (no interactions expressed; signs denote direction of predicted effects) is:

Unionization = a + Inflation

– Unemployment + Strikes

+ Unionized sector – Service sector

– Civilian labor force + Left party

± Catholic population + CD party

+ Left corporatism + State

centralization – State traditionalism

+ Ghent-unemployment

interaction. (1)

The model, then, would predict that inflation, strikes, unionized sector employment, Left party strength, CD party strength, left corporatism, and state centralization would all have positive effects on unionization. Unemployment, service sector employment, civilian labor force, and state traditionalism should have negative effects on unionization. The interaction between Ghent and unemployment should have a positive effect on unionization (i.e., unemployment should have a positive effect on unionization in Ghent countries). Note that Catholic population size could affect unionization either positively or negatively in the simple additive model.

In a second round of analyses, we estimate interactions between effects of Catholic population size and a measure of CD party rule. To do this, we use models that incorporate statistical interactions in the following form:

Unionization = $a + L^*$(Catholic population)

$+ M$(CD party)$+ XB + e$; (1a)

$L^* = L + N$(CD party). (1b)

Figure 4.12 continues

Table 2. Variable Definitions

Variable	Definition
Unionization	Union members as a proportion of the dependent labor force
Non-Catholic unionization	Non-Catholic union members as a proportion of the dependent labor force
Inflation	Annual rate of change in consumer price indices
Unemployment	Unemployed workers as a proportion of the total labor force
Strike volume	Work days lost to strikes divided by total (approximate) number of work days (dependent labor force multiplied by 250)
Unionized sector	Proportion of the labor force working in mining, manufacturing, construction, public utilities, and transportation
Service sector	Proportion of the labor force working in wholesale and retail industries, finance, real estate, and all other services
Civilian labor force	Natural logarithm of the mean civilian labor force (civilian workers plus unemployed workers)
Left party strength	Average proportion of Cabinet portfolios controlled by Left party over the past four years
Catholic population	Proportion of the total population that is Catholic
Christian Democratic party strength	Average proportion of Cabinet portfolios controlled by the Christian Democratic party over the past four years.
Left corporatism	Scale of long-term working-lass mobilization and political-economic integration (composed of union strength, centralization, class mobilization, and Left party rule from 1946 to 1960)
State centralization	Scale of state centralization and welfare program consolidation (composed of revenue centralization, state centralization, and welfare program consolidation)
State	Scale of long-term absolutist legacy (composed of the administrative share of welfare outlays, state absolutism, resistance to mass enfranchisement, and class rigidity)

Note: Refer to Appendices A and B for data sources.

Figure 4.12

THE CASE FOR DIFFERENCE MODELS IN CROSS-NATIONAL RESEARCH

Because of its concern with the harmful long-term effects of foreign investment, dependency research's objective is to estimate *long-run* effects. Because cross-sectional relationships tend to reflect adjustments to change over the long run (Kuh 1959), cross-sectional data are appropriate for estimating long-run effects (Hu 1973:96–98). Until the middle or late 1970s, most cross-national studies in sociology used cross-sectional data, but most studies now use two-wave panel data. We argue that the use of panel data is appropriate for the questions raised by dependency theory, but the particular method used in dependency research is suspect.

Consider the following model for N nations, measured first at time 1 and again at some later time 2:

$$Y_{i1} = \alpha_1 + \mathbf{X}_{i1}\beta_1 + \mathbf{Z}_i\gamma_1 + \varepsilon_{i1},$$
$$i = 1, 2, \dots N; \qquad (1)$$
$$Y_{i2} = \alpha_2 + \mathbf{X}_{i2}\beta_2 + \mathbf{Z}_i\gamma_2 + \varepsilon_{i2}; \qquad (2)$$

where $\mathbf{X}$ and $\mathbf{Z}$ are vectors of causal variables, and β and γ are vectors of parameters. If there are p variables in vector $\mathbf{X}$, then $\mathbf{X}$ has dimension $1 \times p$ and β has dimension $p \times 1$; similarly, for q variables in vector $\mathbf{Z}$, $\mathbf{Z}$ is $1 \times q$ and γ is $q \times 1$. Usually Y, $\mathbf{X}$, and $\mathbf{Z}$ are logged to reduce the influence of outliers, but this has no bearing on our conclusions.[3]

---

[3] For the usual case in which a logged dependent variable is regressed on logged independent variables, let $Y = \log(Y')$, $\mathbf{X} = \log(\mathbf{X}')$, and $\mathbf{Z} = \log(\mathbf{Z}')$ in equations 1 and 2. This modification implies a multiplicative model in the original metric, but does not alter our argument. (We must also assume that the logarithm is defined for the variables in the model, but that usually is not a problem in cross-national research because a nation's levels of GNP, foreign investment, export activity, etc., are never negative.)

The distinction between $\mathbf{X}$ and $\mathbf{Z}$ is critical to the argument. $\mathbf{Z}$ represents variables that differ across nations but are constant for nation i from time 1 to time 2 (there is no sec-

ond subscript for $\mathbf{Z}$, because $\mathbf{Z}_{i1} = \mathbf{Z}_{i2} = \mathbf{Z}_i$), whereas $\mathbf{X}$ denotes variables that differ across nations and are *not* constant for nation i from time 1 to time 2. The variables ε_{i1} and ε_{i2} are random disturbances, and we assume:

$$E(\varepsilon_{i1}|\mathbf{X}_{i1}) = E(\varepsilon_{i1}|\mathbf{X}_{i2}) = E(\varepsilon_{i1}|\mathbf{Z}_i)$$
$$= 0 \text{ for all } i, \qquad (3)$$
$$E(\varepsilon_{i2}|\mathbf{X}_{i1}) = E(\varepsilon_{i2}|\mathbf{X}_{i2}) = E(\varepsilon_{i2}|\mathbf{Z}_i)$$
$$= 0 \text{ for all } i. \qquad (4)$$

β_1 and γ_1 can be estimated without bias by least squares (regress Y_{i1} on $\mathbf{X}_{i1}$ and $\mathbf{Z}_i$); similarly, β_2 and γ_2 can be estimated without bias by least squares (regress Y_{i2} on $\mathbf{X}_{i2}$ and $\mathbf{Z}_i$).

Summarizing, then: β and γ reflect long-run effects under the usual econometric assumptions. Because the objective of dependency research is to estimate long-run effects, the general model given by equations 1 and 2 applies widely in cross-national research. And the model can be estimated using least squares. In principle, then, the estimation of long-run effects is straightforward. As a practical matter, however, there are complications.

Bias Due to Omitted $\mathbf{Z}$ Variables

Enduring traits of individual units are hard to measure and often remain unmeasured (Liker, Augustyniak, and Duncan 1985). Although the authors cited individual human traits, like "taste," to illustrate the difficulty of measuring "constant" individual traits, their point applies equally to nations. Nations are unique, and it is not hard to think of constant (or nearly constant) unmeasured national characteristics that could have substantial effects on the outcomes development sociologists study. Examples include a nation's location, topography, climate, rainfall, mineral resources, type and quality of soil, access to seaports, history, culture, economic system, political system, legal system, city system, religious composition, relationship with neighbors, and so on. The importance of such national attributes depends on the issue studied, of course. The point here is that,

Figure 4.13   continues

because enduring national attributes often are hard to quantify, they are rarely included in the data used by development sociologists. Thus, when enduring attributes *are* important—as we suspect they often are—the results of quantitative cross-national research can be seriously biased because the assumptions expressed in equations 3 and 4 in general will not hold when $\mathbf{Z}$ (or some relevant component of $\mathbf{Z}$) is omitted.

Difference Models

A simple solution to the problem of unmeasured $\mathbf{Z}$ variables is to use a difference model (Allison 1990; Liker, Augustyniak, and Duncan 1985; Rodgers 1989) formed by subtracting equation 1 from equation 2:

$$Y_{i2} - Y_{i1} = \alpha^* + \mathbf{X}_{i2}\beta_2 - \mathbf{X}_{i1}\beta_1 + \mathbf{Z}_i\gamma_2$$
$$- \mathbf{Z}_i\gamma_1 + \varepsilon_i^*$$
$$= \alpha^* + (\mathbf{X}_{i2} - \mathbf{X}_{i1})\beta_2$$
$$+ (\beta_2 - \beta_1)\mathbf{X}_{i1} + \varepsilon_i^*, \qquad (5)$$

where $\alpha^* = \alpha_2 - \alpha_1$, $\varepsilon_i^* = \varepsilon_{i2} - \varepsilon_{i1}$, and (we assume) $\gamma_1 = \gamma_2$. Unless the effects of $\mathbf{X}$ change from time 1 to time 2,[4] $\beta_1 = \beta_2$ and the model reduces to:

$$Y_{i2} - Y_{i1} = \alpha^* + (\mathbf{X}_{i2} - \mathbf{X}_{i1})\beta_2 + \varepsilon_i^*. \qquad (6)$$

There are three important points about the difference model (also called the "first-difference" model [Liker, Augustyniak, and Duncan 1985] or "fixed-effects" model [England, Farkas, Kilbourne, and Dou 1988]). First, the effects of the $\mathbf{Z}$ variables are removed even though the variables are not actually measured. This follows from the equivalence of γ_1 and γ_2, so that $\mathbf{Z}_i\gamma_2 - \mathbf{Z}_i\gamma_1 = 0$ in equation 5 (this difference is approximately zero when $\gamma_1 \approx \gamma_2$). Second, all variables are measured as change scores. This feature distinguishes the "true" difference

[4] Isaac and Griffin (1989) discussed the issue of "periodizing" data to get constant effects in time-series models (short-run or medium-run effects). With difference models, we can test the assumption of constant effects by using equation 5 instead of equation 6. In any case, when using a difference model we want the time interval to be sufficiently long so that observed change is not largely measurement error or transient fluctuation.

model from the "semi-difference" model of dependency research, in which some variables are measured as change scores and some are not. Third, under the usual assumptions about the disturbances given by equations 3 and 4, β can be estimated without bias by an OLS regression of change in Y on change in $\mathbf{X}$, because:

$$E\left(\varepsilon_i^* \middle| \mathbf{X}_{i2}\right) = E\left(\varepsilon_{i2} \middle| \mathbf{X}_{i2}\right) - E\left(\varepsilon_{i1} \middle| \mathbf{X}_{i2}\right)$$
$$= 0 \text{ for all } i, \text{ and}$$
$$E\left(\varepsilon_i^* \middle| \mathbf{X}_{i1}\right) = E\left(\varepsilon_{i2} \middle| \mathbf{X}_{i1}\right) - E\left(\varepsilon_{i1} \middle| \mathbf{X}_{i1}\right)$$
$$= 0 \text{ for all } i. \qquad (7)$$

Because $\log(Y_2) - \log(Y_1) = \log(Y_2/Y_1)$, and $\log(Y_2/Y_1)$ measures the growth rate of Y (Jackman 1980; Firebaugh 1992:equation 3), the difference-of-logs model is a growth-rate model.[5] Put differently, a difference model is a growth-rate model if the variables are logged. This feature of the difference model bears directly here because cross-national regressions often employ variables in their logged form. The difference-of-logs form has three advantages: It tends to yield more robust results because outliers exert less influence; it avoids out-of-bounds estimates (although it can give out-of-bounds estimates for infant survival probability); and its coefficients have a ready interpretation as the effect of one rate on another.

Semi-Difference Models

Cross-national research in sociology currently is dominated by estimation models of the form:

[5] The term "rate" here means *rate of change* in some quantity. Thus, for example, GNP growth rate from time 1 to time t refers to the level of GNP at time t relative to its level at time 1 (similarly for foreign investment rate and the other variables used here). Percentage change, defined as $100(Y_t - Y_1)/Y_1$, is a simple rate measure. A percentage change does not take into account the length of the time interval, however, so the annual rate of change—defined as $[t^{th}$ root of $Y_t/Y_1]$ − 1 where t is measured in years—is often used instead. For cross-national data, an annual growth rate is virtually equivalent to the difference-of-logs measure ($r > .999$ between the two measures for the variables used in this analysis). We use the difference-of-logs measure here for theoretical reasons, to difference out $\mathbf{Z}$ (equation 5).

Figure 4.13

ment that do not refrain from counting (income, infant mortality) but that do not allow method—here, modeling—to think for us. The authors claim that a true difference model bests the semi-difference model of dependency research, resolving the dispute about whether capitalist modernization actually benefits people in peripheral nations. Yet modeling is merely discourse, a way of figuring data that do not speak for themselves but are merely frozen pieces of history. No matter how convincing the methodological argumentation, modernization theorists and dependency theorists will view the same "facts" differently, constituting them through the lens of their own totalizing, comprehensive theory. Thus, method will not resolve this argument outside of argument itself, which method eschews as prescientific.

INVERSION OF TEXT AND FIGURE

Although any skilled reader will want access to technical details of measurement and modeling, both to aid understanding and to sample the data directly instead of relying simply on prose descriptions, what I am noticing here is that the traditional relationship between prose, which constituted the main text, and figure, which used to occupy the margins as supporting material, has been inverted in the discussion-of-findings section of the positivist journal article. As I just observed, the boundary between technical prose and methodological figure or gesture has faded to the point of indistinguishability under sway of method, which invades thought and theory, bending them to its rules of computation, inference, generalization. Even before we notice the blurring of this boundary, we see the inversion of text and figure.

In figure 4.14, consecutive journal pages litter the methods section with, first, a large table summarizing coefficients and t-values in an event history analysis of promotion from associate professor to full in biochemistry and then, on the next page, with two graphs of the expected probability of promotion from associate to full by years in rank. These are facing pages; the reader who opens the article to pp. 716 and 717 is overwhelmed by the auratic work of figural gesture. Not only do these figures diminish surrounding prose, which is itself already highly technical, hence figural. The text is squeezed from below by footnotes 9 and 10 that further explain the details of method. Prose is nearly eclipsed by this figural extravaganza. This is carried to the extreme in figure 4.15, where pp. 92 and 93 of an article on religious participation in early adulthood are totally occupied by tables of probit coefficients for various regressions (p. 92) and percentage-point changes from a 50 percent probability (p. 93). These tables consume the entirety of both pages. Given that certain technical details are reserved for appendices and footnotes, both of which appear in smaller-point type than is found in the main body of the journal page, one wonders why these tables could not be reduced in size, if not scope, thus allowing surrounding prose to peek through. I am not questioning the value of a table with about 300 regression coefficients; as I said before, the presentation of the full text of data realizes certain literary economies and, as well, gives the reader access

Table 6. Event History Analysis for Promotion From Associate Professor to Full Professor: Ph.Ds in Biochemistry, 1956–1967

Variable	Unstandardized Coefficient			t-Value	Percent Change in Odds of Promotion for:	
					Unit Increase	Std. Deviation Increase
Non–Time-Varying						
Prestige of Ph.D. department	.242*			2.52	27	25
Citations to mentor (square root)	.006			.30	1	2
Doctorate in medical area	−.017			−.11	−2	—
Articles prior to rank (square root)	.072			.49	7	9
Citations prior to rank (square root)	.022			.72	2	11
Years between Ph.D. and rank	−.162***			−4.64	−15	−42
Time-Varying						
Inbred	.156			.69	17	—
Change in institution	.072			.20	7	—
Married	.091			.33	10	—
Years in rank	3.252***			4.14	—	—
(Years in rank)^2	−.438***			−3.03	—	—
(Years in rank)^3	.023			2.14	—	—
(Years in rank)^4	−.000			−1.49	—	—
Coefficients for Women						
Constant	−10.604***			−6.65	—	—
Prestige of current department	−.739***	†		−3.18	−52	−45
Articles in rank (square root)	1.008***	††		4.23	174	253
Citations in rank (square root)	−.011			−.26	−1	−5
Coefficients for Men						
Constant	−10.538***			−6.82	—	—
Prestige of current department	−.181	†		−1.41	−17	−14
Articles in rank (square root)	.313*	††		2.25	37	48
Citations in rank (square root)	.065			1.72	7	33

* p < .05   ** p < .01   *** p < .001 (two-tailed tests)
† p < .05   †† p < .01   ††† p < .001 (two-tailed tests)

Note: Daggers indicate significance levels of differences between coefficients for men and women. Likelihood ratio χ^2 = 382.0, d.f. = 20, p < .001

for men and 6.9 for women) the sex difference is highly significant (p < .001). Nevertheless, sex differences in citations in rank are not significant. Finally, women continue to be significantly less likely than men to be married, and they have significantly fewer young children.

Sex differences in promotion. The first logit model for promotion from associate professor to full professor includes only a dummy variable indicating the sex of the scientist. In any given year, the odds of being promoted from associate professor to full professor are 40 percent lower for women than for men (p = .001,

two-tailed). When control variables are added, the disadvantage for females decreases to 20 percent and is no longer statistically significant. This model, however, assumes that the effects of all variables are identical for men and women. Significant sex differences emerge for the effects of publications in rank and the prestige of the current department.[9] Table 6 dis-

[9] The effects of changing institutions were just barely significantly different by sex. In the restricted model, the effects were no longer different by sex, and consequently the effects were constrained to be equal.

Figure 4.14   continues

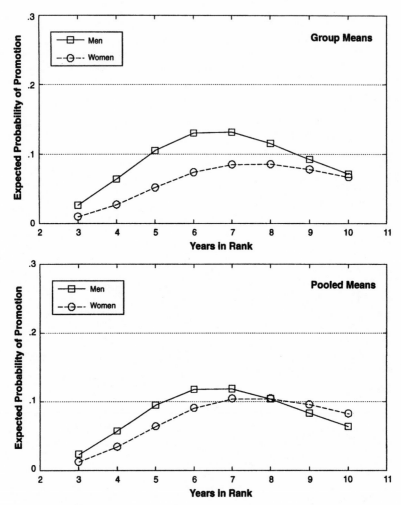

Figure 2. Expected Probability of Promotion from Associate Professor to Full Professor by Years in Rank: Ph.D.'s in Biochemistry, 1956–1967

Note: Models include sex-specific coefficients for prestige of current department, publications in rank, and citations in rank.

plays the results for a model in which the coefficients of publications in rank, citations in rank and prestige of current department are allowed to differ by sex.[10] Allowing the effects

[10] While no sex differences emerged for the effects of citations in rank, these coefficients were allowed to differ by sex in order to compare the effects of publications and citations in rank by sex.

of the remaining variables to differ by sex did not improve the fit of the model (likelihood ratio $\chi^2 = 13.03$, d.f. $= 13$, $p = .45$).

Sex differences in promotion to full professor are summarized in Figure 2. We use the logit estimates in Table 6 to compute the expected probability of promotion for a given year in rank. In the top figure, group means, i.e., separate means for men and women, for

Figure 4.14

Table 2. Probit Coefficients for Regressions of Religious Participation on Selected Independent Variables, by Year: High School Seniors of 1972

Independent Variable	1976 (Age 22)		1979 (Age 25)		1986 (Age 32)	
	Beta Coefficient	t-Statistic	Beta Coefficient	t-Statistic	Beta Coefficient	t-Statistic
Intercept	-2.268***	-12.38	-2.298***	-13.65	-2.480***	15.34
Black	.199***	4.32	.177***	3.87	.303***	6.61
Hispanic	.073	1.00	-.119	-1.65	-.039	-.55
Asian	.051	.38	.066	.50	-.244	-1.87
Parents' education	-.004	-.59	.004	.66	-.002	-.30
Small town	-.091*	-2.44	-.089*	-2.42	-.103**	-2.86
Medium city	-.131**	-2.72	-.182***	-3.86	-.158****	-3.41
Medium suburb	-.185**	-3.13	-.097	-1.71	-.227***	-4.02
Large city	-.097	-1.88	-.092	-1.82	-.127*	-2.54
Large suburb	-.191***	-3.44	-.164**	-3.02	-.223***	-4.23
Very large city	-.156*	-2.41	-.121	-1.92	-.250***	-4.02
Very large suburb	-.133*	-2.13	-.239***	-3.87	-.191**	-3.23
South	.099***	3.42	.140***	4.95	.130***	4.64
Education	.054***	5.94	.039***	5.33	.056***	8.93
Protestant	.503***	6.55	.583***	7.52	.548***	7.68
Catholic	.249**	3.17	.428***	5.41	.439***	6.03
Other Christian	.498***	6.16	.568***	6.98	.489***	6.48
Jewish	-.086	-.68	.164	1.35	.101	.89
Other religion	.206*	2.31	.078	.89	-.047	-.54
Religion missing	.237**	2.62	.381***	4.24	.428***	5.10
Past religious participation	1.139***	31.24	.850***	23.72	.695***	19.09
Marriage value	.099**	3.24	.176***	5.91	.150***	5.05
Kid opportunity value	.008	.36	.009	.43	.006	.31
Family near value	.087***	4.16	.035	1.73	.099***	4.97
Cohabitating	-.424***	-5.75	-.386***	-5.87	-.391***	-5.07
Married	.098*	2.42	.029	.69	.207***	4.04
Disrupted cohabitation	-.290*	-1.98	-.383***	-3.62	-.315***	-3.86
Disrupted marriage	-.104	-1.40	-.063	-.98	.191**	2.81
Children age < 1	.009	.18	.138***	3.38	.067	1.64
Children age 1	-.006	-.11	.219***	4.67	.083*	2.02
Children age 2	-.135*	-2.03	.158**	3.28	.134**	3.26
Children age 3	-.041	-.57	.188***	3.61	.237***	5.75
Children age 4	.048	.44	.117*	2.05	.252***	6.29
Children age 5	-.184	-.97	.049	.78	.297***	7.29
Children age 6	.730*	2.03	.157*	2.29	.212***	4.93
Children age 7	.000	.00	-.038	-.36	.282***	6.16
Children ages 8–9	.000	-.00	.178	1.17	.227***	6.56
Children ages 10–12	.000	.00	.000	-.00	.058	1.74
Male	-.093*	-2.24	-.254***	-5.30	-.130*	-2.10
Male × Past religious participation	-.072	-1.34	.151**	2.83	-.035	-.66
Male × Married	.067	1.20	.174**	3.13	-.047	-.72
Male × Disrupted cohabitation	-.164	-.62	.119	.70	.355**	2.73
Male × Disrupted marriage	.022	.19	.000	.00	-.441***	-4.31
Number of cases	11,523		11,613		11,453	
Pseudo R	.423		.379		.358	
Log–likelihood	-6101.5		-6498.4		-6816.2	

*p < .05   **p < .01   ***p < .001 (two-tailed t-tests)

Figure 4.15   continues

Table 3. Percentage-Point Changes from a 50-Percent Probability of Religious Participation Produced by a Unit Change in the Independent Variable, by Sex and Age: High School Seniors
of 1972

	Female			Male		
Independent Variable	1976 (Age 22)	1979 (Age 25)	1986 (Age 32)	1976 (Age 22)	1979 (Age 25)	1986 (Age 32)
Black	7.9	7.0	11.9	7.9	7.0	11.9
Hispanic	2.9	-4.7	-1.5	2.9	-4.7	-1.5
Asian	2.0	2.6	-9.6	2.0	2.6	-9.6
Parents' education	-.1	.2	-.1	-.1	.2	-.1
Small town	-3.6	-3.5	-4.1	-3.6	-3.5	-4.1
Medium city	-5.2	-7.2	-6.3	-5.2	-7.2	-6.3
Medium suburb	-7.3	-3.9	-9.0	-7.3	-3.9	-9.0
Large city	-3.9	-3.7	-5.0	-3.9	-3.7	-5.0
Large suburb	-7.6	-6.5	-8.8	-7.6	-6.5	-8.8
Very large city	-6.2	-4.8	-9.9	-6.2	-4.8	-9.9
Very large suburb	-5.3	-9.4	-7.6	-5.3	-9.4	-7.6
South	4.0	5.6	5.2	4.0	5.6	5.2
Education	2.2	1.5	2.2	2.2	1.5	2.2
Protestant	19.3	22.0	20.8	19.3	22.0	20.8
Catholic	9.8	16.6	17.0	9.8	16.6	17.0
Other Christian	19.1	21.5	18.8	19.1	21.5	18.8
Jewish	-3.4	6.5	4.0	-3.4	6.5	4.0
Other religion	8.2	3.1	-1.9	8.2	3.1	-1.9
Religion missing	9.4	14.8	16.6	9.4	14.8	16.6
Past religious participation	37.3	30.2	25.7	35.7	34.2	24.5
Marriage value	3.9	7.0	6.0	3.9	7.0	6.0
Kid opportunity value	.3	.4	.3	.3	.4	.3
Family near value	3.4	1.4	4.0	3.4	1.4	4.0
Cohabitating	-16.4	-15.0	-15.2	-16.4	-15.0	-15.2
Married	3.9	1.2	8.2	6.6	8.1	6.4
Disrupted cohabitation	-11.4	-14.9	-12.3	-17.5	-10.4	1.6
Disrupted marriage	-4.2	-2.5	7.6	-3.3	-2.5	-9.9
Children age < 1	.4	5.5	2.7	.4	5.5	2.7
Children age 1	-.3	8.7	3.3	-.3	8.7	3.3
Children age 2	-5.4	6.3	5.3	-5.4	6.3	5.3
Children age 3	-1.6	7.4	9.4	-1.6	7.4	9.4
Children age 4	1.9	4.7	9.9	1.9	4.7	9.9
Children age 5	-7.3	1.9	11.7	-7.3	1.9	11.7
Children age 6	26.7	6.2	8.4	26.7	6.2	8.4
Children age 7	.0	-1.5	11.1	.0	-1.5	11.1
Children ages 8–9	.0	7.1	9.0	.0	7.1	9.0
Children ages 10–12	.0	.0	2.3	.0	.0	2.3

Note: Male and female effects shown in this table differ only for variables that interact with the sex
variable. Effects were evaluated at a 50-percent probability of religious participation.

Figure 4.15

Table 2. Variables Used in the Analysis: 65 Countries

Country	Year of Survey	Step Parameter	Percent not in Agriculture	Per Capita Energy Consumption	Political Democracy Index	Dominant Religion	Techno- logical Background	Number of Cases
Australia	1981	−.564	91	4,795	100	2	0	19,173
Austria	1982	−.682	83	2,887	97	1	0	7,485
Bangladesh	1975[a]	−.725	13	20[b]	63	3	1	3,122
Belgium	1979	−.573	94	4,424	100	1	0	1,615
Benin	1981	−.583	48	50	25	0	2	3,007
Brazil	1980	−.962	51	447	61	1	1	30,486
Cameroon	1978	−.754	14	72	56	0	2	5,518
Canada	1976	−.696	88	5,941	100	5	0	32,233
China	1982	−.702	30	647	16	0	1	56,802
Colombia	1976	−.865	50	522	71	1	1	2,328
Costa Rica	1976	−.787	50	235	90	1	1	2,364
Czechoslovakia	1980	−.679	78	5,560	21	1	0	22,246
Denmark	1979	−.648	85	3,415	100	2	0	1,327
Dominican Republic	1975	−.629	39	158	39	1	1	1,555
Ecuador	1979[a]	−1.132	45	247	45	1	1	3,644
Egypt	1980	−.704	44	333	39	3	1	6,212
Fiji	1974	−.697	43	350[b]	70[c]	0	1	4,341
Finland	1972	−.755	61	1,034	97	2	0	437
France	1979	−.716	82	2,824	91	1	0	1,426
Ghana	1979[a]	−.688	38	118	24	0	2	3,003
Guyana	1975	−.654	62	566	53	0	1	2,580
Haiti	1977	−.869	21	37	21	1	1	1,549
Hong Kong	1971	−1.023	48[d]	255	70[c]	4	1	3,312
Hungary	1973	−.890	60	1,907	12	1	0	13,698
India	1971	−.740	26	122	91	0	1	1,814
Indonesia	1976	−1.026	26	137	10	3	1	31,828
Ireland	1979	−.907	69	2,164	97	1	0	1,522
Israel	1970	−.760	84	734	97	0	0	1890
Italy	1979	−.913	76	1,661	97	1	0	1,417
Ivory Coast	1980[a]	−.763	13	169	46	0	2	3,835
Jamaica	1975[a]	−.727	61	521	90	2	1	1,094
Japan	1971	−1.192	59	544	100	4	0	1,307
Jordan	1976	−.841	65	206	31	3	1	3,136
Kenya	1977[a]	−.662	15	143	58	0	2	4,222
Lesotho	1977	−.529	8	10[e]	40[c]	5	2[f]	2,484
Malaysia	1974	−.809	36	258	80	0	1	4,744
Mexico	1976[a]	−.862	46	936	75	1	1	4,480
Morocco	1980	−.832	40	180	32	3	1	2,533
Nepal	1976	−.731	5	4	29	0	1	3,851
Netherlands	1977	−.570	90	3,136	100	5	0	51,952
New Zealand	1981	−.678	87	2,780	100	2	0	39,983

(Table 2 continued on next page)

Figure 4.16 continues

(Table 2 continued from previous page)

Country	Year of Survey	Step Parameter	Percent not in Agriculture	Per Capita Energy Consumption	Political Democracy Index	Dominant Religion	Techno- logical Background	Number of Cases
Norway	1972	−.602	79	2,267	100	2	0	510
Pakistan	1975	−.759	38	68	63	3	1	3,136
Panama	1975[a]	−.947	49	616	77	1	1	2,393
Paraguay	1979	−.974	45	106	45	1	1	2,166
Peru	1977[a]	−1.184	49	520	87	1	1	4,283
Philippines	1978	−.904	41	173	93	1	1	7,764
Portugal	1979[a]	−1.201	62	567	39	1	1	4,451
Rwanda	1983	−.337	6	14	30	0	2	2,769
Senegal	1978	−.545	17	128	54	3	2	2,702
South Korea	1974	−1.395	33	211	53	4	1	4,664
Sri Lanka	1975	−.716	44	110	86	0	1	4,884
Sudan, North	1978[a]	−.806	15	69	38	3	1	2,259
Sweden	1972	−.621	85	3,075	100	2	0	520
Syria	1978	−.753	47	351	20	3	1	3,341
Taiwan	1970	−.955	51	381	23	4	1	1,256
Thailand	1975	−.999	16	62	17	0	1	2,549
Trinidad	1977	−.787	79	2,233	85	5	1	2,728
Tunisia	1978	−.874	45	219	64	3	1	3,261
Turkey	1978	−.595	27	329	76	3	1	3,353
United Kingdom	1972	−.470	96	4,834	99	2	0	5,426
United States	1980	−.779	95	9,031	92	5	0	26,077[a]
Venezuela	1977	−.790	67	2,780	73	1	1	1,899
West Germany	1979	−.739	89	4122	89	5	0	1,541
Yugoslavia	1971	−1.007	31	593	51	0	0	1,709

[a] Data collection continued into the next year.

[b] Estimated using information for the 1970s.

[c] Estimated using information from Banks (1977) and Taylor and Hudson (1972).

[d] Average of Taiwan, South Korea, and Japan

[e] Information was available only after 1979, indicating Lesotho has the lowest value of all our African countries. Therefore, we assigned a value somewhat below that for Rwanda.

[f] Coded as industrializing horticultural.

planatory variables. The country characteristics used are the level of economic development, degree of political democracy, dominant religion, and the technological background of the least-developed countries. These characteristics are operationalized as follows. We use two different measures for the *level of economic development*: the percentage of the labor force *not* in agriculture and the natural logarithm of per capita energy consumption (in kilograms of coal equivalents). These two measures are used as interchangeable indices. This allows us to

perform a more rigorous test of our hypotheses regarding the effects of the level of economic development. Because these variables are designed to measure the same phenomenon and are highly correlated ($r = .90$), we do not include them both in a given model.

Political democracy is measured with a democracy index developed by Bollen (1980). The index runs from 0 (very undemocratic) to 100 (very democratic). For *dominant religion*, we use a six-category variable: 0 = other, 1 = Catholic, 2 = Protestant, 3 = Muslim, 4 = Confucian, 5 = mixed

Figure 4.16 continues

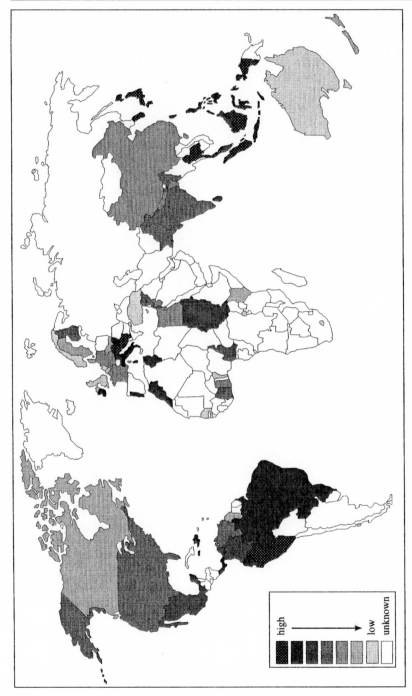

Figure 1. Level of Educational Homogamy in 65 Countries

Figure 4.16   continues

Table 3. Loglinear Coefficients for the Bivariate Effects of Selected Independent Variables on Educational Homogamy: 65 Countries

Model	Independent Variable	Coefficient	Standard Error	Percentage Reduction in G^2
(1)	Proportion not in agriculture	−.287**	.008	21.9
(2)	Proportion not in agriculture	1.329**	.048	40.2
	(Proportion not in agriculture)^2	−1.367**	.040	
(3)	Per capita energy consumption (ln)	−.047**	.001	19.1
(4)	Per capita energy consumption (ln)	.170**	.010	25.9
	(ln Per capita energy consumption)^2	−.016**	.001	
(5)	Political Democracy Index	−.188**	.006	16.3
(6)	Dominant religion			50.3
	Catholic	.251**	.007	
	Muslim	.284**	.009	
	Confucian	.564**	.021	
	Catholic/Protestant	.047**	.006	
	Other	.099**	.007	
(7)	Technological background			35.3
	Industrialized countries	.035**	.009	
	Agricultural background	.228**	.009	

Note: Reference categories are "Protestant" for dominant religion and "horticultural background" for technological background; N = 486,931.

$^*p < .05$ $^{**}p < .01$

Protestant/Catholic. A religion is considered dominant if the majority of a country's population belongs to it, and if there is no other religion to which a substantial part of the population belongs. The "other" category is a residual category. It contains countries in which another religion is dominant and countries with more than one dominant religion (except the mixed Catholic/Protestant countries). For the *technological background* of the least-developed countries, a three-category schema presented by Lenski and Nolan (1984) is used: 0 = industrialized countries, 1 = industrializing agrarian countries, and 2 = industrializing horticultural countries. For practical reasons (to prevent the parameter values from becoming very small), the percentage of workers not in agriculture and the democracy index are divided by 100 before the analysis is performed.[7]

Our data pertain to existing marriages, which were registered before the survey. Because societal factors should have their greatest impact around the time of a wedding, we use country characteristics for a year preceding the survey year (cf. Ultee and Luijkx 1990). The indices for the level of economic development refer to 15 years prior to the survey year. The democracy index refers to 1965. The information on dominant religion pertains to the 1960s and early 1970s. The technological background variable is not time-dependent. Values of the explanatory variables are presented in Table 2.

[7] Sources for the indicators of level of economic development are Taylor and Hudson (1972), World Bank (1979), Taylor and Jodice (1983), ILO (1990), Lane, McKay and Newton (1991), and UNDP (1992). Information on dominant religion was derived from Taylor and Hudson (1972) and Barrett (1982). Because the indices for the level of development were not always available on a year-to-year basis, their values for the target year sometimes had to be estimated. In most cases, linear interpolation could be used, as values for a given year before and a given year after the target year were available. Sometimes, only values after the target year were available. In those cases, linear extrapolation was used.

Figure 4.16   continues

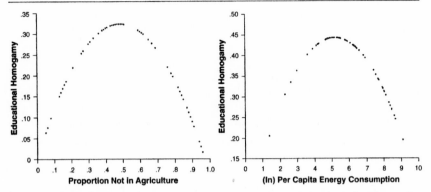

Figure 2. Bivariate Relationship between Indicators of Economic Development and Educational Homogamy: 65 Countries

RESULTS

To study the bivariate effects of the explanatory variables on educational homogamy, we estimated a separate loglinear model for each of the explanatory variables. For the measures of level of economic development, we estimated not only linear models but also models with both a linear term and a quadratic term. The results of these analyses are presented in Table 3. The models in this table and in Table 4 are specified so that a *positive* sign for a parameter means that *high* values of the variable are associated with *more* educational homogamy.

Models 1 and 3 in Table 3 show that level of economic development has significant linear effects on educational homogamy. In both models, countries with high levels of economic development show less educational homogamy. This finding agrees with the romantic-love hypothesis. However, Models 2 and 4 show that adding a quadratic term to the equations leads to a significant improvement of the model.

Figure 2 plots the bivariate relationships between proportion not in agriculture and per capita energy consumption (ln) and educational homogamy. The relationship is about the same for both variables—that is, with increasing economic development, educational homogamy first increases, reaches a peak, and then decreases. This finding agrees with the predictions of the inverted U-curve hypothesis. Educational homogamy is strongest in countries in which about 50 percent of the

labor force worked outside agriculture 15 years before the survey year (e.g., Brazil and Costa Rica). Homogamy is also strongest in countries that had a per capita energy consumption of about 200 kilogram coal equivalents 15 years before the survey year (e.g., Morocco and the Philippines).

The bivariate effect of the political democracy measure is significant and in the expected direction: Countries with high levels of democracy show less educational homogamy. The bivariate effects of the dominant religion and the technological background of the least-developed societies are also significant and in the expected direction. Countries with a predominantly Catholic, Muslim, Confucian, mixed Catholic/Protestant, or "other" population have significantly higher educational homogamy than do countries with a predominantly Protestant population. Industrializing agrarian countries show significantly more educational homogamy than do the industrializing horticultural countries.

In the multivariate analysis, two loglinear models are estimated—Model 1 uses the proportion of workers not in agriculture as the indicator of development, and Model 2 uses the per capita energy consumption. Table 4 shows the parameters of these models. Again, the two indicators of the level of economic development are nonlinearly related to educational homogamy.

Figure 3 shows that the multivariate relationships between the two economic variables and educational homogamy have an

Figure 4.16

to the nuts and bolts of the argument. I am merely observing that this presentation has been achieved at the expense of prose's total eclipse.

In figure 4.16, we find five consecutive pages of an article on educational homogamy in sixty-five countries. This is a data-rich presentation. In the first table, the seven variables being investigated are listed across the table, and the sixty-five countries are listed vertically. This is so voluminous a presentation that it spills over onto the next page, leaving room for only thirteen lines of text, split into the usual two columns (itself a replication of science journals and representing a departure from the *ASR*'s early years, where two columns were eschewed for one full page of text). On p. 277, facing the page onto which the table of sixty-five countries has spilled over, we find a map of the world! Areas are shaded from dark to light in order to indicate level of educational homogamy. I am perhaps too visually illiterate to appreciate this figure. It is difficult to imagine an editor allowing a paper on the dissemination of critical theory to use a similar vehicle in order to demonstrate the diaspora of the Frankfurt School's ideas. On the following page (p. 278) of figure 14.16, we find the top half of the page devoted to a table on loglinear coefficients. Another technical footnote compresses the prose on the page into the equivalent of eighteen lines. Finally, on the last page of this figure, p. 279, we find two parabolic scatterplots of bivariate relationships. These scatterplots end the discussion of method, after which follows a section called "results." These five pages are about 70 percent figure (excluding the note on p. 278). When we look back on *ASRs* of the past, even as recently as the 1960s, we find a very different, less figural approach to writing sociology.

REPRESENTATION

By now, figure is in the saddle, and prose merely supports it. Figure represents and hence reproduces the nature-like status of the social world. The peaks and valleys of graphs suggest peakness and valleyness, subtly persuading the reader that she is in the presence of nature, or at least viewing nature through the refracting lens of research methodology, a silent text. Social science represents nature-like data in order to attain the institutional and societal legitimacy of the hard natural sciences, but, in so doing, unwittingly freezes the peaks and valleys of our present unjust, inequitable social world into nature-like solidity. Even the representationality of the journal page is not a particularly self-conscious stratagem but merely a norm replicated time and again by journal authors who figure their work lavishly and editors who publish such work. By now, few think twice about pages such as 275 through 279 of figure 4.16. Representation reproduces representation.

Figure 4.17 is taken from an article on the formal modeling of collective action and group heterogeneity. These graphs suggest the peakness and valleyness I talked about above. Interestingly, these three figures are found in a non–data-based article. The non-smooth trajectory of the functions suggests that we are observing a nature-like process or phenomenon, precisely the impact of such figures in journal science. Figure 4.18 is a relatively rudimentary but still representational depic-

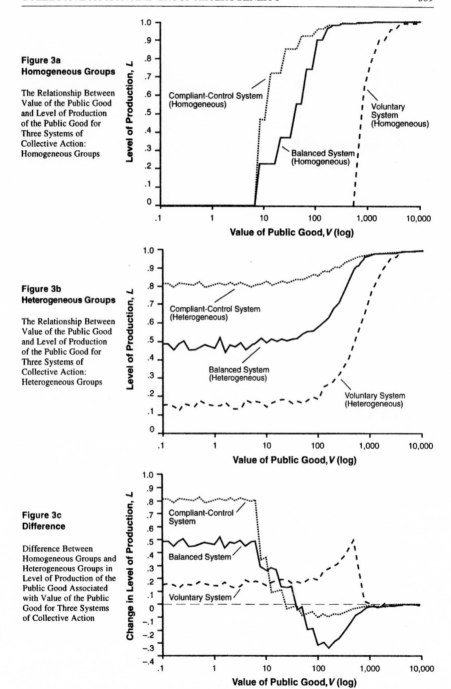

Figure 3a
Homogeneous Groups

The Relationship Between Value of the Public Good and Level of Production of the Public Good for Three Systems of Collective Action: Homogeneous Groups

Figure 3b
Heterogeneous Groups

The Relationship Between Value of the Public Good and Level of Production of the Public Good for Three Systems of Collective Action: Heterogeneous Groups

Figure 3c
Difference

Difference Between Homogeneous Groups and Heterogeneous Groups in Level of Production of the Public Good Associated with Value of the Public Good for Three Systems of Collective Action

Figure 4.17

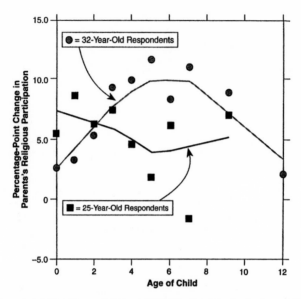

Figure 1. Percentage-Point Change in Parents' Religious Participation by Age of Child, for Respondents Ages 25 and 32: High School Seniors of 1972

Figure 4.18

tion of percentage-point change in parents' religious participation by age of child in a survey of people who were high school seniors in 1972. This figure suggests clearly different patterns of religious participation for twenty-five-year old parents and thirty-two-year old parents. This garden-variety figure suggests an almost nature-like pattern of data, corresponding to an implied iron law of religious participation by age of child. Upon inspection, of course, the curves are not fit perfectly by the data and there are outliers.

Although representation is never claimed by the sociological text, for after all epistemology has been left behind as an unproductive philosophical prolegomenon, it is powerfully suggested by the methods section, which substitutes technical reason, in Weber's terms, for substantive reason. Although I do not doubt the obvious economy of figural presentation, the growing sophistication of research methodology has not been matched by growing attention to matters theoretical. Articles have not gotten longer. Thus, in the zero-sum game of the struggle for pages, increasingly elaborate figural representation comes at the expense of reasoned prose, including theory. And, as I will discuss later, even theory has become figural in its own way.

This is where the positivism of mainstream U.S. sociology really resides: method is a gestural text that represents a static objective world drained of history or what people of my persuasion call historicity, our location in a history essentially open

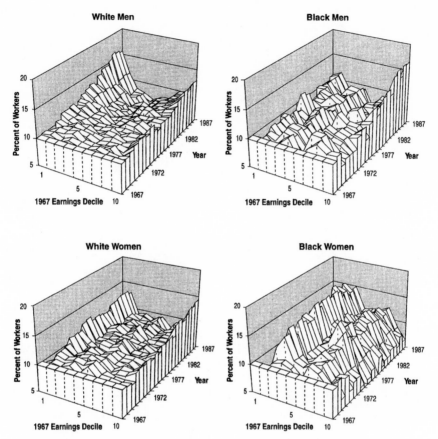

Figure 4. Changes in the Relative Distribution of Earnings by Race and Gender: Full-Time, Full-Year Workers, 1967 to 1987

Figure 4.19

to change, to be achieved through human agency including writing. It is method's representational quality that sociologists use to convey their status as scientists (scientificity, in my language).

Figures 4.19 through 4.24 present other examples of figures that represent nature-like processes or phenomena. Figure 4.19 suggests an almost geological sedimentation. Figure 4.20 suggests a complicated, physics-like system of interrelated parts, here of variables related to economic and political development. Figure 4.21, a nature-like distribution and differentiation of variables represented by scatterplots, each within its own rectangle piled one upon another, suggests a modernist cityscape. The "rate of population increase" is preceded by the adjective "natural."

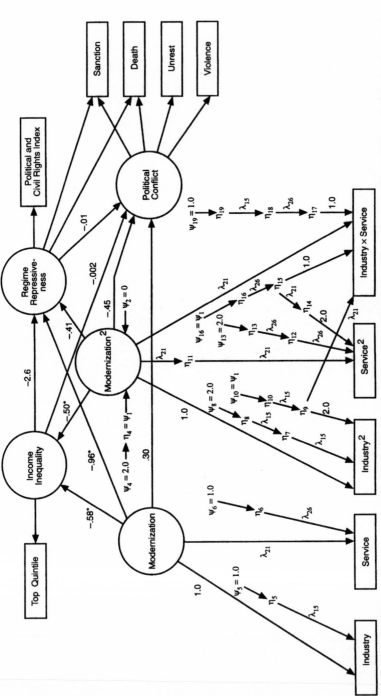

Figure 1. The Path Diagram and Standardized Structural Coefficients of the Curvilinear Model Linking Modernization, Income Inequality, and Regime Repressiveness to Political Conflict ($\chi^2/df = 427/41$; GFI = .60)

$^*p < .05$ (one-tailed tests); other structural coefficients are not significant.

Figure 4.20

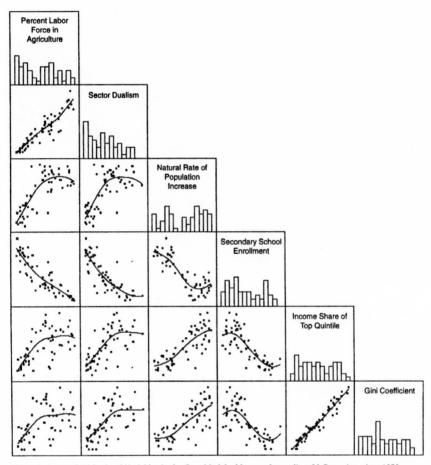

Figure 5. Scatterplot Matrix of Variables in the Core Model of Income Inequality: 56 Countries, circa 1970

Figure 4.21

Figure 4.22 depicts a feedback loop that could as well be found in an electrical engineering publication. Figure 4.23, which appears in a non-data-based article on the micro-level legitimation of power, suggests a chemical reaction. Figure 4.24 combines the engineering-like and chemistry-like connotations of figures 4.22 and 4.23 in a complicated page of an article on self-esteem and delinquency. A different reading of 4.24 suggests cosmological implications. To my eye, none of these figures enhances explanation or provides the reader with data that go beyond the text.

Science's figural gestures suggest that science is a mirror of nature (Rorty 1979), in sociology's case, of social nature. These gestures produce what I am calling the science aura, the impression that one is reading a text so intimately bound up with

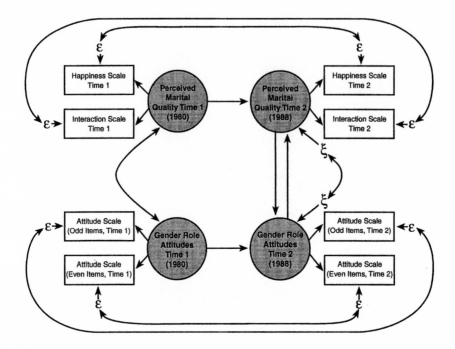

Figure 1. Diagram of Model 1: A Test of the Reciprocal Relationship between Gender Role Attitudes and Perceived Marital Quality among Husbands and Wives

Note: Time 1 = 1980 and time 2 = 1988. Model 2 (not shown) is identical to Model 1 except scales measuring negative marital quality (disagreement, problems, and divorce proneness) replace the happiness and interaction scales (which, in Model 1, measure positive marital quality).

Figure 4.22

the world's *thingness,* objectivity, factuality, that we can reasonably conclude that the world is governed by cause and effect patterns. Although sociologists are careful not to claim lawfulness for their work just yet, their science being avowedly immature by comparison to geology or biology, they get around this by portraying the world as if it could be explained causally once method is powerful enough to probe its deepest mysteries. The science aura, what looks like physics or engineering, is bestowed by gesture, not by argument.

Let me return to the sentence above: "The peaks and valleys of graphs suggest peakness and valleyness. . . ." This sort of construction invites positivists to lampoon the apparent silliness and wordplay of postmodern theory. The term *peakness* will be dismissed as a neologism by sober sociologists, who themselves proliferate technical terminology—my peakness for Long's polynomial. However, form bears content where the issue is the language game of research's presentation. "How" we express our findings does more than influence the findings. "How" constitutes findings, as any research methodology seminar will instruct, given the perspectival,

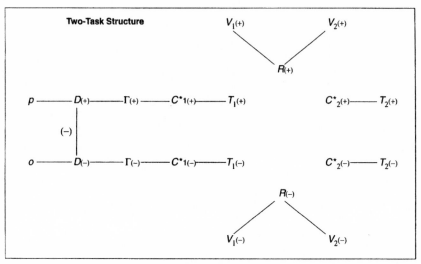

Figure A-1. A Two-Task Structure Showing Interrelations among Actors, Characteristics, and Outcome States

Figure 4.23

indeed constitutional, nature of survey instruments, data collection, and data analysis. This is precisely why methodologists spend so much time designing studies carefully, recognizing that issues of reliability (getting consistent findings) and validity (getting accurate findings) bedevil sloppy research findings. They recognize that bad methods produce bad findings, just as texts write authors.

No methodological scribe will confess to figuring her paper with peaks and valleys in order to produce the impression that science mirrors nature. Graphs will be defended conventionally, as the ways that people figure data in order to aid comprehension. Positivists do not plot to produce the nature-like appearance of society in aid of a conservative political agenda. Most of my sociological colleagues, past and present, support "choice," oppose the deforestation of Oregon, and want to raise the minimum wage. But, since Comte, the project of social physics has evolved in such a way that today, in the early twenty-first century, positivism, which has inevitable conservative consequences given its metaphysical belief in social laws such as capitalism and patriarchy, is a discursive program reproduced thoughtlessly in the ways that writers write and teach their students how to read and write in order to build careers.

Social physics has taken a figural turn as sociology's fortune in the university has slipped since the recession of the 1970s and then the Reagan presidency. Sociological journal writing resembles science in order to re-legitimize sociology at a time when deans and funding agencies want payoff for their investments. Peaks and

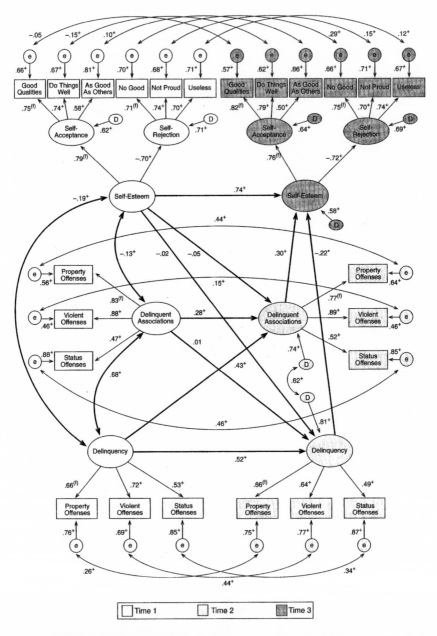

Figure 1. Estimated Model of Self-Esteem, Delinquent Associations, and Delinquency for Total Sample: Rochester Youth Development Study

Note: Fixed coefficients are indicated by (f); N = 780; RMSEA = .05; NFI = .87; fit ratio = 3.10.

+*p* < .05 (one-tailed tests)   **p < .05 (two-tailed tests)

Figure 4.24

valleys in articles convince deans and their superiors that the sociology department deserves another hire, a computer lab, more travel money, a bigger Ph.D. program, an outside chairperson found in a national search. With increasingly corporate management cultures in U.S. universities, micromanagement takes the form of central administrative control of departments' and faculty members' intellectual agendas. I have never worked in a university in which administrators above the level of the department refrained from allowing their prejudices about sociology to inform their decision making about resources and personnel. Peaks and valleys of graphs, equations, statistics, Greek mathematical symbolism, pages of tables of correlation coefficients, all convince administrators, policymakers, and the public at large that sociology has arrived as a hard science. The science aura translates into resources and leverage.

There is something to be said for this, especially where universities are run by administrators from outside of the liberal arts. Since Washington University closed down its intellectually enlivening, if fractious, sociology department in the 1980s, departments have been threatened with "retrenchment," the administrative technical term for elimination. For those who remember how sociology alliterated with socialism, social work, and the sixties, only a partial misconception at the time, the science aura is much-needed, especially where faculty members seek external or extramural funding. Now that even public universities are bankrolled more by private sources than by their state legislatures, sociology's very survival might seem to depend on demonstrating both resemblance to science and relevance to policy, which go hand in hand where policy issues, such as crime and health, are readily quantifiable. The more distance contemporary sociologists put between themselves and sociology's more activist phases, going all the way back to Durkheim and Weber who, with Marx, were quite critical of emerging capitalism for its human costs, the better. Even sociology's beginnings in the United States, with the Chicago School in the 1890s, were directly grounded in sociologists' attempts to ameliorate urban problems and had little to do with the pursuit of scientific status.

For those who would produce the science aura, and hence earn institutional and societal legitimacy, sociology must abandon not only Marx and postmodernism, which make easy targets, but sociology's original engagement with social issues. Although Comte modeled sociology on the natural sciences, I have already indicated that he, Durkheim, and Weber wanted sociology to smooth out the path of evolutionary progress, producing an ideology that helped people seek fulfillment and betterment in everyday work and leisure while foregoing revolution. When Parsons introduced these classical sociologists to the United States in his *Structure of Social Action* and transformed them into apologists, not simply ideologists, for the status quo, U.S. sociology lost the thread of social criticism from its European progenitors and the urban activism and reformism of Chicago School sociology. Although Parsons was not a discursive positivist in the quantitative tradition, in Americanizing angst-ridden European sociology by flattening out its ambivalence about "progress" into celebration, he prepared the way for quantitative journal sociology some fifty years later. The Parsonian turn extirpated social criticism from American sociology, at least until the social movements of the 1960s.

Parsons was challenged during the 1960s and 1970s by radicals and liberals who, with Gouldner and Mills, wanted sociology to help explain and even resolve the social crises of the Vietnam War, civil rights movement, and emerging women's movement. Sociology's temporary radicalism from about 1965 to the end of the Vietnam War ceased when the war ended, the civil rights movement had been derailed, and the women's movement became institutionalized in policy and consciousness. At the same time, sociology was increasingly pressed to defend itself in the university and with funding agencies during what was emerging as a difficult period of declining support for public universities and especially the social sciences and humanities. As well, sociology in the large Midwestern-empiricist departments was rapidly becoming methodologically sophisticated as the first quantitative generation began to train and publish with a second generation, who earned doctorates and entered the academic labor market beginning in the mid-1970s.

The radicalism of the sixties—both 1860s and 1960s—never entirely disappeared, as Jacoby has traced in *The Last Intellectuals.* Sixties radicals such as Jacoby, Todd Gitlin, and Sidney Peck entered graduate school and then the professoriate. They began to read the recently translated works of European Marxism and critical theory. Paul Piccone, the founder of *Telos,* the main U.S. organ of critical theory and Left European philosophy that was begun in 1969, taught sociology at Washington University and was a colleague of Gouldner. This *Telos* generation retreated from the increasingly conservative political fray and learned broad-gauged social and cultural theory, drinking deeply of the Frankfurt School and French theory, such as the work of Derrida and Foucault. The radicalism of the 1960s became largely theoretical, both within and outside of sociology. Necessarily, this theoretical discourse was difficult, requiring a philosophical background, and for the most part had little influence on the rapidly flowing quantitative sociological mainstream, which had come to control most sociology departments, especially at public universities, by the end of the 1970s. Erstwhile movement radicals did not submit their work to the *ASR* but instead published books of theory read by hundreds, not hundreds of thousands, as Jacoby has lamented.

By now, the positivist hegemony of the 1980s and 1990s has begun to erode slightly, as theoretical radicals such as Steve Seidman, Norman Denzin, Patricia Clough, Charles Lemert, and Joe Feagin have established productive academic careers, publishing widely and training doctoral students who are entering the field. The angry young men who founded and wrote for *Telos* are now in their forties and fifties. They are no less committed to a critical perspective on late capitalism; this perspective is, if anything, deepening as scholars address globalization (Robertson 1992). For the most part, they are nonquantitative. And yet many have come to understand that obscurantism is self-defeating, instead broadening their work to speak to empirical sociologists, students, and members of the literate public at large.

Although I do not want to overdraw the portrait I am painting of the hegemony of positivism in U.S. sociology today—and it has eased somewhat since the beginning of the 1990s, with developments in critical theory, cultural studies, and feminism—I think it is undeniable that the disciplinary power centers remain the large, grant-oriented midcontinent sociology departments and their major organs such as Penn State and the *ASR,* North Carolina and *Social Forces.* A recent president of the American Sociological Association (ASA) estimated to me that about 75 percent of working U.S. sociologists are quantitative empiricists. She and I realize that the rump of 25 percent represented an increase in the number of nonmainstream qualitative, theoretical sociologists over the past decade. This is a sensitive issue: Has American sociology significantly changed in order not only to make room for nonpositivist alternatives but to assign them legitimacy? There is evidence both to support and reject this. *ASR* under the editorship of Paula England opened itself somewhat to nonmainstream articles; it even ran a debate about the relevance of Derrida for sociology! But it could be argued that this was false ecumenism inasmuch as the *ASR* is now back in the hands of mainstream empiricists who are returning the journal to the old ways of positivist discourse.

Recently, Joe Feagin, a noted radical sociologist who has published many galvanizing books on race, sex, and class as well as on urban problems, was elected president of the ASA, representing an arguably seismic shift in sociological sensibilities. Feagin told me that he thought he owed his election mainly to women and minority sociologists as well as the few of us ex-'60s radicals who lucked into tenure! Although Feagin is far to the left of another recent ASA president, the late James Coleman, Feagin's own work is, if not highly quantitative, at least accessible, conceptually framed empiricism—the type of work frequently published in the journal *Social Problems,* which, in some circles, is considered the fourth most prestigious U.S. sociology journal, after the "big three" of *ASR, American Journal of Sociology,* and *Social Forces.* Although politically radical, Feagin is not postmodern, does not write convoluted prose, and is engaged with practical questions of social injustice and social change. For example, his and Vera's (1995) book *White Racism* is politically outraged but carefully argued.

In Immanuel Wallerstein's terms, this is largely, I suspect, a matter of core and peripheral spheres of influence, to borrow a phrase from his world-systems theory. Positivist journal discourse, grants, the *ASR* are "core." "Peripheral" are the Society for the Study of Symbolic Interactionism, which has been infiltrated by the postmodern feminist Left; the work of Stanley Aronowitz, a prolific sociologist from CUNY-Graduate Center; and the writings of Dorothy Smith, a Canadian feminist epistemologist. Joe Feagin crosses over from periphery to core or, in terms of the chronology of his own career, from core to periphery. He is one of the only sociologists I know who has become more radical with age! Paula England is on the soft fringe of the core, using quantitative method and engaging with "hard" literatures of economic sociology, but a committed feminist and even a reader in feminist spirituality. Sociological theory, a microcosm of sorts, is split between the establishment—Jeffrey Alexander at UCLA, Charles Camic at Wisconsin—and its own Left—Charles Lemert at Wesleyan, Aronowitz at CUNY, Norman Denzin at Illinois.

One might conclude that sociology has become increasingly contested, with Leftism having begun to inform both substantive and epistemological debates. Words such as *postmodern, feminist, cultural studies* are now displayed prominently in book reviews, at the book display at the ASA, in graduate student dissertations. It is virtually impossible to examine a publishing house's list and not find scores of titles in postmodernism, feminist theory, cultural studies, critical theory. Books of such an ilk abound, and not only in the avant-garde quarters of humanities disciplines. Even sociologists are writing such books, as a glance at the lists of Routledge, Blackwell, Rowman & Littlefield, and Westview suggests. Although these trends are important and say much about how the boundaries between disciplines, even between the social sciences and humanities, have begun to blur, necessarily representing liberating intellectual decentering, they should not be exaggerated: what Marcuse (Wolff, Moore, Jr., and Marcuse 1969) called "repressive tolerance" allows the dominant culture or core to use a few examples of negativity in order to demonstrate its tolerance, openness, pluralism. This "artificial negativity" (Piccone 1975; Luke 1975) is even produced by the dominant order to generate new, system-serving but risky ideas. Totalization, in Lukacs and Adorno's original senses, leads to stagnation, or even to the impression of a counterdemocratic authoritarianism.

The few scholars who do cultural studies, feminist theory, postmodernism, and critical theory are, at best, weird and exotic species on display for the delectation of those temporarily wearied by positivist business as usual. And intellectual bohemians are usually isolated so that they do not attain critical mass and threaten the dominant order. Even empiricist sociology departments hire a theorist to teach the history of the discipline, such as Alan Sica at Penn State, and to demonstrate the department's ecumenism. Although productivity expectations for these isolated theorists may be somewhat different than for empiricists—fewer grants expected, few articles placed in mainstream journals—it is not uncommon to find job openings for theorists who possess what are called substantive areas (that is, they do empirical research) and who publish in journals. Recently, I applied for just such a job at Berkeley. While it is possible to publish essentially curatorial articles on the history of theory in the *ASR,* to expect theorists to publish in such outlets as well as to conduct empirical research in substantive areas essentially neutralizes the theoretical project. In this view, theory is not speculative critical thought but merely a prosthesis of mainstream empiricism, which, through method's peculiarly deauthorized discourse, at once makes an argument and conceals argument.

5

Concluding Science

UNDECIDABILITY AND DEFERRAL

$\mathbf{A}$s we have just seen in the methods sections, authors, reviewers, and editors narrow arguments and militate against intellectual risk taking. Although figure dominates the pages of method, prose is interspersed. Figure and prose coexist tensely, with prose pushing outward on the technical constraints imposed by method, especially by the statistics used. Even prose of a highly technical kind, usually found in the methods sections, is reduced to figure, gesturing a methods-driven sociology. As ever, authors explore their freedom, writing beyond the limit of their narrow topic and the constraints imposed by method. After all, method is an argument not only for a theory but for a world. Positivism proselytizes, albeit secretly. In this section, I examine the ways in which authors conclude, claiming little answers for the research just reported but deferring big questions until later; hence, deferral, based on intellectual circumspection, is programmatic, calling for its own reproduction.

Although method carefully conceals its authorial tracks, by reading attentively we learn that method does not solve intellectual problems in their own right but involves us in what Derrida terms *undecidability* and *deferral*. Even science itself acknowledges fallibility, deconstructing its postured objectivity or what Derrida calls its logocentrism—a place outside of the text from which we can represent the world in all its mystery. By undecidability Derrida refers to the ways in which language creates new problems of meaning by solving other problems of meaning. Every version of the world entails lacunae, blind spots, incomplete definitions, the clarifications of which entail further lacunae and blind spots. Meaning involves circularity because language is opaque to itself.

Let's begin with a simple example. Durkheim in *Rules of Sociological Method* defined "social facts" as instances of human behavior's determination by external social forces that act upon the individual. By now, after Durkheim, Weber, and Marx, we clearly recognize that our social existences are riddled with such episodes of determination. We are products of our social class, gender, race, religion, nation, region, hometown, generation, size of family, proximity to cities. Although we are also products of heredity and physiology, sociology, unlike psychology, concentrates on the social forces that make us what we are. Durkheim helped us understand how our religious affiliation, in particular whether we are Protestant or

Catholic, has direct impact on the likelihood that we will commit suicide when we are faced with serious difficulties in our lives. Durkheim theorized that Protestants are more likely than Catholics to commit suicide, all things being equal, because the Catholic Church, in its tight-knit community, helps provide people with a sense of belonging that we lack in industrial-age societies, breeding what Durkheim called *anomie*—alienation. Thus, he analyzed religion and suicide as social forces or social variables that could be systematically analyzed by the sociologist, equipped with the proper data and research methodology. What is undecidable about his definition of social facts is that Durkheim does not spell out clearly what he means by either the notion of social forces or determination. These are terms he uses to define social fact. He does not pause to define them lest he become involved in a process of infinite regress, offering definitions of terms that themselves need to be defined.

The conclusion of an article is framed by the way in which the author views her work after reviews have been considered and revisions completed in their light. Reviews and the editor's mediation provide authors with self-consciousness, allowing them to see how other disciplinary professionals view their contribution. Most reviews constrain arguments, urging authors not to speculate beyond their data or their statistical techniques. Reviewers discipline authors, moving them back into charted territory. Authors are urged to claim less in the way of intellectual gain than they had originally intended. In addition to producing a text that is highly figural, indeed that drives out prose or marginalizes it, the discussion of findings and conclusion are written in a tone of extreme circumspection, refusing to go beyond the data. The paper ends with a whimper, not a bang, auguring further research in the programmatism of most conclusions: "It has been demonstrated that further research is needed. . . ." This caution is a discursive hallmark of journal positivism, guaranteeing that findings will represent only piecemeal progress in the field that has been stipulated in the opening literature review section.

Figure 5.1. Clearly, further analysis of the intrametropolitan system of cities is warranted.

Figure 5.2. This analysis focuses on only one aspect of marital organizations—bank accounts—but the findings argue for broader attention to transaction cost considerations in families. A certain rationality underlies family organization. The collectivist orientation, non-market regulation of exchange, and common ownership that characterize family life can be seen as reasonable adaptations to the continuity, sunk costs, and metering ambiguity associated with transactions between kin. As separate bank accounts make clear, family life may

The author of figure 5.1 ends her paper with a final sentence to the effect that "further analysis . . . is warranted." The authors of figure 5.2 begin the final paragraph of the paper with an acknowledgment of the paper's undecidability. The analysis is incomplete, engaged in deferral (of the truth) because it "focuses on only one aspect of marital organization." Immediately, within the very sentence, this issues in a programmatic call "for broader attention to . . . [questions that have gone unanswered in the paper]." As the final sentence

take on more individualized or privatized arrangements under different conditions. On one level, this is a question of how preordained family units opt for one form of internal organization over another. On another level, the transaction cost approach raises fundamental questions about what constitutes a family, particularly where its boundaries are drawn. This approach can be fruitfully extended to other aspects of family life, including bequests, cohabitation, intergenerational support of the aged, child support by custodial and noncustodial parents, and divorce.

Figure 5.3. Ultimately, however, establishing the causal importance of industrial restructuring for earnings inequality will require qualitative work. We need a better understanding of how firms have changed their production processes and the skill levels they require. We need to identify the consequences of these changes for wage hierarchies and segmentation. And we need to know if the survival of firms in the post-industrial economy is dependent upon the continued creation of low-wage jobs.

Figure 5.4. To inform development policy, we need further research on the size of welfare returns to economic growth and the conditions that maximize those returns. Comparative research in sociology should examine the effects of rising income on living standards in the Third World because that issue bears on the daily experience of billions of people.

Figure 5.5. Future research on religious behavior would benefit from a renewed focus on the effects of attitudes, along with attention to the intermingling of age and family life cycle effects. The family life cycle concept should expand to include the diverse and often chaotic forms that modern family life assumes.

Figure 5.6. Our study is one step in the development of a demography of interorganizational relationships. It complements the field of organizational ecology, which focuses on the

indicates, "this approach"—the one proposed by the authors—"can be fruitfully extended to other aspects of . . . [marriage]." Here, the acknowledgment of undecidability, a hallmark of bench science, is made good by a programmatic call for further research, probably including the authors' own.

In figure 5.3, the authors call for "qualitative work," which, they contend, is required in order to "establish the causal importance of industrial restructuring for earnings inequality." This is an unusual sort of programmatism in that the authors do not call for more of the same work but for a significantly different, qualitative, type of sociology. The three authors of the paper are assistant professors, perhaps not yet acquiescent to the norms of self-producing programmatism. Nonetheless, they construe the problems facing future researchers as largely ones of measurement: "To answer these questions, we must directly confront the problem of independently measuring the skills required by jobs . . . and skills possessed by workers. . . . Neither of these tasks is trivial." They wend their way between the Scylla of journal programmatism and the Charybdis of straying too far from method.

The authors of figure 5.4 combine sociological programmatism with a nod toward policy. They contend that development policy needs to be informed by "further research" on the question of whether rising national income levels raise living standards, a serious point of contention between modernization theorists and world-systems theorists. The authors of fig-

demography of organizational populations (births and deaths of organizations). Our results show that the mortality of market relationships is a function of the institutional rules of exchange created during the emergence of the market, which are supported, reinforced, violated, and transformed over the years by the interplay of competition, power, and institutional forces. A next step is to examine the birth of market relationships as a function of the original rules of exchange as they are maintained and undermined by the same three forces. Finally, just as organizational ecology has analyzed interactions across organizational populations (Hannan and Carroll 1992), a demography of interorganizational relationships can examine the diffusion of rules of exchange across markets. The continued development of a relational demography would enhance the sociological understanding of a defining principle of modern society—the right to make and break relationships (Coleman 1974:24–25).

Figure 5.7. Ridgeway et al.'s (1994) study provides support for our theory with regard to the impact of *consistent* status characteristics, and the external cultural support they provide, on the likely legitimation of power and prestige orders (Theorem 1 in our formulation). The next task is to conduct independent tests of other specific and general theoretical consequences of our formulation. While our primary need at present is for research specifically designed to test this formulation, there is still a broad range of theoretical problems to be addressed. We need to understand, for instance, how the delegitimation process is affected by the mechanisms groups sometimes use to cope with situations in which performance expectations become incongruent with the legitimated structure and threaten to undermine it.

Sociologists have long been interested in legitimation processes and have accumulated a rich body of theoretical ideas and empirical knowledge. However, to the best of our knowledge, there have been few attempts to develop formal theories of this process. We think the

ure 5.5 do not mention policy explicitly. Their programmatism takes the form of a comment to the effect that future research needs to account for issues such as people's attitudes and the lifecycle perspective in order to understand why people with families do and do not attend church. Although these authors do not mention policy explicitly, it was difficult for me to read their paper without concluding that they view religious nonparticipation as a social problem. As scientists, they do not say this, nor do they exhort people to worship.

Figures 5.6 and 5.7 offer weak and strong versions of programmatism respectively. The authors of figure 5.6 spend only a sentence in the last paragraph of the paper indicating what a "next step" in their research agenda would involve. They also situate their work, in the first sentence of that concluding paragraph, in a cumulating body of work that they characterize as "a demography of interorganizational relationships." I have never heard of that field. In a stronger agenda, the authors of figure 5.7 call for empirical testing of their theoretical formulation of legitimation, stemming from the work of Ridgeway, who is one of the coauthors. Interestingly, just above, they suggest that "Ridgeway et al.'s (1994) study provides support for our theory. . . ." Ridgeway provides support for Ridgeway. They characterize the empirical testing of her theory as the "next task." Figure 5.8 also provides a strong programmatic agenda, devoting the final two paragraphs to a discussion of what needs to occur next in the author's field. This author does

time has come for sociologists to tackle this task.

Figure 5.8. Future research should systematically evaluate the assumption that whites' reactions to black numbers is a threat response, while acknowledging the distinction between personal and collective threat, the multiple types of threat, and the interdependence of perceived threat with other social psychological states.

Finally, a better understanding is needed of the dynamics that account for the observed macro/micro links (House 1977; Pettigrew 1997; Taylor and Johnson 1986). For black numbers to have the effects demonstrated in this study, the physical presence of African Americans in localities must be accompanied by public discourse that heightens the salience of race and encourages negative interpretations. Years ago, Blumer (1958) insisted on the pivotal role played by elite leaders and interest groups in defining racial matters adversely "in the arena of public discussion" (p. 7). By implication, local media, politicians, and other opinion leaders are central. A crucial next step, then, is to consider the local social processes that may mediate observed effects of local black numbers on whites' racial views.

not cite herself here, nor does she portray her field as smoothly advancing.

Although conclusions are circumspect, they also rehash the new territory claimed by the article, demonstrating incremental progress in moving the field forward. It is moved forward far enough by the research that the research can be viewed as having been warranted. At the same time, additional research is called for, providing the author and others of her ilk with careers. This is often warranted on technical grounds: bigger data sets need to be assembled, better statistics used, more variables tested. Inevitably, this will require additional grant money. And this is a bridge to policy considerations, which now help frame the author's request for additional external support by the National Institutes of Health or National Science Foundation. Grants are tight and need to be argued for in terms of social policy considerations, such as the amelioration of a pressing social problem—teenage crime or drug use, insufficient prenatal care in inner cities, the impact of divorce on employed mothers.

However much is claimed for the findings when one establishes one's warrant for journal space in the move to differentiate one's contribution from the emerging literature, the findings are inherently trivial in the sense that they do not come close to approximating the causality sought by Comte in his metaphor of social physics. They merely represent a puzzle piece. The world is so complex, with so many continually interacting variables, not all of which have been understood (controlled for) by the sociologist, that a particular research rarely escapes the narrowness destined for it by the choice of a topic that differentiates it from the surrounding literature but does not lose its intellectual anchor in that literature.

Authors are hesitant about their findings both because they need to remain squarely within the gravitational field of their discourse community, not straying too far into uncharted territory in which hard-and-fast data may not yet exist, and because they need to prepare the way for the programmatism of the concluding section, where they call self-servingly for more research. Authors spend whole careers researching narrow topics carved out of their doctoral dissertations; their expertise becomes ever-expanding as they refine methodological techniques, lay their hands on new data, and continue to rephrase their findings in order to get published and win grant money. Circumspection is both a hallmark of the piecemeal advancement of science within fields and a career necessity. The more stringent the review process, the less is ventured in the way of intellectual risk, especially where reviewers find fault with methodologies, notably statistical techniques, that reviewers claim are not perfectly suited to the topic at hand or are misused by authors with inadequate technical skills.

Circumspection is an important Derridean script, a discursive outcome representing the struggle between prose and figure. Circumspection is usually driven by technique—research methods and statistics—that curbs speculative reason. It is accentuated in the revision process, as authors respond to reviewers' cautions about overstepping the implications and requirements of their methods and statistics, claiming in prose what is disallowed by the techniques used in the article. Frequently, one or more of the reviewers is methodologically expert, more expert than the author. For this reason, most reviews focus on technique and suggest improvements, even whole new statistical programs. This can delay revision, as the author learns the latest technique in logistic regression and LISREL, perhaps even attending a workshop or conference in order to stay contemporary. The reviews also require the author to rewrite, constraining claims made in prose that are not strictly warranted by the statistical or methodological program in use.

Circumspection signals the author's sense of the undecidability of her quest for truth. Methods-driven papers are especially likely to acknowledge undecidability in that they confess the limitations of their data set, measurements, statistical analyses, merely middle-range theoretical grounding. I applaud these acknowledgments because they are precisely in the nature of any quest for truth in that they are confined to their own frameworks, grand narratives, language games. However, such confessions by the authors of science give the lie to the scientific project as outlined by the Enlightenment *philosophes* and then Comte, who conceived science as a project of total understanding and control. For science to confess its own vulnerability, especially on the terrain of methods, should be taken very seriously by readers who mistrust science's claims to advance from a partial to a progressively more total understanding of the world through the process of cumulation and methodological refinement. Interestingly, most sociology articles, even the most technically sophisticated ones, acknowledge their own limitations, as we see below.

In figure 5.9, the authors acknowledge, near the end of their article, that their study of the rank advancement of biochemists may not be generalizable to other fields, an especially serious problem for those who seek an understanding of rank advancement in their own field, sociology. The authors devote three paragraphs to a discussion of the limitations of their research, involving shortcomings in methodology and problems comparing their research to others' published research on the subject. Interestingly, in the last two sentences of the paper, the authors cite one study that does suggest the generalizability of their work—a study coauthored by one of the coauthors! Scott Long's research findings support Scott Long's research findings. Undecidability is made good by way of self-citation.

In figure 5.10, a subtle acknowledgment of undecidability is offered. The authors are examining income inequality in their paper. They state that it is a convention to count number of workers, not number of jobs, at each level. Figure 5.10 is followed by a statement about "the difficulty of measuring skills directly. . . . The inadequacy of current measures is particularly acute when studying trends over time. . . ." Using a term of art, they characterize this substitution of a less significant variable for a more significant one as a "proxy": number of workers is a proxy for number of jobs. They resort to a proxy measure because, they say, "the primary reliable data sets take the individual, not the job, as the unit of analysis." Hence, they confess their research's undecidability on grounds of missing or unobtainable data. Many of the articles surveyed use the term "proxy" for this sort of methodologically driven substitution, which almost automatically signals a confession of the work's undecidability, its inability to answer intellectual questions without begging new ones. Proxies are used because sociologists do not have access to data regarding the variables for which they are placeholders—signifiers, in poststructural terminology. The very concept of a proxy variable, which is fundamental to late twentieth-century methods-driven sociology, is poststructural, suggesting that variables are but signifiers of various "signifieds" and that signifiers acquire meaning in relation to other signifiers to which they are nonidentical— "dog" is defined by the fact that "dog" is not "cat." The variable "social class" is necessarily an abstraction in that social class is "operationalized," transformed into steps of measurement that allow sociologists access

Figure 5.9. To what extent can our findings be generalized to scientists in other fields and different cohorts? A definitive answer is not possible. While many of our results are consistent with past research, direct comparisons are difficult. With few exceptions, other studies have not dealt adequately with complications introduced by censoring. Further, none of the past studies has included all of the variables included in our analysis. For example, to our knowledge, our study is unique in including both number of publications and citations to those publications.

Our own data suggest that these results do not generalize to cohorts receiving their degrees prior to 1956. Data were collected on 153 female biochemists who received degrees from 1950 to 1955. While the percentage of this cohort that entered the ranks of assistant and associate professors was similar to that for the female biochemists analyzed here, logit models predicting advancement in rank found none of the variables to be statistically significant, including years in rank. Reviewing the biographical histories of these women suggests that this may be because many of these scientists had "courtesy" appointments rather than true tenure-track positions.

In addition, our data are limited to the period before 1981. During the 1980s, universities were under increasing pressure to demonstrate that they were not discriminating against women. The effect of these pressures on processes of promotion remains to be seen. The generalizability of our results to other fields is indicated by recent work by Allison and Long (1987, 1990). This work, which considers scientists in chemistry, physics, mathematics, and biology generally corroborates results based on biochemists.

Figure 5.10. We adopt several common conventions in our analysis. First, while much of the debate is about changes in the number of *jobs* at different wage levels, our analysis uses the number of *workers* at each level. This proxy is used out of necessity, since the primary reliable data sets take the individual, not the job, as the unit of analysis.

Figure 5.11. If the continuing effect were a result of the divorce rather than unmeasured factors, it would suggest that this childhood event can set in motion a chain of circumstances that affects individuals' lives even after they have left home, married, and entered the labor force. The exact nature of these continuing effects cannot be determined from the NCDS data.[10]

Figure 5.12. As Mayer points out, these procedures are not without their problems. If families anticipate future income changes and adjust their consumption accordingly, and the consumption changes benefit or hurt children, then future income does indeed play a causal role. The likely measurement error in income sources such as dividends and interest will impart a downward bias in their coefficients. Moreover, interest and dividends are almost universally absent from the income packages of families at or below the poverty line.

Figure 5.13. Finally, given several limitations in our data, future research should consider the following.

Figure 5.14. Future comparisons will clarify these possibilities. The design employed here was limited in that it covered only the first two years following the imposition of macroeconomic reforms. Later waves of data may show

to the complex reality of class and socioeconomic inequality. Thus, sociology only knows the world inasmuch as it can measure the world, with one set of operational indicators—variables—differing from another. A proxy, then, is a signifier that signifies in place of another signifier—in figure 5.10, number of workers (a variable) is a proxy for number of jobs (also a variable), both of which represent a certain "signified," in this case the structure of occupations in this society.

In figures 5.11 through 5.14, undecidability revolves around methodological issues: In figure 5.11, the data do not permit a certain interpretation; in figure 5.12, certain technical "procedures are not without their problems"; in figure 5.13, there are "several limitations in our data." Interestingly, this issues in programmatism—"future research"—that could be considered an instance of deferral: problems are deferred until the future, when presumably they will be resolved (but rarely are). In figure 5.14, the research "design employed . . . was limited. . . ." Again, the problem is deferred: "Another database, now in preparation, will allow further explorations." These four acknowledgments of undecidability are typical in that they do not acknowledge limitations of theory or concept formation but strictly of method, to be made good with resort to better methods. This is unsurprising in light of the methodological preoccupations of a great deal of journal sociology today. A Derridean would applaud the avowed

a different picture, and also will allow us to investigate more standard organizational survival outcomes. Finally, the design we followed here did not consider small SOEs or new private firms founded since 1989. Another database, now in preparation, will allow further explorations.

sense of limits, of basic corrigibility, of this methods-oriented sociology, but would lament the ways in which undecidable sociology promises resolution in the methodological Hereafter, once techniques have been refined. Thus, journal sociology is only partly and, I would hasten to add, disingenuously a Derridean text: limitations of analyses are confessed as a rhetorical strategy of normal science. In reality, the positivist writers believe that the truth is hard and fast—and quite attainable, given time, hard work, and sufficient grant support. Few of the scribes whose work I have cited are losing sleep over the quandaries of method; nor are they reading Derrida in order to play philosophical catch up. They write the way they do because they recognize that method is a tool kit, even a version. But they seek bigger and better tools as they continue to build their vitae, careers, and the canons of their fields.

It is precisely this circumspection that mires sociology in an eternal present, concealing the historicity and agency that characterize all social orders. The data, pieces of frozen social history, exercise centrifugal pull on arguments that point beyond data, either toward unusual interpretations or whole new worlds. The paradigm of this sort of dialectical reason is Marx's claim at the beginning of Volume One of *Capital* that "commodity fetishism," object-like relations between people who treat themselves and their labor as objects, tends toward its own abolition as the giant and existential structures of capital subvert themselves through "tendential laws" that undo capitalism. Marx refused to freeze the *fictio juris* of the wage-labor contract, according to which workers give up ownership and control of their production in exchange for a living wage (the cynical "family wage," feminists would add later), into the cement of social laws. He refused the postulate of social laws and social physics, contra sociology, because he wanted to exploit the tendencies of unjust social and economic orders to undo themselves, moving history forward through dialectical transformations.

Although Marx littered *Capital* with figures, for example the important gesture "C-M-C," these figures did not drive out thought or critique, constraining them. His chapter titled "The Concept of Relative Surplus Value," although technical, does not sacrifice reason to technique but allows them to inform each other. Not an easy read, *Capital* allows itself digressions, self-clarifications, examples in order to render its estimable conceptual and technical apparatus accessible. Marx was in effect reinventing economics, using its timeworn bourgeois categories against themselves in order to see the world in a new way. As such, his treatment was thoroughly technical, working within established categories of value, exchange, and labor, although without ignoring the inherence of these categories in theoretical perspective and position. Marx refuses to extrapolate the present into eternity, but digs beneath it in order to recognize its historicity—its susceptibility to being changed, given its own dialectical tendencies. One need not embrace the discourse of the dialectic in order to write sociology with an eye toward publicity and an ear toward the suppressions and deferrals of one's own argument.

Marx recognized that the data do not simply present themselves, making themselves available for mathematical manipulation. The data, but not the world, are thoroughly products of theory. They are artifacts, outcomes of authorial artifice. They are no less real for all that. When Marx discusses the commodity, he uses the term in ways radically different from bourgeois economics. And yet he never pretends to be merely describing, not also arguing or theorizing. Positivist sociology buries argument in technique and uses technique to limit argument in the inversion of figure and prose. Although Marx deploys figure, in fact his book is scarcely imaginable without phrases such as C-M-C, he does not overburden his argument with figures that substitute for argument. In journals, by contrast, the declining rate of prose mirrors and reinforces the declining rate of intelligence (Jacoby 1976), concealing argument underneath technique and limiting science to incremental gains in understanding.

Marx felt that he could disclose the world and pierce ideology through a straightforward language of critique. This may have been appropriate to Europe of 1867, *Capital*'s year of publication. In the meantime, the Frankfurt School argued, straightforwardness has been co-opted by positivists and technocrats who operationalize truth as its measurement. Instead, they recognize that truth is approached only indirectly and by allusion, leading Adorno in his (1974a) *Minima Moralia* to compose philosophy in aphorisms. Subtitled *Reflections from Damaged Life*, *Minima Moralia* contains neither figure nor sustained argument. Adorno refracts truth through small phrases, analogies, examples, much as Walter Benjamin had earlier praised the fragment as an antidote to the fascist tendencies of the total system. Paraphrasing Hegel, who wrote before the Holocaust and Hollywood, Adorno said that "the whole is false" at a time when everything is slogan.

Adorno did compose journal articles! (See Adorno 1945, 1954, 1974b.) By contemporary editorial standards, they were too dense and too long. They did not have subheadings, literature reviews, technical descriptions of method and measurement. There were too many assertions and too few proofs. Adorno would not have been published by the *ASR*, nor would he have submitted there. He adopted a studied disdain for linearity and clarity, refusing to solve intellectual problems with glossaries. Yet it is difficult to find a spare word in his writing. He labored over revisions (see Adorno 1997: 361–66), wanting to find the right phrase and pursuing the internal logic of arguments. He wrote social criticism using the approach of immanent critique, unraveling concealed arguments through a relentless digging at their roots, an approach that closely resembles Derrida's deconstruction, as Ryan [1982] has argued. It is difficult to imagine Adorno acquiescing to reviewers' suggestions simply to move his career forward. I doubt that he thought he had a career at all.

Why consider Adorno in the same breath, or chapter, as other sociologists who ply their trade in the journals, with method? Did Adorno write sociology? Surely he did, in places. He was one of the authors of a book titled *Aspects of Sociology.* He played a major role in writing *The Authoritarian Personality,* a component of a larger project on authoritarianism called "studies in prejudice." The 1950 *Authoritarian Personality* is cited in virtually every introductory sociology textbook. Adorno is thus found in more sociological bibliographies than I am. By that standard, he wrote sociology. And many of his studies of the production and reception of culture were sociological in content and approach, an unsurprising fact given his collaboration with Paul Lazarsfeld after Adorno fled Germany for New York and then Los Angeles. The point is that sociology is not restricted to what is published in its official house organs, and thus there is no rigid formula that we must follow regarding how we write up our research, for example with respect to the ratio of figure to prose. Quantitative *ASR* articles are replete with figure; Marx used figure more sparingly in his twelfth chapter on relative surplus value; Adorno used figure not at all. All used "methods," although not necessarily the methods of survey research, secondary data analysis, and inferential statistics. It is difficult to imagine Marx or Weber objecting to logistic regression per se, although Marx as a non-positivist would have insisted that data be viewed as molten pieces of social history and not as nature-like sediments of a deeper, timeless causality.

Marx and Adorno differ with latter-day journal scribes' insistence on generalizing from the particulars of the contemporary moment to world history, even if Adorno felt that the grand narrative of progress needed to be treated with caution, given its tendency to flatten individuals. Although both used data, after a fashion, they were not hemmed in by the demands of technique, which are, after all, only theoretical versions in their own right. They objected to circumspection as a truncation of imagination, and hence liberation. In a 1964 essay on Weber, Marcuse (1968) exposed technical reason as a form of substantive reason that only reproduces the status quo by failing to pierce its framework of guiding assumptions and operations. The same argument could be applied to journal sociology: Authors are prevented (prevent themselves) from going beyond their data in assaying sweeping interpretations, just as they are limited by their own methods and statistics to incremental advances in knowledge that are really advances in method.

MARGINALIA: NOTES, BIBLIOGRAPHY, ACKNOWLEDGMENTS, TITLE

Earlier, I noted that method squeezes out reasoned argument, thus becoming an even more compelling argument for a frozen world. In denying its authorial role, method authors a world frozen in time, thus freezing it. In reflecting an inert world, science's text authors that world, recognizing that it is a strong version, not a mirror of nature. It is in this sense that positivism is ideology, reproducing the world through a representation that compels conformity to the supposed universals of modernity—private productive property, patriarchy, the protestant ethic. Ideology is discourse that permeates our everyday lives, situating itself in our familiar land-

scape of lived experience as second nature, not as considered argument—a deliberate text. This is what I have called dispersed textuality, a topic of critical deconstruction. Far from being value-neutral tools or techniques, the methods-driven
pages of sociological journal articles situate themselves in everyday worlds of professional readers and writers who come to believe that the social world, a "social
fact," can be represented in a way that drains society of history or the dialectical
potential for change. Journals silently recommend a lawful world and thus, in their
ways, help bring it about.

Reason is displaced by method into what I call marginalia. If anywhere, this is
where real argumentation takes place or, at least, where clues about argument can
be found. By *argument* I mean position taking that acknowledges one's own intellectual investments, implicitly accepting that others invest differently. The marginalia are argument's traces that remain after method has drained reason from the body
of the text. The best evidence of authorial sensibility can be found in marginalia,
especially in notes and acknowledgments. The marginalia are by and large imper-
vious to the encroachments of method, which deems them unimportant, merely
conventional gestures that bear no meaning. By contrast, inspection of marginalia
reveals the displacement of authorial presence, of argument, that helps shed light
on the empirical sections of the paper or monograph. Marginalia demonstrate that
the announcement of the death of the author has been premature, even though
their existence on the margins suggests that all is not well with the main body of
the text, which has been reduced to a mechanical protocol that systematically elim-
inates authorial subjectivity as a threat to objectivity.

As I observed above, there are no hard-and-fast literary rules or norms governing the preparation of the abstract, apart from length guidelines. As I said, most
notable is the *idea* of an abstract, implying that science articles can be reduced to a
hundred descriptive words. Similarly, notes, bibliography, acknowledgments, and
title are relatively unencumbered by rules, apart from the style guide used by the
journal in question governing preparation of notes and bibliography. Frequently,
the *Chicago Manual of Style* is the final arbiter of taste in this respect. But, again, as
with abstracts, reviewers and editors rarely comment on these marginalia; stylistic
changes in notes and bibliography are usually left up to the copyeditor, who
removes inconsistencies and checks for obvious errors in citations. I have never read
a review that dealt substantively with any of the marginalia, except titles, where a
reviewer or editor might suggest a more appropriate title. Even this is rare. It is not
an exaggeration to observe that almost anything goes in ways that authors compose
marginalia, except where issues of length and house style are concerned.

The history of the note or footnote (see Grafton 1999) suggests that, over time,
many disciplines have moved away from lengthy notes in the interests of parsimony
and cost cutting. Footnotes, printed at the bottom of the page, often give way to
endnotes or simply notes, published at the end of the paper or monograph. The
fact that notes have been relegated to the back of the work makes it more difficult
to read them as either elaboration of, or counterpoint to, the argument made in the

text. Where notes—footnotes—were formerly printed at the bottom of the page in which their superscript identification occurred, it was much easier to read them in dialogue with the main text, making for interesting revelations about the nature of the argument. Footnotes have fallen out of style and even notes have been reduced in both length and number, giving way to the style of purely parenthetical citation (and, frequently, citation without specific page references), as I discussed earlier. Notes are increasingly a thing of the past, removing a vital source of authorial self-consciousness, self-criticism, reflexivity, and suggestions for further reading—intertextuality, to use a postmodern referent.

The decline of the note reduces the role of reasoned prose still further. References are confined to parenthetical citation sausages, without explication or discussion. Articles are monologues, lacking intertextuality and reflexivity. Of course, that is the goal of the science text, suggesting a powerful, machine-like evolution that need not equivocate or digress. Even twenty years ago both journals and monographs in social science devoted more space to notes, reflecting a more rudimentary but intertextually richer era of authoriality. With progress in method has come regress in authorial presence, here indicated by the decline of the note. Notes are so important because they allow readers to explore a kind of parallel universe in which the author adopts a different voice and vision, playing with her argument as it might have developed in different directions; engaging cited authors in dialogue; demonstrating often complex intellectual lineages; teasing out unforeseen implications that could lead to new research programs; nailing down arguments with a meticulous scholarship that takes other versions so seriously that they are cited and discussed, chapter and verse. I have heard the objection raised that if notes are so important, their discussion belongs in the body of the text. But sociology articles have become shorter and more methods-driven, allowing even less room for one's primary argument. Perhaps the most important signifier of authorial presence and erudition, notes' decline has elevated methods even more.

In journal sociology, notes tend to be methodologically oriented, describing the research protocol in even greater detail than the main text permits and anticipating readers' methodological concerns. *ASR* articles retain footnotes, printed at the bottom of the page. And they supplement footnotes with lavish methodological appendices. Interestingly, footnotes have become so technical that, like the prose contained in the methods sections of the main text, they often resemble figure—dense pastiches of minute technical concerns that constitute gestures more than considered arguments. Although there is a great deal of congealed intelligence in the methodological discussions of the main text, notes, and appendices, representing extraordinary skill and training, for the most part this intelligence does not double back on itself and exhume deep assumptions and invite arguments about these assumptions from readers less concerned with method than with substance. The eclipse of the discursive note has given way to the rebirth of notes as figures, further reducing the space allotted to prose in the main body of the article.

In an article on modernization and dependency, the authors compose three consecutive footnotes, found in figure 5.15. All are densely methodological, presenting equations and using mathematical notation. Interestingly, in footnote 9, the authors state that they "update missing cases in the original data source" with additional data, rectifying undecidability in this way. Figure 5.16 includes two footnotes that are also densely methodological. One is hard-pressed to differentiate the level of technical specificity and detail of the footnotes from that of the main text, printed directly above. To an uninitiated reader, it is not immediately clear why the material contained in the notes would not be retained in the main text. Both are technical to the point of being gestural.

Finally, in figure 5.17, we find four lengthy footnotes packed with methodological detail. Footnote 2 lists data sets used in the study. Footnote 4 spills over onto the next page. Although all of this information appears relevant to the article, it is clear that footnotes of this length and detail not only displace the prose of the main text but become gestures in their own right. Consider footnote 2, listing all of the many data sets used. This information would prove vital only if other scholars attempted to replicate this study; replicability is a hallmark of good science. But no one will replicate the study, reanalyzing the data with either the same techniques used here or new techniques. This is the sort of article not destined to help sociology cumulate, although its theoretical position is interesting and potentially controversial. There is no need to list all of the data sets, or at least they could have been listed in an appendix that did not interrupt the flow of prose in the main body of the article. I submit that the authors chose to pack the list of data sets into footnote 2, occupying parts of two journal pages, precisely in order to produce the science aura—"this is what good science looks like."

Bibliographies have declined as well. Where twenty years ago a bibliography could contain material not cited in the text or in notes, today bibliographies restrict themselves to material cited in the body of the text. This may well be enforced by the copyeditor, who scrupulously checks the bibliography against material cited in the text, attempting to guard against bibliographical sprawl and catch instances where textual citations are not entered into the bibliography. Again, this robs the reader of leads, new directions, intertextuality, full citations of material buried in notes. Like notes, bibliographies can be read for traces of authorship, demonstrating what the author has read and takes seriously. The more bibliographies are allowed to range beyond parenthetically cited material, the greater access we have to the author's own intellectual formation, especially if, as detectives, we examine the evolution of an author's citations as evidence of her own intellectual growth.

Initially, the graduate student cites too little, not having read widely in the literature of the field. Over time, the bibliography expands as the student-author reads more widely. As this happens, bibliographies across the field tend to take on a sameness inasmuch as they correspond to the citation of a relatively homogeneous literature in the opening section of articles. In this sense, bibliographies are not particularly interesting where they are driven by the exigencies of canonical

measured in terms of forced incorporation by a dominant power, it was not methodologically correct to attribute the presence of separatist sentiment to social differentiation produced by the modernization process, as Hibbs (1973) suggested. I decided, therefore, to follow Boswell and Dixon (1990) and consider separatism as an exogenous variable having independent effects on regime repressiveness and political conflict.

Peripheralization

Peripheralization involves foreign capital penetration and trade dependence. *Penetration* is measured by the total stock of direct foreign investment in 1967, weighted by capital and labor.[8] Trade dependence is measured at the level of external trade using two variables. The first is Galtung's (1971) *Trade Composition Index* (TCI) and is intended to measure the relative concentration between raw materials exported and manufactured goods imported.[9] Countries ranking low on this 1973 measure tend to import raw materials and export manufactured products (i.e., they are developed core countries), while high ranking countries specialize more in raw material exports and exhibit high levels of dependence on manufactured imports (i.e., they are less developed peripheral countries). The second mea-

sure of trade dependence specifies the degree to which export production is concentrated by commodity. This variable, the *Commodity Concentration Index* (CCI), measures the percentage contribution of 175 individual export commodities to total exports in 1973.[10] Taken together, both measures of trade dependence specify the degree to which domestic production has been distorted to produce an export enclave economy that is dependent on the dictates of international capital and the world economy.

Vulnerability

Since export production is one of the primary economic mechanisms through which peripheral countries become vulnerable to the world economy, I use fluctuations in total export earnings to measure vulnerability. This is calculated using the United Nations Conference on Trade and Development (1976:69) Index of Fluctuation as the sum of the absolute value of the annual average percentage deviations from the expected trend values in a period given that growth or decline in exports is constant for the entire period.[11] Because the magnitude of the effects of export fluctuation depend on the relative size and composition of the export sector, these values are taken as the ratio of ex-

---

[8] This formula is measured by Bornschier and Chase-Dunn (1985) as:

$$\frac{\text{Foreign Capital Penetration}}{} = \frac{\text{Total value of foreign direct investment}}{\sqrt{\text{Domestic capital stock} \times \text{Size of labor force}}}.$$

The total population is used as a proxy for the labor force.

[9] The formula for computing the Trade Composition Index is:

$$TCI = \frac{(A+B)-(C+D)}{A+B+C+D}.$$

where A equals the dollar value of raw material imported, B equals the value of processed goods exported, C equals the value of raw materials exported, and D equals the value of processed goods imported. To maximize the number of observations, I updated missing cases in the original data source (Ballmer-Cao and Sheidegger 1979) using more recent data from United Nations Conference on Trade and Development (1979). Index signs were reversed to scale this measure in the same direction as the other variables.

[10] Commodity Concentration Index, C_{jx}, for any country j, is calculated using the Gini-Hirschman coefficient:

$$C_{jx} = \sqrt{\sum (X_{ij}/X_{.j})^2},$$

where X_{ij} is exports of good i by country j, and $X_{.j}$ is total of exports of goods by country j. This coefficient is computed using 175 (SITC 3 digit) export commodities.

[11] The absolute value is necessary because the positive and negative deviations cancel each other out, providing an incorrect value for the extent of export fluctuation.

$$\text{Export fluctuation} = \frac{100}{n}\sum_{i=1}^{n}\frac{|x_i - x_i'|}{x_i'},$$

where x_i is the value of exports at time i, x_i' is corresponding trend value, and n is number of years. Trend value is computed as

$$x_i' = (x_o)(x_n/x_o)^{t_i/n},$$

where x_o is the value of exports in 1975, x_n is the value of exports in 1980, n is total number of years (and is equal to 5), and t_i is the year (varies between 1 and 5).

Figure 5.15

ment, Kuznets (1955) placed considerable emphasis on the dualism between traditional and modern sectors of the economy of developing societies. The economy of a society in the early stage of industrialization can be represented schematically as being composed of a small modern sector with high productivity and high wages encroaching on a large traditional agricultural sector with low productivity and low wages. With industrial development an increasing proportion of the labor force shifts from the low-income traditional sector to the high-income modern one. These population shifts between sectors produce, *as an automatic numerical consequence*, a trajectory of income inequality that increases, levels off, and then decreases, with a peak at some intermediate stage of development.

The mechanisms by which these population shifts generate an inverted-U shaped inequality trajectory can be demonstrated with numerical experiments following Kuznets himself ([1955] 1965:270), as well as Robinson (1976), Lydall (1977:205–25), and Lecaillon et al. (1984:16–22). The numerical experiments assume a simplified division of a national economy into two sectors: a traditional (agricultural) sector A and a modern (nonagricultural) sector B. Development typically entails a shift of population from sector A to sector B, which contains the growing "modern" industrial and service activities. If, as is usually the case, average wages are higher in sector B than in sector A, these population shifts away from the traditional sector will produce a trend over time in which inequality increases at first, then levels off and decreases. This trend occurs, even if it is assumed by simplification that there is no inequality *within* sectors.[6]

---

[6] The outcomes of population shifts are more varied when incomes are allowed to vary within sectors. The U-shaped pattern may be more or less pronounced depending on the relative degrees of inequality within sectors. For outcomes of experiments assuming various degrees of inequality within sectors, see Kuznets ([1955] 1965:270–75) and Lydall (1977:205–25). Fields (1980:33–58) proposed a more refined decomposition of the basic model of dualistic development that distinguishes between modern sector "enlargement" and "enrichment." He showed that, in the case of modern sector enlargement (with no change in the income differential between sectors), the inverted-U pattern always arises, even

The phenomenon is presented in Figure 2, which shows the evolution of income inequality as the proportion of the labor force (p) in the traditional sector A declines from 90 percent to 10 percent as the labor force shifts to the modern sector B. Income is assumed to be constant within each sector. Income inequality is measured in two ways—by the Gini coefficient and by Theil's inequality index based on information theory.[7] The horizontal axis shows decreasing values of p, consistent with a direction of development from left to right. The inverted U-shaped evolution of inequality is shown as a function of p. When the income differential between sectors B and A is high (4:1) the Gini coefficient starts with a low value of .21 when the proportion in sector A is .9, reaches a peak of .33 for p between .7 and .6, and declines thereafter as sector A continues to

---

when income inequality is greater within the traditional sector.

[7] The Gini formula for dualism can be derived as a special case of a formula for the Gini coefficient proposed by Nygård and Sandström (1981: 292, eq. 8.10):

$$R_L = p_{k-1} - \sum_{i=1}^{k-1} L(p_i)(p_{i+1} - p_{i-1}),$$

where the p_i's are cumulative population shares, and the $L(p_i)$'s are the corresponding cumulative income shares, the pairs $(p_i, L(p_i))$ being points on the Lorenz curve for income category boundaries $i = 0,...,k$. With only the two categories, agriculture and nonagriculture, $k = 2$ and the formula reduces to the simple expression $D_G = R_L = |p - L|$, with $p \equiv p_1$ and $L \equiv L_1$. The absolute value is used to guarantee a positive value of dualism, even in the hypothetical situation in which the agricultural sector is relatively more prosperous than the nonagricultural one.

Following Lecaillon et al. (1984), sector dualism can also be calculated using Theil's information theory-based inequality measure using the formula (Theil 1967; 1972:58, eq. 1.3):

$$D_T = L \ln \frac{L}{P} + (1 - L) \ln \frac{1 - L}{1 - p},$$

where ln is the natural logarithm.

In the numerical experiments of Figure 2, the income share L of sector A is calculated as

$$L = I_A p / (I_A p + I_B[1-p]),$$

where I_A and I_B denote income in sector A and sector B, respectively, and inequality is then calculated using the formulas above.

Figure 5.16

these countries. In horticultural societies, the degree of social inequality was generally lower than in agrarian societies (Lenski 1966; Lenski, Lenski, and Nolan 1991). In horticultural societies, not all of the land was used, so it was relatively simple to start a new garden. As a result of the lower levels of inequality, status considerations were probably less important in partner choice. Furthermore, women in horticultural societies contributed much more to subsistence activities than they did in agrarian societies (Van den Berghe 1979), which gave them a stronger position in society. This also may have given them more freedom in marriage choice. Such differences between horticultural and agrarian societies in the "openness" of marriage patterns may have become part of their cultural heritage and continue to affect marriage behavior, even after the onset of the industrialization process. Thus, regarding the effect of the technological background of developing countries, we hypothesize that educational homogamy will be lower in industrializing horticultural societies than in industrializing agrarian societies.

MEASUREMENT AND DATA

Special techniques are required to measure the degree of educational homogamy in the 65 countries we study. The association between the educational levels of spouses reflects not only the degree to which persons *prefer* a spouse with a certain educational attainment, but also the *availability* of spouses with that educational level. If fewer women than men go on to college, as is the case in many countries, some of the men with a college education will not find partners with their same educational level. These men are "forced" to marry women with lower educational levels, regardless of their preferences. Because the total number of homogamous marriages in a country depends to a certain extent on this structural factor, this total number is not a good indicator of social openness. To get a better measure, it would be necessary to control for differences in the educational distributions of husbands and wives and to measure what is called *relative homogamy* (Ultee and Luijkx 1990). This will be done here by using loglinear analysis (Agresti 1990).

To study the association between the educational levels of spouses, we collected data sets with individual-level data on married persons for 65 countries.[1] For most countries, we used large representative samples of the whole or almost the whole population. Exceptions include the data set for Sudan, which represents only the northern part of that country; the data set for the former republic of Yugoslavia, which represents the republics of Croatia, Serbia, Slovenia, and Macedonia; and the data set for India, which represents the states of Andra Pradesh, Gujerat, Uttar Pradesh, and West Bengal.[2]

---

[1] In addition to legal marriages, in several countries other kinds of permanent or semi-permanent unions can be found. Our use of the term marriage includes these other kinds of relationships.

[2] The following data sets were used: Australia 1981, Census of Population and Housing, 1-percent sample; Austria 1982, Mikrozensus, berufslaufbahn; Bangladesh 1975/76, World Fertility Survey; Belgium 1979, Poverty Study Europe; Benin 1981, World Fertility Survey; Brazil 1980, Demographic Census, .8-percent sample; Cameroon 1978, World Fertility Survey; Canada 1976, Census, 1-percent sample; China 1982, Census of Population, 1-percent sample; Colombia 1976, World Fertility Survey; Costa Rica 1976, World Fertility Survey; Czechoslovakia 1980, Census (table); Denmark 1979, Poverty Study Europe; Dominican Republic 1975, World Fertility Survey; Ecuador 1979/80, World Fertility Survey; Egypt 1980, World Fertility Survey; Fiji 1974, World Fertility Survey; Finland 1972, Scandinavian Welfare Survey; France 1979, Poverty Study Europe; Ghana 1979/80, World Fertility Survey; Guyana 1975, World Fertility Survey; Haiti 1977, World Fertility Survey; Hong Kong 1971, Census of Population and Housing, 1-percent sample; Hungary 1973, Social Mobility and Occupational Changes in Hungary; India 1971, Political Participation and Equality in Seven Nations; Indonesia 1976, World Fertility Survey (SUPASII); Ireland 1979, Poverty Study Europe; Israel 1970, Israeli Culture Survey; Italy 1979, Poverty Study Europe; Ivory Coast 1980/81, World Fertility Survey; Jamaica 1975/76, World Fertility Survey; Japan 1971, Political Participation and Equality in Seven Nations; Jordan 1976, World Fertility Survey; Kenya 1977/78, World Fertility Survey; Lesotho 1977, World Fertility Survey; Malaysia 1974, World Fertility Survey; Mexico 1976/77, World Fertility Survey; Morocco 1980, World Fertility Survey; Nepal 1976, World Fertility Survey; Netherlands 1977, Labor Force Survey; New Zealand 1981, Census of

Figure 5.17 continues

To limit the possibility that our results would be affected by fluctuations in the world economy or in the general level of technology, we tried to find data sets for a particular time period. Our goal was to obtain data sets collected in the 1975–1980 period. For 45 countries, we found data for this period; for 6 countries, the data were collected after 1980; for 14 countries, they were collected before 1975. The oldest data sets are from 1970; the most recent one is from 1983. We do not know whether differences in the years of data collection affect our analysis. However, the distortions are not likely to be large because an important period-dependent variable—the level of economic development—is an explanatory variable.

We restricted our analyses to wives ages 20 to 49 and husbands ages 23 to 52. The upper age of 49 for women was chosen because some of our data sets contain information only for women under 50 years of age. The age limits for husbands were set somewhat higher than those for wives because married men are generally somewhat older than their wives. For several countries, this age classification was not possible, either because only the age of one of the spouses

Population and Dwellings (table); Norway 1972, Scandinavian Welfare Survey; Pakistan 1975, World Fertility Survey; Panama 1975/76, World Fertility Survey; Paraguay 1979, World Fertility Survey; Peru 1977/78, World Fertility Survey; Philippines 1978, World Fertility Survey; Portugal 1979/80, World Fertility Survey; Rwanda 1983, World Fertility Survey; Senegal 1978, World Fertility Survey; South Korea 1974, World Fertility Survey; Sri Lanka 1975, World Fertility Survey; Sudan 1978/79, World Fertility Survey; Sweden 1972, Scandinavian Welfare Survey; Syria 1978, World Fertility Survey; Taiwan 1970, Value System in Taiwan; Thailand 1975, World Fertility Survey; Trinidad and Tobago 1977, World Fertility Survey; Tunisia 1978, World Fertility Survey; Turkey 1978, World Fertility Survey; United Kingdom 1979, Oxford Social Mobility Inquiry; United States 1980, Census of Population and Housing, B-sample, 1/1000; Venezuela 1977, World Fertility Survey; West Germany 1979, Poverty Study Europe; Yugoslavia 1971, Political Participation and Equality in Seven Nations. Because the numbers of cases in the data sets for China, Czechoslovakia, Indonesia, New Zealand, and the United States are very large, the homogamy tables for these countries are based on random samples of the original data.

was available or because the age variable was measured in intervals rather than in years. For these countries, we used age classifications that resemble our preferred classification as much as possible.

Information on the educational levels of husbands and wives was used to construct a table for each country in which the educational levels of spouses were cross-classified. Because loglinear parameters can be influenced by the number of categories of a classification (Dessens, Jansen, and Verbeek 1984), education variables with the same number of categories had to be created for each of the countries. The number of categories was set to four because, in some of the data sets, education was measured using only four categories. Within countries, the same education classification was used for husbands and wives.[3,4]

[3] Further information on data sets, age selections, and education classifications are available until April 2000 at FTP.FRW.RUU.NL in subdirectory EDUHOMASR. This FTP site also makes available other information about this study, including the homogamy table used.

[4] In light of our decision to use relative education variables, for each country an education classification had to be used that reflected as well as possible the educational distinctions that were important in that country. We assumed that this was the case for the original educational variables in the data sets. If a country's lowest educational category was "completed primary or lower," there probably would be few persons in that country with no education or incomplete primary education. And if the education classification does not differentiate between lower secondary and higher secondary education, this distinction is probably not very important in that particular country.

For countries whose education classification had more than four categories, some categories had to be merged. For this purpose, each educational scheme was carefully examined using information from encyclopedias and education yearbooks (UNESCO 1970–1983) as well as the frequency distributions of the education variables themselves. Most combinations involved merging categories of general education with categories of vocational education, or merging empty or nearly empty categories with a neighboring category. Sometimes we had to split an educational level (e.g., to divide primary education into a lower and a higher level). In those cases, we tried to get a smooth education variable without high peaks or deep troughs.

To test whether the degree of educational ho-

Figure 5.17

scholarship that, in effect, reproduce what others have cited. Bibliographies have great utility in this sense, providing a relatively accurate and timely barometer of people's respective standing in the field. No longer a means of exhuming a scholar's own intellectual itinerary, bibliographies reflect the value of one's occupational stock. The more professionalized the young author becomes, the more her bibliography will accurately reflect the pattern of reputations in the field inasmuch as the bibliography will have been professionally prepared, reproducing the field's canon.

Although the intellectual functions of notes and bibliography have declined with the rise of journal science, which drives out all undisciplined discourse, it is easier for authors to resist the truncation of notes and bibliography than to buck the formulaic structure of the text's body. Reviewers and editors, if not copyeditors, are less likely to care about marginalia as long as they are formatted in the journal's or house's standard style. By the time a busy editor considers a submitted manuscript that has already been revised twice and read the reviews of that manuscript, she may not notice nuances in the presentation of marginalia, instead turning these matters over to the copyeditor. Authors traditionally negotiate "small changes" with copyeditors, who are, in the case of book publishers, often freelancers with doctoral degrees much less invested in disciplinary strictures, even if they defend the *Chicago Manual of Style* to the death! Although copyeditors for journals are usually employed by the journal to edit copy of all accepted articles and thus have a greater investment in consistency, it is not impossible for authors to succeed in the negotiation of small changes, and to resist recommended changes. Again, marginalia matter less than does the body of the text. For this reason, deft authors can sometimes defend notes and bibliography against truncation, thus resisting the total eclipse of authorial presence in the text.

All books begin with acknowledgments, in which the author thanks others for help, both intellectual and emotional. Even articles allow authors to acknowledge help, either at the bottom of the first page or buried at the back of the article.

The author of figure 5.18 thanks twenty-eight people in her acknowledgments! These people read and commented on various drafts of the paper. Some are graduate students and colleagues at Wisconsin. Others are big names in the field. Although it is professionally courteous to thank people who read one's work before publication, voluminous acknowledgments produce what Baudrillard (1983) calls "sign value." It certainly does not hurt the author's cause to cite people like Theda Skocpol and Bob Connell. This suggests that she is appropriately networked and has sufficient standing with these busy scholars to warrant their attention. That is not all. She acknowledges support afforded by a National Science Foundation grant. She thanks three presumably anonymous *ASR* reviewers. (This is common practice for *ASR* authors today.) Interestingly, she says that "earlier versions of [the] paper were presented at meetings, workshops, and seminars in the United States, Sweden, Germany, and Australia"—a total of three continents! Clearly, the author wants us to believe that this paper has been heavily vetted by distinguished scholars the world over, some of whom are her friends and colleagues. I find this claim eminently believable. Here, I am interested in acknowledgments as gestures that increase an article's sign value, its science aura. Or to put this more prosaically, authors go to certain literary lengths to persuade us that their work deserves its pedigree.

In figure 5.19, the author thanks twenty-three scholars, four anonymous *ASR* reviewers, and the *ASR* editor! Her list of twenty-three readers includes several luminaries. She acknowledges research support from Princeton, Michigan, and the National Endowment for the Humanities. She indicates that the paper was presented at various seminars in Chicago, Ann Arbor, New York, and Princeton. She thanks participants in these seminars for their comments. The authors of figure 5.20 acknowledge readings by twelve scholars, the parallel research efforts of four scholars who are said to constitute a study group, and four *ASR* reviewers. They acknowledge various types of research support and indicate that their paper was given a trial run in presentations throughout the United States and in Germany. Finally, the authors of figure 5.21 thank eleven scholars by name; they acknowledge various funding agencies; and they indicate that their paper was read at a national meeting in November 1993. (I accompanied my spouse to that meeting, and the weather in Baltimore was beautiful.) As noted in chapter 3, an e-mail address is provided for contact with the authors.

A glance at the first page of the respective articles on which the acknowledgments are printed reveals that abstract, title, and acknowledgments occupy most of the page. Prose has been severely displaced just where one would expect it most—at the beginning. This gives the impression of science: the paper has a lengthy, science-like title; an abstract, usually printed in italics; and a substantial set of acknowledgments, indicating the good

Figure 5.18. Direct all correspondence to Ann Shola Orloff, Department of Sociology, University of Wisconsin, 1180 Observatory Drive, Madison, WI 53706. This research was partially supported by a grant from the National Science Foundation (SES 8822352) and is being carried out jointly with a project on "The Gender Regimes of Liberal Welfare States" with Dr. Sheila Shaver and Dr. Julia O'Connor. Earlier versions of this paper were presented at meetings, workshops, and seminars in the United States, Sweden, Germany, and Australia. For their comments on drafts of this paper, I thank: Julia Adams, Janeen Baxter, Jane Collins, Bob Connell, Linda Gordon, Alex Hicks, Barbara Hobson, David James, Jane Jenson, Trudie Knijn, Walter Korpi, Marilyn Lake, Christiane Lemke, Leslie McCall, Eileen McDonagh, Margit Meyer, Pavla Miller, Deborah Mitchell, Renee Monson, Julia O'Connor, Joakim Palme, Wendy Servasy, Sheila Shaver, Birte Siim, Theda Skocpol, Barbara Sullivan, Pamela Walters, Dorothy Watson, and three *ASR* reviewers. Leslie McCall and Heather Hartely provided research assistance.

Figure 5.19. Direct all correspondence to Margaret R. Somers, Department of Sociology, University of Michigan, Ann Arbor, MI 48109. This research was carried out in part under the support of a Research Fellowship from the Shelby Cullom Davis Center for Historical Research, Princeton University; a National Endowment for the Humanities fellowship, UCLA; and Rackham Faculty Recognition and Rackham Faculty Support Grants, both from the University of Michigan. Earlier versions of this paper were presented at the Center for Transcultural Studies in Chicago; the Council of European Studies Europeanists' Conference in Chicago; the University of Michigan Center for the Study of Social Transformations; the Russell Sage Foundation Politics and Culture Seminar in New York; and the Princeton Department of Sociology Colloquium. I thank members of those seminars for their thoughtful comments. For their generous feedback on written drafts I thank Julia Adams, Elizabeth Anderson, Renee Anspach, Daniel Bell, Rogers Brubaker, Geoff Eley, Gloria Gibson, Walter Goldfrank, Thomas Green, Miguel Guilarte, Miriam King, Richard Lempert, Mark Mizruchi, Moishe Postone, Jane Rafferty, Sonya Rose, Howard Schuman, Bill Sewell, Marc Steinberg, Arthur Stinchecombe, Charles Tilly, Marty Whyte, Mayer Zald, four anonymous *ASR* referees, and the *ASR* Editor.

Figure 5.20. Direct correspondence to Wayne Baker, Department of Organizational Behavior, University of Michigan School of Business, 701 Tappan Street, Ann Arbor, MI 48109-1234 (wayneb@umich.edu). This research was supported by a grant from the American Sociological Association, Fund for the Advancement of the Discipline. Versions of this paper were presented at the Interdisciplinary Committee on Organizational Studies (ICOS) at the University of Michigan, the Rational Choice Conference in New York City, the Department of Organizational Behavior at Northwestern University, the Department of Social and Decision Sciences at Carnegie Mellon University, and the Euro Conference on Social Research (ICOR) held at Friedrich-Alexander Universität, Erlangen-Nuremberg, Germany. We are grateful for helpful comments received at these presentations and to Douglas Anderton, Phillip Bonacich, Ronald Breiger, Kathleen Carley, Michael Cohen, Randall Collins, Jane Dutton, David Krackhardt, Roseanne Martorella, Anjali Sastry, Harrison White, and Kazuo Yamaguchi for comments on various drafts. We acknowledge the research efforts of "The Madison Avenue" study

standing of the author or authors. Although marginalia could, as I noted above, be an occasion for an author to compose a nonformulaic piece and to situate, in acknowledgments, the work for curious readers, all too frequently marginalia such as acknowledgments and notes are formulaic, simply reproducing the extant disciplinary style. Practitioners of the art—those who publish in journals—may well defend this by suggesting that acknowledgments or other marginalia don't matter to science. They are merely conveniences, composed conventionally. Acknowledgments may be defended as courtesies to those who have spent time and effort reading various drafts of papers. My and Russell Jacoby's critique may seem cranky, even reflecting the fact that we don't have many friends!

The acknowledgments found in books sometimes run to two pages, packed with names of friends and loved ones who lent assistance, a topic touched on by Jacoby in *The Last Intellectuals,* where he laments the decline of the autonomous author who is not ensconced in the dense web of academic networks. I share Jacoby's critique of acknowledging as a possible mode of sycophancy and name-dropping that establishes one's normalcy as a person with a tenured or tenure-track job who has many friends. The acknowledgment of help surely becomes excessive when the count of acknowledged names reaches 100! I observe that there is an inverse relationship between the N of names dropped in the acknowledgments and the number of publications the author

group, and especially the work of Dee Weber. Heather Noseworthy, Melissa Bator, and Doug Myers. We thank the four anonymous *ASR* reviewers for their helpful and insightful comments and suggestions.

Figure 5.21. Authors' Note: This article was prepared for a symposium at the November 1993 annual meeting of the National Council on Family Relations, Baltimore, MD. This research was completed with generous support from a Crossroads grant funded by the state of Indiana and the Purdue University Cooperative Extension Service. The contributions of time, thought, and energy by research participants are deeply appreciated. We also are grateful for assistance from Annette Becker, Mary Kay DeGenova, Gabriela Heilbrun, Chris Hetrick, Mary Clare Lennon, Thomas Luster, Stephen Marks, Elizabeth Menaghan, Eileen Newman, Stephen Small, and Laura Wittig. Support from the Krannert Graduate School of Management and the Department of Child Development and Family Studies is appreciated. Address correspondence to 1267 CDFS Building, Department of Child Development and Family Studies, Purdue University, West Lafayette, IN, 47907-1267. E-mail: shelley@vm.cc.purdue.edu.

has to her credit. Simply put, one is more likely to acknowledge a lot of people in one's first book than in one's sixth. There is something cloying about flowery acknowledgments that never seem to quit. Although it is reasonable to thank one's mentor and perhaps one's closest colleagues if they have actually read and commented on the manuscript, and perhaps even one's long-suffering partner, it adds little to lard acknowledgments with dozens of names quite remote from the work in question—past colleagues, graduate school cohort mates, childhood friends. As Jacoby indicates, acknowledging can be read as a self-conventionalizing account.

However, if approached differently, acknowledging can be a way of resisting the domestication of one's work if one avoids name-dropping and instead gives a brief account of how one's work can be situated in one's oeuvre and perhaps how it arises out of one's life. It is of moment that Todd Gitlin, a culturally oriented sociologist at NYU, was a founder of the SDS (Students for a Democratic Society). I want to know that Gitlin's (1980) book on the media coverage of the 1968 Democratic Convention in Chicago, *The Whole World Is Watching,* was written by the same person who wrote (1987) *The Sixties: Years of Hope, Days of Rage,* an excellent movement ethnography written from the perspective of a participant as well as a latter-day sociologist. Self-contextualization is different from self-conventionalization, in this respect. It is useful to know that Gitlin acknowledges Tom Hayden's help with his manuscript, just as Hayden (1988) acknowledges Gitlin; this need not be read as name-dropping.

Many authors employ acknowledgments to disclose themselves as situated beings. Although Jacoby is certainly correct to notice that some use the occasion of acknowledging cynically to drop names and cement connections, for many, especially journal writers, the acknowledgments are the only place where they may situate themselves as real people without fear of surveillance and discipline. It is widely accepted that acknowledgments are off limits to reviewers and editors, even some laissez-faire copyeditors. This is so not because acknowledgments have been formally restricted from editorial intervention by gatekeepers aware of the death of the author but simply because no one cares about acknowledgments in the world of science. But who among us does not read acknowledgments before we delve into the body of the piece, realizing that it is in this brief piece of text that we are most likely to detect the authorial heartbeat, which we need in order to situate the rest of the text? I suspect that professional readers are torn between flipping first to the bibliography, to see whether they are cited, or to the acknowledgments, to get a feel for the author. I know that I am!

This is not to say that acknowledgments are written without formula. Certain things are inevitable these days. One thanks one's mentor, especially if it is one's first book, and perhaps one's whole dissertation committee. One thanks a number of one's colleagues, probably including the chairperson, who may have helped the author obtain a leave in order to write. One may even thank the dean, if the dean needs buttering up! If one knows the identity of her reviewers, they will be named. One thanks one's editor if it is a book, and perhaps other people at the house involved in the book's production. One thanks people who have read the manuscript, beyond reviewers. Immediately thereafter, one absolves one's prepublication reviewers of responsibility for a bad book by indicating that the author is responsible for the ultimate literary outcome—the bound book, for better or worse. Or one may say, artfully, that the reviewers are responsible for the good parts and the author for the bad parts—a demonstration of humility. Finally, one thanks one's partner, spouse, offspring for their emotional work toward the finished product. Inasmuch as many academics are coupled with other academics, frequently in the same field, one may thank one's partner not just for tender loving care but also for reading and commenting on the manuscript. (One wonders how such tightly bonded dyads can stand so much togetherness.)

Although this sounds tongue-in-cheek, there are perfectly valid reasons for naming and thanking all of the aforementioned if they helped one publish. While I share Jacoby's cynicism about too much of a good thing, I applaud acknowledgments when they situate one in a genuine community of intellectual and personal support and thus reveal connections between one's work and life. I have written my share of such acknowledgments. I even dedicated a book to my mentor (and he expressed pleasant surprise). The point here is that acknowledging is governed by certain conventions that may have the effect of reducing acknowledgments to rather uninspired protocols that do little to liberate authorial sensibility. I know of a respected sociologist who acknowledged his typewriter.

Finally, there is the matter of the title. Titling is not always left up to the author, especially in book publishing, where editors and publishers seek to maximize books' marketability. Even journal editors and reviewers may comment on working titles, ensuring a close fit between the title and the topic covered. Typically, sociology authors will use a technical field-based subtitle, which narrows a catchy title: "10,000 Maniacs: Resistance to Change in a Small Nevada Town, 1945–56—A Test of Social-Capital Theory."

The title of the article in figure 5.22 is typical: colloquial, chatty title, descriptive subtitle. The title of figure 5.23 involves descriptive title and subtitle. The title of figure 5.24 reverses form: literary subtitle, science-seeming title. Figure 5.25 does away with the subtitle altogether. Most books sport subtitles, which also narrow, although perhaps not as far as do journal articles, which must locate themselves in an established field. Books' subtitles may confine themselves to a large field or multiple fields, which could be said to constitute a subdiscipline, such as social psychology or social theory. This wide scope of coverage is often claimed in the case of textbooks, which seek market across a whole subdiscipline, collecting many particular fields.

Figure 5.22. MONEY IN THE BANK: TRANSACTION COSTS AND THE ECONOMIC ORGANIZATION OF MARRIAGE*

Figure 5.23. EDUCATIONAL HOMOGAMY IN 65 COUNTRIES: AN EXPLANATION OF DIFFERENCES IN OPENNESS USING COUNTRY-LEVEL EXPLANATORY VARIABLES*

Figure 5.24. HOW WHITE ATTITUDES VARY WITH THE RACIAL COMPOSITION OF LOCAL POPULATIONS: NUMBERS COUNT*

Figure 5.25. A WITHIN-INDUSTRY COMPARISON OF EMPLOYED MOTHERS' EXPERIENCES IN SMALL AND LARGE WORKPLACES

Although titles are remembered, especially in the world of books, they are less well remembered than are the author or authors who wrote them. After all, the last name of the author is entered into the literature of the field, which is parenthetically cited in future articles and books. Authorship, not the paper itself, replete with title, is canonized—for example Davis and Moore 1945. The author's intervention in the field counts for more than the paper as such because, after awhile, the paper is not read or read carefully by subsequent practitioners. The paper becomes its citation, the author's last name. Although it is possible for the author to discuss the paper in the body of the text with reference to its title, this rarely happens in sociology because it rarely happens in science. It is more likely to happen in the book world, although even there one finds a tendency for fields to congeal around literatures, which reduce articles and books to authorial naming.

Perhaps it is better that we remember the author rather than title. This may preserve what earlier I called authorial presence in the text. What is really happening, however, is that papers and books, once canonized, receive only superficial, if any, close reading by people who cite them in subsequent work. In an age of fast literary capitalism, discourse declines where people write too fast and read only cursorily, giving articles and books the shelf life of potato chips or blockbuster movies. The decline of titles in favor of parenthetically cited authors, with their dates of publication, reflects a decline of careful reading, which characterizes both society at large—Jacoby's point in *The Last Intellectuals*—and scientific writing, where writers force the writings of others through the meat grinder of literature reviews without considering carefully how other authors view their problem, both in agreement and counterpoint.

THEORY'S SCIENCE ENVY

Sociological theory is not immune to the tendencies I have described in this and the preceding chapters. Theory has become obstructed writing, riddled with citations, and devoted to issues of exegesis and intellectual filiation that bear scant resemblance to the grand theorizing of Marx, Durkheim, and Weber. Theorists may explicate the founders, including Parsons, and not more contemporary work, thus playing an important canonical role in the discipline. Sometimes theory is not theory at all but middle-range concept formation that frames empirical research—the theory of demographic transition, resource-mobilization theory, status-attainment theory. Although a good deal of creative writing in social theory, broadly understood as a multidisciplinary project that addresses the social, does not obstruct its reception or submerge authorial presence, there is a striking tendency for journal theory, published in the leading sociology journals, to imitate the worst tendencies of journal science, notably obscurantism. I contend that this is a product of theory's science envy, its effort to produce the science aura, albeit without resort to the auratizing techniques of method. Absent method, theorists can still manage occasionally to find their ways into print in the most prestigious sociology journals as long as they obstruct their writing and avoid overly broad topics, including social criticism, that are seen to subvert sociology's claim to be science.

How do theorists convert prose into figure in order to allay their science envy and boost their chances of publication? First, they clog their writing with parenthetical citations, preferably of the founders' writings, and perhaps even quoted material, which is discussed. These citations and quotations impede reading, reducing the apparent discursive textuality and narrativity of the article or monograph. Science defends itself against the literary by refusing to compose a seamless text, with all of the accoutrements of narrative and literary felicity. Although passable grammar is not objectionable, turgidity, elaborate use of figure, the passive voice all obstruct readings that are thus prevented from engaging with the text and even engaging it in dialogue—future versions. The more obstructed writing is, the more it is thought to resemble science in simply reporting "findings." The problem for theory is that it lacks the usual empirical findings of mainstream sociology. It does not employ data sets, methods, or statistics. Absent data, it must manufacture its own data—exegesis and explication of others' works, notably of the sociological founders. Here data are not individual responses to survey instruments, income means, or crime rates. Data are the raw material of the founders' translated prose, which, in theory's equivalent of the findings section of the paper, submit themselves to explication, explanation, and interpretation, for example, a paper on Durkheim's theorizing on crime. Sometimes the issues treated are intertextual—Parsons's relationship to Weber. In all such cases, theory produces data by citing and quoting elaborately. Figure lies close to the ground, in parenthetical citation sausages and italicized quotations, which may be indented on the journal page. In this respect, theorists figure their work, relieving its inveterate narrativity, albeit without recourse to the standard quantitative method.

Why would editors publish theory at all, given the scarcity of journal space? They do so in order to demonstrate a balanced view of the discipline, allowing the occasional theorist her day. They also do so because journal theory, established sociological theory, helps the discipline canonize the founders as objects of intellectual and social history but not of living engagement with contemporary issues. Where mainstream empirical authors cite work published only in the past five or ten years, risking disciplinary amnesia in this, theorists do curatorial work by reminding us that sociology extends further back in time and has canonical roots in the writings of Comte, Durkheim, Weber, and Marx (but only insofar as Marx can be viewed as a safe conflict theorist, not a revolutionary dialectician).

Journal theory canonizes the founders, plumbing their work interpretively and thus implying that important theory ceased a century ago. The well-founded tendency to extend sociological theory, which treats only of the classics and drinks deeply of the positivist project, into social theory, incorporating insights from European theory and cultural studies, is resisted. Theory obstructs reading by clogging itself with citations and quotations. It may develop its own obscure technical language. Even what passes for theory is rather unclear, especially as middle-range theorists, rational-choice theorists, and theory constructionists intrude upon the domain of speculative theory. Certain empiricists attempt to organize their literatures and findings into what Merton called middle-range theory, theory that does not explain the world globally but descends to a description and explanation of social processes addressed by particular disciplinary subfields such as criminology and demography. This version of theory merely organizes data and insights, as Merton recommended. It does not explain globally or structurally, as some of us contend theory must. Rather, middle-range theory is what Turner and Turner call "theories of."

Figure 5.26. My main theoretical claim is that the local protest movement in Birmingham was responsible for the successful outcome of this campaign. This argument contrasts sharply with the "violence thesis" which argues that a third party—the federal government—was responsible for the local victory. I use the Birmingham case to crystallize my conceptual argument, which differs from the "violence thesis" and related formulations that credit third parties with being the crucial factor leading to protest success. My formulation also has general implications for social movement theory.

Figure 5.27. Quantitative cross-national research and historical case studies should be complementary. Such complementary research is especially important for connecting middle-range theories to grand theories. It would also open up a little explored but fruitful avenue for examining the contemporary

In figure 5.26, taken from the excellent and atypically unfigured article on the civil rights movement in Birmingham discussed earlier, the author characterizes his contention "that the local protest movement was responsible for the successful outcome of this campaign" as his "main theoretical claim." Remaining in the middle-range, he claims that his research "has general

relevance of Marx's theory. Exploitation was exceptionally high in the state socialist countries of Eastern Europe, so the contemporary relevance of Marx's theory may be greatest for countries where it is least expected.

Figure 5.28. We use agency theory to analyze the development of the tax collection system in Prussia between 1640 and 1806. The Prussian tax system was one of the most efficient in early modern Europe.

Figure 5.29. We attempt to integrate, elaborate, and test competing theories of why religious participation increases with age during young adulthood.

Figure 5.30. Theory development is facilitated when one study builds on another as "[n]ew data exert pressure for the elaboration of a conceptual scheme" (Merton 1949:102). Our study builds on the prior study of client-auditor dyads in three ways.

Figure 5.31. Finally, we propose a theory of market-tie dissolution that subsumes the conceptual framework of the study of client-auditor dyads and lifts the analysis of the right "to establish and break relationships" (Coleman 1974:24–25) to a higher theoretical level.

Figure 5.32. It remains to be seen whether there is also a trend toward more openness, as predicted by industrialization theory (Kerr et al. 1960; Treiman 1970).

Figure 5.33. I seek to explain the emergence of social differentiation. While it is always possible to explain one outcome with a theory that is devoted solely to explaining that one outcome, the challenge is to explain that outcome with a theory that has the three properties that are desirable of any theory: "(1) that . . . [the theory's] assumption set be as short as possible; (2) that its observable implications be as many and as varied as possible; and (3) that its observable implications include phenomena or relationships not yet observed"

implications for social movement theory." In figure 5.27, the authors argue for a combination of quantitative research and case studies, claiming that this will help connect middle-range to grand theories. These are the authors who are attempting to test Marx empirically. In figure 5.28, taken from a dense treatment of Prussian taxation between 1640 and 1806, the authors invoke what they term "agency theory," a middle-range theory. In figure 5.29, in their abstract, the authors propose to test theories of "why religious participation increases with age during young adulthood." As with figure 5.28, this directly links middle-range theory to empirical testing. In figure 5.30, citing Merton 1949, the authors state that "[t]heory development is facilitated when one study builds on another. . . ." Again, this links empirical testing and the goal of scientific cumulation with middle-range theory building. In figure 5.31, a theory of "market-tie dissolution" is proposed as a "theory of continuity and discontinuity." In figure 5.32, the authors attribute predictions to "industrialization theory," behind which they cite Kerr et al. 1960 and Treiman 1970. In figure 5.33, the author develops what he calls "a theory of information and social structure," supplementing Spencer and Durkheim. This is middle-range theory on the high end, attempting to do more than explain the fit of two correlated variables. The theory offered by the author makes Spencer's and Durkheim's theories of social differentiation "more precise." Citing Jasso, the author, a formal theorist, goes on to suggest that theories must have three properties—their assump-

(Jasso 1988:1). In addition to these characteristics, which can be evaluated independently of empirical findings, it is also important
for a theory's predictions to be accurate
(Heckathorn 1984; Jasso 1988). These arguments establish criteria against which theoretical work can be judged. I demonstrate that the
theory of information and social structure
scores well against these criteria.

Figure 5.34. Status construction theory
argues that structurally constrained interaction
plays a crucial role in the construction and
spread of status value beliefs (Ridgeway
1991).

Figure 5.35. The theory of reward expectations (Berger et al. 1983, 1985) describes the
process by which expectations for rewards are
formed in status situations, the interrelations
between reward expectations and performance expectations, and how the allocation of
rewards, in itself, can create performance
expectations. The theory introduces the concept of referential beliefs and distinguishes different types of such belief structures.

tions be as few as possible, that observable implications of the theory be as
many as possible, and that its observable
implications include phenomena as yet
unobserved. Figure 5.34 refers to "status
construction theory," figure 5.35 to "a
theory of the social construction of status value," figure 5.35, using the concept of "referential beliefs," to a "theory
of reward expectations."

For that matter, some people defend
ethnomethodology and ethnography,
especially feminist and African American versions, as theoretical. There is a
whole literature in feminist sociology
(e.g., Dorothy Smith 1987) that argues
that theory, for women, is necessarily
more grounded in everyday life than it
is for men, who can afford to disdain the
minutiae of the everyday in favor of
grand systemizing. Thus, theoretical
accounts, it is argued, must be
grounded in people's narratives about
their own lives. Although I am in sympathy with the contention that theory
should arise from people's, including the theorist's, lives, a claim also made by phe-
nomenologically oriented critical theorists such as Piccone (1971), Paci (1972), and
O'Neill (1972, 1974), it is not clear that the narrativization of social theory, either in
the directions of ethnomethodology, symbolic interactionism, or feminist epistemology, is sufficiently generalizing, universalizing, or totalizing to "count" as theory. This
reopens an issue raised by postmodernists such as Lyotard, who declare "grand narratives," which explain with global scope, defunct, indicting such aggrandizing narratives as inherently authoritarian in their alleged disrespect for difference.

Much of this narratively oriented work is good and interesting, especially for
someone with my critical perspective. Whether it should "count" as theory is rather
unimportant, except to notice that mainstream sociology journals publish little
ethnographically oriented work (but see the article cited for figure 3.21). This is so,
I suspect, because ethnographers do not frequently have science envy and they
write in ways that do not obstruct reading. The whole phenomenological movement (see Natanson 1970; Spielberg 1982) grounds knowledge, including philosophy and theory, in unmediated everyday experience, implicitly defeating the generalizing, reifying tendencies of quantitative method that cover over the grounding
of knowledge in interest and experience.

The theory published by the mainstream outlets is theory that canonizes the founders, obstructs reading in order to mimic the science format, and conceals its own literariness. Theorists produce data by citing and quoting. Empirical theory, on Merton's middle-range model, is also published. This is a pale copy of speculative theory, residing squarely within empirical fields. Theorists who seek to publish in mainstream outlets can occasionally find ways of doing so, given the right approach, a good letterhead, and connections. Increasingly, the high-output, grant-oriented quantitative sociology departments view theory as a sociological subspecialty among many others, to which a graduate course or two will be devoted. Instead of being a means of configuring the whole discipline, theory has been reduced to canonical curation. Compounding this problem, sociological theory in its official version has been inured to interdisciplinary developments in social and cultural theory, rejecting much of this work as political and jargon-laden. Needless to say, social theory's discursive turn is roundly rejected by positivists who view discourse-driven analysis as insubstantial and who do not view their own scientific work as discursive.

6

"Maybe the Reviewer Is Just Dense": Review and Revision as Argument

METHODS-DRIVEN REVIEWS

In this chapter, I examine prepublication reviews of articles, re-reviews of revised papers, authors' letters to editors accounting for why they made certain changes but not others, and editors' letters to authors providing rationale for their editorial decisions. I have collected files of reviews of papers submitted to mainstream sociology journals and the related correspondence. I am interested in the review and revision process as one of argument, position taking, perspective, and even politics. This process is largely governed by methodological concerns, leaving certain other issues aside. I consider reviewing as a language game, proceeding according to certain informal rules within specific contexts that call forth predictable speech acts. According to Wittgenstein, there are many types of language games and of corresponding rules. The rules of reviewing for social science journals are clear, if not explicit. They are reproduced by reviewers who are also authors, whose own submitted work is reviewed. Reviewers are also sent other readers' evaluations of a given paper, and the text of the subsequent editorial decision about publishability. Reviewers are thus both readers and writers. I argue that reviewing produces two quite distinctive kinds of writing or language games: It produces reviews, in the image of the reviews that the reviewer has read, and it produces papers that are written according to the expectations conveyed by reviews. Reviews reproduce themselves and papers in their image.

For Wittgenstein to call language a game does not mean that it is trivial or capricious. He is simply situating language in performative contexts within which people attempt to arrive at understandings within the frames of references called forth by what they are doing. Shopping, getting one's car fixed, talking to one's children, teaching a class, writing an article all involve certain linguistic games that are transacted among speakers who understand the rules of the particular game in play, or think they do. It is a very short step from Wittgenstein's comments about language in *Philosophical Investigations* to social phenomenology (Schutz 1967) and ethnomethodology (Garfinkel 1967), both of which suggest that people engage in practical reasoning guided not by transcendental or formal rules of meaning but by the everyday exigencies of sense making—a teacher who tries to bring her class to order on an early spring day when the students would rather be outside, a parent attempting to explain to her four-year old why it is not okay to pinch his classmates, or a junior sociologist trying to reconcile contradictory reviews of her article in order to get published and thus gain a toehold on the tenure track. All of these are games in that they challenge people's discursive intelligence and inventiveness.

Garfinkel has brilliantly showed that people make sense in spite of profound barriers to understanding. Everyday language is often sloppy to the point of incoherence. Imagine calling 911 in the middle of the night with an account of a burglar next door. One's heart is pounding; one has stumbled into furniture en route to the telephone; one's glasses are out of reach; one's adrenaline is flowing. In the context of this frenzy, one may not make perfect sense to the person at the other end of the 911 phone line. And that person's responses may be misunderstood. Yet sense emerges, even out of chaos, given people's discursive abilities to fill in gaps and transcend inconsistencies, grounding understanding in the contextual contingencies of the moment. We are adept at working the language games through which we pragmatically transact meaning with others because we have lived in the world and possess the power to reason practically, if not always purely.

Wittgenstein and Garfinkel enable us to view articles and reviews as governed by certain conventions that may, from the distance afforded by theory and critique, not make the best sense, given available discursive options. Anticipating chapter 8, I would like to see the *American Sociological Review* (*ASR*) and other mainstream sociology journals and monograph publishers return to aspects of the more open journal discourse of the 1930s, 1940s, and even 1950s, yet abandon the doctrinal positivism of early American sociology. I do not want to turn back the methodological clock but to make sociology available to those who may not be able (or need) to understand LISREL, t-tests, or heteroskesdasticity in order to enter profitably into sociological argument. Lemert, like Peter Berger (1963) and C. Wright Mills before him, argues in (1997) *Social Things* that sociology is a practical project of everyday understanding, a key theme also of ethnomethodology—for example, John O'Neill's *Making Sense Together*. To say this does not require sociology to drop its vernacular, including method and figure. Theory is a challenging language game whose rules may also need to be reconsidered, especially in light of Habermas's arguments about critical theory's responsibility to create a democratic public sphere based on widely distributed dialogue chances, as he calls them. How sociology writes matters precisely because sociology is one of the ways in which we understand the historicity of our social world, its susceptibility to change.

Reviewing reproduces normal journal science where reviewers focus on common themes that appear regularly in the reviews. These issues emerged from my reading of over 150 reviews of seventy articles submitted, either in first-generation or revised-generation drafts, to major sociology journals such as *ASR, American Journal of Sociology (AJS), Social Psychology Quarterly, Demography, Journal of Marriage and the Family, Journal of Family Issues, Sociological Quarterly, Gender and Society,* and others in the discipline. About 14 percent of these papers were accepted, most after at least one revision. Thirty percent were given initial revise-and-resubmit decisions; that is, the reviewers found enough merit in the submitted article that the editor invited the author to revise the paper in light of reviewers' and the editor's own suggestions, with no explicit promise of eventual acceptance. Fifty-six percent of these seventy articles were rejected, usually upon original submission but sometimes after the revision was completed. In this sample, the *ASR* (under two editors) was the most likely to reject papers, with *Journal of Family Issues* and *Journal of Marriage and the Family* being the most likely to accept. (Official acceptance/rejection rates are available from each of these journals.)

Reading through this thick pile of reviews, editors' letters to authors, re-reviews of revised drafts of the papers, and authors' accounts of how they revised their papers in order to please first-generation reviewers revealed remarkable similarities in how reviewers compose themselves. Eight key issues emerged from reviews of original submissions. We find many comments on method: suitability of data, measurement, statistics used, and interpretations constitute the main focus of most reviews. We also find comments on the quality of literature reviews, the articles' theoretical grounding, the papers' style, the papers' contributions to their fields, authors who go beyond their data in offering bold but unwarranted interpretations, figures used in the text, and footnotes that either need to be added or redone.

We find somewhat different themes in comments on revised papers, especially where the reviewer in the second round has reviewed the paper in the first round. Re-reviews frequently evaluate the author's responsiveness to first-round reviews, deciding, in that light, whether the paper has been improved enough to warrant publication. Where reviews of the original submission often run to a single-spaced page or two (and sometimes more), reviews of resubmissions are much briefer, sometimes, in the case of affirmative reviews, only a few lines: "The author has done an admirable job in meeting my and the other reviewers' suggestions in the revised draft of the paper. I particularly like the way in which s/he has responded to suggestions about tests of reliability. This paper will make an important contribution to the literature. I recommend that you accept as is." By contrast, original reviews are packed with comments about detail, as well as more general comments about suitability. Sometimes original reviews are divided into major criticisms and minor criticisms, with appropriate subheadings.

Reviews are, in the first place, methods-driven. I did not read a single review that did not foreground methodological issues. This is not to say that these comments were picayune. Just as most papers are smart and well wrought, if not immediately publishable, reviewers' comments represent congealed intelligence and sophistication. For the most part, editors seem to choose reviewers wisely, identi-

fying people in the field who are close to the relevant literatures, theoretical apparatuses, and methods used to study particular topics. Frequently, these reviewers are
identified by editors because they have been cited in the submitted paper, suggesting their centrality to the literature in question.

Reviewers focus on method because authors focus on method. Reviewers
review what is given to them. The many pages and gestures devoted by authors to
matters methodological call forth reviews that argue for or against logit and probit
analyses, additional R-squareds (a correlation coefficient), different tests of significance, better specified models relating dependent and independent variables, and
alternative or supplementary data sources. Authors may not have received the same
level of graduate school training in methods and statistics, resulting in ragged papers
that require further work. And in the case of very positive reviews, especially of
revised and resubmitted papers, methods' centrality in reviews simply reflects the
centrality of methods in submitted papers and in the discipline as a whole. Or to
put this another way, reviewers virtually never praise a paper that does not pass
methodological muster simply because the paper happens to make an otherwise
important substantive contribution.

Here is perhaps the most important issue in a critical analysis of reviewing: the
distinction between a paper's substantive contribution to the field's literature and
its methodological virtuosity tends to fade precisely because so-called substantive
advances tend to be advances in method, at least since the 1970s. By the same token,
papers found to be insignificant or insubstantial are faulted primarily for weaknesses
of method. I have already suggested that the model of a cumulating sociology is
belied by the narrow specialization of articles that tend to make their claims to dis-
tinctiveness on the basis of treating different independent variables—for example,
the impact of number and age of children on church attendance—than others
have, not in making fundamental conceptual advances. Reviewers' comments
about method tend to bleed into their comments about the paper's substantive contribution. Limitations of method constrain the reviewer's enthusiasm about the
paper's overall contribution to the field. Rarely do reviewers indicate that a paper
is limited by its theoretical formation, narrowness of topic, or misleading use of literature. Although comments are made about these areas, the reviewer's overall
assessment of the paper reflects her evaluation of the methods used, or, put differently, the overall evaluation of the paper's contribution closely resembles the
reviewer's evaluation of the methods used.

This is because, since about 1970, papers are inseparable from their method.
Method constitutes the paper's contribution, which is framed in terms of the
author's handling of independent and dependent variables. Substantial contributions deal carefully with these multiple variables, both in terms of measurement and
statistical interpretation, allowing the author to identify possible patterns of causa-
tion. Lesser contributions, which are sometimes reduced to research notes by the
editor, are more descriptive and less explanatory. They make fewer claims to contribute to an evolving literature than do full-fledged articles. Authors sometimes

compose papers as research notes. Frequently, though, editors downgrade submitted articles to research notes because reviewers have cast doubt on the explanatory significance of their contribution. Research notes do not have elaborate methodological apparatuses; as research reports, they merely present data.

The boundary between method and substance is defended by those who claim that empirical journal articles are theoretically driven; that is, articles are said to derive testable hypotheses from research literatures held together by middle-range concepts such as demographic transition, family exchange, power control, rational choice. A good "test" of this proposition is found in the reviews themselves: rarely do any of the 150 reviews I sampled praise a paper's method but fault its theoretical contribution or derivation. Although, as we shall see, questions of theory are sometimes raised, what article writers and reviewers call theory is not grand by any means but problem-dependent; theory for article writers and reviewers is explanation (or, as methodologists might say, it is a "proxy" for explanation). Most of the 150 reviewers' recommendations to accept, reject, or revise are based on perceived problems of method and measurement and not on inadequate theory. These issues may blur inasmuch as reviewers pay lip service to the compartmentalization of method that treats method as only one of eight or more important issues to be evaluated.

What I found, then, is that most reviews of quantitative empirical articles tend to focus on method, even though they also make comments on other issues such as theory, literature review, significance of contribution, and style. That they make comments on other issues appears to compartmentalize or circumscribe method such that we maintain the illusion that sociology is driven by substantive, conceptual concerns and not simply by technique. Although smart reviewers no doubt have things to say about nonmethodological issues that are especially important when they recommend revision and resubmission, these issues are largely secondary, judging by the amount of space devoted to methodological criticisms and suggestions. Perhaps many reviewers focus on method because method can be "fixed." It is finite, technical, specific, well understood by sociologists trained in the contemporary era. Few of the reviewers who found fault with method suggested that the paper was irretrievable by careful revision. Papers recommended for revision were usually accompanied by specific suggestions for methodological fine-tuning that most people would view as "do-able," not involving thoroughgoing rewrites.

This is not to say that reviewers always agreed in their methodological criticisms. One of the most interesting aspects of reviewing and revision is the sheer contradictoriness of reviews. Following from this, another important issue is the likelihood that revised papers are not sent to all of the same reviewers who read the original manuscript but only to one or two of them, thus exposing the paper to new readings and therefore the potential for new contradictions. Rarely did I find a consensus among reviewers about their ultimate recommendations, leaving the field open to the editor, who would need to exercise her discretion in deciding whether or not to publish. There was less than perfect consensus among reviewers in most cases even about seemingly "objective" issues such as method, raising questions about blind reviewing as a supposed hallmark of the community of science.

Perhaps the most consistent theme in reviewing that concentrated on methodological issues involved the perceived sophistication of the mathematical analyses performed on the data at hand. Frequently, the reviewers' comments could be read as a primer of sorts, giving the author advice on how to make the analyses more sophisticated by the standard of today's cutting-edge statistical sociology. The technical nature of reviewers' discourse about method closely resembles the thick discourse of the methods sections of published articles. Sociologists unfamiliar with the ins and outs of quantitative method and statistics would be hard-pressed to read through many of the reviews sampled here with a clear sense of what is at stake. This is not to say that the reviewers were purposely obscurantist. They write for authors at or near the reviewers' level of training in method, who share a common discourse. I would guess that most reviews in my sample were written by sociologists somewhat more advanced in their careers than the authors of the seventy submitted manuscripts simply because junior sociologists, who must publish to get tenure, are probably overrepresented in the sample of authors. Reviewers are already known to the editor (or made known to the editor by virtue of having been cited in submitted papers) on the basis of established scholarly reputations. Although graduate students and junior sociologists may do some reviewing, especially if they are members of the editor's own academic network, reviewers tend to be selected because they have already published in the field, on the basis of which they have acquired visibility that destines them for selection as reviewers.

In this context, methodologically sophisticated reviewers tutor more junior or otherwise less technically sophisticated authors, who in effect complete their professional training by writing and getting reviewed. Not only do reviews reproduce the discursive norms of the discipline by disciplining submitted writing, they also teach, where graduate training leaves authors less than fully prepared for the rapidly evolving world of statistics and methods. One could say that all readings edify. However, there is a specific sense in which sociological article reviews raise authors to the level of high-powered methodology by filling gaps in knowledge. One of the best ways for graduate students to test the level of their acquired methodological expertise is to submit their empirical work to the *ASR* or *Social Forces,* awaiting the reviews as one would await comments from their mentors. Although this can be a damaging experience, especially where one has received high grades in college and graduate school and suddenly confronts harsh professional criticism, there are few better ways for advanced graduate students to work their chapters and articles into shape than to submit them for publication. One's expectations of quick success should be low, although if one coauthors with one's graduate school mentor (and if one's mentor is accomplished), publication may be just around the corner. At the very least, one will learn how to read reviews and write better papers, especially in the methodological sense, allowing one to undertake revisions with the hope of eventual publication, if not at a high-status outlet then perhaps at an outlet of somewhat lesser prestige.

Most reviewers, no matter how trenchant their methodological criticisms may be, do not acknowledge that their evaluations of submitted papers are methods-driven. Thus, they consider larger and different questions in their reviews. They may address the literature review, which needs to be complete and support the hypotheses derived from it. About a quarter of the 150 reviews I read made explicit comments about how the literature review could be improved, both by adding cites and by better teasing out the implications of one's constitution of a field through citation for the work at hand. Comments about the adequacy of literature reviews are sometimes linked to comments about a paper's theoretical formation: some reviews indicate that the author's assemblage of citations into middle-range theories such as the rational-choice perspective or the institutional perspective is incorrect or could be improved, whether by clumping together different permutations of citations or by renaming the middle-range theories surveyed in the opening literature review section. This can be a devilish proposition where, in effect, the author conjures theories out of thin air, assembling citations into perspectives unified around certain common themes. As I have said before, one of the essential contributions of literature reviews is to frame the problem at hand in the currency of a field that could be said to be cumulating through piecemeal research. Where the author wants to break new ground by unifying or transcending apparently competing perspectives, thus enabling us to see a particular aspect of the empirical world in a new way, literature reviews provide a perfect staging area for middle-range theoretical discussion, which summarizes commonalities and differences without a great deal of—or any—specific discussion of pages and passages.

Literature reviews may be faulted either for shortcomings that manifest themselves in inadequate theoretical formulations or for tenuous connections to the hypotheses or propositions tested in the paper. This latter problem is especially troubling to reviewers where the literature reviews seem to promise more than the meager payoffs produced by the subsequent data analysis and conclusions/discussion. Literature reviews may get the author into trouble when, in fact, her topic is derived not from careful combing of the existing empirical and theoretical literature of the field but rather from expediency such as the availability of data sets or a particular interest in statistical techniques that yield little in the way of substantive sociology. The methodological focus of most reviews accurately reflects the circumstantial nature of most topics, which are derived not deductively from prior research and theory but framed by both data availability and the author's own career contingencies such as the need to publish quickly. Papers relate dependent and independent variables using contemporary methodological and statistical techniques. Literature reviews situate papers in substantive sociology by contextualizing the manipulation of variables, explaining the genesis of "the research question." Where hypothesis testing appears to flow seamlessly from the stage-setting literature review, reviewers either say nothing about the literature review or praise it. But where literature reviews and data analysis are not cleanly meshed, reviewers may find fault and recommend revisions. Or, alternatively, they may dismiss the focus of the paper as too narrow, not sufficiently justified by the author's attempt to situate the paper's topic in existing research and middle-range theory. This may be an irremediable problem because it is more difficult to correct a paper's insubstantial contribution than it is to make modifications to the literature review.

Most reviewers do not fault papers' overall disciplinary contributions. Only about ten percent of the sampled reviews found the overall contribution wanting, which, as I just said, was often evaluated in the context of the literature review connecting topic to existing field. Where contribution was questioned, it was often flagged in the reviewer's private comments to the editor, who, especially in the case of the *ASR*, asks reviewers to comment on the extent to which a paper's treatment of a topic will be of interest and importance to general sociological readers. This is a less salient criterion for specialty journals such as *Journal of Marriage and the Family*. Many *ASR* reviewers in my sample explicitly commented that a paper was not at a level of interest and importance to warrant publication in the journal, which is said to have higher standards and require a more general substantive contribution than lesser journals. *ASR* reviews were often more acerbic and less forgiving than other reviews in the sample, although they were no less methods-driven. Indeed, *ASR* reviews are among the most detail-oriented when it comes to comments about method, which preoccupy them. It is another question whether the *ASR* actually publishes more significant work and work of more general sociological interest than do the *AJS, Social Forces,* and specialty journals. I am not persuaded that it does, although it appears from my sample that accepted *ASR* papers undergo more stringent and lengthier processes of revision than do accepted papers at other journals. As I will discuss below, a paper in my sample of particular interest to me accumulated fully fifty-three single-spaced pages of reviews and letters from author and editors. This thick text of reviews and editorial and authorial comments accumulated over the span of two *ASR* editors, two revise-and-resubmit decisions, and a final round of author-induced revisions.

Reviews for the *ASR* differ somewhat in tone, if not substance, than for other journals. They do not apologize for what might be viewed as nitpicky criticisms and suggestions for revision. As one reviewer said, "After all, this is [the] *ASR*." Not only must papers make significant contributions to general sociology, they must also use sophisticated methods and cite literatures exhaustively. At least in *ASR* reviewers' discourse, the *ASR* is a cut above other journals in its exacting standards. The reviewers expect more substance, more method, more literature reviewed. And *ASR* editors put papers through more revision than do other editors, at least judging from this sample. This is not to say that acceptance rates at the *AJS, Social Forces,* and *Demography* are substantially higher than the *ASR*'s; they are not. But when *ASR* editors give authors revise-and-resubmit decisions, they put revisions through exhaustive processes of editorial scrutiny and even re-revision and review, if they think it is warranted.

Where issues of method are paramount and where reviewers also comment on papers' significance, often in ways that reflect their view of papers' methodologi-

cal adequacy, and where they touch on both literature review and papers' theoretical formations, they also address style, albeit in minor ways. Frequently, reviewers
provide "running" commentaries, with page by page references, on obvious gaffes
in grammar; spelling; punctuation; references in the body of the paper that are missing from, or misidentified in, the bibliography; other mistakes in citation; and missing pages from their copy of the manuscript. Almost by definition, problems with
style can be corrected, as reviewers imply or state. Occasionally, serious problems
with style are included in a list of irretrievable faults of the paper in support of recommendations not to publish, or not even to invite a revision. In most of these
cases, one suspects that the paper has been written by a first-timer, either in or just
out of graduate school. But while particular points about style are made, never is a
paper discussed as a discursive or literary act, its narrativity, language game, form of
life made a central topic in a review. Not a single review discussed figures as a form
of rhetoric, of argument, although comments about the suitability of figures are
sometimes made. By the same token, reviewers never comment on the almost figural quality of the methods discussion in papers as a critical topic, probably because
reviewers do not reflect on the literary conventions of sociological journal articles
as things that can be addressed, let alone changed, by the singular author or author
team.

Although reviewers frequently comment on matters of style and figural presentation, they never treat journal articles as discourse, pregnant with assumptions and
implications about the social world and about sociology's inherence in that world.
Reviews are not sociologies of sociology, although they may contain many comments about the state of particular fields and about articles' relations to those fields.
I suspect that this is because reviewers feel it necessary to review the articles presented to them, not the state of sociology, methods, theory, let alone the state of
the world. They feel that it is their professional responsibility to review the article
"as it is," not as it should or could be, except for recommended changes to be made
within its language game. Professional norms regarding objective reviewing require
reviewers to distance themselves from critical questions about discourse, especially
about the politics of discourse. Again, Stanley Fish has written about the myth of
objectivity in reviewing, arguing persuasively that reviews are necessarily interested
and situated documents that exist in political relationships with the articles they
review. Hence, he argues against blind reviewing as a distortion of what is really at
stake in reviewers' reading of articles whose authorship they may suspect they
know. Or in my terms, sociology, however much its authorship is disguised, is
secret writing—the more secret, the more powerful an authorial act it is for all that,
given its unavoidable argument for one state of affairs or another.

Reviewers do not treat sociological articles as arguments; nor do they view their
own critical work as rhetorical. Instead, they assess objectively the truth-value of
articles read as scientific contributions. In particular, they assess the adequacy of the
methods used to study an aspect of the social world. Although they pay lip service
to the role of middle-range theory in concept formation necessary to conduct

research, this theorizing is clearly subordinate to the rigors of method. But this is not method read as a language game, with its own rituals and exclusions. It is method thought to be governed by incontrovertible rules of procedure that determine scientific outcomes. I prefer to view method as a way of making an argument that could be posed, and resolved, differently. Although I do not doubt that sophisticated reviewers have much to say to less-sophisticated authors about their techniques, and even about the role of middle-range theory in concept formation and problem formulation, the 150 reviews sampled here bespeak an almost universal concern for method's techniques and a universal neglect of method as a discursive strategy that conveys the appearance of science as well as science—substantive research findings. Method can be read both ways, in terms of its own internal rules of procedure and in terms of its thickness and busyness on the page, which exclude other versions that lay no less credible a claim to objectivity.

In addition to comments about method, papers' overall contributions (as a "proxy" for comments about method), literature reviews, middle-range theory, and style, reviewers also remark in passing about figures, footnotes, and authors who are said to "go beyond" their data in the conclusion/discussion section. Figures and footnotes are usually minor issues, extending method's imperial march. Figures are deemed helpful or unhelpful, usually in terms of the work they do in the methods section. "Hard to read," "useful," "unarticulated with the text" are sample comments. Detailed suggestions for revisions of figure are offered. Footnotes are rarely recommended for revision. However, it is standard fare for reviewers to recommend adding technical footnotes in order to clarify arcane methodological issues, just as it is commonplace for authors undertaking revisions to add footnotes in order to deal with reviewers' concerns. Authors account for these footnote additions in their letters to editors explaining what changes they have made in their revision, prompted by original readers' criticisms. In this sense, footnotes echo dialogue between author and reviewers, sometimes mediated by editor, in which the authorial heartbeat is to be detected. Unfortunately, footnotes are marginal to the main text, and the sort of footnotes added in response to reviewers' comments are highly technical, regarding method. As I have argued above, footnotes, like the main text of the methods sections, have become nearly figural, gesturing science in their incredible degree of methodological detail. This counteracts the dialogical potential of notes. In the best of all possible worlds, notes exemplify what Habermas calls ideal speech, allowing authors to explore the unexamined assumptions and unintended resonances of their postures and thus inviting argument—toward consensus—from readers.

ASR footnotes have never been happy hunting grounds for reflection on one's subtext. From the 1930s through the 1950s, notes mainly contained publication references for cited works. Occasionally, there were digressions and clarifications. Even from the beginning, *ASR* notes contained technical references. Rarely did notes essay the implications of the author's assumptions. With the advent of mandatory bibliographies ("references") at the end of papers, footnotes have become almost entirely technical. There has never been a golden age of notes in

American journal sociology. With the compulsory bibliography, notes have declined still further, enabling authors to respond to reviewers' fine-grained comments about method and little else. This belongs to the general trend away from page-driven and passage-driven discussion of other works and toward parenthetical citation sausages that constitute the field but do little more in the way of exploring intellectual topographies.

The final matter sometimes discussed in methods-driven article reviews is the author's tendency to "go beyond" her data. In my sample, this was mentioned in fewer than 10 percent of the reviews. This is an intriguing criticism: the author is being taken to task for having insufficient data to support her interpretations, which are usually founded in the "discussion" section of the article. The paper's methodology is insufficient to support conclusions and interpretations. Caution is urged by these reviewers, or perhaps a different research design. This is probably the only place in reviews where reviewers acknowledge—and oppose—the undecidability of social research that occurs in the important transition between the methods section and the following discussion or data analysis section of an article. This transition is, of course, a rhetorical one, moving from the gestures of method and statistics to a narrative about what the data disclose about the social world. No matter how figured the discussion section may be, no matter how tightly packed with instrumental rationality, discussions necessarily take liberty with method inasmuch as they translate method into meaning, putting words and concepts to sheer technique. (Of course, method is not sheer technique, as I have argued, but merely one discourse among many.)

I am not denying that authors can commit errors of interpretation. If someone proposes to study the impact of divorce on future earnings for both spouses and collects information about income only during the year after divorce, one cannot legitimately—that is, within the language game of method—conclude that divorce has lifetime effects on earnings. If one assays that interpretation, one can be said to have gone beyond one's data, which derive from the research design. The claim that one has gone beyond the data can only be formulated as argument within a language game that proceeds according to certain rules and engages in certain exclusions and deferrals. That is, going beyond one's data is not self-evident outside of argument, theory, method, context. One needs to make the case that collected data are not appropriate to their interpretations, which overreach them.

This notion of going beyond one's data constrains both research and theorizing. It encourages caution and discourages boldness. It also reinforces methods-driven sociology where it finds fault with essayistic, narrative treatments that extrapolate from particular results speculatively. Although constraints imposed by interpretation are derived from a language game of method, there are other language games that permit less-than-tight fit between results and interpretations, especially games that recognize the discursive nature of data, method, figure, statistics. Data, as Durkheim and other positivists view them, are frozen pieces of social history—capitalism, patriarchy, racism, the domination of nature. Thawed, these data can be viewed dialectically, as their potential to become something other through critique and action. The data must be narrated by the sociologist. This narration is always selective and subjective, no matter how strict the protocols of method may be. My point here is that data can be narrated differently, according to the interest and perspective of the narrator, who needs to take responsibility for her interpretations without simply falling back on the unexplicated notion that interpretation "goes beyond" the data at hand.

THE AUTHOR ARGUES

When an author is given a revise-and-resubmit decision, she is invited—and often required—to respond to criticisms of the first-round submission of her paper when she submits the revised version. This is copied and sent to the second round of reviewers, at least some of whom usually include people who read the paper the first time around. The author is asked to explain how she revised the paper in response to first-round reviews. Especially important is the author's account of why she decided not to make certain changes recommended by an original reviewer. Many journals instruct authors to submit the statement in multiple copies so that second-round reviewers, who are also supplied with first-round reviews, know how the author handled the first-round criticisms and suggestions for revision. Editors state explicitly that this authorial statement plays an important role in the evaluation of the resubmitted manuscript. Judging by the length and detail of many authors' statements that I culled from my sample, authors take this occasion for explanation and self-justification seriously indeed.

This communication among author, editor, and reviewers is interestingly dialogical, inviting the self-accounting of authors who situate their writing as an outcome of particular discursive choices they have made. The statements authors provide to the editor and second-round readers burst with literary presence: such accounts are usually composed in the first person. They explain authorial intent. They acknowledge disagreements among reviewers, a central issue, as we shall see later. They treat reviews as versions in their own right, disclosing the reviewer's authorial interests and perspectives. This is not to say that they are typically cavalier or dismissive. Most authors, especially junior ones, recognize that they need to come more than part way in order to placate second-round reviewers. Authors' statements frequently run to three or more single-spaced pages. Often, they list each and every criticism by reviewers and indicate what authorial "action" they have taken in order to meet or rebut these criticisms. This is often a very involved and twisted account inasmuch as most reviews are minutely methods-driven, concerning all sorts of detailed comments about the fine points of method and statistics. It is involved because the issues are fine-grained and difficult. It can be twisted because there may be much disagreement about technical details—the regression equation, how big or little the R-squareds should be, the use of dummy variables, logit, probit, pooled data. Although these can be important issues, especially where authors' technical skills lag behind the reviewers', they frequently are not cut and dried; they are murky, elusive, open to dispute. In a word, they are undecidable.

In this context, the author labors both to revise the paper in light of first-round reviews and to prepare a statement about why she did what in the way of these revisions, with specific reference to the texts of first-round reviews. The author's statement is above all an argument, an exercise in rhetoric, where she attempts to persuade both second-round reviewers and editor about the reasonableness of her revisions and, implicitly, about the overall publishability of the paper. Although one stops short of naked advocacy, the author is much more exposed in these comments than she is in the thick underbrush of the science text, whether first- or second-round, except, perhaps, in certain marginalia. Motives are acknowledged, choices defended, the paper's approach and topic justified. Successful authorial statements side-step defensiveness, meet the reviewers part way (where possible), and defend one's artifact against misunderstandings. It is difficult for a person with my dialogical agenda for a social science that would help create a democratic public sphere not to applaud the possibility of dialogue between author and reviewers. On the other hand, such dialogue coexists contradictorily with the monological, de-authored quality of science-like papers. One wonders why papers couldn't be written in the same engaged, disclosing prose as authorial statements to editors and reviewers, with the author unashamedly arguing.

Pity the poor author! She is trying to get tenure or be promoted to full professor. Selective journals such as the *ASR,* the *AJS* and *Social Forces* have acceptance rates not much higher than 10 percent of submitted manuscripts. Reviewers are technically sophisticated and often doyens of their fields. For many educators at less-than-elite public universities (and some private universities), teaching loads are rising as faculty are held "accountable," with increasing surveillance of how they use their time. Undergraduate education is at a premium, especially as state budgets erode and universities depend directly on tuition and fees as well as formula-driven state funding. In this context, a revise-and-resubmit decision from a leading journal requires many hours of tribulation and travail, both in revising the paper for second-round evaluation and in composing the author's statement. Many of the first-round reviewers' comments may seem trivial, contradictory, wrong. But certain Carnegie-classified "Research I" universities will not tenure and promote faculty in sociology without a number of "big three" journal articles in print or in press. In a competitive job market, revise-and-resubmit decisions cannot be blithely ignored, especially inasmuch as submission to another journal chews up many additional months and may result in yet another r-and-r editorial decision.

Getting published, especially at the beginning of one's career, is difficult, time-consuming, and stressful. Although one's mentors can provide valuable advice and assistance, they, too, are busy building their own careers. Authors pull out their hair in exasperation as they deal with rejection and revision. Careers and personalities self-destruct in the competitive and unforgiving world of high-octane academia. There is a certain desperation written into the tone and texture of authorial statements, as the author argues both for her revised article and for survival—publication, tenure, a livelihood, a personal and family life.

This marketplace of ideas, as John Stuart Mill called it, is heavily weighted in favor of those who are already secure—people with prestigious letterheads, ample vitae, networks, reputations, methodological expertise (or coauthors who possess it). Although junior faculty from obscure universities can and do break into the pantheon of those who publish, eventually publishing their way out of obscurity, these faculty are the exceptions, not the rules. Most faculty in the United States don't publish at all, or they publish very little. The best faculty at research universities publish in the most prestigious outlets, but others, even those who earn tenure, publish in lesser outlets—so-called second- and third-tier outlets. I have never submitted an uninvited article to a journal with the words *sociology* or *sociological* in the title. I have never submitted an article to a specialty journal in sociology, nor to an ASA dues-supported journal. I published an invited comment on Derrida in the *ASR* during Paula England's somewhat unusual editorship. (I did publish an invited paper in the graduate-student run *Berkeley Journal of Sociology,* which has little cachet except among people in theory and on the Left.) I do not lack "numeracy"(as I recall, my SAT math score was 710 or thereabouts). My father was a quantitative political scientist who littered our house with IBM cards. Many of my most productive faculty colleagues in sociology have been quantitative. My wife, a sociologist, is quantitative. I have hired, tenured, and promoted many quantitative sociologists.

I have managed to build a career around the edges of the discipline, and in commerce with other theoretically oriented disciplines such as English, comparative literature, history, and anthropology. I have published articles in the late Stanley Diamond's *Dialectical Anthropology,* a journal practically invisible to sociologists. Most of my writings are books, which only certain sociologists view as legitimate academic production. One of my former demographer colleagues told me grudgingly: "At least you get your work out the door," high praise from a person who publishes regularly in the mainstream journals. The point here is that authorial responses to reviews need to be read as if they are inflected with career-building interests, not as the accounts of people interested in the cumulative progress of bench science. Tenure, not truth, is at issue here.

My own story suggests that we all have career contingencies, whether or not we submit work to the leading empirical journals. These contingencies, such as getting or keeping a job, require survival strategies that enable us to get published. Even if we land at nonresearch universities, the crowding of disciplinary job markets in the social sciences and humanities creates "buyers' markets" in which applicants need publications in order to differentiate themselves from applicants who have not published. For empirical sociologists, getting published depends on authorial interventions with editors in responding to reviewers' comments. In the bookish social theory world, as well as in the humanities, authorial intervention may eventually involve responding to manuscript reviewers. But in the book world, publication decisions are made earlier in the process, usually after an editor scrutinizes a submitted project and then picks reviewers who she thinks will validate her initial judgment about the manuscript. Savvy authors submit to editors likely to publish their kind of work, who already know them and their track records, and who may be susceptible to influence from disciplinary brokers who introduce the author, especially the junior author. Book publishing, unlike the science-like journal world, largely dispenses with authorial and reviewer anonymity.

Authors, in dialogue with reviewers and editors, have some degree of control over the fate of their submitted work. Literary agency exists. The language games of journals and books are not seamless, although they are powerfully self-reproducing through imitation and constraints imposed by reviewers. Authors can defend themselves, their revisions, why they chose to follow or ignore certain advice. This is not a defense of the open marketplace of ideas or of the self-evident nature of quality and excellence. Good papers get rejected and bad papers published, depending on how the dice are rolled—choice of first- and second-round reviewers, editor's predilections. In the following section, I will examine how editors make decisions to publish or reject and what this tells us about the extent of an author's literary agency. The fact that authors are invited to provide accounts of how they worked from first submission to revised second submission and possibly additional submissions suggests that the marketplace of ideas is not governed by an invisible hand, driven simply by a paper's quality. Instead, submitted papers, reviews, editors' letters to author, and authors' responses to editor are all versions. They all make sense in their own terms and have blind spots, provoking other versions that correct, cajole, criticize.

Derrida suggests that all writing is somewhat deaf to itself, inhabiting a soundless space in which authors, no matter how quiet they are and how acutely they attempt to listen to themselves write, cannot fully explain the significance of what they are doing. Their versions of their versions, such as their accounts of how they revised their first-round submissions, cannot fully account for their choices without entering into infinite regress—explanations of versions requiring further explanations, endlessly. Although the language game of science and science-like sociology is wonderfully enlivened by authors' accounts of their revisions, addressed to the all-powerful editor, there is no authorial ur-text of self-explanation that can be reached through a series of revisions and accounts of revisions. Eventually, closure must be exercised. As one *ASR* editor wrote to an author who had undertaken two revisions and endured countless contradictory reviews, if an editor waited until all reviewers agreed, nothing would get published, suggesting that revising and reviewing are corrigible and not simply corrective.

Ordinary career-building authors are, of course, not in pursuit of an ur-text or subtext. They want to get published. Thus, their letters accounting for their revisions are strategically crafted to demonstrate to the editor and second-round reviewers that they were *responsive* to first-round reviews, even where this required them to fight their way out of disagreements between reviews and otherwise twist their paper into a version that attempts to please everyone but risks pleasing no one.

Responsiveness is an essential feature of dialogue. However, this is a strange dialogue in that second-round reviewers almost always include readers who did not review the paper the first time around. The author's responsiveness to first-round reviews may do nothing for second-round reviewers, who either find the first-round reviewers' comments beside the point or believe that the author, in trying to placate everyone, has fatally undermined the logic of her paper. The ineluctable undecidability of the science text is compounded by authorial responsiveness that is premised on a continuity in readership from the first round of reviews to subsequent rounds that may simply not exist.

This is not an argument against revision. Revision always revises in the direction of the public sphere in the sense that authors respond to criticisms that enable them to make their own logic of argument more accessible and, one hopes, impregnable. Revised papers have at least been read by another set of eyes, mitigating the author's loneliness. Reviewers not only correct obvious errors: misspellings, typographical errors, computational mistakes, bibliographical minutiae. They also help make the revised text more polyvocal, more responsive to actual and potential counterarguments that do not cumulate into truth but ensure that the text is a democratic language game on which a democratic polity can be premised, much as Habermas hoped. The first-round submission is not inferior to subsequent-round submissions. It is simply different, more monological, less attuned to its own aporias and blind spots.

Translation is a kind of revision, a version of versions. Adorno's (1984, 1997) *Aesthetic Theory* has been translated twice into English. The second translation intends to be more literal, capturing the fact that the original German edition was not finished or polished and hence remained unstructured into paragraphs and chapters. This is not necessarily a better translation except in the sense that it presupposes the first translation, to which it adds and from which it differentiates itself. Both are legitimate versions; both derive from a workmanlike knowledge of German and English as well as critical social theory. The second translator revises the first, building the first's version of Adorno into his own account, hence producing a version of *Aesthetic Theory* that is neither Adorno's nor the first translator's but that takes them into account, hence necessarily learning from them. The aim of translation is not to capture authorial intentionality perfectly but to produce a version that can be defended, albeit from within the perhaps quite different perspectives and tropes of one's own language. What makes the three versions of *Aesthetic Theory* interesting is their polyvocality, the dialogues they conduct or imply about the meaning of theoretical phrases. In proposing the superiority of his version, the second translator positions Adorno's wife as an arbiter, a rhetorical device that does not win the day, given the undecidability of versions, but that illuminates the endless iterability of *Aesthetic Theory.*

Why would *Aesthetic Theory* require two translations? Why would *ASR* articles require two or more revisions before publication? Imagine Adorno composing a "discussion" section compartmentalized away from the balance of the article!

Adorno was meticulous about revision, subjecting his work to intense scrutiny, believing that writing constitutes a seamless totality that is altered by even the smallest change in phrasing or structure. He wrote carefully, if against the grain of the orderly text that proceeds from assumptions to data and ends with interpretations. The allusiveness and indefiniteness of his writing was practiced, as he attempted to capture the indeterminacy of the object—late capitalism. Books such as *Aesthetic Theory* and (1973) *Negative Dialectics* traced the negative totalities of bourgeois culture and philosophy in attempts to identify their fissures and hence susceptibility to critique and transformation. Adorno, as I related earlier, even engaged in empirical research during his World War II exodus in the United States, where he worked with sociologists such as Paul Lazarsfeld on topics of mutual interest.

Adorno did not require outside readers' reports in order to hear the echoes of his own writing. He was perhaps his own most acute reader, a real gift. He could gauge his writing's impact on readers and thus anticipate potential problems of reception. This is not to say that he "wrote down" to his audience. The second translator of *Aesthetic Theory* indicates that Adorno returned to Germany after World War II partly in order to have his work published by his friend Peter Suhrkamp, the founder of Suhrkamp Verlag, Adorno's main publishing outlet, allowing him to avoid constraints imposed by the market researchers who then dominated American publishing. Adorno made few concessions to his readers. He offered no glossaries or textbook-like expositions. Like Habermas, Adorno expected his readers to have done the difficult work of mastering oeuvres of Hegel, Marx, and Freud, as well as mandarin culture. Of course, this was an unrealistic expectation for all but a few of his most accomplished readers.

The rest of us benefit from prepublication reviews, which allow us to "hear" our work more acutely. Few of us have Adorno's trained ear. The fine and useful detail of sociological article reviews helps authors revise in the direction of more capable and even more public versions, removing obstructions to understanding. This would be even more the case if editors routinely invited authors to perform "author-induced" revisions, not subject to further review, or gave them conditional acceptances, requiring only the editor's approval before publication. Although such things happen, they usually only occur after several rounds of reviews and revise-and-resubmit decisions. The more seasoned the author, the greater the likelihood that she can revise the paper successfully after first-round reviews, accommodating the suggestions of first-round reviewers and presenting a plausible case for her revision strategies in the author's statement. More junior authors may labor through many reviews and multiple revisions before the editor says that enough is enough and the author has the final cut.

Revision can be viewed as a central ethos of the idea of a self-correcting community of science. Or it can be viewed as a process of producing a more polyvocal version, anticipating readers' responses and thus being clearer about one's argument so that differences with real or imagined readers will be addressed forcefully instead of burying one's assumptions in the subtext of marginalia. It can be both of these things, but it rarely is, because the ethos of science is so strong that polyvocality gets subordinated to truth, or what passes for truth in the quality control process of mainstream sociological journals. I seriously doubt that more than a small handful of mainstream sociological empiricists would subscribe to Derrida's notion of textual undecidability, if they knew what he meant by it. For them, the objectivity of science is patent, even if they acknowledge that methodological immaturity may mean that sociologists require decades of bench science before sociology can legitimately aspire to be called social physics. As such, I doubt that many sociologists view reviews simply as versions that add themselves to the text of the revised paper as interlocutors but not as correctives in the tribunal of objectivist epistemology.

EDITORS' WORK: UNDECIDABILITY AND THE PUBLICATION DECISION

The author who has been invited to revise and resubmit writes the editor what is, in effect, a letter explaining why she has made certain revisions and not others (and, often, how she has dealt with contradictory advice proffered by first-round reviewers). That letter responds to a letter the author has already received from the editor, explaining the initial publication decision in light of the reviews at hand. In the example I mentioned above, a young author submitted a manuscript to the *ASR* during the tenure of a previous editor. After obtaining three reviews, the editor wrote the author a letter informing him that he was being given a revise-and-resubmit decision. The reviewers offered conflicting appraisals of the paper, with one praising it and the others finding room for revision. The author revised the paper and sent the editor a detailed account of how he dealt with the first-round criticisms. After receiving reviews (some from new reviewers, some from original reviewers), the editor gave the paper a second revise-and-resubmit decision. Before the author could revise the paper again, a new editor came on board. In an unusual move, the author sent the first-round and second-round reviews to this editor and asked for advice about how to deal with the contradictory reviews. After a month, the new editor wrote back, offering the author some general advice about how to deal with matters of revision. The author then revised the paper and received third-round reviews. At least one of the third-round reviewers was new, not having seen the paper in the first or second round. When the author submitted his revision, he sent the editor a very lengthy and detailed account of how he had addressed the second-round reviews. The third-round reviews were still indecisive, with one reviewer recommending publication and the other two holding out for additional revisions. On the basis of all this, the new editor finally accepted the paper conditionally. That is, the new editor informed the author that his paper was accepted on the condition that he address and attempt to integrate third-round recommendations for revision. The new editor promised not to have the paper reviewed again but said that her own appraisal of the author's responsiveness to the third-round reviews would suffice. At long last, the paper was published.

As I said above, all of the reviews and attendant correspondence totaled fifty-three single-spaced pages, much longer than the paper itself. It is a particularly dense text in that the reviewers in both rounds have substantial disagreements about the merits of the paper. The author, scrambling to earn tenure in a department that expects articles to have been published in the *ASR,* the *AJS,* and/or *Social Forces,* went to heroic lengths to explore the details of the reviews, seeking safe passage through the minefields of their contradictions. My reading convinces me that the paper would probably not have been published if the author had not done such a thorough and rhetorically skilled job of responding to reviewers in his five-page statement covering his resubmitted paper. Even at that, one of the second-round reviewers suggested that the author had not made all of the changes promised in his authorial statement, in effect deconstructing the authorial statement as a slick job of salesmanship.

What makes this "case study" so intriguing is that this is one of the few *ASR* papers published during the 1990s that breaks the standard mold. Although it is sub-divided in the usual way, literature review leading to methods and then discussion, the author presents no figured data but instead offers a theoretically informed analysis of an important social organization in U.S. society. Offering neither quantitative data, figures, nor a literature review that suggests stable consensus among scholars in the field, the author does qualitative research in order to advance the development of neo-Marxist social theory. Perhaps for this reason the author ran into difficulty with reviewers who could not agree about the merits of the article. These six reviews are among the most passionate in my sample, frequently engaging in hyperbole to criticize or praise the author. I should also add that the paper was accepted by an editor known to have a somewhat iconoclastic view of the discipline and of journal discourse, having read widely in theory and outside of her own empirical specialty areas.

I obtained this thick file of reviews and letters between author and editor by asking the author for it. I first met the author when my former department interviewed him for a tenure-track job in the 1980s. I found his work interesting, and supported his hiring. I have followed his career from a distance, noting that he has published in mainstream sociology journals. Occasionally, we meet and chat at ASA annual meetings. In my reading of journal discourse for this book, I noticed his most recent *ASR* article as a rare departure from form for that outlet. Although I had read some of this author's earlier work, I was unprepared for the mold-breaking nature of this article. In this spirit, I asked him for the file of reviews and letters. I should also add that my former department was quite split about his tenure-track job candidacy. Some of us felt that he did solid and theoretically informed empirical research of the kind that had come to be typical of his doctoral department at Kansas. Others said that he lacked quantitative indicators, as one of my former colleagues put it, and thus could not be said to engage in mainstream empirical research. His critics predicted that he would fail to have his work published in the leading journals!

In the meantime, he found his first job at a college with a high teaching load and few research aspirations, followed by a stint at a utilitarian urban university, albeit in a city with character and a major-league baseball team. Toiling at these institutions for six years, he published well, eventually winning a job offer from a much better university, at which he eventually earned tenure, undoubtedly on the strength of his mainstream publications. The author has two *ASR* articles to his credit and numerous other publications. He has also been rejected by the *ASR,* as have many others. He has published a book summarizing his research agenda to date. Clearly, his career is going well. He has experienced more successes than failures. He works hard, as this thick file on a single *ASR* submission demonstrates.

Fully thirteen pages of this thick file of reviews and letters are devoted to this author's two responses to the first- and second-round reviews. Not only must the author fend off detailed criticisms, acknowledging reasonable ones and arguing against unreasonable ones. He must also make sense of the contradictoriness of positive and negative comments, which abound in these reviews. He takes the unusual step of writing the new *ASR* editor before he undertakes a third revision precisely because he wants guidance in dealing with these two rounds of reviews. Perhaps because I am overly cynical about mainstream sociology and the publishing world in general, I was quite surprised that the new editor responded, in a lengthy and thoughtful letter. Her letter not only addressed issues of substance. She also empathized with the author, who had by then done two arduous revisions and was now being asked by the outgoing editor to do a third. In what I count as a classic phrase, the new editor concedes to the author that one of the reviewers, who the author claims does not understand his paper, is simply "dense," not a typical *ASR* adjective! The editor probably does not believe that the reviewer is simply dense but rather wants the author to think about how the paper might be made clearer for a reader who does not appear to "get it."

After all of this, the author undertakes a third major revision of his paper. He does not want to waste the time and effort already expended, and he wants to vindicate himself, demonstrating that his work is important in the field of the critical sociology of organizations. Two of the crucial issues in evaluating the paper are whether the case study of a large firm can be generalized and what the theoretical status of the issues involved really is. The author argues for his imaginative use of the case study and for a critical perspective on private-sector manufacturing firms that does not recant important Marxist insights about the centralization of power and authority in late capitalism. The author rejects the notion that the era of so-called "flexible accumulation" in "disorganized capitalism" somehow augurs greater decentralization of managerial control. His case study of the firm is meant to demonstrate this. The author does not give ground on these two central issues, although he was willing to make many changes both to clarify his argument and to sharpen the focus of the paper.

I have already indicated that much is at stake in the interesting conversation among author, reviewers, and editor—a first job, tenure, promotion, salary raises, one's career. To be sure, science is at stake too. But this is not the science of myth, with hypothesis testing proceeding objectively and findings subject to replication such that every competent reader will be able to appraise the quality of the work indisputably. This is a cacophonous science, with multiple versions everywhere. Journal sociology is thoroughly Derridean, with undecidable versions of articles, reviews, and authorial accounts proliferating and requiring editors to employ their own perspective-ridden judgment as they make publication decisions. Authors and reviewers argue and editors adjudicate, building careers and establishing disciplinary canons. Here I want to consider editorial agency, which is ample, not as a marginal factor brought to bear only on occasion, when reviewers disagree, but as a constitutional factor in editing and publishing, influencing virtually everything that transpires once work is submitted. Editing is practice, proceeding according to contextualized judgments that take place within language games, not transcendentally, with sheer disinterest. Editors *author*, both the publication decisions they make, the letters to authors they compose, and even the revised articles they eventually publish. This is not to overdetermine the editorial process, vesting it with immense authority, as a positivist conspiracy; that ignores nuance and difference. For example, the recent open-minded *ASR* editor who empathizes with beleaguered authors, publishes mold-breaking non-positivist work, uses words such as *dense* in her letters to authors, and even publishes work on Derrida that not only reverses the momentum of disciplinary positivism but acknowledges the perspectival nature of journal discourse, thus abandoning closure as a realistic goal. And in the future, journals can be edited in ways that democratize author-ity, not being embarrassed by textual undecidability but instead embracing it as an occasion of a talkative public sphere in which the good is talk and all non-positivist talk is good.

Editors memorialize publication decisions in the letters they send to authors announcing the decisions and then copy to reviewers, who are viewed as interested parties in dialogue. Most of the journal editors in my sample, including the *ASR*, write letters that are partly formulaic—"I am delighted to accept your article"— and partly idiosyncratic. These letters are readings of readings, an activity that occupies much of an editor's time. Although the editor encloses the reviews along with her decision letter to the author, the editor glosses the reviews in summarizing prevailing sentiment and perhaps exploring some of the deficiencies and merits of the article. These letters are crucial when they announce revise-and-resubmit decisions. In these letters, the editor tells the reader where the paper has problems; how she may disagree with certain things said by the reviewers, especially where the reviewers offer contradictory appraisals; what general revision strategies the author may want to adopt; and, finally, in this litigious age the editor may estimate the probability that the paper will be published, making clear that the revise-and-resubmit decision, however encouraging, is not a commitment to publish. The estimation of probabilities may well reflect official data kept by the journal on the fate of first-round and revised submissions.

Although editors attempt to ground their publication decisions firmly in the reviews themselves, for example in the case of uniformly bad or good reviews, this rhetorical strategy fails when reviewers disagree. The case study of the industrial firm that is also my case study here involves disagreement among reviewers in all three rounds of reviews. Consensus is totally absent. I suspect that this is so because the author has written a nontraditional article in which he not only eschews the use of survey data, having a sample of only one firm, but also, as an ideologically attentive and theoretically oriented sociologist, the author takes pains to disclose his own investments. These investments, in one or another version of the neo-Marxist sociology of organizations, are precisely what make the article so interesting, where the author attempts to pierce the ideological illusions of managerial decentralization with reference to his own ethnography of decision making in the firm. The readers not only fault, and praise, the author's execution of an argument viewed within his own language game. The negative reviewers also take issue with the whole language game, arguing that the author has fatally neglected intellectual developments in non-Marxist sociology that undermine or trivialize his own findings and his interpretation of them.

Confronted with such rampant disagreement both about theoretical and technical issues, the earlier *ASR* editor asked for two revisions, reflecting indecisiveness about how to handle the lack of consensus among reviewers. The exasperated author appealed to the new editor for guidance before he began the third revision. The new editor obtained third-round reviews. One was very positive, but the other two saw room for improvement in the paper. At this point, the editor accepted the paper conditionally, asking the author to perform yet another revision, but without the threat of external review. The editor herself would determine whether the author had made a good-faith effort to placate the still-negative reviewers, and, if he had, she would publish the paper. This is when the editor told the author that if she waited until all reviewers agreed about everything of substance, she would publish nothing. What we have here, then, is an unconventional paper that underwent three rounds of review, none of which produced consensus among reviewers. Reading through the nine reviews done in all three rounds of evaluation, it is difficult to imagine the paper ever receiving unanimous support or opposition from diverse readers with their own strong investments in the sociology of organizations. In this light, it is easy to see how the new editor dealt with what I would call the undecidability of language games—here, the language game of evaluation—in putting a halt to the evaluation process (in a direction favorable to the author).

Reviews are undecidable because they are rhetorical; they argue, for or against certain positions taken by the author. By *positions* I may mean nothing more than methodological techniques, which are also undecidable, admitting of no final and objective resolution. Like sociological articles, reviews are written in the tone of indubitable objectivity: reviewers declare the truth about method, theory, and literature reviews without necessarily disclosing their own investments that condition their judgment. Three reviewers may make different assumptions about truth and method, and hence produce different readings of submitted work. Although editors can resolve the incommensurability of reviewers' language games simply by counting heads, as the *ASR* editor herself admits, this would seldom produce unanimity about issues regarded as central by the reviewers or even by the editor, who, at the end of the day, asks reviewers for thumbs up or down on submitted papers.

The 150 reviews in the sample evidenced a surprising lack of consensus about submitted work. Although sometimes they agreed in their ultimate recommendations, more often than not there was a split recommendation, requiring the editor to make the final determination. Of course, the editor makes not only the final determination about submitted work but also the first determination inasmuch as she selects reviewers, sometimes with the help of others, such as members of an editorial board. This is not to imply that busy editors always have clear-cut intellectual agendas that they advance by choosing reviewers who, they suspect, will produce predictable outcomes and thus allow the editor to steer the journal in a given direction—more or less quantitative, feminist, macrosociological. Having edited myself, I suspect that editors' assumptions about what constitutes good work inform their evaluations and decisions at the margin: they favor "their" kind of work in small ways, not out of naked favoritism but in the care they give to papers from kindred spirits. These papers are perhaps more likely to have like-minded reviewers chosen for them; they are more likely to receive revise-and-resubmit decisions; and revised papers are more likely to be published. I suspect that many editors do not acknowledge to themselves their investment in a positivist language game but allow such investments subtly, and for that reason powerfully, to influence their decisions, thus reproducing positivist hegemony in the journal world and discipline.

Editors exercise literary agency where they resolve disputes among reviewers and between reviewers and author. They also exercise agency in the letters they write to authors guiding them in their revisions. Some editors are more directive than others. I read multipage letters from recent sociological journal editors in which they pore over the reviews with attention to fine detail and offer their own perspectives on which of the many readers' comments are to be followed in the revision. From my sample, it appears that the greater the editor's involvement in mediating first-round reviews, for example the longer and more detailed the editor's letter to author announcing the revise-and-resubmit decision and offering guidance in revision, the greater the likelihood that the paper will be accepted eventually. The editor's investment of time, effort, and attention in effect incorporates the editor as a coauthor (and the author as a coeditor). There is great variation in the extent to which editors involve themselves directively in interpreting reviews for authors and thus stipulating appropriate paths of revision. There is variation across editors, some being more directive than others. There is variation in a given editor's involvement in particular papers.

I found that editors are more involved in papers close to their own interests. Although this is an almost irresistible temptation to which we all might succumb— I know that I have in my editorial work—this is one of the subtle ways in which editors in effect author the direction of their journals. If submitted papers in editors' areas of interest are more likely to receive their editorial attention in the revision process, and if papers that command their attention are more likely to be published eventually, given the editor's investment in them, the fact that an editor is known to work in particular areas almost destines that journal to move in her intellectual direction. There is another factor at play here: authors who work in the editor's area are more likely to submit to that journal, suspecting that they will receive a sympathetic hearing, appropriate reviewer choice, and prudent adjudication of reviews. Finally, editors are more likely to know personally scholars who work in their area, conditioning the readings they give papers and reviews. I found that when editors address authors by their first name, papers are more likely to be accepted. Or more strictly, editors are likely to use authors' first names when they write them acceptance letters, suggesting that they already know them.

These processes are, of course, not seamless. Friends reject friends; people who work in the editor's area have their work rejected; certain editors bend over backward not to favor like-minded work; editors reject papers in which they get heavily involved. What is crucial to recognize here is that editorial discretion plays a very important role in what gets published both because there is rarely consensus among reviewers, giving the lie to a process of consensus-based normal science, and because reviews do not speak for themselves but must be interpreted. In another theoretical language, reviews are undecidable, no less undecidable than submitted papers. That is, they cannot simply be read in a commonsense way without reference to authorizing assumptions, passions, perspectives, politics. They are versions that call forth other versions, for example editors' letters to authors, in an endless process of iteration. As the recent *ASR* editor admitted to my bruised but indefatigable case-study author, the recalcitrant reviewer may in fact be dense! Although that editor did not have a hand in picking that particular reviewer, who was a holdover from the preceding editorship, even one's own reviewers may be dense, failing to work within the paper's language game in attempting to evaluate it in its own terms.

This brings us to what is perhaps the most perplexing part of reviewing. Authors everywhere, in the book as well as journal worlds, bristle at reviewers who appear to want the author to write a different sort of work, perhaps the work the reviewer herself would have written. Reviewing is undecidable because reviewers may not respect the author's language game, or even understand it as a language game governed by certain rules of inclusion and exclusion that render it incommensurable with the reviewer's game. Clearly, in the example of my case-study author working in the field of the sociology of organization, with the fifty-three-page dossier of reviews and letters, a significant number of his negative reviews came from people who wanted a different kind of paper, not the paper he was trying to write.

Productive academics tend to be control freaks who cannot imagine academic work being done except in the way they do it. Perhaps cosmopolitanism, which not only tolerates but appreciates difference, counteracts disciplinary professionalism in this way. Many professionals would probably profess cosmopolitan values, such as the appreciation of diverse methods and theories. But when it comes to the crunch and they write reviews of papers within their fields that use different approaches from theirs, professionalism takes over and they find fault, in effect urging the authors to write a different kind of paper altogether.

Certain editors who edit with a light hand have theorized this issue of cosmopolitanism, perhaps even linking it to the notion of a polyvocal public sphere in which intellectual differences are both acknowledged and celebrated. Editors need to ask themselves whether they are willing to publish competent work by their intellectual opponents—a critical theorist publishing game theory, an interactionist publishing demography, a rational-choice sociologist publishing antiquantitative versions of feminist theory. Although it is difficult to be selected as an editor in open competitions, often sponsored by professional associations such as the ASA, without an intellectual agenda, this agenda need not exclude other language games, methods, theories, topics, literary styles. But the tension between disciplinary professionalism and (call it) cosmopolitanism makes it very difficult for editors known to be both mold-breaking and polyvocal to acquire significant editorships. Instead, these posts usually go to visible disciplinary professionals known to have strong investments in the positivist language game, even if they claim to be open to diverse work styles. No matter how open they say they are or think they are, professionals tend to want papers to be written in their image. Their strong investment in the language game of their particular work style probably helped them publish and become recognized as opinion makers in the discipline, eventually leading them to be selected as editors.

In my sample, virtually all editors were required to make judgment calls in resolving disputes between reviewers. Some editors strongly intervened in resolving these disputes, giving authors quite directive advice about appropriate revision strategies, while others let authors find their own ways. When editors gave directive advice, they were more likely to accept subsequent revisions. At the same time, they shaped the intellectual agenda of their journal where they played a significant role in guiding the revision of submitted work. Interestingly, although certain editors in my sample at certain times wrote detailed, lengthy letters to authors that suggested appropriate revision strategies, few editors appear to engage in what old-style book editors call line editing, taking a blue pencil to the text in order to improve style and sense. The sociology journal editors in my sample rarely even mentioned style in their letters to authors, except where they may have suggested cutting the length of the paper in subsequent revisions. There was one prominent exception, involving a former editor of the feminist outlet *Gender and Society*. And my own experience with theory journals and certain book publishers suggests that line editing, while uncommon in empirical social science journal editing, has not disappeared entirely.

How frequently did editors in my sample accept papers recommended for rejection by the majority of the reviewers? In the example of my case-study article, as I have already mentioned, a majority of the third-round reviewers still found ample room for revision. But the editor accepted the paper anyway, deciding to put the author, who had worked diligently in revising and then in accounting for his reasons, out of his ill-deserved misery. Although in my sample most accepted papers were supported by a majority of positive reviews, even if only the common slim majority of two "for" and one "against," a significant minority of papers involved acceptances based on a majority of negative or equivocal reviews. Reviews do not sort neatly into the positive and negative, even though most of the journals in my sample asked the reviewer to offer the editor private advice about whether to accept, invite a revision, or reject. Although this enabled the editor to count heads in toting up the number of reviewers for and against publication, in reality reviews were often more nuanced, combining both praise and criticism and thus implicitly leaving the editor room to move. I do not know of a single American sociology journal that formally requires a majority of reviewers to recommend acceptance before articles are, in fact, accepted for publication. Nor do I know of an American sociology journal that has a formal policy requiring a certain number of reviews per submission. In my sample, I was struck by variation in the extent to which a given editor would make a publication decision on the basis of two, three, four, or more reviews. I even found an instance where a regional journal accepted a paper based on a single review. In this case, and, I presume, in other cases, in-house reviewing and vetting took place, with the editor and members of the editorial board offering advice about publishability.

I edited a theory annual for five years, receiving sixty or more submissions per year, some of which were invited. After rejecting papers that were clearly not theoretical at all, according to my conception of theorizing, I reviewed everything else that was submitted. Even though some papers were clearly, to my initial reading, rejects, I viewed it as a professional courtesy to the author, perhaps a junior initiate, to obtain helpful reviews that would show the way toward profitable rethinking and revision. At the other extreme, certain papers were, at face value, likely to be accepted, given the polished state of the submitted draft, the significance of the argument, and the timeliness of the topic. The author's reputation reliably predicted whether the paper was likely to fall into this category. Here, reviews helped authors polish. Papers that did not fall into these two categories were papers whose fate would be largely, if not entirely, determined by reviews. If the theoretical approach used in a paper was quite foreign to me, for example a paper using formal modeling, reviews would help me decide whether to publish. Certain papers, although showing obvious potential upon my initial reading, needed a good deal of additional work to bring them to publishability. In these cases, I would seek as many reviews as possible in order to help the author work through these issues.

I usually made definitive judgments at the front end, refusing to put authors through revision processes that were unlikely to produce acceptable papers. I probably gave fewer revise-and-resubmit decisions than do many mainstream sociology journals. At the other end, though, I was quite nondirective, allowing smart authors to determine the extent to which their revisions would be guided by first-round reviewers' criticisms and suggestions. I never put papers through second-round reviews, exercising closure before we got to that point. Notable to me was how frequently reviewers known to me to be scrupulous and productive scholars would disagree about the merits of a paper, suggesting, again, that reviewers, like authors and editors, are ensconced in their own language games and sometimes have difficulty "transcoding" foreign work into their own frame of reference. This would lead reviewers, however well intentioned, to expect authors to write different papers than they intended to write, requiring me as editor to re-transcode their potentially useful substantive suggestions into the author's original language game. Much of my time was spent in this re-transcoding work, protecting authors from expectations that they write impossibly different papers while allowing my reviewers' ample intelligence and erudition to assist in revision that did not violate the paper's original intent.

When I invited revisions, I allowed authors to make author-induced changes, not forcing them to average the reviewers' criticisms toward a version that pleased no one. Although this risked authors' arrogant imperviousness to reviewers' suggestions, I found that most authors, especially junior ones, conscientiously took reviews into account when they did revisions. And senior authors needed to revise less, given their literary experience. Even when I accepted a paper after the first round of reviews, I asked authors to consider the reviews carefully in making author-induced revisions. At this point, I would offer advice about length, style, and even substance, based on the first-round reviews and on my reading of the paper. Theorists have few publication outlets for article-length work. As a result, I found most authors willing to write and revise in good faith, grateful for the opportunity to publish. Perhaps my greatest challenge as editor was to discipline myself not to rewrite all the papers, especially those in critical theory! My perspective as a sometime-Derridean allowed me to recognize the inherent undecidability of texts and thus to treat papers, revisions, reviews, and my own comments on papers as versions susceptible to endless reworking. I chose to view this reworking not as "getting it right" but as an undercurrent of the public sphere in which dialogue chances are roughly equal and in which people intend to build consensus out of difference, as Habermas has suggested. Although I had no illusion that the annual series *Current Perspectives in Social Theory* (*CPST*), founded by the Kansas theorist Scott McNall, was visible on the disciplinary radar screen, let alone the societal one, I hoped that the people who wrote and reviewed for *CPST* constituted a body politic of sorts—people in theory who do not publish in the mainstream outlets and who crossed disciplinary boundaries in doing French- and German-inspired critical theory and cultural studies.

7

Was Sociology Always Like This?

THE PREHISTORY OF SCIENTIFIC SOCIOLOGY: 1938–1968

The preceding analysis of contemporary mainstream sociology discourse, especially as reflected in the *American Sociological Review* (*ASR*) during the 1990s, begs the question "Can sociology be written differently?" Before I answer that question in my next chapter, I pose a prior question—*Has* sociology been written differently in the United States? That is the topic of this chapter, which is an analysis of changes in *ASR* discourse from 1938 to 1988. I went back one decade at a time, beginning with 1988, in sampling the texts of various *ASR* articles. Of paramount concern here is whether *ASR* discourse was always so methods-driven, especially in its approach to literature review, scientific cumulation, the use of figure, and marginalia. To my surprise, I found that the *ASR* became highly methods-driven only quite recently, although this is not to say that it lacked positivist underpinnings, even in the early years. In this chapter, I report on the prehistory of scientific sociology in order to prepare the way for a discussion of how we should rethink our approaches to sociological discourse.

There are a number of good institutional histories of American sociology. Perhaps the best recent account is provided by Turner and Turner in *The Impossible Science*. In many ways, their study parallels this book, especially in its sensitivity to issues of scientificity. They focus mainly on the history of the American Sociological Society (ASS), later to become the American Sociological Association (ASA), and on the history of extramural support for American sociologists. Their account of the Comteanism of early U.S. sociologists such as Small, Giddings, and Sumner suggests that American sociology was never without pretensions to be a science, although Turner and Turner nicely describe the shift in nuance from the reformist Chicago sociology of the 1930s to the methods-oriented sociology of the present.

Their study, a sociology of sociology in the best sense, underscores the fact that even the earliest American sociologists contended, with Comte, that sociology should aspire to be a science of society, seeking laws of social motion. This was coupled, until after World War II, with an "ameliorism" that sought to solve social problems especially related to industrialization and urbanization. Turner and Turner make much of the fact that American sociology moved away from reform toward science, especially after World War II, when the state funded social scientists and institutionalized sociology grew rapidly, both in the professional associations and the universities (also see Sjoberg and Vaughan 1993). They trace the decline of sociology after about 1975, when student interest in the major and in doctorates began to decline and when universities began to contract, especially in the social sciences. By the mid-1990s, there had been an upturn in both undergraduate and graduate student interest in sociology and a revitalization of the tenure-track faculty job market. It may be that sociology is reemerging as an appealing part of the general education curriculum, offering useful lessons about multiculturalism, ethnic diversity, problems of families, drugs, crime, and other topics of societal concern. After the fragmentation of sociology led to the loss of "specialty areas" such as social work and criminology, which became institutionally autonomous fields, and even departments and programs of their own, weakening sociology's position in the university, sociology is making up lost ground by again stressing a social-problems orientation, both in undergraduate pedagogy and grantworthy research activities.

As we explore the changes in sociological discourse since the 1930s, and there have been significant ones, we need to keep in mind that a scientific, law-seeking sociology has been a recurrent goal since the first sociologies of Small and Giddings. Following Comte, most 1930s sociologists, like contemporary sociologists, believed that sociology should position itself as a lawful science, assembling social facts into general patterns of sociation. What earlier sociologists and then Parsons termed general theory was to summarize laws adduced by busy empiricists who contributed their studies to a cumulating canon of disciplinary knowledge. American sociology has been positivist from the beginning. Having said this, it is also important to recognize differences in presentation and perspective since the 1930s, especially as reflected in the ways in which sociologists composed their journal articles. A 1938 *ASR* article differed in more than cosmetic ways from a 1998 article, if not in commitment to social physics then in the posture struck by the author toward her own literary involvement in the text. Indeed, the *ASR* was rhetorically different, containing rather different components and literary devices than the *ASR* of today. The *ASR* only began to resemble the densely gestural text it is today in the late 1960s and early 1970s, a significant threshold in the discipline's discursive politics.

In 1938, the program of the annual meeting of the American Sociological Society was published in the marginalia of the *ASR*. The meeting was held in Detroit between Christmas and New Year's. It was not a voluminous schedule by today's standards. Many of the participants—Lundberg, Parsons—have become revered figures in the discipline. There is even notice of hotel rates and airline arrangements. A single room at the downtown convention hotel cost all of $3, with a double room costing $4. Less expensive Detroit hotels are also listed. Not only was the program of the ASS annual meeting published in the *ASR*. Until the 1950s, the *ASR* also sported extensive book reviews, research notes, symposia on important issues, debates, and even notices about ASS members—new jobs, promotions, deaths. By the standards of today's *ASR,* the *ASR* of yesteryear was downright chatty, seemingly open to all comers, as long as they were white and male. The journal was less a document of scientific cumulation—for example, papers were not preceded by abstracts until the 1950s—than a gathering point for issues and events of disciplinary relevance.

My study of journal sociology since 1938 suggests both that the discipline of U.S. sociology was positivist from the beginning, judging by the declarations authors made about objectivity and lawfulness, and that only quite recently, in response to sociology's loss of institutional prestige, in the 1970s, has the *ASR* come to resemble a science journal. In the *ASR*'s earlier decades, the writing was essay-istic, dialogical, and replete with authorial presence. Only recently has figure come to dominate the journal page, although rudimentary figures, hand drawn in India ink with the x and y axes labeled in typescript, could be found in the thirties and forties. In the meantime, the 2×2 table has given way to high mathematics as soci-ologists attempt to produce the science aura. In the early days, sociologists claimed that their work was scientific. Today, claims of science give way to gestures demonstrating what is thought to pass for science, notably the eclipse of prose by figure and gesture. Although in one sense this has not changed things, most soci-ologists being positivist both yesterday and today, it has signaled important changes in the ways sociologists compose themselves. The *ASR* of yesteryear, which ended only recently, was more accessible, more literary, more disclosing about deep assumptions than the *ASR* of the 1990s.

In a word, early journal sociology, extending to the end of the 1960s and per-haps even somewhat beyond, was not methods-driven. Nor, as we shall see shortly, was journal sociology premised on the model of connection with/differentiation from a prevailing literature, on the model of scientific cumulation. Methods have become the intellectual driving force only in the past twenty years, with rapid accel-eration since about the mid-1980s, with the growing mathematization of journal discourse. We see this in a variety of ways. In what one could call the prehistoric period, from the 1930s through the 1960s, mathematical notation was rarely used. Figures intending to represent the world in a nature-like way were only occasional. Prose dominated articles, and even footnotes. Figure was not yet in the saddle. This is not to suggest that quantitative methods are totally absent in this prehistoric period. Even in the 1930s, journal articles boasted tables and graphs, summarized data quan-titatively, and employed inferential and descriptive statistics. At no time in the period covered was American sociology not quantitatively oriented, which is unsurprising, given the dominance of positivist aspirations since Giddings. But these methods were not presented as gestures in the articles; they were integrated into the article, explained, and explicated, allowing the reader to understand them in a larger con-text of prose and preventing articles from being dominated by technique.

Prehistoric sociology shows that one can deploy quantitative (and qualitative) method and still write comprehensibly and allow one's work to be driven by intel-lectual, not technical, interests. The freedom from method of prehistoric sociology is quite striking for those who go back and read these early articles. Even into the 1950s and 1960s, when one would frequently find regression coefficients reported, the use of quantitative method in *ASR* articles was far from obscurantist. In fact, it was just the opposite: one finds real efforts by methodologically sophisticated authors to make sense of their techniques for an uninitiated audience and to lay bare the assumptions underlying their methods. At the same time, as one traces the prehistory of methods in American sociology, one can read these earlier articles as laying the foundation for the "mature" methods-driven sociology of the contemporary period in that, even in the 1930s, authors figured their work, albeit in rudimentary ways, and spent considerable time describing their research protocols.

There is a second striking feature of this prehistoric sociology, in addition to the substantive, and not simply methodological, focus of articles. Until the 1970s, the notion of the literature review was nearly absent. To be sure, virtually all articles referred readers to other studies, some of which were discussed in footnotes. But articles did not begin with elaborate literature reviews that grounded the article in a cumulative body of scholarship—a field, as I have called it. These simply did not exist in prehistoric sociology because, I contend, sociologists, albeit positivist in their epistemological leanings, did not view their work as piecemeal contributions to bench science in the fashion of the natural sciences. The early sociologists conducted empirical research and believed that social facts exist independent of the researcher and can be understood objectively, without elaborate conceptual mediations. They also believed that sociology reasonably sought laws of social motion, in the spirit of Comte. But they did not view their own work as deriving from a focused literature or canon, to be cited parenthetically at the beginning of the article. This is a literary technique introduced only in the last thirty years. Before that, articles began with brief substantive discussions of the problem at hand, for example in one 1938 article the subject of elopement, and then moved directly to discussions of the research methods used in the study.

It is also important to observe that the discussions of method were short and nontechnical, by contemporary standards. They were not larded with caveats, technical asides, digressions, quibbles about proxy variables and missing values. It is not enough to conclude that this is simply because sociological method was yet in its infancy, an argument preferred by methodological modernization theorists, who view yesteryear as primitive—a world of 2×2 tables, IBM cards, mainframe computers. Progress may have improved technical skills; after all, as I said earlier, doctoral students now take several methods and statistics courses before they earn their union cards. But the refusal of the early sociologists to substitute method for argument is not owed to method's primitive state as much as a commitment to narrativity—to the notion that sociology is writing, if not all writing sociological. The single columns of discursive, dialectical prose found in *ASR* articles of the 1930s and 1940s suggest a literariness that could have survived the mathematization of method beginning in the 1970s. After all, the early sociologists crunched numbers too, albeit slowly, by hand, without the aid of the computer chip. Advances in technique did not require latter-day sociologists to abandon the discursiveness of early sociology. This abandonment was occasioned by institutional changes in American sociology, notably sociology's decline in the university, and in the choices made by individual sociologists, who sought to build careers by repeating the prevailing norms. How many sociologists trained since 1975 have even read journal sociology from earlier eras?

Although mainly positivist, sociology from 1938 to 1968 refused the hegemony of method. This began to change when sociology fell upon hard times during the 1970s, with cuts in funding and declining numbers of undergraduate majors, graduate students, and tenure-track job opportunities. I have argued that the de-narrativization of sociology, its methodological compulsions, came about largely as a response to the institutional crisis of sociology documented by Turner and Turner. Sociologists scrambled to shore up a declining discipline with a fixation on methods, thus, they contended, imitating the natural sciences (and hopefully imitating their successes too). This turn toward method, for the first time in the history of American sociology, counterposed itself to the politicization of some sociology during the social movements of the 1960s, claiming sobriety through science at a time when sociologists were beginning to have hard times finding jobs, grants, tenure.

Method, especially mathematics, was conceived as a solution to the institutional decline of sociology. The rise of methods-driven articles in the *ASR* coincides almost exactly with the downturn in sociology student majors, graduate enrollments, and funding opportunities during the 1970s. I suspect that a survey of changes in graduate curricula in sociology during that decade would indicate methodological retrenchment as theory and qualitative sociology were increasingly blamed for the institutional troubles of sociology, including, in particular, the demise of sociology at Washington University. This resort to method as a panacea for sociology's decline gathered momentum during the 1980s and 1990s, as journal sociology became even more mathematized, figural, gestural. Ironically, at the same time, an intellectual revolution swept the humanities as European developments in interpretive, cultural, and critical theory replaced the New Criticism and politicized both graduate programs and publication outlets (see Fekete 1978; Ross 1989; Watkins 1989). At the margins, these intellectual developments have begun to affect the social sciences, including sociology. This is why postmodernism has proven so scandalous to mainstream sociological empiricists, who breathed a sigh of relief as the conflict-oriented 1960s were surpassed. These Midwestern empiricists do not welcome the return of an agitational and theoretically driven social science, bordering on the humanities, indebted not to C. Wright Mills but to Derrida and the Frankfurt School, fearing that this will only retard sociology's attempt to resurrect itself as a serious science.

Were it not for these developments in critical and cultural theory, a study such as this would be impossible. Until the French postmodern theorists and the German critical theorists transformed the ways in which we look at textuality, few, even within the Gouldner-inspired tradition of the sociology of sociology, examined disciplinary discourse as a contested terrain. This new approach, largely owed to

European inspiration and intellectual resources, reads disciplinary writing for buried and explicit assumptions about the nature of its subject matter—for its ontology, in different terms. Methods-driven sociology is especially quiet about its investments, given its technical approach to solving intellectual problems. Of course, technical sociologists do not have much patience for meta-analysis of this kind, viewing it as intellectually irrelevant and perhaps even downright seditious, given the alleged need for sociology's legitimation in the academy and beyond.

I harbor no illusions about the ontology of the 1930s to 1960s sociologists. Most of them, following Comte, Durkheim, and parts of Weber, wanted to put sociology on a scientific footing, seeking cause-and-effect understandings of the social. But their approaches to sociological narrativity eschewed method's displacement of substance; the prehistoric sociologists solved intellectual problems with arguments, not techniques. This narrative approach could be a model for future sociologists, even if the overall positivist project is particularly problematic. One can subscribe to a positivist agenda and still refuse to produce an impenetrable, auratic text that keeps outsiders out. In Habermas's terms, one can model the ideal speech community in one's approach to writing and to argument, even if one has certain misguided ideas about sociological lawfulness. That subsequent sociologists have taken the route of method in order to legitimate the discipline does not require all positivists or empiricists to do so. Although I am not a fan of Parsons and Merton, my objections to their writings are substantive, having to do with their deep assumptions and arguments. They wrote appropriately narrative texts that could be grasped from outside their language game and challenged, even as they embraced the positivist program of emerging empirical sociology.

FIGURE AND THE SCIENCE AURA

The use of figure in early sociology must be viewed dialectically, as both different from and yet containing the seeds of present-day sociological discourse. As I said above, one can find rough, handcrafted figures even in the 1930s. The mathematical and representational figures of today had their origins in the gestural work of the early sociologists. Different, though, was the reliance of early sociology on prose, which always dominated the text of journal articles. Also different was the relative crudeness of these early figures; their "production values," to use a Hollywood term of art, were nothing compared to the elegant, computer-generated graphics of today. Finally, early figures were used to illustrate and amplify arguments, not produce the science aura. These are simple, descriptive figures, both from 1938. Figure 7.1 describes radio amateurs per 100,000 people in the United States between particular years. Figure 7.2—a table—presents data about motives for elopement that issue in happy or unhappy outcomes; it is found in an article quaintly titled "A Study of 738 Elopements." There is no subtitle.

By 1948, figures are somewhat more sophisticated, and prose is presented in two columns, resembling science journals. Figure 7.3, another table, describes people's varying familiarity with eight musical genres in an article titled "Social Background and Musical Taste." Figure 7.3 is somewhat challenging to read quickly; a footnote printed directly below the table describes the ratio used. This is by no means impenetrable by non-methodologists. Figure 7.4 is a table with twenty-four cells, describing mean personality adjustment scores for various groups of children by residence and sex. On the preceding facing page, another table was presented, constituting a roughly even ratio of figure to prose on these two pages.

By 1958, we find somewhat more mathematical presentations, as we can see in figure 7.5 and in material on the following page. Mathematical notation is used, although it should be noted that this paper is a foray in methodology, dealing with issues of statistical significance and inference. (Such a paper would not have appeared during the 1930s and probably not during the 1940s.) However, most of this 1958 article is conducted in prose, with few figures. In figure 7.6, we find a straightforward table pulling together a lot of descriptive data regarding the

FIGURE I. RADIO AMATEURS PER 100,000 POPULATION FOR THE UNITED STATES, 1914–1935.*

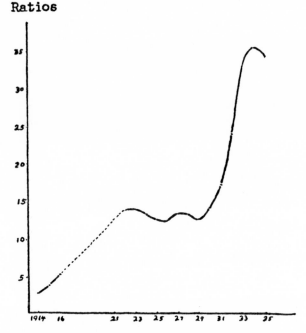

* Data are lacking for 1917–1919 due to the war ban on private radio transmitting. The 1920 figure was not used because of various factors preventing a fair picture of radio participation (See R. V. Bowers, 1934, op. cit.). The 1933 figure is not available.

Figure 7.1

TABLE I. OUTCOME OF ELOPEMENTS

Motive	Happy	Doubtful	Unhappy	Totals	
				Number	Percent
Parental objection	158 45%	28	162	348	46
Publicity	84 60%	8	49	141	20
Economy	55 63%	6	26	87	12
Pregnancy	19 33%	14	25	58	8
Miscellaneous	40 39%	10	54	104	14
Totals { Number / Percent	356 48	66 9	316 43	738 100	100

Figure 7.2

TABLE 2. RATIO[1] OF AFFIRMATIVE TO NEGATIVE
REPLIES BY DEGREE OF FAMILIARITY

Musical Selections	Familiarity Categories		
	Many Times	Several Times	Never
Old Song	45.4	25.7	1.6
Classical	10.9	3.4	.8
Jazz	10.8	3.7	1.3
Modern Classical	9.8	2.0	.5
Old Waltz	118.3	20.4	2.3
Light Classical	152.0	4.9	.9
Popular	103.3	14.0	2.1
Hill-billy	3.0	1.4	5

[1] The ratio may be written, $r = \dfrac{1 + 2l'}{d + 2d'}$, where l equals the number who liked a given selection, l' the number who liked it a great deal, d the number who disliked it, and d' the number who disliked it a great deal. Thus a ratio of 1.00 indicates that the favorable opinion, as measured, just equals the unfavorable opinion.

Figure 7.3

TABLE 2. COMPARISON OF MEAN ADJUSTMENT SCORES FOR THIRD AND
SIXTH GRADE CHILDREN BY RESIDENCE AND SEX

A. Means and standard deviations

Sex and test	Mean Score			Standard Deviation		
	City	Rural		City	Rural	
		Nonfarm	Farm		Nonfarm	Farm
Boys (number)	158	272	190	—	—	—
Self-adjustment	44.33	47.47	46.91	10.35	10.95	10.45
Social adjustment	51.17	54.07	54.15	11.40	10.75	9.80
Girls (number)	127	301	181	—	—	—
Self-adjustment	47.90	50.23	50.61	10.60	10.25	9.60
Social adjustment	57.94	59.68	58.49	8.85	7.70	7.55

B. Group differences

Sex and Test	Farm—City			Farm—Nonfarm			Nonfarm—City		
	Diff.	S.E.	C.R.	Diff.	S.E.	C.R.	Diff.	S.E.	C.R.
Boys									
Self-adjustment	2.58	1.118	2.3	−.56	1.010	0.6	3.14	1.058	3.0
Social adjustment	2.98	1.153	2.6	.08	.964	0.1	2.90	1.118	2.6
Girls									
Self-adjustment	2.71	1.095	2.5	.38	.933	0.4	2.33	1.049	2.2
Social adjustment	.55	.892	0.6	−1.19	.720	1.7	1.74	.844	2.1

Figure 7.4

TABLE 1. NINE MEAN VALUES OF VARIABLE Y

	X_1	X_2	
Z_1	μ_{11}	μ_{12}	$\mu_{1.}$
Z_2	μ_{21}	μ_{22}	$\mu_{2.}$
	$\mu_{.1}$	$\mu_{.2}$	μ_y

Figure 7.5

TABLE 1.—(*Continued*)

Countries by Type of Locality *	Per Cent of Total Population in Localities by Size Ranges **						Per Cent Urban **	Per Cent in Metropolitan Areas ***
	2,000 +	5,000 +	10,000 +	20,000 +	50,000 +	100,000 +		
India, 1951	17.3[1]	16.7[1]	14.4[1]	11.9[1]	9.0[1]	7.2[1]	17.3	7.8
Japan, 1950	59.6[1]	58.0[1]	50.7[1]	42.1[1]	33.2[1]	25.6[1]	37.5	36.3
Malaya, 1947	24.3	21.2	19.0	17.1	10.2	7.4	26.5	12.7
Mexico, 1950	45.5[1]	34.6[1]	28.9[1]	24.0[1]	18.7[1]	15.1[1]	42.6[1]	20.3
New Zealand, 1951	65.7	60.2	57.0	54.2	41.6	32.8	61.3	43.6
Nicaragua, 1950	28.0	21.7	19.0	15.2	10.3	10.3	34.9	13.3
Panama, 1950	42.5	33.8	27.8	22.4	22.4	15.9	36.0	23.9
Paraguay, 1950	28.1	20.2	18.4	15.2	15.2	15.2	34.6	15.6
Peru, 1940	25.5[1]	20.4[1]	17.5[1]	13.9[1]	10.5[1]	8.4[1]	36.1[1]	10.4
Philippines, 1948	21.0[1]	13.8[1]	8.9[1]	6.3[1]	4.1[1]	3.4[1]	24.1[1]	10.3
Thailand, 1947	9.9[1]	9.8[1]	8.9[1]	6.7[1]	4.5[1]	4.5[1]	9.9	6.8
Turkey, 1950	28.7	22.4	18.7	14.5	10.1	8.2	21.9	14.0
Union of South Africa, 1951	39.8	36.2	33.2	30.7	28.2	24.0	42.6	31.5
United Kingdom, 1951	79.7[1]	77.6[1]	74.0[1]	66.9[1]	50.8[1]	36.1[1]	80.3[1]	77.0
United States, 1950	59.8[1]	54.4[1]	49.0*	43.0*	35.3[1]	29.4[1]	64.0[1]	55.9
Venezuela, 1950	49.7[1]	42.4[1]	36.8[1]	32.2[1]	24.7[1]	20.6[1]	53.8	26.2
Type C								
Austria, 1951	65.7	49.3	43.1	39.8	35.2	32.9	49.2	38.9
Belgium, 1947	82.3	62.7	46.6	32.0	17.9	10.5	62.7	41.4
Egypt, 1947	90.9	64.1	40.3	29.1	22.7	19.3	30.1	19.6
France, 1954	62.6	49.8	41.5	33.3	23.1	16.8	55.9	34.4
Germany, East, 1950 [f]	70.1*	57.2*	47.7[1]	39.2[1]	25.6[1]	20.8[1]	67.6[1]	37.9
Germany, West, 1950 [g]	72.5	59.5	50.9	44.1	35.7	30.3	72.4[1]	51.2
Greece, 1951	55.4	42.0	36.3	28.1	16.2	12.7	36.8	22.0
Iraq, 1947	99.9	99.5	94.7	76.9	34.9	16.6	33.8	17.5
Italy, 1951	93.1	73.9	55.4	41.2	28.0	20.4	40.9[1]	27.3
Japan, 1950	98.0	75.1	53.9	42.4	33.2	25.6	37.5	36.3
Philippines, 1948	99.4	97.2	85.7	55.5	17.5	9.3	24.1	10.3
Spain, 1950 [h]	83.2	66.3	51.8	39.8	30.3	24.1	37.0	24.2
Switzerland, 1950	68.1	48.1	36.4	29.1	24.7	20.6	36.5	41.2
Thailand, 1947	100.0	99.9	99.4	95.2	57.4	13.3	9.9	6.8

* See text for a description of the three types of localities.
** Unless designated otherwise the percentages shown in these columns are based on figures reported in the *Demographic Yearbook, 1955*, Tables 7 and 8.
*** Based on provisional figures prepared by International Urban Research.
[a] Excluding the Faeroe Islands; [b] Per cent urban for the year 1952; [c] 1951; [d] Urbanized Areas and incorporated or unincorporated places outside of Urbanized Areas treated as localities; [e] Estimate made by International Urban Research; [f] Including East Berlin; [g] Including West Berlin; [h] Including Canary Islands; [1] Census reports or official yearbooks used as source.

Figure 7.6

percentages of population by country in communities of various sizes. Although this figure is denser than many found in the 1930s and 1940s, it is not particularly challenging to the non-methodologist. And the content bears directly on the substance of the discussion being conducted in parallel prose.

By 1968, the next point in my sample of articles, we find the beginnings of a transition from simple and substance-driven methodology of earlier years to more methodological elegance, although this is not to flower fully until the 1970s. The 1960s was very much a period of transition for American sociologists, moving away from the essayistic approaches of earlier years toward methodologically dense

TABLE 4. GUTTMAN-LINGOES OUTER-POINT
SCALOGRAM ANALYSIS COORDINATES
FOR A TWO-SPACE

City Number	Axis	
	Horizontal	Vertical
1	−0.504	0.259
2	−0.519	−0.392
3	−0.431	−0.894
4	−0.373	−1.000
5	−0.690	−0.448
6	−0.701	0.980
7	−0.600	−0.339
8	−0.684	0.741
9	−0.188	0.702
10	0.399	0.205
11	−0.586	0.258
12	−0.544	−0.398
13	−0.431	−0.640
14	−0.350	0.092
15	−0.389	−0.770
16	−0.299	0.846
17	−0.320	−0.090
18	−0.182	−0.317
19	−0.498	0.264
20	−0.260	0.152
21	−0.357	−0.308
22	−0.395	0.162
23	0.542	−0.092
24	0.369	−0.289
25	−0.343	−0.001
26	−0.614	0.755
27	0.331	−0.178
28	0.340	−0.224
29	0.795	0.179
30	0.689	0.178
31	0.428	−0.217
32	0.179	−0.147
33	0.614	−0.161
34	0.790	0.184
35	0.712	0.302
36	0.582	0.198
37	0.761	0.084
38	0.610	0.167
39	0.821	0.163
40	0.458	−0.268
41	0.063	−0.163
42	0.301	0.425
43	0.080	−0.162
44	0.394	0.202

Figure 7.7

TABLE 3. EXCESS OF HYPERGAMOUS TO HYPOGAMOUS MARRIAGES (IN THOUSANDS) FOR EACH INTERCLASS COMBINATION

| | Older Group (Wives 42–61) Spouse B's Father's Occupation | | | | |
	I	II	III	IV	V
Spouse A's Father's Occupation					
I. Professional and managerial	...	...	...	...	...
II. White-collar	−11	...	...	...	...
III. Upper blue-collar	−54	0	...	...	...
IV. Lower blue-collar	−8	10	73	...	...
V. Farm	−52	39	−73	−169	...

| | Younger Group (Wives 22–41) | | | | |
| | | Spouse B's Father's Occupation | | | |
	I	II	III	IV	V
Spouse A's Father's Occupation					
I. Professional and managerial	...	...	...	...	...
II. White-collar	−14	...	...	...	...
III. Upper blue-collar	−14	110	...	...	...
IV. Lower blue-collar	−6	77	−32	...	...
V. Farm	−44	−1	−88	−265	...

Figure 7.8

presentations. In the article from which figure 7.7 is taken, we find the first examples of representational figures, depicting the proximity of race riots to cities, a topic of relevance during the late 1960s. Figure 7.7 itself presents Guttman-Lingoes outer-point scalogram analysis coordinates for a two-space. (My graduate education has left me ill-prepared to read this table!) The table occupies an entire column, and faces a whole tabled page titled "matrix of coded conditions." I should add that the representational figures mentioned above appear on every single one of the remaining ten pages of the article. Coupled with figure 7.7, these gestures produce what in 1968 must have passed for the science aura. In figure 7.8, also from 1968, we find a table titled "Excess of Hypergamous to Hypogamous Marriages (in Thousands) for Each Interclass Comparison." The author comments in the text that this table "may be of value to demographers concerned with the flow of population across class lines." Just over 20 percent of this article is taken up with figures of one kind or another.

As I said, this late-1960s sociology was the end of an earlier genre of substance-driven sociology and the beginning of high method. By 1978, articles sport representations, tables of regression coefficients, and mathematical notation. This is a far cry from the rudimentary method of the 1930s, 1940s, and 1950s. It is a qualitative leap beyond the 1960s as well. The coauthored article from which figures 7.9, 7.10, and 7.11 are taken is not atypical of sociology of this period. Figure 7.9 is a nearly page-long representation of various models of psychological modernity effects. Relations among variables in these models are depicted graphically. By the standards of today, these are not particularly elegant representations. It appears that the text

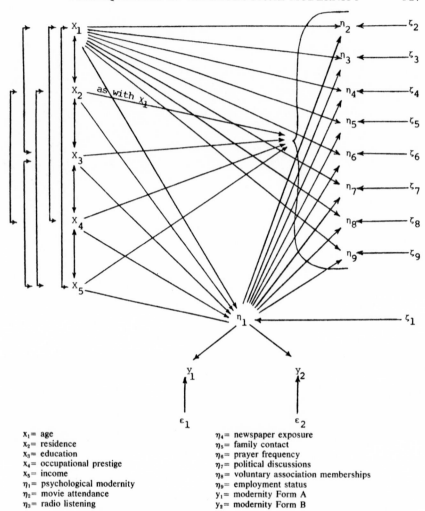

x_1 = age
x_2 = residence
x_3 = education
x_4 = occupational prestige
x_5 = income
η_1 = psychological modernity
η_2 = movie attendance
η_3 = radio listening

η_4 = newspaper exposure
η_5 = family contact
η_6 = prayer frequency
η_7 = political discussions
η_8 = voluntary association memberships
η_9 = employment status
y_1 = modernity Form A
y_2 = modernity Form B

Figure 3. Seemingly Unrelated Regression Structural Model of the Eight Total Sample Behaviors

$\eta_1 = \gamma_{11}\chi_1 + \gamma_{12}\chi_2 + \gamma_{14}\chi_4 + \gamma_{15}\chi_5 + \zeta_1;$

$\eta_2 = \gamma_{21}\chi_1 + \gamma_{22}\chi_2 + \gamma_{23}\chi_3 + \gamma_{24}\chi_4 + \gamma_{25}\chi_5 + \beta_{21}\eta_1 + \zeta_2;$

$\eta_3 = \gamma_{31}\chi_1 + \gamma_{32}\chi_2 + \gamma_{33}\chi_3 + \gamma_{34}\chi_4 + \gamma_{35}\chi_5 + \beta_{31}\eta_1 + \zeta_3;$

•
•
•

$\eta_9 = \gamma_{91}\chi_1 + \gamma_{92}\chi_2 + \gamma_{93}\chi_3 + \gamma_{94}\chi_4 + \gamma_{95}\chi_5 + \beta_{91}\eta_1 + \zeta_3;$

and the fallible measurement structure is given by:

$y_1 = \lambda_{11}\eta_1 + \epsilon_1;$
$y_2 = \lambda_{21}\eta_1 + \epsilon_2.$

We estimated the model with a full-information maximum likelihood (FIML) program (Jöreskog and Sörbom, 1976). This program is well-suited for present purposes since it allows a simultaneous estimation of all model parameters including correlated disturbances and the measurement structure. Additionally, the program provides a likelihood chi-square goodness-of-fit test and matrices of first-order partial derivatives of the fitting function (F) with respect to the individual

Figure 7.9

Table 1. Effects of Background Variables and Psychological Modernity on Behaviors of Costa Rican Adult Males

Dependent Variable	Background Variables					Psychological Modernity	R²	N
	Age	Residence	Education	Occupation	Income			
	Standardized Regression Coefficients							
(1) Attend Movies	.368*	.183*	.271*	-.111	.049	—	.334	208
	.371*	.182*	.288*	-.110	.054	-.029	.334	
(2) Listen to Radio Often	.002	.025	.053	-.074	.135	—	.025	209
	.000	.026	.037	-.075	.129	.029	.025	
(3) Read Newspapers Often	-.015	.052	.522*	.120*	.144*	—	.441	207
	-.026	.059	.424*	.113	.113	.170*	.455	
(4) Organization Memberships	.020	-.065	.181*	.242*	.100	—	.177	210
	.022	-.066	.191*	.243*	.103	-.018	.177	
(5) Discuss Politics	.123	.007	.309	-.006	.082	—	.168	208
	.105	.018	.153	-.017	.033	.272*	.203	
(6) Employed/Unemployed	-.056	-.122	-.349*	.393*	—	—	.205	207
	-.061	-.119	-.401*	.387*	—	.079	.208	

Figure 7.10 continues

Table 1. Continued

(7) Less Family Contact	-.023	-.050	-.302*	-.025	-.123	—	.159	209
	-.020	-.052	-.270*	-.023	-.112	-.056	.161	
(8) Less Frequent Prayer	.082	.194*	.185*	.020	.059	—	.111	207
	.064	.205*	.028	.008	.009	.274*	.146	
(9) Age at Marriage	-.234*	-.016	-.199	.273*	-.052	—	.119	99†
	-.234*	-.017	-.187	.275*	-.044	-.028	.120	
(10) Fewer No. of Children	.307*	.041	.513*	-.195	-.030	—	.323	99†
	.307*	.041	.488	-.199	-.048	.056	.329	
(11) Ever Use Contraceptives	.003	.089	.222	.063	.067	—	.105	83††
	-.010	.088	.127	.050	.012	.200	.126	
Wife is Not Forbidden to:								
(12) Take a Job Outside Home	.058	.131	.004	.273*	-.067	—	.094	99†
	.058	.131	.011	.274*	-.062	-.014	.094	
(13) Join in Visits with Men	.033	-.150	.142	.043	.203	—	.141	97†
	.034	-.149	.099	.035	.172	.098	.145	
(14) Talk to Men You Don't Know	.163	-.008	.104	.112	-.078	—	.062	98†
	.164	-.006	.051	.102	-.116	.120	.068	
(15) Visit Women You Don't Know	.072	.002	.091	-.075	.049	—	.019	98†
	.071	.000	.139	.067	.084	-.110	.025	
Mean	31.60	1.50	7.90	28.40	2.20	.66		
Standard Deviation	10.40	.50	5.10	25.30	.69	.22		

Note: All background variables are ordered in the direction of theoretically predicted positive association with modernity, e.g., old age to young, rural to urban residence, etc. Variable identifications are Age: self-reported years; Residence: rural (small settlements 15 to 60 kilometers from San Jose)=1, urban (San Jose)=2; Education: self-reported years of schooling; Occupation: self-reported description coded to Duncan SEI scores; Income: self-reported income below ₡300=1, ₡300 to ₡800=2, above ₡800=3, where 1 colones=12¢; Psychological Modernity: Inkeles and Smith's OM-11 scale based on mean scores (0.00 to 1.00) across ten dichotomous items coded traditional=0 and modern=1. Items and distributions are available on request.

* Statistical significance of p≤.05.
† Married subsample (N=99).
†† Married, Catholic subsample (N=89).

Figure 7.10

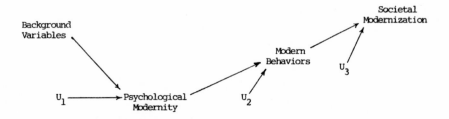

A. Traditional model of psychological modernity effects.

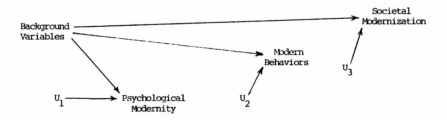

B. Alternative model of psychological modernity noneffects.

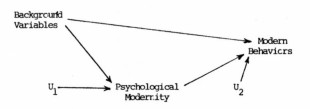

C. Model estimated in this research.

Figure 1. Models of Psychological Modernity Effects and Noneffects

Figure 7.11

describing the variables in the models has been typed. Figure 7.10 is a large table spilling over onto the next page that describes many correlation coefficients, one of the hallmarks of contemporary sociology. Figure 7.11 is a high-mathematical representation at its best, auguring the elaborate figural work of the 1990s. Figure 7.9 is titled "Seemingly Unrelated Regression Structural Model. . . ." The accompanying text says that the model was estimated "with a full-information maximum likelihood (FIML) program. . . ." Figure 7.11 occupies the entire journal page and is followed by a similar model two pages later. Footnote 6, which begins on p. 326, describes figure 7.11 in structural equation models, phrased in mathematical notation. These dense journal pages represent a clean break with the more open texts of the past and augur the methods-driven discourse of the 1990s.

By 1988, journal sociology is nearly as mathematized as in 1998. Although there was less formal mathematical modeling than today, virtually every 1988 *ASR* article contains elaborate figural work. And, as we shall see later, all of the other components of journal science are in place—abstract, coauthorship, acknowledgments, technical footnotes, literature review, methodological detail, inversion of text and figure, programmatic conclusion. Perhaps most important, the boundary between figure and text begins to disappear, as it has in the 1990s, with text becoming so technical and dominated by mathematical symbolism that it could be viewed as a methodological gesture in its own right.

In figure 7.12, three-quarters of a journal page is occupied by a table describing thirty-two variables treated in the study. This is in the midst of a section on methods ("data and measurement"). Toward the bottom of the page, we find equations in mathematical notation. The top half of the next page is given over to a table of regression equations, using three different models estimated in the paper. In figure 7.13, a 1988 journal page is littered with a representation (involving social networks), equation, text so technical that it could be regarded as figure, and technical footnote. An interactional "experiment" involving undergraduate student subjects is mentioned. Network analysis was a particularly compelling tool of the 1980s.

It is clear from examining changes in the use of figures in *ASR* articles that only in the past twenty years have figures transcended their previous role as, in effect, part of the text itself, subordinate to the arguments they supported. The use of figures only became figural and gestural, conveying meaning by producing the science aura, in recent sociology, largely, I contend, to check the decline of sociology in the United States. While some would defend the elaborate use of figure, including mathematics and representation, as progress in sociological method, figure began to add value—science aura—to sociology only since the end of the 1960s, timing that I contend is no accident, given the larger institutional decline of U.S. sociology. Where before figure supported text, text now supports figure, becoming figural itself. This is what I mean by methods-drivenness—a concern with method so obsessive that substantive sociology is squeezed out by the technical advances that are claimed.

This has been a dialectical process. Scientific method, and with it a reliance on method (including math) to solve intellectual problems, was foundational as doctrine in positivist U.S. sociology since the 1930s and, through the twists and turns of institutional and intellectual history, flowered into methodological fetishism some fifty years later as positivist doctrine became unexamined positivist discourse, gesture replacing argument. This was not preordained; it was only one possible vector of intellectual development among others. It was conceivable that the narrativity of early journal sociology could have become a form of what Marcuse (1969)

Table 1. Variable Names and Descriptions

Variable	Descriptions
LNWAGE	Natural logarithm of mean weekly earnings.
WAGEGAIN	Negative of the residual from a market earnings regression for LNWAGE (note 8).
%GAIN	WAGEGAIN/LNWAGE.
LOSEJOB	"How likely is it that during the next couple of years you will lose your present job and have to look for a job with another employer?" (1 = not at all likely; 4 = very likely)
BENEFITS	Scale constructed by counting the number of benefits the respondent receives on the current job. The benefit categories were retirment program, life insurance, savings plan, paid vacation, medical insurance, paid sick leave, dental and eyecare benefits, and, for women only, paid maternity leave and maternity leave with full re- employment rights.
TENURE	Years of service with employer.[1]
AGE	Respondent's age in years.
LFEXP	Respondent's years of labor-force experience.
SUPERVISOR	Dummy coded 1 if respondent supervises the work of others.
UNION	Dummy coded 1 if respondent's job is covered by collective bargaining agreement
FIRMSIZE	Number of people who work for employer at same location as respondent.[1]
CORE	Dummy coded 1 if respondent's job is in "core" sector as defined by the Beck, Horan, and Tolbert (1978) typology.
BIGCITY	Dummy coded 1 if respondent resides in the central city or suburbs of the 12 largests SMSAs.
WEST	Regional dummy coded 1 if respondent resides in the West.
FEMALE	Dummy coded 1 for female respondents.
NONWHITE	Dummy coded 1 for nonwhite respondents.
SCHOOLING	Respondent's years of schooling.
OTHERINCOME	Respondent's annual earnings expressed as percentage of total annual family income from all sources.
OTHERJOB	Dummy coded 1 if respondent works for pay on a job other than his main job.
MARRIAGE	Dummy variable coded 1 for married, spouse present.
KIDS<6	Number of children less than six years old in household unit who are respondent's or respondent's.
KIDS<18	Number of children age 6–17 in household unit who are respondent's or respondent's spouse's.
HOURSWORK	Mean number of hours worked on main job per week.
PROFESSIONAL	Dummy variable for respondent's major Census occupation.
MANAGERIAL	Dummy variable for respondent's major Census occupation.
CRAFT	Dummy variable for respondent's major Census occupation.
OPERATIVE	Dummy variable for respondent's major Census occupation.
OFFERS	"About how easy would it be for you to find a job with another employer with approximately the same income and fringe benefits you now have?" (1 = not easy at all; 3 = very easy)
UNUSED SKILLS1	A scale (Cronbach's α = .79) constructed from the following terms: "My job lets me use my skills and abilities." (4 = strongly disagree; 1 = strongly agree); "I am given a chance to do the things I do best." (4 = not at all true of job; 1 = very true)
UNUSED SKILLS2	"Do you have skills from your experience and training that you would like to be using in your work but can't use on your present job?" (1 = yes; 0 = no)
LACK RESOURCES	A scale (Cronbach's α = .72) constructed from four items of the form, "I have enough [help and equipment, information, authority, time] to get the job done" (1 = very true of job; 4 = not at all true of job).
SCREEN	"In general, how well would you say your job measures up to the sort of job you wanted when you took it?" (5 = not very much like; 1 = very much like)

[1] The *QES* records this variable as a set of class intervals; workers were assigned the midpoint of their respective classes.

Figure 7.12

called "new science," following on remarks he made in *Eros and Civilization* about the possible "erotization" of science and technology under a regime of noninstrumental, nonsurplus repressive rationality—much the same vision early Marx had where he talked about the liberation of the five senses, and thus of praxis (self-creative activity), under socialism. This notion of a dis-alienating, nonsurplus repressive science will be crucial to my comments about a new sociology in chapter 8, where I suggest alternative conceptions of sociological discourse that follow from the deconstructive analyses of these preceding chapters. With Marcuse and

and h the longest such path from i in that domain. Only paths within a domain's boundaries are counted. As illustrated in the graphs, each path begins and ends with circles, between which there are either no positions or only boxes. Position i's GPI within the domain is[14]

$$p_{id}(e_d) = [1/e_d] \sum_{k=1}^{h} (-1)^{(k-1)} m_{idk} \quad (2)$$

$p(e)$ is closely related to $p(1)$ and similarly calculated. Multiplying the summation by $1/e_d$ simply places $p(e)$ and $p(1)$ values on the same scale.

Let us apply equation 2 (which now substitutes for Axiom 1) to network 4a, with $e = 2$. The two dyadic domains are indicated by (AB) and (AC) subscripts. We see that $p_B = p_C = p_{A(AB)} = p_{A(AC)} = (1/1)(1) = 1$. Each position has, in each of its domains, exactly one one-path and one exchange. Therefore, A has no power advantage in either of its domains. Similar results obtain in Figure 4b.

The 4c network has (AB) and (DE) dyadic domains and power domain (BCDF). Again, $p = 1$ for members of dyadic domains. However, for the power domain we calculate $p_{C(BCDF)} = (1/2)(3) = 3/2$, and for B, D, and F, $p = (1/1)(1-1) = 0$. Thus, C has a power advantage in both of its exchanges, B and D have low power in one of their exchanges and equal power in the other, A and E have equal power in their one exchange, and F has low power in its one exchange.

We may also calculate an *average power index*, $\bar{p}_i$, as the mean of i's indices across domains. In 4c, $\bar{p}_C = 3/2$; $\bar{p}_A = \bar{p}_E = 1$; $\bar{p}_B = \bar{p}_D = (1 + 0)/2 = .5$; $\bar{p}_F = 0$.

The Figure 5a network is the same as Figure 2, but redrawn using the circle and box notation. When $e = 1$, the network is a single domain and only the Es are high-power positions. In 5b, where $e = 2$, the situation is drastically altered. Only D has power advantages, with the Es all having low power relative to D. Furthermore, the E-F relations form three equipower dyadic domains.

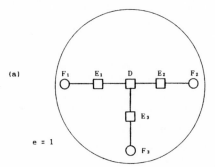

(a)

$e = 1$

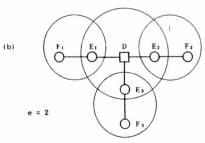

(b)

$e = 2$

Fig. 5

The 5a and 5b networks tested the GPI generalization. The two networks have identical shapes. Only the number of exchanges per round differs. Cook et al.'s (1983) simulations found the Es to be high-power positions in this network; $p(e)$ concurs, but *only* for the special case of $e = 1$.

EXPERIMENT 2

Experiment 2 tests the Figure 5 networks under $e = 1$ and $e = 2$ conditions. In spite of their identical shape, our analysis indicates that these networks should exhibit radically different profit distributions.

Method

Procedures for this experiment were similar to those used in Experiment 1. In this case, however, each subject negotiated from the different network positions under both one-exchange and two-exchange conditions, controlling for any personal characteristics of subjects that might confound the test.

Instructions for the one- and two-exchange conditions were identical, save for the

---

[14] For clarity, i subscripts have been suppressed for the e and h variables, d is suppressed for h, and p_{id} (e_d) will be written as $p(e)$ or p. Note that Axiom 1 is now comprised of the more general equation (2).

Figure 7.13

other members of the Frankfurt School, I believe that one can develop a science and technology that play with concepts and nature, respectively, combining objectivity and a playful, nonalienated subjectivity that does not regress behind the many marvels of Einsteinian physics and a powerful industrial technology.

Early sociological writing provides only one example of empirical research and theoretical writing that does not allow the use of figures to become gestural—representational, compulsively mathematical, the inversion of reasoned prose. Figure and quantitative method are acceptable as long as they are viewed as rhetoric, vehicles of argument that are not privileged by comparison to other modes of talking about and depicting the world. A dis-alienated sociology would endorse figures, statistics, theoretical phrases, ethnography, and historical studies as equally legitimate modes of rhetoric as long as these vehicles, these methods, do not become reified as we delude ourselves that method solves intellectual problems in its own right. The rudimentary tables and graphs of 1938 are not intrinsically superior or inferior to the sophisticated scatterplots of the 1990s; both versions can be harnessed to positivist or non-positivist agendas. What is important is how they understand themselves as discourse. In 1938, the author of an article on 738 elopements, although perhaps a positivist, probably did not believe that his method, and especially his method's gestures, would unlock the secrets of the connubial world. By the 1990s, most sociological articles are methods-driven, substituting what Weber called instrumental reason for substantive reason. It is my perspective that this needs to be opposed if sociology is to become critical and enlightening once again.

LITERATURE REVIEW AND CUMULATION

One of the biggest surprises of my historical study of *ASR* sociology since the 1930s is that the literature review is a relatively recent artifice. Even by 1968, the literature review was not a compulsory piece of the sociological script. Before 1968, articles began with only cursory statements of their problems, virtually none of which was anchored in an existing literature that was cited parenthetically, usually without particular page references. For that matter, with some exceptions, we do not see extensive bibliographies of cited works, such as the field's literature, until the 1960s. Both literature reviews and bibliographies are relatively recent developments. What work is cited is usually noted and sometimes briefly discussed in footnotes. And, until the 1950s, a good deal of cited or noted work is from sociological textbooks, which, unlike in Europe, were a legitimate mode of research presentation until mass-market omnibus textbooks designed only for classroom use came to dominate textbook publishing in the late 1950s and 1960s. By the standards of today's meticulous and lengthy literature reviews, which both constitute the field and provide a point of departure for the author's differentiation of her topic from other published work in the field, all of this is very strange.

Not only are literature reviews absent until the 1970s, when we begin to see full-blown treatments of a field's literature. We also find few references to scientific cumulation in sociology until the 1970s. These two things go hand in hand: literature is reviewed mainly to suggest a cumulative process within scientific fields that warrant the present research, which positions itself to add to the existing literature and move it gradually forward. Without literature, there can be no cumulation, a hallmark of science. Without the prospect of cumulation, individual research loses its warrant. It could be argued by historians of science that disciplines in their infancy by definition cannot have canons of research and theory with which to orient individual researchers. However, in the United States, there was virtually no movement toward clearly discernible literature reviews until the past twenty or thirty years, suggesting that cumulation was not taking place even as late as the 1960s. For those of us who reject the goal of cumulation in the human sciences, which are necessarily framed by theory, paradigm, and perspective—Ritzer's (1975) multiparadigmatic sociology–the lack of literature reviews is not problematic. Indeed, it is a cause for celebration inasmuch as sociologists before 1970 did not feel that they needed to ground their work in the illusory notion of a preestablished and forward-moving field to which they make an incremental contribution.

Methodologically adept sociologists produce mountains of piecemeal research simply because they are able to identify "variables"—for example, ethnicity and decisions about housing for the elderly—that are shown to vary together in statistically significant ways. One test of the proposition that post-1970 sociology does not really cumulate is to trace carefully the development of fields constituted by individual researchers' many literature reviews. Are people citing work that gradually builds into a significant literature based on clear advances in sociological knowledge? Are a host of sociologists working in parallel ways on the many problems identified by journal articles, correcting each other through processes of replication? Another way to demonstrate that post-1970 sociology does not tend to cumulate is to notice the extent of undecidability and programmatism that qualify the results of particular researches and call for further research within the same narrow niche. Sociologists confident that they are advancing their fields would not acknowledge so many limitations of their research, particularly their methodologies.

In 1938, 1948, and 1958 we see virtually no literature reviews; very little literature is even cited. Between 1958 and 1968, we notice a transition of sorts, as authors increasingly cite or footnote others working within the same general field. However, even in 1968, the full-blown literature review is not a standard prolegomenon in sociological journal articles but more an emergent property of brief introductions that attempt to situate the author's problem either in prior sociology or in the social world. A 1938 article begins with this sentence: "The major portion of the literature on social change provides little basis for penetrating insights into the nature of the processes involved." Data analysis begins at the top of the article's second page. The balance of the first page is taken up with a brief description of the author's project. "Being a first study its methodology and its conclusion are crude." The author promises to test a hypothesis. The only footnote references to other literature draw attention to the author's doctoral dissertation at Minnesota and to a 1937 *ASR* article by the author.

Another 1938 article claims that its topic, elopement, "has received more attention in drama and fiction than in social science." The only literature cited in the article is a coauthored paper by the author published in a journal called *Mental Hygiene*. Yet another 1938 article cites more extensive literature, including two *Social Forces* papers by the author and the author's coauthored social psychology textbook. He cites a number of other textbooks on social psychology, as well as papers from the *Encyclopedia of the Social Sciences, ASR,* and the *American Journal of Sociology (AJS)*. In total, there are seven footnotes, all of which cite literature— three textbooks and seven articles, an extensively documented paper for the 1930s. There is even a hint of the possibility of scientific cumulation: "Elsewhere studies which seem to confirm the foregoing position have been reported in detail." However, on the article's first page, the author laments that surveys of attitudes have been "taken up by journalists and radio broadcasters" and thus "such questionnaires will probably go out of style among academicians."

The final 1938 article I examined did not use subheadings. The discussion of the topic segued smoothly into the methods discussion. Three long paragraphs introduce and situate the problem—occupation choice and intelligence. The balance of the article, ten pages in all, presents and discusses the empirical findings. By the standards of 1938, there is a good deal of figural work, including tables and even a footnoted equation describing the ratio of the difference of means to the standard error of the difference of means. The relative sophistication of the methods used and the surprising extent of figural display match the relatively extensive citation of literature in the opening three paragraphs—nine studies in all. These studies demonstrate that "the distribution of intelligence ratings . . . of the group [of children] conformed closely to the prestige ratings of the fathers' occupations." Virtually all of the studies cited appear to have been published in psychology journals. Unlike latter-day literature reviews, this discussion of parallel sources does not ground the work in a field supported by middle-range sociological theory that would help explain the correlations found. Nonetheless, in these opening paragraphs, we find the rudiments of what later came to be called the literature review.

The four papers sampled from 1948 *ASRs* do not demonstrate a marked trend toward more extensive literature reviews. One of these articles is a theoretical piece by Robert Merton, in which he cites himself extensively. In only one of the three empirical articles are more than a couple of citations provided. The first article begins this way:

> The notion that individual taste is not fortuitous but rather is controlled by cultural standards may be regarded as a truism. However, few empirical studies have been concerned with the manner in which difference in cultural backgrounds is associated with variation in the content of musical taste. The present study sought to determine whether

difference in socio-economic background is associated with a significant variation in musical taste.

That is the extent of the pre-methods discussion! In the body of the methods/findings discussion, a few methodological citations are offered. In the next 1948 article, nothing is cited except previous work by the author distributed by Ohio State, his home institution, and a research monograph published under the auspices of Ohio State's Bureau of Education Research. The article begins "This paper presents some results of a study of personality adjustment of school children in Miami County, Ohio." Nothing more is claimed for the results in the way of connection to a literature or generalizability. This is pure bench science.

The final empirical article from 1948 presents more literature, especially in its discussion of existing "marriage prediction" scales. The article positions itself as an analysis and critique of such existing scales, necessarily requiring the citation of literature. Eleven sociological works are cited, some of them unpublished, with the citations interwoven at various places in the descriptive section of the article. A modest attempt at the assessment of the extent of cumulation is made: "In sum: the content of the existing marriage prediction scales invites little trust in the prognostic value of these scales. . . ." This should be considered a proto-literature review, providing an early model for full-blown literature reviews since the 1970s.

Merton's theoretical article is a special case. He cites nineteen works, four of which are authored or coauthored by him. "With a few exceptions," he writes, "recent sociological discussions have assigned but one major function to empirical research: 'testing' or 'verification' of hypotheses." Merton cites nothing here to support his characterization of recent sociological discussions. In the balance of the article, he makes a reasoned argument for the role of empirical research in theory formation, citing authors from Pierce and Parsons to Durkheim and Tarde. In this conceptual article, Merton seamlessly weaves references to other literature into footnotes supporting the main body of the text. Although Merton does not present a systematic literature review at the beginning of the article, he certainly reviews and builds upon extant "literature" in the course of his argument, which posits what has come to be regarded as a quite significant relationship between theory and empirical research and that formed the basis of his own later conception of "middle-range" theorizing (theorizing supported by, and informing, data).

By 1958, sociological authors were still not producing literature reviews of the contemporary variety. And yet sociology was very much in transition between the late 1950s and late 1960s, underneath the surface of sociological writings. Although one could surmise that in the 1930s there simply wasn't any literature to review, by the late 1950s the ASS had reached a kind of adolescence, if not full maturity, and the number of publishing sociologists had expanded considerably since the beginnings of U.S. sociology. By 1959, the ASS had changed its official name to American Sociological Association, marking a degree of disciplinary maturity and institutionalization. It is not a coincidence that the professionalization and administrative rationalization of the ASS/ASA occurred during the Sputnik era, when American science and higher education geared up to thwart emergent Soviet superiority in science and technology. Although "modernization" was always latent in the project of American sociology, given its Comtean roots, and although epistemological modernization was not to become manifest until the 1970s, when the institutional decline of sociology prompted it, the late 1950s and then the Kennedy presidency were an occasion for rethinking the role of sociology in the academy and society. Sociology became institutionalized during the 1950s and 1960s with the expansion of faculty numbers, graduate programs, and publication outlets. The "scientization" of post–World War II empirical sociology was just around the corner.

That the institutional and societal decline of sociology occurred in the wake of the social movements and social conflict of the 1960s misled sociological opinion makers to conclude that sociology's decline could be explained by its erstwhile activism. But I contend that sociology's activist moment during the 1960s was fully consistent with its modernizing project, as Comte and later Giddings conceived it. Although sociology was to be science, it was supposed to solve social problems through science. Sixties activism was blamed for the delegitimation of sociology in the academy and society, leading to loss of majors, loss of funding, and loss of public confidence. The mathematizing compulsions of the present-day discipline were understandable in light of both sociology's response to declining fortunes during the 1970s and its own inveterate positivism—"social physics." Whether a mathematized, auratic sociology must completely cut off its connection to the public sphere, sought by both Comte and Marx albeit in different ways, is another matter. The year 1958, then, saw little change in journal discourse, but the rapid social changes in postwar U.S. society that began to occur augured imminent changes in the ways American sociologists understood their project. For some like Mills and Gouldner, sociology was to be a harbinger of progressive social change. When post-1960s positivist sociologists looked back retrospectively on the decline of sociology that began in the 1970s and continued for the next two decades, they concluded that sociology's activism doomed the positivist project by reducing sociology to advocacy.

In the first 1958 article that I sampled, the literature review amounted to two introductory paragraphs positioning the author's perspective against the argument advanced by Hanan Selvin in a 1957 *ASR* article. The issue is how sociologists should view matters of statistical significance in their research. On the same opening page, the author cites two letters to the editor of the *ASR* by other sociologists responding to Selvin. On the next page, an article in a statistics journal is cited, followed a page later by the citation of a monograph on probability theory. A page later another statistics text is cited. No other work is cited until the article's final page, where another statistics text is cited. In the next 1958 article, a coauthored treatment of international urbanization, no literature whatsoever is cited. The first sentences of the article read this way:

Most of urban sociology rests upon observations made in countries representing a small and biased sample of the world as a whole. Any attempt, however, to remove this narrow restraint—that is, any attempt to extend comparative urban analysis to include all parts of the earth—runs into the complex problem of comparability. In the present paper, we have no solution to offer for this problem, as it affects all aspects of urban sociology, but we do have some information bearing upon the validity of one type of international comparison—namely, the degree of urbanization as between one country and another.

Not only do the authors fail to marshal literature in order to demonstrate the disciplinary context and relevance of their problem; they do not even promise to solve their own problem! The article is so disconnected to field and so ungrounded in middle-range theory that it promises nothing more elaborate than "some information."

The next 1958 article, on intergenerational occupational mobility in the United States, is methodologically sophisticated and relatively figural for its time. But literature review is virtually nonexistent, consisting of four opening paragraphs, preceding the section on "methodology and findings." The article begins with a reference to Sorokin, who was already thirty years in the past. A hint of scientific cumulation opens the second paragraph of the article: "To be sure, progress has been made in the investigation of societal trends. Since the 1920s several excellent studies of mobility trends . . . have been made. . . ." At this point, a textbook summarizing some of these studies is cited. After the next sentence, a research monograph is cited. Finally, the author suggests that "only two studies have dealt with the problems of *trends* at the societal level. . . ." Here, a chapter from an edited book and a research monograph are cited. That is the extent of the author's review of the literature.

In the final 1958 article to be sampled, on fertility and marriage, four introductory paragraphs precede a discussion of "the data." The article has three authors. A single article, from the *AJS,* is cited. Two of the 1958 article's authors are authors of the *AJS* cite. To be sure, additional cites are found in the section on "variables," following the section on data. These cites constitute a ground-level literature review, tracking recent empirical articles on, or related to, variables treated by the authors. Four of these citations mention one or more of the authors' own articles, diluting the survey of the literature somewhat. Additional cites later in the article are primarily technical and methodological in nature. Even as recently as 1958, what we have come to know as the literature review was still not a prominent literary form in journal sociology.

In 1968, we witness the introduction of the bibliography in *ASR* articles. These are called "references," keyed directly to the citations in the text. Notes have begun a steady decline; if they appear at all, they are usually technical explanations that, as I have argued above, begin to blur with figure itself. The major difference between 1968 and post-1970 articles is that the latter articles indulge heavily in figural gestures designed to produce the science aura. The 1968 articles are still this side of the great methodological divide, the far side of which is the figural sociology of the present. Although we have found figures even in the 1930s, and certainly by the 1960s, 1968 was at least half a decade and probably a full decade behind the advent of the contemporary sociology science article, as we have come to know it, in that figure had not yet become text and the literature review, connecting a study cumulatively to a claimed field, was still relatively uncommon. The absence of literature reviews in 1968, except in rudimentary forms, is rather surprising, given the dramatic changes that were to follow in the next few decades.

The literature review was definitely in transition by 1968. Although we do not find the exhaustive parenthetical citation sausages of the present, we find longer introductory stage settings, in which topics are situated in a field, than we did in the 1950s and before. In the first 1968 article, we find only one citation in the body of the introductory section. That is because the author is reanalyzing data collected by two other authors, on the social and demographic circumstances of urban race riots. Their reanalysis employs a new methodological technique called multidimensional scalogram analysis. Fully eight papers that bear on this technique are cited, constituting a kind of literature review. This is perhaps a symptom of growing interest in method and technique during the 1960s, coming to a head some twenty years later as sociology became more fully mathematized. This paper has no bibliography, unlike many of its 1968 counterparts.

The second 1968 article comes equipped with bibliography. The author spends the first three pages of her article discussing her research problem in the context of what other sociologists have to offer about it. The paper is about what she calls commitment mechanisms in utopian communities. Instead of constituting a tight field centered around a parenthetically cited canon of related works, the author ranges more widely and plumbs sociology for theoretical and empirical statements about commitment, citing Becker, Parsons, and Shils and Kelman, among others. In the body of her empirical discussion of her data, other authors, such as Coser and Stinchcombe, who more directly contribute to an understanding of her problem are cited and discussed in the text. Footnote 14 on p. 510 reads, "The common threat or shared fate as a builder of cohesiveness is widely documented. See, for example, Simmel (1964); Coser (1964); Blumer (1953); Freud (1962:61). A field experiment by the Sherifs demonstrates the phenomenon rather dramatically. (See Sherif and Sherif, 1953)." This footnote comes very close to constituting a miniature literature review, suggesting both cumulation/consensus and bringing together diverse citations parenthetically, without argumentation. This brief footnote gesture is certainly a harbinger of later literature reviews, in both style and intent. This article was highly readable, unreliant on high methodology but not eschewing method and data analysis. It was theoretically grounded in important sociological literature and it was written accessibly and engagingly. The author did not allow her method or theory to get the better of her analytical eye, which remained sensitive and inquisitive.

In the third and final 1968 article, on whether American women "marry up," a total of eleven citations are found in the opening section, which takes up just over two pages at the beginning of the article. The first two cites, with which the paper begins, are textbooks—handbooks, to be precise. Near the beginning of the article, the author states, "That women tend to marry up (and men to marry down) the socioeconomic ladder in some societies is a well-documented fact." The author then goes on to document this fact, with reference to the research of others. A number of these cites are from more than ten years ago, suggesting that the author had to dig deep in order to locate his research problem in a cognate literature that could be viewed as cumulating. This 1968 article is not yet a full-blown science article. Interestingly, in his conclusion, the author anticipates a trend in later journal sociology: he acknowledges the undecidability of his research where he concludes that "the present data clearly do not permit an ideal test of the hypergamy hypothesis." Such a test would require different, better data. The *ASR* issue from which this article is taken is typical of *ASR*s of that era in that only one of the six articles published in that issue has more than one author. Again, 1968 journal sociology has not yet crossed the threshold of later team science.

By 1978, what we know as the standard sociological journal article format has come into clear view, especially with regard to a full-blown literature review that grounds the topic cumulatively in an existing field. By 1978, many articles are co- or multiauthored. They have begun to be quite methods-driven, relying heavily on figural displays in the body of the text as well as in the margins, which become figural in their own right. The main 1978 example that is reviewed here cites more than twenty sources in the opening literature review, which is conducted in the first three pages of the article. Not only are many other studies cited, but they are sausaged into parenthetically encased strings that produce a version of consensus among quite disparate authors. Here, for example, something called the modernity thesis is characterized this way: "Central to individual modernity theory is the assumption that psychological modernity leads to modern behavior, which contributes to or is necessary for modernization of societies. . . ." Nine studies are cited parenthetically immediately after this formulation, followed by a short passage from another source. The quotation of this short passage in order to elaborate the sentence above is anachronistic by the standards of 1990s literature reviews, which generally do not descend to specific quotes, with page numbers.

Beginning in the 1970s, the standard-form *ASR* article rapidly emerges. Although there is more mathematics by the late 1990s than during the 1970s or even 1980s, a threshold of scientificity had been crossed by the time the 1960s ended. In 1988, literature reviews generally sport more than twenty citations, and sometimes many more than that. Fields are constituted in this way, and they are portrayed as governed by intellectual consensus. Literature reviews frequently segue into a discussion of testable hypotheses that frame the methods sections of articles. The term *model* appears frequently in the 1980s and beyond. Mathematical notation abounds, especially during the 1980s and 1990s. In the third paragraph of the first 1988 article sampled, the author says that "over the last two decades, the marriage of human capital and information theory has produced an array of economic models that provide a rich theoretical portrait of the decision calculus surrounding job mobility. . . ." A parenthetical string of citations follows. The first sentence of the second 1988 article reads this way: "Although no single exchange theory dominates the social sciences, a fairly coherent social-exchange perspective exists." The three authors, working on power relations in exchange networks, conceptualize their task this way: "We propose and test a theory that predicts relative power for network positions." Throughout the first section of the paper, various authors are cited who pursue similar lines of research.

The third 1988 article cites more than twenty authors in the opening literature review, which occupies the first four pages of the seventeen-page article. The literature review concludes with two paragraphs summarizing the exploration of literature and then connecting it to the methods sections of the paper. "In conclusion, the evidence above suggests that collective-action organizations' members are motivated to become involved by their interests in a variety of incentives." By *evidence,* the author means evidence cited. He goes on to say that "the chief analytic task of this paper is to determine the relative impact of various types of incentives on members' involvements in their associations." The paper concludes with a good deal of hesitation: "Not all the theoretical expectations were confirmed." This is met with programmatism: "The analysis of incentive systems must be integrated into a larger framework of organizational political economy. . . . Formal and substantive organizational democracy lies at the political heart of this explanation, and the polity's connections to the incentive economy should be the critical focus of future reports." A bibliography, "references," follows.

We have seen how the literature review emerged over the past half century. In the 1930s, papers began abruptly, with few or no references to other work (and, even then, sometimes to textbooks). Until the late 1950s, this practice continued. Authors did not pretend to connect their work to an existing field or body of knowledge, which they depicted as advancing slowly but surely, through the piece-meal findings of bench science. By the late 1960s, papers were beginning to be framed in terms of emerging bodies of knowledge, even if fewer references were cited than routinely occurs today. But only in 1978 do we see real literature reviews of the kind to which we have become accustomed, with scores of cites arrayed parenthetically at the beginning of papers, after which authors frequently derive testable hypotheses.

MARGINALIA

Some of the most interesting changes over the past sixty years in American sociology articles occur at the margins—titles, abstracts, number of authors, acknowledgments, notes, one-column or two-column pages, bibliographies. As I have indicated earlier, science increasingly recruits marginalia to produce the science aura, although this effort is not always entirely successful. Instead, writing at the margins, if read deconstructively, conceals the beating heart of authoriality, which chafes against its confinement by the literary norms of science. As we are learning here, the literary norms of science did not apply to sociology much before the 1960s and 1970s. Or, perhaps better said, the literary norms of social science were quite different, allowing the margins a resonant voice and not simply subordinating them to science's totalizing project. Indeed, the authorial meanderings of sociology's contemporary marginalia were not relegated to front matter, back matter, or bottom matter but were more likely to be integrated into the text itself, undercutting the hierarchy of text over subtext, center over margin. This refusal to hierarchize one text over another within a single oeuvre is one of the hallmarks of good sociological writing, as I understand it.

Let me begin with titles. I cannot find a single subtitle, qualifying the main title, before 1958, and only one in 1958. Beginning in 1968, the vast majority of articles sport subtitles, typically providing a lengthy technical description qualifying a flashier main title. If science establishes its identity with technical subtitles, sociology was prescientific until the late 1960s, at the earliest. One also observes a generalizing intent in many of the early titles: "Differential Intensity of Intra-societal Diffusion," "The Sociological Significance of Measurable Attitudes," "Social Background and Musical Taste." Contrast these with more contemporary titles: "Determinants and Behavioral Consequences of Psychological Modernity: Empirical Evidence from Costa Rica," "Action and Information in the Job Mobility Process: The Search Decision." This is not a seamless pattern; one finds articles without subtitles (and with sole authors) in the contemporary period. However, science-like titles definitely belong to the post-1970 period in U.S. sociology, signaling the discipline's collective effort to reinforce its eroding legitimacy in the wake of the fractious social movements of the sixties.

Just as telling, we do not find abstracts until the 1960s. As I said earlier, the assumption that articles *can* be abstracted is a hallmark of bench science. The more sprawling and essayistic the article, the less appropriate abstracts are. It is no accident that the shift toward methods-driven bench science in the 1970s and after coincides with the *ASR* requirement that articles begin with abstracts. Minor technical innovations in treating various "variables" lend themselves to being summarized at the beginning of the article. This is not to suggest that 1930s or 1940s articles were always global grand narratives; a few were, but most were not. It is to suggest that minor advances in method did not command journal space in the pre-1970 period. Abstracts belong to the literary arsenal of a cumulating discipline in the sense that they tersely summarize advances in objective knowledge. The contribution of such articles is not the totality of the presentation but merely *findings,* which, once found, can be summarized in a hundred or so words. Abstracts are a hallmark of bench science, producing the literary impression that findings that advance the field slightly have, in fact, been found. The 1938 article on elopement, however fine-grained by the prevailing standards of the discipline, did not position itself as bench science adding to an existing stock of knowledge about marriage and family. Instead of beginning with a dispassionate, italicized account of the article's findings, positioned at the top of the first page underneath a science-like title, the 1938 article begins quite discursively: "Why do people elope?" Why, indeed.

It is not assumed that we already know a good deal about elopement. It is not assumed that elopement has generated a field of parallel and cumulating research studies. "Why do people elope?" could as well begin an essay in *Time* magazine or *Redbook*. This is not to denigrate the rigor of the method used in the 1938 article but only to notice the essayistic, accessible style of journal sociology until about 1970, when method came to rule. Titles and whole articles invited readers into the text, refusing to sacrifice substance on the altar of technique, something that would not happen on a wide scale until the 1970s. Although 1938 articles were positivist in the sense that most of their authors subscribed to the tenets of Comtean social physics, it was a considered positivism that could be argued, and opposed. Although not an open forum of social and literary criticism—not *The New Republic,* let alone *Les Temps modernes*—the *ASR* in the 1930s and 1940s was more diverse, open and dialogical than the *ASR* today, which has become nearly a monolith of mathematics. How else do we explain the fact that Leo Lowenthal, a charter member of the Frankfurt School, authored an *ASR* obituary of Else Frenkel-Brunswik, one of Adorno's empirical coauthors? Although this effort to read titles and even obituaries may be viewed as a frivolous exercise in reading tea leaves—marginalia!—the fact that the *ASR* no longer runs obituaries and mimics science titles, in addition to littering its pages with figural gestures, suggests that the journal is less an open forum than it used to be. As I have been saying throughout, it is less an open forum of methods and theories because there has been a kind of methodological and theoretical closure since 1970, as speculative sociology has been driven out by technical work framed as cumulative empiricism.

Although the *ASR* before the 1970s published its share of mundane descriptive pieces that did not test or advance larger theories, this was leavened by pieces authored by the likes of Parsons and Merton on the appropriate scope and method of sociology. Although both are positivist in their ways, bending theory to the exigencies of empirical investigation in what I contend were wrong-headed ways, Parsons and Merton violated the discursive program of positivism at every turn, writing sweeping essays littered with literary references that required readers to have an un-American cultural formation. One of the main problems of American sociological theory, I contend, is that few readers shared Parsons's erudition and thus they accepted at face value his appropriation of European theoretical themes. Parsons, Weber, and Durkheim became America's Weber and Durkheim, omitting their angst and implicit critique of capitalist alienation and thus transmogrifying them into partisans of Eisenhower's America. An alternative Weber, Durkheim, and Simmel could be read as harbingers of the Frankfurt School's critique of domination.

Titles and abstracts are only the tip of the iceberg. The whole apparatus of journal sociology before 1970 bespoke a different conception of its discourse and thus of its world. Before the 1970s and 1980s, most sociology is composed by single authors. In 1938, I sampled one coauthored paper. In 1948, there were none in my sample that were not sole authored. In 1958, two out of four were coauthored. In 1968, none were coauthored. After 1968, many articles were coauthored or multi-authored. In the 1970s, sociologists began to work in teams, including colleagues and graduate students at their home institutions and at other institutions, supported by large grants and involving complicated data sets. By now, the majority of main-stream sociology and political science articles are authored by more than a single person as empirical social science has become a team enterprise, mobilizing both per-sonnel and resources. Hiring and promotion and tenure committees "control for" coauthorship in weighing an individual scholar's credentials: Does the person coau-thor with peers or with senior colleagues and former dissertation supervisors? Has the person ever published alone? Does order of authorship reveal inequality of con-tribution? Sometimes, one's coauthors are asked for testimonial statements about the extent of one's contribution. In the major research-oriented sociology departments, it is common for scholars to be tenured and then promoted to full professor on the strength of records in which coauthorship is the norm, not the exception.

For scholars from the more genteel quarters of the university campus, this can be disturbing, especially by the standards of lonely scholarship in the humanities. I deaned a College of Liberal Arts skewed toward the humanities. There was gen-eral suspicion about social science team authorship and an expectation that faculty needed a book for tenure and ideally a second book for promotion to professor. Not only was this oblivious to the norms prevailing in empirical social research today; it also peculiarly overvalues the effort expended in publishing one's first book, almost always the dissertation, and then a second book, often the humanist scholar's only major research project after graduate school. In this context, some of the most prolific social science faculty can be systematically undertenured and underpromoted where the humanities model of book production holds sway and, with it, a somewhat antique conception of sole authorship as the sine qua non of academic advancement. Prejudices of this sort flow both ways: article writers in the social sciences frequently view books as derivative scholarship less worthy than arti-cles. A former chairperson of mine told me that I could not photocopy my book manuscripts on the departmental Xerox machine because "books only report research, whereas articles are research." Article producers who "count" books as legitimate scholarship sometimes propose an algorithm according to which one book is "worth" six articles.

These debates are not simply about disciplinary norms and interdisciplinary intol-erance. They reflect deep intellectual and political investments in various models of scholarship. An epistemological pluralist, I am intolerant only of intolerance! That is, the positivist program as I understand it necessarily excludes non-positivist ways of knowing and writing. I do not oppose quantitative empiricism and its var-ious figural and methodological strategies unless those strategies exclude nonquan-titative work as a demonized literary Otherness. We get into trouble only where positivists claim to exhaust empiricism, as they frequently state or imply.

So titles, abstracts, and number of authors signal important things about the ways in which sociologists compose themselves. As well, one of the most marginal pieces of marginalia, acknowledgments, tells a lot about the discipline. As with other aspects of sociological journal articles, only in the 1970s do we begin to see acknowledgments that resemble the floral, elaborate acknowledgments of the present, attesting to an author's proximity to a disciplinary power center and to nodes of funding. Not a single 1938 article in my sample offered acknowledgments. By 1948, terse acknowledgments appear in half of the sample articles. One example reads: "The substance of this paper was delivered in an address to the American Association of Marriage Counselors, April 10, 1948. The writer wishes to thank Dr. Herbert S. Conrad, who critically read this paper in manuscript and offered valuable suggestions." The other 1948 article thanked two prepublication readers. In 1958, only one of four sampled papers acknowledged others' help. A sociologist is thanked for providing data, and three other sociologists are acknowledged for having read and commented upon the manuscript.

Articles from the 1968 sample all include acknowledgments. One briefly acknowledges the indispensable help of a senior scholar in the field. He is not credited with having read the manuscript. Another thanks a single scholar for his help. A third is lengthier and acknowledges grant support from the National Institute of Mental Health and a center at the University of Michigan. The author indicates that the article is based on her Michigan dissertation and thanks six people for their help, one of whom is presumably her spouse. Some of the others were probably on her Michigan dissertation committee. This set of acknowledgments edges closer to the contemporary model, which thanks everyone under the sun. In 1978, both articles sport acknowledgments. In each case, three scholars are thanked for having helped with the ideas and/or the manuscripts. (In one case, the people thanked were probably members of the author's dissertation committee at Berkeley.) In the second case, granting agencies are acknowledged, as are scholars who read the manuscript and three people who helped in data collection and with editorial work. Some or all of these people may have been graduate students at the authors' home institutions. Finally, we see the first acknowledgment in the sample of an anonymous *ASR* reviewer.

In 1988, all three articles sampled bear acknowledgments. Two are brief, thanking editors, anonymous readers, and named readers as well as a funding source. The third is lengthy, thanking four readers by name, as well as anonymous reviewers, and acknowledging support by the National Science Foundation and the Russell Sage Foundation. Data sources at Indiana and Minnesota are acknowledged. Finally, the audiences at two presentations of this paper are thanked—one at the ASA and the other in the Indiana University Sociology Department. This latter gesture has become common in 1990s sociology, suggesting both that the paper has been given a dry run or two and that the authors have sufficient visibility to conference widely. Although 1988-style acknowledgments do not differ much in format and content from those in the late 1990s, in the decade since 1988, acknowledgments have become denser with names of people and organizations to be thanked. Authors construct themselves as having worth because they received extensive support from faculty, graduate students, and agencies in their research efforts. Although it is ungenerous not to give credit where credit is due, acknowledgments construct authorial identity as much as express gratitude for minor favors.

The fact that authorial identity is constructed in these peripheral ways suggests that the text of sociological science excludes or extirpates identity, requiring subjectivity to secure any moorings available, even in agate type at the bottom of the opening page. There is a certain desperation entailed in positioning oneself as a networked, conferenced, granted author with friends in high places. It is the desperation of virtually everyone at a time when subjectivity is assailed from all sides by what the Frankfurt School theorists, with prescience, called "total administration." *ASR* articles of the present are totally administered and administering, reproducing a science-like format formulaically and enduring editorial and review processes that further constrain both argument and authoriality.

Since the 1930s, notes, like other marginalia, have evolved. Until the 1960s, there were no bibliographies or "references" listing the sources cited parenthetically in the body of the text. Notes contained references, which in itself gave notes a certain substantive importance. I calculated the mean number of footnotes in each of the years since 1938 from which I drew samples. An interesting pattern emerges. If one considers the years between 1938 and 1958, during which time there were no bibliographies, the mean number of footnotes per article in the sample was twelve. Between 1968, the first sample year in which there were bibliographies, and 1988, the mean number of footnotes per article was 10.2, representing some decline with the inception of the bibliography. Examining the number of footnotes per article decade by decade, we find that in 1938 there were 9.25 notes per article, fifteen in 1948, 11.8 in 1958, nine in 1968, 8.5 in 1978, and thirteen in 1988. Between 1948 and 1978, then, there was a steady rate of decline in the number of footnotes per *ASR* article in the sample. This might be characterized as the first stage or phase in the discipline's scientific prehistory. But there is a distinctive second phase, beginning with an upturn in the number of notes per article in 1988. Thus, there were two sharp upturns in notes per article, first between 1938 and 1948 (an increase of 5.75 per article) and second between 1978 and 1988 (4.5 per article). The second upturn represents what I am calling the second wave of the discipline's approximation of science, which corresponds with other developments in disciplinary discourse such as the increasing use of mathematical notation and figures in articles. Predictably, notes dominating journal discourse in 1978, 1988, and 1998 are highly technical in nature, with notes in quantitative articles almost always dealing with arcane issues of methodology.

Although *ASR* notes have always been somewhat technical in the methods sections, before 1968 notes, as I just observed, contained publication references of works cited in the body of the text. Although a subset of notes in pre-1968 articles were technical in nature, after 1968 virtually all notes are technical, with an increase in the number of notes between 1978 and 1988 corresponding to the recent turn toward high science and high methodology after the 1970s. Interestingly, since 1988, there has been a leveling off, after the second wave of scientific elevation. Between 1993 and 1998, the average number of notes per sampled article is thirteen, with virtually all notes concerning methodology. In 1998, the number of notes per sampled article is also thirteen. Although the average number of notes per sampled article is roughly the same in 1948 and 1998, in 1948 the notes were more likely to be publication references of cited work, whereas in 1998 the notes are more likely to be methodological clarifications now that citations are connected to full publication references listed in the bibliography. From this, it could be concluded that we are actually seeing an ascendance of the footnote in journal sociology, although this is not the antique footnote in the philosophy treatise or the work of speculative sociological theory, in which the author plumbs an issue or dispute for nuances, but the contemporary footnote given over to methodological technique and clarification. It may well be that the proliferation of footnotes is the author's way of responding to reviewers' technical comments and suggestions in order to satisfy editors that they have covered their bases before publication, as we saw in the preceding chapter.

Let me add a methodological aside. The average nonquantitative article in my sample of *ASR* articles between 1993 and 1998 had a larger number of notes than the average quantitative article during the same period. This is because such articles have to work overtime in order to produce a semblance of the science aura, laboring to introduce technical detail as well as textual differentiation (e.g., fine print) where they were denied access to quantitative gestures by the nature of their method. The nonquantitative articles published between 1993 and 1998 that I surveyed were dense with parenthetical citations, quotes in the body of the text, many footnotes, and even the occasional representation—for example, the map of England or transcripts of conversations I mentioned earlier. Absent data, the authors of such articles need to produce the impression of technical virtuosity, if not the virtuosity of sheer method. Footnotes and parenthetical citations are ways of producing this impression; they are figural gestures. However, one must not overgeneralize: one of the only examples of a recent qualitative *ASR* article with absolutely no figural gestures disdained footnotes altogether. This article, on the civil rights movement in Birmingham, also eschewed the literary norm of acknowledging the gradual cumulation of the literature in the field. As we recall, this author, a Northwestern sociologist, positioned his study against the weight of prevailing consensus about his topic. In general, it is safe to say that there is a tendency for qualitative and theoretical articles published in mainstream sociology journals to proliferate more footnotes and longer bibliographies than quantitative articles, which produce the science aura through methodological gestures.

Footnotes have a rather different role and scope in theory. During the mid-1990s, *Sociological Theory,* the ASA dues-supported theory journal, had an average footnote rate of fifteen notes per article. Most of the notes are short, citing additional material or offering interpretive asides. This rate of fifteen notes/article is not significantly different from the current *ASR* rate of thirteen notes/article. But theoretical and qualitative articles in the *ASR* tend to have many more notes than either of these averages, suggesting that theory behaves differently in mainstream journals than in theory journals, given the differences in context. Nonquantitative authors behave like quantitative authors in order to get published: they figure their work, with such embellishments as notes if not mathematical notation.

I have already mentioned the decision of *ASR* editors in 1943 to move from one-column to two-column journal pages, emulating the natural sciences. Interestingly, *Sociological Theory* has made a point of sticking to one-column pages, suggesting an essayistic, non-positivist quality. It is worth considering changes in the graphic design of the *ASR* over the years. At first glance, apart from the move to two-column pages, there has been little change. Article title is printed in all caps, below which, in smaller-point type, we find the author's name, also in all caps. In minute type, below the author's name, we find her institutional affiliation, italicized. In 1959, abstracts are introduced. Printed in italics of apparently the same-point type as author's affiliation, abstracts are interposed between author's affiliation and the beginning of the text. However, upon close examination, we notice a 1971 change in the *ASR*'s first page, which, like other changes such as one-column presentation, signals the journal's move toward science. Between the author's affiliation and the abstract, we find the full publication reference of the article—"American Sociological Review 1978, Vol. 43 (April):177-198." This gesture is a labor-saving device. It allows readers who may photocopy the article or request a reprint from the author to situate the paper correctly. Ten years later, in 1981, an even more science-like signature is adopted by the *ASR*: full *ASR* publication references are moved to the bottom of the first page, a product label that warrants the product's authenticity and scientificity.

Finally, there is the matter of bibliographies, called "references" in *ASR* science parlance. Bibliography connotes a broader tableau of cited and uncited works that not only provides textual references but suggests further reading. References are only those publications cited, usually parenthetically, in the text. References are a signature of science, signifying the literature cited in the opening literature review. They make footnote references to other texts unnecessary, leaving the field of notes open to technical sidebars. Although there is a certain undeniable economy in bibliographies/references that are clustered together, the movement of citations from notes at the bottom of the page to the end of the article disrupts intertextual readings that move quickly from text to the works cited in the text. This is the beauty of footnotes: they allow text and subtext to play off against each other without the labor of moving from page to end of article or book. In this way, footnotes acknowledge the undecidability of texts that allow for digressions, deferrals, intertextuality, and polyvocality without fearing the loss of legitimacy. Footnotes are echoes of other voices contained within the text's own voice.

In 1968, the *ASR* began publishing bibliographies or references. This caused the rate of footnotes per article temporarily to decline, until the 1970s, when the rate of footnotes began to incline, caused by methodological preoccupations that translated into technical notes. As I said above, some of these notes are probably driven by reviewers' concerns. In the 1968 articles I sampled, the average number of items in the bibliographies of articles was twenty-five. In 1978, the average was forty-two. A theoretical article from 1978 was an outlier, with fully 181 bibliography items, again suggesting the need for theory to produce the science aura in ways that do not rely on quantitative method. This huge theory bibliography could be viewed as a figural gesture in its own right. By 1988, the average number of bibliography items was fifty-one. The rate of incline in the volume of bibliographies suggests not only the proliferation of literatures that authors feel they need to cite in order to claim comprehensiveness, with each bibliography reproducing the one before it and adding new cites. It also suggests that bibliographies have become a form of figure, as they certainly are for nonquantitative articles with hundreds of cites. Bibliographies in *Annual Review of Sociology* articles are often sprawling, even by the standards of the *ASR,* inasmuch as *Annual Review* pieces intend to provide authoritative reviews of the respective literatures of various fields.

The growth of bibliographies corresponds to a general growth of marginalia by comparison to rather more parsimonious *ASR* articles of the prescientific, pre-1970 period, especially the one-column presentations of the 1930s. I contend that these marginalia—abstracts, dense titles, acknowledgments, technical footnotes, bibliographies, and appendices—can be interpreted either as science-like gestures that legitimize sociology in an era of institutional contraction or as the beating heart of authoriality—the survival of the subtext in which authors step outside the lines of journal strictures and compose themselves in relatively unsupervised ways. As I said earlier, no one edits or critically comments on the abstract or acknowledgments. Marginalia are unsupervised territory, allowing authors to be authors. This is not to deny that marginalia are governed by certain literary norms; as I have amply demonstrated, *ASR* marginalia reproduce themselves, evidencing a striking commonality. It could be said that marginalia are a contested terrain on which an autonomous literary subjectivity vies with the forces of disciplinary power and control for the right to breathe.

8

Sociological Writing in the Wake of Postmodernism

RETURNING TO SOCIOLOGY'S NARRATIVE PERIOD?

In this book, I have found much fault with contemporary sociology, judging from the forty articles I surveyed that were published between 1995 and the present and the 150 reviews and authors' and editors' letters that I read. I have also traced the history of *American Sociological Review* (*ASR*) discourse since 1938, demonstrating that the resemblance of contemporary journal sociology to the discourse of the hard sciences only began in earnest in about 1970, although I took pains to show that the seeds of both doctrinal and discursive positivism were planted nearly half a century before. I hope that my analysis has been of value to apprenticing sociologists as they contend with the submission of their work for publication and confront the language games, as I am calling them, of positivist sociological writing. Also, I hope to have shed light on shortcomings of these language games, especially where they are not only impenetrable by technically unsophisticated readers but also tend to replace reason with method, thus undermining the potential of sociology to enlighten and criticize.

My purpose, though, is not merely to find fault. In this chapter, I want to explore alternative modes of sociological discourse that do not betray the empiricist project and suggest how these would affect the activities of authors, reviewers, and editors. This is necessarily a utopian chapter, going beyond critique toward practical alternatives, where possible. Unfortunately, although pre-1970 sociology has a great deal to recommend it, whether the essayistic and technically undemanding meanderings of 1930s and 1940s *ASR* articles or C. Wright Mills's *Sociological Imagination,* I am not suggesting that we return to a golden age, before methodology, when U.S. sociology belonged to the public sphere. There was no such age. However, there was a narrative period during which method had not become gestural and the main text of writing was text, not figure. I contend that narrativity can be retrieved, using the prehistory of *ASR* articles and many other book publications in sociology as useful models.

By *narrativity* (see Jameson 1981) I mean the way in which writing acknowledges that it is, indeed, writing, an authorial practice and product. The opposite of narrativity in this sense is *representation,* where writing purports to reflect a world "out there," without authorial mediation. The most extreme case of representation occurs in natural science and in the science-like social science disciplines, where the use of mathematics as what I call gesture, connoting the "science aura," lards the text, squeezing out prose and reducing the impression of the text's narrativity, its having-been-written by an author with perspective. Although one can embrace positivism as a theory of knowledge that seeks to describe natural or social laws, precisely Comte's agenda, and still exhibit narrativity in one's writing, the tendency since about 1970 in U.S. sociology is for non-positivists to embrace narrativity and for positivists to expunge it, where possible, from their writing—hence my term *secret writing* for journal discourse. Postmodern theory is read by many positivists to embrace narrativity, especially where Derrida said that "there is nothing outside the text," which is misinterpreted to mean that there isn't a social or natural world but only texts about the world. Postmodernism *does* embrace narrativity as a vital recognition of the discursive constitution of social and cultural reality. However, this gets confused by opponents of postmodernism with Lyotard's contention in *The Postmodern Condition* that a "grand narrative," a total science or theory, of the world is impossible or at least undesirable, given the tendency of totalizing systems to issue in authoritarian political consequences. Thus, partisans of a positivist sociology, who reject Lyotard's critique of grand narratives, reject all narrative-like writing, writing that makes the author present and opens itself to debate.

In the first instance, I contend that we in sociology would be better off if we practice and preach *author-present* writing, which is another term for narrativity. Although I do not endorse the notion of a sociological golden age, to which we should turn back the clock, it is clear from my reading of pre-1970 *ASR* articles that narrativity was abundant in journal sociology until mathematics became gesture during and since the 1970s. Although most U.S. journal sociology embraces positivist doctrine, notably Comte's suggestion that sociology seek to describe social laws as a kind of "social physics," this was not inconsistent with narrativity, or author-present writing, until the death of the author occurred in about 1970. Although positivism always intended the death of the author, or it contained premises about the relationship between knowledge and the world that required that the author be removed from the text of science and social science, the author was not vanquished by positivists until the sociological establishment decided that sociology's declining institutional and societal fortunes during the 1970s could only be reversed by legitimating sociology as science, which, they thought, required the de-narrativization of sociological discourse through mathematics. This did not happen in a smoke-filled room filled with the leading theorists, methodologists, and epistemologists but occurred gradually, as graduate training began to emphasize advanced methodology, academic administrators placed a greater premium on obtaining outside funding for one's research, journal editors published mathematized work, and sociologists presented such work at national and regional meetings. Over time, these practices reproduced themselves in the work of a younger generation of sociologists, who have taken the cue from disciplinary changes that occurred during the 1960s and 1970s. And accompanying all of this was a rapid contraction of the tenure-track sociology job market through the decade of the 1970s, making it very difficult for junior sociologists to compete successfully unless they were perceived to do cutting-edge, fundable, highly figured work.

In the past ten years, non-quantitative sociologists have begun to re-narrativize sociological writing at the margin. This has necessarily been a marginal, although quite visible, movement, among symbolic interactionists; critical theorists; feminists; and students of race, gender, and culture. It has been marginal because graduate training and hiring in the most prestigious departments are still by and large controlled by positivists who view narrativity writ large (postmodernism, critical theory, feminist theory) as a threat to sociology's newfound legitimacy. Scholars such as Charles Lemert, Steven Seidman, Norman Denzin, John O'Neill, Stanley Aronowitz, Patricia Clough, Laurel Richardson, and Richard Harvey Brown have endorsed European theoretical developments that allow us to read and write sociology as a "text" driven by certain political and social interests. Although the book display at the annual meeting of the American Sociological Association (ASA) boasts many titles that drink deeply of these theoretical and interpretive developments—think of the lists of Routledge, Blackwell, Sage UK—for the most part these intellectual developments have been marginalized and are likely to remain marginalized in U.S. sociology until these visible senior faculty train doctoral students who find tenure-track jobs in the leading departments.

Nevertheless, narrativity has reentered American sociology, if only through the backdoor. It will be difficult to vanquish it, even if the *ASR* does not publish many narrativizing articles such as those by Aldon Morris, Karin Martin, and Harland Prechel that acknowledge that they are perspectival, passionate, even polemical, let alone articles by prominent postmodernists, feminist theorists, and critical theorists. The genie of narrativity is out of the bottle, as faculty and students question the meaninglessness of mathematized sociology, much as we questioned the relevance of Parsonian structural-functionalism in the late 1960s, when an engaged sociology helped us understand and restructure our world in turmoil. Sociologists, like fellow academics in neighboring disciplines such as anthropology and history and more distant disciplines such as English, are beginning to think sociologically about their writing as discourse, containing assumptions and values that, they argue, need to be spelled out, given the undecidability of all texts and their constraint by their own language game. Derrida meets Wittgenstein.

Think of it this way. Texts, including that of science, are undecidable because they cannot define all their terms without resorting to terms that remain undefined. Ice is frozen water. But what does it mean to freeze? H_2O freezes below thirty-two degrees Fahrenheit. But what is Fahrenheit? Social facts are behaviors caused by external forces. What is causality? This is why Derrida said that all texts necessarily defer their meaning, awaiting definitions of definitions and clarifications of clarifications. Wittgenstein said that meaning is captive of language games, specific rules of usage in the practical discourses of everyday life. Methodology is one such language game, or, actually, many language games. One's speech and writing acquire meaning only in the context of the language game one inhabits, whether building a house, solving a riddle, or testing a theory. Unfortunately, certain critics of postmodernism conclude that these notions make science impossible in that they thwart objectivity and undermine the community of science. I contend that if science is viewed rhetorically, as scholars in the sociology of science have begun to do (see Mulkay 1979, 1985; Knorr-Cetina 1981), one can salvage objectivity as a goal and at the same time open science to many users, democratizing it and the society in which it is anchored. This is precisely Habermas's aim where he wants to rebuild the public sphere, a theme in his work since the early 1960s.

Narrativity, as I call it, undergirds a public science and social science, which play a role in creating a viable public sphere. In the following section, I outline the implications a public science would have for disciplinary discourse—writing, reviewing, editing—and for the organization of disciplines. Sociology has a great deal to offer in the way of conceptualizations of structured social inequality, including insights about how to bring about progressive social change. Unfortunately, Comte and the Enlightenment saddled sociology with scientific pretensions, seriously diminishing sociology's effectiveness as an agent of change. A potentially public social science fulfilled Comte's ambition for it by the 1970s, having become, at least rhetorically, a version of social physics. There is no getting around the fact that the past three decades of quantitative, grantworthy, highly figural sociology have produced very little enlightenment. Instead, sociologists have built careers, obtained outside funding, and piled up citations.

American sociology is a mature discipline and discourse in the sense that it is well organized, highly differentiated, and stratified, rhetorically formulaic. It is regaining institutional and societal prestige since its mathematization during the 1970s, competing successfully with "hard" disciplines such as psychology and economics for the ears and favors of academic administrators. Only a decade ago, following the lead of Washington University's administration, deans threatened to close down sociology departments because they were not paying their own way and appeared somewhat intellectually fragmented by comparison to the natural sciences and harder social sciences. In its degree of newfound politicization and intellectual fragmentation, English resembles the engaged sociology of the 1960s, disrupting the calm waters of academia as trends like cultural studies (Grossberg et al. 1992) and queer theory (Seidman 1996) scandalize. Stanley Fish is the Alvin Gouldner of the 1990s, publishing widely and cultivating his ever-widening spheres of influence in the discipline of English. Like Gouldner, he exudes self-confidence, drawing fire like a lightening rod. English has replaced sociology as the enfant terrible of the university. A few years ago, I attended a conference for new deans. We went around the table and indicated our most "difficult," obstreperous department. There was much laughter when everyone present said "English!" (including deans from the discipline of English). I am sure that many of us said this with tongue in cheek, recognizing, as surely we must have, that English is a site of intellectual energy and creative contention, much as sociology was in the 1960s.

Where English has become exciting, sociology has become drab, with its prosaic rhetorical rituals and pedestrian Midwestern empiricist departments, driven by scientism. Looking backward, I contest the claim that sociology fell on hard times because of its radicalism. First, many 1960s sociologists were never radicals, not only doing mainstream empiricism but also opposing or ignoring various new social movements. The war in Vietnam was not universally unpopular among the professoriate. Many sociologists were garden-variety empiricists who swore theoretical allegiance either to Merton's middle-range conception of theorizing or to Parsons's canonical functionalism, even if their empiricism was not particularly guided by it.

Although there was an important radical current in American sociology that gave birth to all sorts of interesting intellectual and political engagements, including the founding of the journal *Telos* in 1969 by Paul Piccone, these were developments against the grain. A young graduate student in philosophy who later became a tenure-track sociologist at Washington University, Gouldner's department, only to be denied tenure in spite of support from scholars as diverse as Jurgen Habermas and Daniel Bell, Piccone helped translate and explicate important developments in western Marxism and critical theory, including his own work in phenomenological Marxism, for a theoretically inclined generation of young social theorists attempting to make sense of the impasses of post–World War II capitalism and authoritarian state socialism (see Piccone 1983). Lukacs's 1923 *History and Class Consciousness* was translated into English two years later, followed the year after by Horkheimer and Adorno's *Dialectic of Enlightenment.* In 1973, Martin Jay, a Harvard Ph.D. in history, published *The Dialectical Imagination,* a history of the Frankfurt School from 1923 to 1950. Russell Jacoby, one of Marcuse's former Brandeis students and a regular correspondent for *Telos,* published *Social Amnesia* in 1975, signaling the emergence of a distinctively American voice in critical theory. William Leiss, another Marcuse student, published *The Domination of Nature* in 1973, a book blending Frankfurt School themes with issues raised by the nascent environmental movement and New Left.

These important intellectual developments growing out of and offering a retrospection on the antiauthoritarian themes of the American New Left—developments that spurred many an academic career in critical theory, including my own—had virtually no impact on American sociology. Although Gouldner's *Coming Crisis of Western Sociology* was published in 1970 and although Gouldner tried to protect the interests and tenure of his Washington University colleague Piccone, the Americanization of critical theory, which I regard as one of the few bright spots in post-1970 American academic life, had little impact on disciplinary sociology. Piccone lost his tenure fight. Tenured sociologists whose primary identity is critical theory can be counted on the fingers of two hands, with some left over: Stanley Aronowitz (CUNY-Graduate Center), John O'Neill (York in Canada), Ray

Morrow (Alberta), Craig Calhoun (NYU), Robert Antonio (Kansas), myself. Timothy Luke at Virginia Tech is a political scientist. He graduated from Washington University and participated in the *Télos* group. Doug Kellner (UCLA) is a philosopher by training. Mark Poster (Irvine) is an historian, as is Martin Jay (Berkeley). I have already addressed the multidisciplinarity and interdisciplinarity of critical theory. The fact remains that critical theory, which flourished on the American intellectual margins beginning in the late 1960s, has had little impact on sociology, in spite of caricatures offered by mainstream empiricists who sought to curtail theorizing of all kinds as a response to the delegitimation of sociology during the 1970s.

Critical theory is but one model of a public social science. Interestingly, Habermas, who has attempted to integrate bourgeois social theory into his overall perspective on a communicatively oriented critical theory in books such as *Theory of Communicative Action* and (1996) *Between Facts and Norms,* has been virtually ignored in American sociology, save for a handful of gratuitous cites. His integration of bourgeois social theory, especially Durkheim, Weber, and Parsons, into the project of critical theory has not been similarly integrated into the agenda of empirical sociology. His mastery of both diverse empirical and theoretical literatures has not been matched by workaday sociologists, who view Habermas's theorizing as non-sociology for its challenging style, affiliation to the Frankfurt School, and seemingly ungrounded formulations such as the "project of modernity." I contend that Habermas's work is immensely helpful for a discursively oriented sociology of sociology, or critique of disciplinarity, in that he draws attention to the ways in which language games encode political dynamics that need to be understood in the interest of both critique and enlightenment. Although clearly frustrated by disciplinary constraints, Habermas recognizes that critical theory must master the disciplines in transcending them toward a clearer understanding of what Hegel unashamedly called totality.

Disparaging mainstreamers say that Habermas's literary style defeats his own call for a revivified public sphere. His densest work is as impenetrable to amateurs as *ASR* mathematized sociology. Yet that is where the similarity ends: Habermas intends critical theory as a totalizing framework that includes public speech as one of its desiderata. Mathematized sociology has no apparent political telos, nor an address to totality. It is merely gesture. Its highly differentiated subject matter, treated in my earlier discussion of fields, attempts to move away from totality toward a mundane bench science that inches along toward the certainties of social physics. But as Hegel argued, particulars are imbued with the universal—here, the differentiated topics of journal sociology reflect larger theoretical assumptions and political preferences about the world. I contend that sociology secretly argues for the world it captures representationally, a world governed by intractable patterns, approaching iron laws, of social inequality—class, race, gender, technological, even religious. As I have said, most contemporary sociologists favor the liberal welfare state and want to see social problems, as Merton called them, alleviated. A few may even be socialist in their understanding of the relationship between bourgeois civil society and capitalist political economy. But their science is conservative in the sense that it portrays human beings as essentially manipulated by larger, intractable social forces, thus reducing their human agency. Although most people for the last 2,000 years have been held captive by overarching institutions and ideologies, this is *unnecessary* in Marx's sense; these large structures can be overthrown and overcome through people's, including writers', concerted efforts.

Liberal sociologists practice conservative science in order to legitimize their discipline during difficult times. Sociology's legitimation crisis is resolved with positivist journal discourse, grants, mathematically oriented graduate programs, the demonstration of societal relevance in addressing issues such as crime and health care. But the price of legitimation has been high: sociology has lost its critical edge, except at the margins of the discipline, especially as occupants of these margins cross into other, more engaged disciplines such as English and anthropology. For me, at least, this cost has been too high: mathematical elegance replaces sociological imagination. These are, of course, viewed as disjunctive alternatives, a hairy, muddle-headed Mills-era sociological activism posed as the only alternative to the seamlessness of current *ASR* discourse.

To be sure, qualitative sociologists and postmodern theorists embrace this disjunctive alternative, refusing the possibility of what Marcuse called new science. Too many non-positivist scholars reject science when, I would argue, they should only reject positivism, a particular theory of knowledge that has untoward ontological and social implications but that does not exhaust methodical knowing—science, by another name. Marcuse's concept of a new science drew on Freudian–Marxist impulses that allow science to be conceptualized as a vital, nonalienated human project that need not enslave people in the way that too many Enlightenment projects have. New science is praxis, cognitive self-externalization. In *Eros and Civilization,* Marcuse uses Nietzsche's image of a gay or happy science to describe playful knowing that does not violate nature nor reify concepts that take on a forbidding life of their own, as positivist concepts have. Although Habermas rejects the image of a new science as an unfortunate instance of original Frankfurt School romanticism, his stress on a public science enriches Marcuse's concept of new science by grounding new science and new technology firmly in the public sphere (Agger 1992).

What critical theory has lacked until recently is a foundation in discourse, which is broader than Habermas's concept of communication. Discourse includes disciplinary literary practices—academic writing as social practice, as Brodkey has called it. Inasmuch as science and social science are crucial to late capitalism, scientific discourse is a key political factor. This insight helps us theorize journal practices as political ones, not only criticizing positivist discourse as a means of domination but thinking beyond positivism toward new modes of scientific discourse and writing that have impact on the very organization of academic life in late capitalism. This is a topic not usually treated by theorists on the Left, who themselves may drink deeply of academic language games, sometimes losing the ability to position their critique of domination outside of, or beneath, high theory.

Much of my own work has failed to conduct the critique of the decline of discourse in sufficiently public terms. After all, in 1987, the year Jacoby published *The Last Intellectuals,* a book in which he lamented the academization of critical theory especially on the part of faculty then under forty-five, I was thirty-five, having received tenure just four years earlier. I was tenured, barely, on the strength of interpretive works of critical theory, which I attempted to defend as a legitimate species of academic social theory. My tenure was in the balance because I did not publish in mainstream sociology journals. I required fourteen outside letters evaluating my tenure case from scholars such as Martin Jay in history at Berkeley and Joe Feagin in sociology, then from Texas-Austin, before I was granted tenure at SUNY-Buffalo. This extensive vetting went far beyond what was expected of my quantitative colleagues. This is not to whine but to situate the relative obscurantism of my work in the need to legitimize my scholarship by grounding it in a tradition. Over time, as I began to understand the language game of positivism by listening to and reading my colleagues and by talking with doctoral students pressed to reproduce the mainstream intellectual styles of most of my colleagues, I realized that critical theory desperately needed a discursive perspective in order to understand what I called fast capitalism. Borrowing selectively from postmodern theory, I incorporated discursive issues into my work, leading me almost inevitably to the sociology of sociology. The more discursive my work became, the more I recognized the obligation to address critical theory's own discursive blind spots, much as Jacoby had done in *The Last Intellectuals,* albeit not as intellectual history, his approach, but rather as a critical reading of my own discipline and an attempt to compose public books and articles.

This reading of disciplinarity must augur a public sociology and not simply denounce mathematized journal discourse for its figural fetishism that diverts attention from the historicity of the social, of domination. As a Marxist, I view this historicity as the possibility of social change that emerges from the ashes of the old, dialectically. Social facts—structured social inequality—can be thawed by a perspective that views them both as what they "are" and what they are not yet. This dialectic eludes a mathematizing, reifying sociology that freezes the historical present into eternity, laws, much as Comte, Durkheim, Weber, and Parsons did. Although all acknowledged the irrationality of overly severe inequality and exploitation, sociologists could only ameliorate these manifestations of an inexorable historical reason, which flowers in the eternal present of late capitalism. Only Marx viewed domination and exploitation as eradicable, under the gaze (and, I would add, discourse) of the dialectical thinker who imagines things as what they appear to be *and* as their possible negation. In this way, a public sociology must articulate clearly how social facts are defined by their historicity, which could lead these facts to be negated through both critique and action.

It is not enough to assert the historicity of social facts, although that is a beginning. The world must be imaginatively portrayed as fluid, available to transformation, in the various milieux in which people live their lives. This is an everyday sociology inasmuch as we must connect people's lives and the enveloping structures conditioning them. The model for this is found in both Marx and Mills, where they called for a sociological imagination linking public and private. I am trying to ground sociological imagination in sociologists' discourse, much as Lemert tried to ground sociological imagination in a historically based account of how people can view their biographies sociologically and thus, in effect, become amateur sociologists and hence better citizens.

> There are many different kinds of sociologies, some of them academic ones, but the most important ones are the sociologies whereby people make sense of their lives with others. Literally speaking, sociologies are nothing more than logics of social things. Though some persons are specially trained in the logic, or science, of social things, even this qualification begins where it begins for us all. Advanced education is not required for a person to recognize the truth of some things. (Lemert 1997: x–xi)

This is very much the spirit of ethnomethodologically oriented sociologies, beginning with Garfinkel (also see Berger and Luckmann 1967 and O'Neill 1974). However, Lemert retains a duality of perspectives, both from ground up and structure down. Garfinkel removed sociology's prior privilege by suggesting that sociology, like all other everyday projects, is practical reasoning done in the natural attitude, as Husserl called it, enjoying no distance from the fray. Although sociology is practice and discourse, immersed in its own language games, Garfinkel essentially denies the reality of social structure, to which Lemert and O'Neill provide correctives. Lemert inverts Garfinkel where he suggests that everyday life can be sociological, with people bringing elevated wisdom and pre-theoretical sophistication to their practical involvements. This is emancipatory where it suggests the possibility of a democratic public sphere grounded in everyday settings in which people not only make sense together but make sense of society together, reasoning about freedom and justice in sophisticated ways.

For his part, Mills in the late 1950s did not confront a maturely mathematical discipline, although he recognized the early signs of sociology's methodological compulsions.

> Probably no one familiar with [the] practitioners [of quantitative sociology] would care to deny that many of them are dominated by concern with their own scientific status; their most cherished professional self-image is that of the natural scientist. In their arguments about various philosophical issues of social science, one of their invariable points is that they *are* "natural scientists," or at least that they "represent the viewpoint of natural science. . . ." What [these sociologists] have done, in brief, is to embrace one philosophy of science which they now suppose to be The Scientific Method. This model of research is largely an epistemological construction; within the social sciences, its most decisive result has been a sort of methodological inhibition. By this I mean that the kinds of problems that will be taken up and the way in which they are formulated are quite severely limited by The Scientific Method. Methodology, in short, seems to determine the problems. (Mills 1959: 56–57)

I concentrate on writing because writing connects graduate education to what lies beyond in one's emerging professional career. What and how students learn to write in graduate school has impact not only on their careers, such as where and what they publish, but it also has impact on the discipline, which is reproduced and potentially redirected through the next generations of sociologists. The *ASR* could not freeze social facts into our fate without the literary interventions of positivist sociologists who write, review, and edit, disguising ideology as sheer representation. The earlier that students pay attention to issues of narrativity, the more clearly will they recognize that their discursive investments in one version of sociology or another are choices that could be made differently. Scientific sociology does not fall from the sky but is the artifact of thousands of busy scribes who, at some level of consciousness, recognize that they are writers. As I said, sociology is secret writing. The first step in the transformation of our discipline is to realize that sociology is writing, embracing narrativity—the writer's presence. Only by recognizing this can we recognize that sociology authors a world that is susceptible to different versions, especially non-positivist versions allowing for fundamental social change. If sociology's narrativity is rejected in favor of an image of sociology as representation, we necessarily freeze the present world into place. Social facts become our social fate.

> To think sociologically is to dwell upon a question we have answered long ago: How it is that men belong to one another despite all differences? This is the task of a *wild sociology,* namely, to dwell upon the platitudes of convention, prejudice, place, and love; to make of them a history of the world's labor and to root sociology in the care of the circumstance and particulars that shape the divine predicaments of ordinary men. The work of sociology, then, is to confront the passionless world of science with the epiphany of family, of habit and of human folly, outside of which there is no remedy. This is not to deny scientific sociology. It is simply to treat it as a possibility that has yet to convince the world. (O'Neill 1974: 10)

Like Lemert and Mills, O'Neill does not reject a methodologically inclined sociology but reads method as a discourse no more or less compelling on its face than other discursive formulations of sociology's task, or of other human tasks. A phenomenological Marxist who has learned from ethnomethodology, O'Neill wants wild sociology, as he calls it, to change the world, but he is fearful of absolute knowledge that pretends to solve the riddle of history from outside of history. This is very much Horkheimer and Adorno's critique of the Enlightenment, which, they contend, betrayed its own emancipatory aims by counterposing mythology and science, which they argue has become a new mythology. O'Neill endorses Marcuse's argument for a new science, although he grounds it somewhat differently, in Vico and Merleau-Ponty. Unless one pays close attention, positivists may be so threatened by O'Neill's critique of science that they presume, mistakenly, that he opposes all science. The following passage, although serpentine, demonstrates otherwise.

I do not want to settle before I begin the question of the relation of scientific languages to everyday speech and talk. I have begun by trying to show a concern for how it is we manage any departure together, how we approach understanding building upon the great platitudes of our experience as embodied beings, with our speech set in local needs and circumstances. To say that we are sociologists is only to remark on the materials at hand, upon the necessity of working on this rather than that. We must first raise the question of what it is that is presupposed by the field we have chosen to work. The practice of sociology, like any other discipline, is precarious. It soon leaves us unable to remember our first motives for doing it at all. The aim of method, as I understand it, is to test in us that strange distance between our work and those for whom we intend it. Sociologists are particularly attached to methods for the sake of their claim to scientific status; I am concerned with the poetic claims of method. (O'Neill 1974: 12)

O'Neill could as well have said *the discursive claims of method*. Very few working sociologists would characterize the "aim of method" as a test of "that strange distance between our work and those for whom we intend it." O'Neill is here reflecting on the distance that sociology seeks between itself and everyday life, recognizing that distance is possible but only a distance premised on connection. Sociology is borne of everyday life and necessarily returns to it as "practical idealism."

Method plays the music in what is of interest to us; it shapes our sensibilities, determines our passions, and defines our world. Method is our practical idealism; it is the opening in things and of ourselves toward them. This is possible because we are able to convert our private enthusiasms into objective enterprises that, in turn, are never accomplished once and for all and so require of us a constant response according to our own need. (O'Neill 1974: 12)

O'Neill says that we come to sociology with "private enthusiasm" and we transform this into a project, an "objective enterprise." This project is never complete and so we return to its origins in our original need to embark on the sociological path, whether we seek only to understand ourselves and our fellows better or also to modify social arrangements. The two, of course, do not contradict each other. My wife began to read and write in the field of the sociology of adoption, departing somewhat from her earlier interests in the sociology of household labor, when we adopted two children. Her intellectual interest in adoption does not remain outside of her other concerns but informs them, and they it, as her personal and professional lives intersect and interact.

I have picked Mills, O'Neill, and Lemert because they all address the narrativity of sociology, one from the late 1950s, one from the 1970s, and one from the 1990s. All of these passages are examples of good writing, as I see it, resonating with authorial presence, which is ill-concealed, indeed, which is celebrated as the occasion of the authors' sociological interests. In the case of O'Neill's *Making Sense Together,* from which I have drawn three passages, the sense of narrativity is accentuated for me because I was his student at the time he wrote the manuscript of the book, which was eventually published by Harper & Row. Earlier, I described how

O'Neill launched me on the road to academia, exposing me to the craft of his own writing. I remember well how O'Neill shared the typescript of *Making Sense Together* with his students and how excited I was not only to read about the inherence of the sociological craft in "practical idealism" but also to witness sociological authorship in the flesh, as it were. O'Neill inspired authorship by authoring. Previously, he had shared other drafts. And I observed how he had piles of pages written in his circular longhand stacked on his bookshelf. He also shared with me a set of galley proofs of a forthcoming book on phenomenology, as I recall, by Richard Zaner, a philosopher at Southern Methodist in Dallas. These proofs were yellow and printed on flimsy paper. O'Neill explained that proofs are an intermediate stage between scribbling and publication, allowing an author—again, that word!—another chance at revision and tweaking.

I was seventeen years old at the time. These experiences of vicarious authorship were gained in a freshman seminar on Marx and Hegel at York University near Toronto. We read *Phenomenology of Mind* and the *Economic and Philosophical Manuscripts.* I should say that we tried to read them! We met weekly and O'Neill gave us strong Canadian beer and tried to make sense of the relevance of these writings for sociology and social thought. We had to give presentations. I remember that he advised me to read a book by Kojève on Hegel that would help me understand the *Phenomenology.* For me, at least, Kojève was every bit as difficult! Although I cannot remember the exact timing of my decision, sometime during that first year of college I decided to become a social theorist, like O'Neill, our teacher and author. In retrospect, the example of his own self-consciousness as a writer, his narrativity, was the major reason I chose what I imagined would be a very exciting life. A few years later I published a book review in *The Canadian Forum,* the *New Republic* of Canada, and my own authorial career was launched. I remember my first flash of authorial self-consciousness when I saw the short review in print.

What makes Lemert, Mills, and O'Neill good writers, in my estimation, is that they tell their readers that they are engaged in the act of writing, which is necessarily a personal one. All three have strong sociological agendas—and much the same agenda, I should add. They do not hide behind a de-authorizing method, nor do they oppose method, especially where, as O'Neill says, "method . . . test[s] in us that strange distance between our work and those for whom we intend it." He, Mills, and Lemert recognize that this "strange distance" that separates sociology from life lived in the natural attitude can be shortened, especially as everyday life is edified and elevated through critical insights afforded by sociology. Lemert wants people to live a sociological life, a life informed by their reflections on how their biographies have been shaped by, and in turn shape, larger social forces that he as a critical sociologist attempts to portray as subject to transformation. This requires a literary posture that thaws social facts into the deliberate acts of men and women. Mills put this well.

Nowadays men often feel that their private lives are a series of traps. . . . Yet men do not usually define the troubles they endure in terms of historical change and institutional contradiction. The well-being they enjoy, they do not usually impute to the big ups and downs of the societies in which they live. Seldom aware of the intricate connections between the patterns of their own lives and the course of world history, ordinary men do not usually know what this connection means for the kinds of men they are becoming and for the kinds of history-making in which they might take part. They do not possess the quality of mind essential to grasp the interplay of man and society, of biography and history, of self and world. They cannot cope with their personal troubles in such ways as to control the structural transformations that usually lie behind them. (Mills 1959: 3–4)

Mills goes on to say that "the history that now affects every man is world history," revealing, again, his Hegelian–Marxist roots. These roots have gone virtually unnoticed in American sociology as his book *The Sociological Imagination* has been domesticated into a staple of introductory sociology courses that grab students' attention, which is then diverted into the dreary study of scientific method and conservative theory.

Good sociological writing is unashamedly narrative, revealing the act of artifice. Sociology is, after all, an act of work, of literary work. In *Social Things,* Lemert grounds his sociological story, which is intended for beginning sociology students, in his own life and work—his neighborhood in Brooklyn; his family life, which involved divorce and his custody of sons; his new wife and new life. The milieu of his neighborhood is a leitmotif as he recounts the murder of the immigrant proprietor of the small deli where he buys the *New York Times.* Lemert's sociology unfolds as his effort to understand this world, which stands alongside the everyday efforts of the people whose lives he describes.

O'Neill in *Sociology as a Skin Trade* talks of his father's and mother's hands, connecting his investment in sociology to his working-class roots in suggesting that sociology is no less an act of labor than working with one's hands.

I am a Marxist without a revolution, though my mother and my father still work. My mother's hands. My father's hands. How shall I separate what is cruel from what is beautiful in the story of their lives? The rest of my family I do not know: They are workers. (O'Neill 1972: 264)

Evidence is the stack of manuscript written in longhand on O'Neill's bookshelf that I mentioned above. For his part, Mills attached an appendix to *Sociological Imagination* titled "On Intellectual Craftsmanship," in which he offers literary advice to aspiring sociologists, the "young academic man," as Mills quaintly calls him! Mills recognizes that the work of building a career and of doing good work is primarily literary work, craftsmanship. He worries that the craft is being badly learned as Method, his term, claims intellectual imagination and public vernacular as its casualties.

In many academic circles today anyone who tries to write in a widely intelligible way is liable to be condemned as a "mere literary man" or, worse still, "a mere journalist." Perhaps you have already learned that these phrases, as commonly used, only indicate the spurious inference: superficial because readable. The academic man in America is trying to carry on a serious intellectual life in a social context that often seems quite set against it. His prestige must make up for many of the dominant values he has sacrificed by choosing an academic career. His claims for prestige readily become tied to his self-image as a "scientist." To be called a "mere journalist" makes him feel undignified and shallow. It is this situation, I think, that is often at the bottom of the elaborate vocabulary and involved manner of speaking and writing. It is less difficult to learn this manner than not. It has become a convention—those who do not use it are subject to moral disapproval. It may be that it is the result of an academic closing of the ranks on the part of the mediocre, who understandably wish to exclude those who win the attention of intelligent people, academic and otherwise. (Mills 1959: 218)

PUBLIC SCIENCE AND SOCIAL SCIENCE:
NEW DISCOURSE AND DISCIPLINES

Writers, thus, must confess their craft, recognizing that their work is literary. It is not only literary, though. Alone, the narrativity of writing is not enough to qualify writing as good and imitable. As Mills says, writing must address public issues in an accessible way, eschewing turgidity and formulaic technical prose. Writing must be *public*, both about public issues and composed for the public or publics, as it were. Roland Barthes, the French critic, wrote playfully, exhibiting the literariness of his work at every turn. But this does not qualify his writing as suitably public, either about public issues or destined for a public unschooled in his literary techniques. A public social science grounds private troubles in public issues, connecting them for all to see. Books such as Mills's (1956) *The Power Elite,* his approach to a critical sociology of stratification, stand as enduring examples of public sociology. Anticipating the criticism that this is only journalism, muckraking journalism at that, Mills in *Sociological Imagination* appended the comments above about intellectual craftsmanship, urging "young academic men" to rise above disciplinary status-seeking and instead write important work for broad audiences.

Mills traces his own interest in stratification to his reading of Thorstein Veblen, who he characterizes as a translator of Marx for Americans. But Mills did not have to be a Marxist, as he was, to have endorsed public sociology. After all, this was very much the sociology of Durkheim and Weber, too, treating large issues in terms of their implications for individual lives and meanings. That Mills appended "On Intellectual Craftmanship" to his book was unfortunate in that this marginal status tends to dilute its message. However, many a graduate student has heavily underlined the appendix, especially where Mills describes how he kept files of notes and clippings that he regularly plumbed as he developed ideas for new works. Although there are of course many ways to approach the literary craft of writing, Mills is making the point that writing, which is both serendipitous and studied, needs to resist its disciplining by Method, as he calls it, in order to have maximum impact on the world around it. One could observe that sociological authors divide around which metaphor they prefer—research, no writing, as method, or as craft. It should be clear where my sympathies lie.

O'Neill, Lemert, and Mills argue for a public sociology that carefully considers its audience as it listens to itself write.

> [F]inally there is the question of those who are to hear the voice—thinking about that also leads to characteristics of style. It is very important for any writer to have in mind just what kinds of people he is trying to speak to—and also what he really thinks of them. These are not easy questions: to answer them well requires decisions about one-self as well as knowledge of reading publics. To write is to raise a claim to be read, but by whom?
>
> One answer has been suggested by my colleague, Lionel Trilling, who has given me permission to pass it on. You are to assume that you have been asked to give a lecture on some subject you know well, before an audience of teachers and students from all departments of a leading university, as well as an assortment of interested people from a near-by city. Assume that such an audience is before you and that they have a right to know; assume that you want to let them know. Now write. (Mills 1959: 221)

Mills, like Trilling, taught at Columbia. He ran in rarefied circles, as his acknowl-edgments indicate, although he was a populist. His dusty roots in Waco, Texas, also known as the birthplace of Dr. Pepper and the site of the immolation of religious cult members at the nearby Branch Davidian compound, render this populism per-fectly plausible. In the late 1950s, this populism, like that of Trilling, was more pos-sible than it is today, as Jacoby argues in *The Last Intellectuals.* Forty years have passed since Mills wrote *The Sociological Imagination,* in which, as I observed earlier, he introduced the term *postmodern.* In the meantime, academics have demonstrated a failure of nerve in refusing to go public, having succumbed to self-enclosed disci-plinary language games.

Yet we must not overdraw the contrast between the 1950s and today, refusing to allow nostalgia to get the better of us. Even in 1959 Mills portrayed the acade-mic organization person in terms that have changed little today.

> The interest of businessmen in the new practicality usually seems clear. But what about the professors? What are their interests? In contrast with the business spokesmen, they are not primarily concerned with the pecuniary, the managerial, or the political mean-ings of practicality. For them, such results are primarily means to other ends, which center, I think, upon their own "careers." (Mills 1959: 97)

Mills goes on to describe "new job opportunities" in consulting becoming avail-able to academics, especially in the social sciences. (He was writing on the eve of Project Camelot.) "In response to these outside demands, the centers of higher learning tend increasingly to produce seemingly a-political technicians."

The academic profession in America, I think we must recognize, has often failed to make ambitious men contented with merely academic careers. The prestige of the profession has not been proportionate to the economic sacrifice often involved; the pay and hence the style of life have often been miserable, and the discontent of many scholars is heightened by their awareness that often they are far brighter than men who have attained power and prestige available in other fields. For such unhappy professors the new developments in the administrative uses of social science offer gratifying opportunities to become, so to speak, Executives without having to become Deans. (Mills 1959: 98)

I wish I had known that before I became a dean! (Of course, as a critical theorist I had nothing of value to sell to the state or business.) Mills continues with a bitter indictment of Eisenhower-era social science:

The academic community in America as a whole is morally open to the new practicality in which it has become involved. Both in and out of the university, men at the centers of learning become experts inside administrative machines. This undoubtedly narrows their attention and the scope of such political thinking as they might do. (Mills 1959: 99)

Things have become worse since he wrote those lines, as universities more closely resemble "administrative machines," run by CEOs recruited from the private sector in order to exact faculty "accountability," a key organizational noun of the nineties. Chairs and deans become expert in the surveillance of labor, which tends to replace labor—thought and writing. Left politics subsists only on the distant fringes, among the people Jacoby describes as having been academized and tenured.

As a group, American social scientists have seldom, if ever, been politically engaged in any large way; the trend toward the technician's role has strengthened their a-political outlook, reduced (if that is possible) their political involvement, and often, by disuse, their ability even to grasp political problems. That is one reason why one often encounters journalists who are more politically alert and knowledgeable than sociologists, economists, and especially, I am sorry to say, political scientists. The American university system seldom if ever provides political education; it seldom teaches how to gauge what is going on in the general struggle for power in modern society. Most social scientists have had little or no sustained contacts with such sections of the community as have been insurgent; there is no left-wing press with which the average academic practitioner in the course of his career could come into mutually educative relations. There is no movement that would support or give prestige, not to speak of jobs, to political intellectuals, and the academic community has few if any roots in labor circles. (Mills 1959: 99)

Some of this was about to change, as Leftish academics were caught up in the maelstrom of the antiwar and civil rights movements. But the change was not permanent, especially for sociologists who, as I have been saying, reacted to the institutional retrenchment of sociology during the 1970s with careerist science, not public sociology. Mills was correct not to overestimate the political engagement of academic social scientists or, I would add, of academics generally, who were under-workers in the increasingly bureaucratic university world—organization men, as Whyte (1957) might have called them. By the late 1990s, universities increasingly resemble private-sector bureaucracies administered by managers and accountants with nonacademic values. For their part, senior academic administrators read Steven Covey (1990) and Bill Gates (1995), not Russell Jacoby (1987) and Gerald Graff (1992), in order to deal with the privatization of universities. A corporate managerial culture is found in most contemporary American universities, whose problems are addressed by constraining faculty viewed as hostile to change, indolent, insensitive to students. I attended conferences and retreats of administrators that were designed to enhance "team building" among an embattled officer corps; I wondered whether *retreat* was a verb or a noun! In this environment, research—intellectuality—is de-emphasized as irrelevant, even selfish, unless it leads to large grants, and teaching and community service are valorized. The shift away from research and the redoubled emphasis on undergraduate teaching not only cheapen the cost of faculty labor, especially where a great deal of instruction can be out-sourced to part-timers. The attack on research also ensures that faculty view themselves as teachers, not as cosmopolitan intellectuals situated in the public sphere. The remedialization of college curricula goes hand in hand with the decline of public intellectuals and the entrenchment of corporate university management.

Tenure and teaching loads are under siege nearly everywhere as universities contract, downsize, and otherwise become more "accountable" to taxpayers and tuition payers. This follows in the wake of the Reagan-era critique of academic life as a "scam" (see Sykes 1990), with faculty members staying home to tend their gardens instead of attending to the needs of students. *Student-centeredness* has become a slogan of both public and private universities seeking to persuade would-be students and their parents that faculty are not self-serving researchers who care more about their careers than about young minds. Tenure has been under assault at least since the 1980s, constituting the greatest threat to academic freedom since McCarthyism. Of course, job security confounds academic managers who seek fiscal flexibility at the margins, for example when the decision is made to downsize the department of English and grow the department of communication. University administrators and legislators propose and implement post-tenure review as a way of giving themselves what they regard as much-needed flexibility, although they defend post-tenure review as a reasonable measure of faculty accountability. Post-tenure review, they contend, allows unproductive "deadwood" among the faculty to be pruned, even after the tenure decision has been made. Especially pernicious is the fact that faculty are supposed to axe their own colleagues, pitting them against each other and destroying whatever remains of the fabric of academic community and mutuality.

Mills's comments on the *disciplining* tendencies of bureaucratically organized academia in the 1950s and the toll this takes on intellectual imagination and social criticism need to be kept firmly in mind so that we do not promulgate a myth of an academic golden age. There was never a time before time when American academics were Gramsci's "organic intellectuals," moving fluently among their roles as scholars, teachers, social critics, and citizens. What is so valuable about Mills's critique is that he champions the concept of the public intellectual, even where he recognized that American sociology in the 1950s was growing inimical to public social science as sociologists became careerist professionals, not pundits. Mills's example is much prized by Jacoby in *The Last Intellectuals*, where he approaches "academization" from the perspective of intellectual and social history. Mills is one of the few sociologists lauded by Jacoby for his radical engagement and literary accessibility. As Jacoby observes, some of Mills's works such as (1951) *White Collar* sold hundreds of thousands of copies, establishing Mills, at least temporarily, as a serious public intellectual who could cross over between academic work and social commentary, even unifying them in a singular voice that was impossible to ignore.

Mills was a spiritual guardian of the New Left. Tom Hayden, the prime author of the Students for a Democratic Society's founding 1962 Port Huron Statement (see Lemert 1993: 383–86), which was indebted to Mills's radical populism, wrote a thesis on Mills. Mills launched the Madison-based journal *Studies on the Left* that was a gathering point for many younger radical intellectuals of the time. Jacoby emphasizes the irony in the fact that many New Leftists retreated to academic life after the social movements of the 1960s had crested, losing the public voice that Mills prized.

> The generation born around and after 1940 emerged in a society where the identity of universities and intellectual life was almost complete. To be an intellectual entailed being a professor. This generation flowed into the universities, and if they wanted to be intellectuals, they stayed. The issue is not their talent, courage, or politics. Rather, the occasion to master a public prose did not arise; consequently, their writings lacked a public impact. Regardless of their numbers, to the larger public they are invisible. The missing intellectuals are lost in the universities. (Jacoby 1987: 16)

Jacoby does not simply "blame" former members of the New Left for decamping to universities and writing for tenure. Blame is beside the point. He examines changes in post–World War II American society, all the way from the growth of suburbs and decline of urban bohemia to monopoly publishing and the rapid post-Sputnik growth of universities, for the absence of an intelligentsia in the United States.

Jacoby combs the decades from the 1930s to 1960s, including Mills, for examples of worldly intellectuals who wrote accessibly but without condescension for a general reading public, the sort of people who subscribe to *The Nation* and *Dissent*. Much of his argument about the academization of critical theory echoes Mills's claim that "there is no left in the U.S." For Jacoby this had as much to do with intellectuals' employment conditions—the fact that they now wrote for tenure and thus embraced obscurantism and worldly disengagement—as with McCarthyism and then the eclipse, or simply petering out, of the New Left, in which he was a participant. His is partly a story about missing intellectuals, who became academics, and partly about the dearth of radical politics and oppositional social movements after the Vietnam War. Jacoby's book has earned much enmity from Leftist academics who believe that they are exceptions to Jacoby's characterization of a missing intelligentsia and who thus accuse him of painting with too broad a brush.

As an intellectual historian, Jacoby does not explore what has fashionably come to be called "discourse" except to point out some extreme examples of theoretical academics' labored prose—for example, Fredric Jameson's 1984 *New Left Review* article on "Postmodernism, or, the Cultural Logic of Late Capitalism," in which he "reads" the Hotel Bonaventura in Los Angeles as a social text, apparently ignoring its site in the urban political economy of greater Los Angeles (also see Jameson 1991). Jacoby lampoons inflated theoretical discourse but does not theorize discourse as a language game in which disciplines trap academic participants, who reproduce that discourse in order to get published and build careers. Jacoby would probably regard the word *discourse* as part of the problem, not the solution!

In my view, his and Mills's analyses of the obfuscating and conformist tendencies of post–World War II academia are essential to understand the decline of social criticism as a structural and cultural feature of advanced capitalism and, through that, the eclipse of critique and reason in society at large. Mills and Jacoby are saying that America has no intelligentsia, without which it has no source of critical ideas. Although the white-collar professions, including academia, are full of well-educated, reasonable, and literate people, anger and vision have no outlet now that academia has become yet another career ladder. Their critiques are deepened if we attend to the ways in which disciplinary discourses, such as that of sociology, obstruct lucid intelligence and public vernacular in the interest of scientism—what Mills called, in capital letters, The Scientific Method. Disciplines discipline rebels such as Mills and Jacoby. It is difficult to imagine Mills attending a 1990s American Sociological Association annual meeting and presenting a paper on a delimited topic, which he later submits to a refereed journal. For his part, Jacoby remains outside of academia, never having held down a tenure-track job, even though he has published half a dozen books with leading publishers. By way of explanation, it is said that he is "difficult," absolving academia of failing to recognize one of its shining stars—a real intellectual by any reckoning. I once tried to convince an administrator above me to hire Jacoby, offering his recently published *The Last Intellectuals* as testimony to his intellectual gifts. The administrator read the book and proclaimed that, in light of the book's message, it would be unfair to tempt Jacoby with an academic post. This single episode was one of the reasons I decided to try my hand at administration, although, in truth, I accomplished little in my stint as dean, given the nearly intractable realities of disciplinary language games, academic conformity, compulsive faculty accountability, and student-centeredness, all of which have been redoubled since Mills wrote.

Good sociology, then, admits that it is a story, a piece of rhetoric, no matter how sophisticated its methodological techniques, and it composes itself for an educated public, not only for other disciplined professionals. Professionals will protest that the pages of the *ASR* should be reserved for cutting-edge disciplinary work, for science by another name. Let public intellectuals publish in the *New Republic,* do television commentary, contribute op-ed pieces, and send their manuscripts to Basic Books (recently resurrected under the umbrella of Perseus). I suppose one could say that public intellectuals are necessarily polyvocal in our multimedia environment, wearing different literary hats and employing diverse styles. However, the fact remains that sociology is not simply discourse but is also organization, discipline, institution. Sociology becomes ideology through the institutionalization of its positivist discourse. Virtually all North American colleges and universities have sociology departments in which faculty teach, conduct at least a little research, and perform what administrators call community service. What and where sociologists publish reflects sociology's worldview and how that worldview is received by the public and policymakers. Without fail, national wire services pick up topical papers presented at the ASA annual meetings, reporting their findings as breaking news—divorce is declining, extramarital sexuality has been exaggerated, more blacks are entering the middle class. These findings are chilled into social fate, both by their mainstream authors and by journalists who report them. Although these findings are usually interesting and even demystifying, they are reported as science, representing the representations of journal sociology as objective news.

Sociology becomes ideology where it remains sheer representation, the language game of positivism. As sociology is promulgated both by teachers who use omnibus introductory textbooks that proclaim sociology's scientificity and by those who report sociology's already frozen findings and use them for "policy" purposes, we become even further removed from sociology's original promise as social criticism. For sociology to confess and even embrace its narrativity and to go public in addressing important social problems transforms ideology into critique, the project of Marx and Mills. Positivists reserve social criticism for their roles as citizens, repeating Weber's famous duality of professionalism and citizenship, science and advocacy. The argument I am making will be dismissed as ideological by those who reject the premise that positivist discourse, in freezing the social world representationally, is ideological itself. Positivists defend the project of an objective social science, disagreeing with me that "objectivity" is no less an undecidable language game than polemic and rhetoric.

One does not need a particular version of left-wing politics—mine, for example—to agree that sociology needs to be written differently, telling a public story. There are different stories, publics, and public issues. In acknowledging its narrativity, sociology invites other versions, creating a public sphere in which people with trained minds, good theories, and rigorous methods debate what ought to be done. If there is one story, there are necessarily many. These stories are not equally true or good, but they cannot be resolved with reference to knowledge outside of argument itself. Although I contend that we can create a classless society, I cannot demonstrate this conclusively to people who would tell a different, perhaps more

Platonist or Weberian, story. My story, however well told, involves a certain circularity—my definition of social class, my theory of inequality, my conception of the good—that begs questions that cannot be answered without inviting further circularity.

NARRATING A PUBLIC SOCIOLOGY

A book such as this cannot end without desiderata! It is not enough to quote Lemert, Mills, and O'Neill as exemplars of good writing. There is plenty of good writing in sociology, but precious little of it in the empirical journals. Occasionally, public sociology can even be found in the journals, especially journals off the beaten path that have lower disciplinary prestige and are more open to iconoclastic and interdisciplinary work. This fact alone makes the point that "discipline" is not seamless; editors as well as authors fall through the cracks and are allowed to go their own ways, relatively unencumbered by the strictures of normal science's language game, which drives out thought and critique. The lack of seamlessness suggests that rebellious and imaginative authors and editors can make a difference, albeit swimming upstream against a powerful current. By *good writing* I do not necessarily mean felicitous writing or writing that has been carefully crafted. Although I support literary felicity and craft as much as the next person, I am not calling for pretty writing as much as I am calling for writing that listens to itself write, disgorging what some might call its subtext of assumptions, positions, and echoes, and then invites others into one's argument. Good sociological writing, or public sociology, admits that it tells a story, invites other stories and addresses important public issues. To put this as concisely as possible, and stripping away theoretical obstructions to common understanding, public sociology addresses social problems accessibly. Good sociology is unashamed of its advocacy, grounding objectivity in choices clearly made about topic, method, theory, discourse.

These choices are not made for one, except where scientists engage in what Sartre (1956) call "bad faith," pretending that their life is not their own, absolving them of responsibility for their own circumstance. Sartre, like Marx before him, is dealing with Hegel's discussion in *Phenomenology of Mind* of the dialectic of master and slave. Hegel argues that slaves are, at a basic level, free in that masters depend on slaves not only for uncompensated labor but also for "recognition," validation of the master by his subordinate. For Marx and Sartre, this key insight is the basis of liberation, which, they understand more fully than does Hegel, confronts sometimes enormous practical obstacles such as poverty, isolation, violence. Sartre attempted to ground Marxist humanism in an existentialist ethics and metaphysics that, in his terms, placed existence prior to essence, people's lives and choices prior to discussions of the nature of the world, of being. Sartre in *Being and Nothingness* concluded that people are their projects, their acts of what Hegel and Marx viewed as their self-externalization in the world through work, politics, and culture—and, one would add today, science and technology. This potentially emancipatory existentialism began with Heidegger, who in (1962) *Being and Time* argued that philosophy's most fundamental recognition is that people choose their lives once they confront their mortality, which both grounds and limits their choices. Roughly put, science is a choice, both existential and literary.

Sociological Desiderata

1. Sociological writing must *reveal the author,* presenting itself as a literary act and outcome. This does not undermine its claim to be science but rather opens science to different versions grounded in diverse language games. Author-present writing refuses to cleanse the text of authorial fingerprints as if the text simply mirrors nature. Instead, the author acknowledges that her text both constructs the world and intervenes in it deliberately. This doesn't reduce society to writing but acknowledges that writing is a social act and the world a social text—an accomplishment of writers and readers.

2. Sociological writing must *engage in self-translation,* disclosing its animating assumptions and confessing its intellectual and social interests. This does not mean that sociologists will write primers, dumbing down the *ASR,* but rather that they will refuse to gloss over what will prove nettlesome and controversial for readers. When I wrote my (Agger 1994) short note on Derrida for the *ASR,* I imagined myself in the mainstream reader's shoes, puzzling over why Derrida might matter for workaday sociology. This includes acknowledging the work's inherent undecidability, its inability to define all of its terms or defend all of its assumptions, even as it attempts to lay bare its definitions, theoretical investments, and methodological underpinnings. This sort of self-translating writing models dialogical relations with readers and other writers who are invited to correct one's own work with their versions. This prefigures a democratic public sphere characterized by endless talk about truth and the good. In short, sociological writers must write publicly, accessibly, openly, recognizing that they will not have the last word and inviting rejoinders. This recognition informs the tone of public sociology, which eschews absolutes.

3. Sociological writing must address *major public issues,* attempting to influence the public and policy. Marx, Mills, Durkheim, and Weber all addressed such central issues of social structure and culture, refusing to be confined by method, which necessarily takes a back seat. This does not mean that otherwise technically motivated papers will include a concluding section on policy or social problems; that only marginalizes what should be a central concern of sociology. Instead, an address to public issues should inform the whole paper, driving it where today method drives many papers.

Writing's narrativity opens itself to other versions that constitute a public of democratic speakers, modeling a democratic public sphere. I am saying that good writing produces a good polity, creating a critical community of writers and readers, who are also citizens. This is important in its own right. But sociological writing must then go public, addressing desperate issues of our time. William Wilson (1987) has done this in his book on the inner city, *The Truly Disadvantaged;* Joe Feagin and Herman Vera have done this in their book *White Racism.* Although I maintain that good writing, as I understand it, will advance the discipline, this is much less significant than are the benefits reaped by writing that prefigures a democratic public sphere and writing that dissects domination in all of its modalities. By now, thirty years since the end of the 1960s, both conservative politics and postmodern cynicism militate against the radical engagements of the likes of C. Wright Mills, let alone Marx. These developments must be resisted, especially as they insinuate themselves into positivist disciplinary discourse and institutional practices, such as the valorization of grants as publication equivalents, that position sociologists to recoup lost prestige in an age of decline.

Writers play an obvious role in narrating a public sociology. By writing differently, beyond the strictures of *ASR* sociology, sociological writers encourage different sociologies. We must also edit differently, not allowing methods-driven reviews to make our judgments for us. Editors necessarily make these judgments anyway, given the contradictoriness of many reviews. Editors displace their literary authority where they hide behind reviews that represent nothing more than the reviewers' worlds. Reviewers must be reviewed by editors and authors, just as reviewers review submitted work. Much more interesting than a paper decentered by numerous methods-driven revisions dictated by many reviewers through multiple iterations of the submitted draft is a revised version that incorporates dialogue with reviewers and editor, disgorging the many, often competing, authorial interests animating the complex minuet of refereed scholarship. Good editors encourage this sort of revision, taking care not only to pick reviewers who acknowledge their own corrigibility but also to read reviews as the rhetorical versions they are. The anonymous referee process does not produce or attain objectivity but simply grounds scholarship in a talkative community in which it is not necessarily clear that revised versions best original versions. Revision mediated by methods-driven reviewers (who may contradict each other) and editors can do violence to the original draft, reducing its contribution by averaging reviews toward a banal middle ground, dominated by technical detail.

Although it can be said that all work benefits from readings, it could also be said that all readings do violence to writing, wrenching it out of its frame of reference. Every particular revision requires revision of the whole text in its light. Few positivist writers, struggling to build careers on a path strewn with rejections and revise-and-resubmits, have the time, skill, or editorial encouragement to do careful revisions that recognize the totality's inherence in every particular. Instead, writers, reviewers, and most editors take a rough-and-ready approach to textual editing, focusing on details of method to the exclusion of almost everything else.

In a new sociological order, method would not be less sophisticated, but it would intrude less in texts. In the era of the information superhighway, authors could promise inquisitive readers the full account of their method, to be delivered through electronic or old-fashioned mail, much as drug companies promise consumers detailed information about product testing and epidemiological studies. One already finds occasional articles that promise such methodological appendices, to be supplied upon request. Editors need to encourage authors to cut down on technical detail in the methods section, particularly by publishing articles that are short on method and long on narrative. If authors insisted on retaining fine-grained technical detail, they must argue for the necessity of such gestures for the overall meaning of their articles. It is perfectly plausible for authors to write papers on method as long as they explain the significance of these arcane matters for a public sociology. By the same token, theorists can write interpretive papers as long as they shoulder the burden of explaining why Bourdieu and Baudrillard should be read by people seeking a better world.

My conception of public sociology resurrects the role of what Antonio Gramsci called the "organic intellectual," an intellectual in dialogue with ongoing social movements. Mills was an organic intellectual. Jacoby laments the academization of such intellectuals at a time when we sorely need them. There are other names to describe this sort of committed intellectual sensibility, whose image has become a staple on the Left among theoretically minded thinkers attempting to merge theory and practice in the example of their own lives. I continue to return to Jacoby's condemnation of academic critical theory because, with him, I believe that academization has exacted a huge toll on the public Left in the United States. (See Mark Kann's [1982] *The American Left* for another perspective on the possibilities of American populist radicalism.) It is not as if critical intellectuals in this country have had many places to turn in the way of organized alternatives to the two established political parties, which now mirror each other. We have no Labour Party (England), no New Democratic Party (Canada), to which Leftist intellectuals could affiliate themselves. And our social sciences, by comparison to social sciences in the United Kingdom, Australia, and even Canada, have been much more conservative and positivist, making theorists' post-1960s retreat to the university all the more unfortunate, essentially abandoning organized politics altogether. The last social scientist to have had much impact on federal policy and politics in the United States was probably Michael Harrington, whose *The Other America* helped persuade Kennedy and later Johnson to launch a war on poverty.

It is not impossible for public intellectuals to make a difference, even in our ideologically impoverished political climate. Public feminists such as Susan Brownmiller and public sociologists such as William Wilson have readerships far beyond academia. They craft their work for the reading public; they do not conceal their position taking; they address vital contemporary issues such as violence against women and the plight of the urban poor. Although Wilson has published academic sociology, he pushes beyond the boundaries of sociological language games, much as Harrington did nearly forty years ago. It might be objected that authors such as Wilson can issue their book-length work either with academic publishers who seek a readership beyond academia or with trade publishers who publish books for educated readers. Leave the journals to the scientists. However, the boundary between journal prose and book/monograph prose is not clear, especially where houses such as Academic, Sage, and Aldine de Gruyter publish social science monographs that are, in effect, expanded journal articles, with their densely figured prose and methodological compulsions. The contention that the sociological book world and journal world are distinct, with two different language games—one laconic and essayistic, the other taught and scientific—is somewhat problematic, especially given the tendency of article authors to write monographs in order to win promotion to professor.

Books are not necessarily public, acknowledging the author, engaging in self-translation, and addressing public issues. Journal articles are not necessarily composed in the private language of high methodology, as the occasional unusual *ASR* articles demonstrate. Most book manuscripts undergo the referee and revision process, bending their arguments toward a middle ground on which all or most reviewers have their criticisms addressed. Of course, book editors ask manuscript reviewers whether a project is likely to recoup the publisher's investment—a notable difference from journal editing. Another difference is that the identity of the author is likely to be disclosed to referees, unlike in journal reviewing, where reviewers are left to guess about the author's identity. In the book world, the reviewers are not known to the author unless, once the project has been accepted for publication, they agree to contribute testimonial "blurbs" for marketing purposes.

Most publishing sociologists write both books and articles. A few quite visible scholars have never published a book, and a few visible book writers do not publish articles in significant sociology journals. The fact that most publishing sociologists cross over between the two art forms suggests that there is nothing inherently different between their language games; methods-driven article authors are likely to write methods-driven monographs. But book writers who compose what I call public sociology are not likely to have their work accepted by the leading sociology journals, or even by second- and third-tier refereed journals, unless they change their tune and clutter their writing with method. Few sociologists or social scientists who write public books bother to submit to mainstream journals, not wanting to make major intellectual compromises in order to have their work accepted. They recognize that this will domesticate their work too much, and instead they invest their energies in finding outlets for their book-length manuscripts.

Unfortunately, the book world itself has undergone profound changes in the past ten years and is likely to undergo further changes as information technologies evolve. In the past decade, culture industries have become increasingly centralized and vertically integrated in vast empires controlled by a few very wealthy magnates such as Rupert Murdoch, who control the film industry, television, newspapers, mass-market magazines, professional sports teams, college and high school textbook publishing, and even trade and academic publishing. Independent (noncorporate) publishers have nearly disappeared as prestigious imprints such as Basic Books, Pantheon, and Westview have been acquired by corporate parents that have changed their editorial agendas almost beyond recognizability. University presses enjoy less support from their home institutions than they did a decade ago, and as a result many of them have begun to publish trade books and even textbooks in order to survive. Acquisitions editors have become experts in market research and marketing, for the most part abandoning intimate involvement with the development of manuscripts under their stewardship. They involve themselves heavily in signing projects, based on reviewers' and their own estimates of potential market, especially in college classes, and then abandon the writer to write. They may also oversee revisions, which are largely market-driven. These editors are employees, evaluated by their supervisors at the corporate parent in terms of the sales of "their" books.

Old-fashioned substantive editing, where acquisitions editors contribute to the intellectual development of their authors' projects and engage in painstaking line editing of submitted manuscripts, has largely gone the way of independent publishing houses renowned for the publication of high-quality work, activist editors, and loyal authors, who come to be identified with the house that publishes their oeuvres. Sartre had his Gallimard, Adorno his Suhrkamp, Marcuse his Beacon, Mills his Oxford. All of this suggests that the book world is not a world apart, especially as the culture industry becomes big business. Manuscripts are "product," and authors are, at best, independent contractors seeking the path of least editorial resistance.

All of us have our publishing war stories, about both the journal and book worlds. These stories suggest that sociology journal discourse is methods-driven whereas book publishing is increasingly market-driven. These stories suggest a general failure of nerve among authors, editors, reviewers, and academic administrators. Yesterday's work is reproduced as tomorrow's breakthroughs. The failure of nerve is conditioned by changing institutional circumstances: sociologists seek the aura of science in order to shore up a declining discipline, where book publishers and their acquisitions editors need books to be profit centers, not loss leaders. Although certain sociology books break free of formulaic, methods-driven journal discourse, they become formulaic in a different way: they are written for "adoption" by faculty who assign them in their college classes.

It is to be noticed here that college teaching is not what it used to be: At most nonelite universities, faculty are under increasing pressure to accommodate ill-prepared students in order to augment enrollment-driven institutional budgets. They simplify their courses, assigning less and easier reading in the name of student-centeredness. At some enrollment-driven institutions, faculty are even held accountable for student "retention"—staying enrolled. Publishers' concern with books' "adoptability" is entirely consistent with the nationwide emphasis on student-centered undergraduate education, which combines remedialized curricula and campus entertainment in the name of student consumer sovereignty. In this context, faculty park at the back of the lot and write textbooks. Those who may romanticize the book world as a world apart need look no further than trends in both publishing and undergraduate pedagogy that have spelled the decline of independent publishing and substantive editing and lower expectations of students, who are viewed as customers to be entertained. In this latter context, the accompaniment of introductory level textbooks with "learning" aids such as CDs, videos, computer files of practice examination questions, and the like has become a mini-industry, required by textbooks in order to earn market share.

The decline of an urban intelligentsia, situated in bohemia, was addressed by Jacoby as a factor in the decline of public intellectuals. One symptom of this decline is the eclipse of the independent bookstore, replaced by mass-market chain bookstores such as Waldenbooks and Barnes & Noble and by Internet book retailers such as Amazon.com. Writers read. To browse among the stacks in academically oriented bookstores and libraries is essential for readers who would write, providing inspiration, a window on what is current in the disciplines and an occasion for discovering surprising intertextual connections. In Buffalo, we enjoyed a decent university library and an excellent independent co-op bookstore, Talking Leaves. SUNY faculty assigned books in graduate seminars that could be purchased at Talking Leaves, thus giving the bookstore a lifeline and acquainting students with a real bookstore, not the campus Follett's. We all depended on our favorite bookstore for intellectual sustenance and knowledgeable service and, as a bonus, it was next door to the North Buffalo Food Co-op, another important cultural asset in the City of No Illusions.

Talking Leaves is one of the things I miss about Buffalo. Although Arlington, Texas, has great weather and major-league baseball, there is no intellectual community partly because there is no intellectual gathering point, such as an academic bookstore. The local university, a utilitarian commuter school specializing in vocational fields such as engineering, architecture, and nursing, boasts an essentially undergraduate library, with few amenities. The university has plans to build a Follett's chain bookstore, replete with a yuppie coffee bar. Arlington, like neighboring Dallas and Fort Worth, has many chain bookstores such as Barnes & Noble and Borders. But these do not have many academic books, catering instead to consumers who want "fast" books, calendars, cappuccino, dates. The male protagonist of the blockbuster movie *You've Got Mail* says about his Barnes & Noble-like chain bookstore, "It's a piazza," in self-mocking self-justification. In the suburban hinterland, and increasingly all across America, academic readers must purchase mail-order books or books off the Web. It is difficult to be a public sociologist in a metropolitan area that is, in effect, a series of contiguous suburbs—no bookstores, no bohemia, no real university libraries. Interlibrary loan takes days, and sometimes weeks, and it is a poor substitute for browsing among the stacks, a basic requirement of intellectual serendipity.

Walter Benjamin in his studies of the built environment of Paris idealized the "flaneur," the person who strolls amidst her urban milieu, prepared to be delighted and surprised at every turn. The flaneur embodies purposive purposelessness, precisely the mien of the urban intellectual. This is as much a state of mind as of body and venue. Benjamin's flaneur requires and constitutes the public sphere, in which diverse individuals rub shoulders, trade ideas, argue, politic. Public writing is the essential circuitry of this sort of civic society, linking people in argumentation, if not in bohemian coffee houses. Kellner (1995, 1997) argues that the Internet is a potentially emancipatory element of a technopolitics that creates an electronically mediated public sphere through which people not only participate in direct democracy via electronic plebiscites but also write back and forth in public discourse (also see Luke 1998 on the Internet's impact on higher education). Kellner and some of his and my graduate students put up a critical theory "page" called "Illuminations" on the World Wide Web. This site has been "visited" by more people than read my specialized academic books! Although I share Kellner's optimism about the Web, it is also clear, as he notes, that the Web can be used in the opposite direction, facilitating commerce and the accumulation of capital in a frenzy of consumption that entails very low transaction costs. One can buy critical theory books from Amazon.com with "one-stop shopping," once one has supplied a credit card number and e-mail address. Although this helps mitigate the lack of good bookstores in the north Texas suburbs, this does nothing for the public sphere and, in fact, drives the few remaining independent bookstores out of business—one of the storylines of *You've Got Mail*.

Sociological journals in the United States have never inhabited the public sphere. I have never seen the *ASR* for sale anywhere. My favorite Buffalo bookstore did carry *Telos, New German Critique, Salmagundi, Signs, Feminist Studies*—academic journals on the Left. The bookstore also carried *The Nation, Dissent, The New Republic, Utne Reader,* periodicals that publish critical essays and commentaries without footnotes. The *ASR* is not sold because it is not an outlet for public writing. It would probably not have been sold in the 1930s, when its articles were more essayistic, less larded with figure, less firmly anchored in a confining literature that inches forward in the baby steps of academic accumulation. As I said above, I am not lamenting the passing of U.S. sociology's golden age, before methodology ruled. There was never a golden age because positivism always dominated sociological epistemology in the United States. Although figures were rudimentary in pre-1970 journal sociology, the hand-drawn tables and graphs of the 1930s, 1940s, and 1950s augured the discipline's subsequent mathematization. Yet it is not unreasonable to hope that people like C. Wright Mills and Charles Lemert, whose books are sold at Talking Leaves, could have their work published by leading academic sociology journals as these journals turn away from method and toward both public writing and public issues. Utopian though it might be, I have hope that the *ASR* could become *Les Temps Modernes,* the periodical that Sartre and Merleau-Ponty founded, or *Telos.* Scholarly rigor would be mixed with perspective and passion, turning sociology outward toward a world that calls it forth.

Certain liberals and postmodernists would agree that there should be multiple language games in sociology, and elsewhere. Let the hard-core methodologists have the journals, or at least certain journals. The softer, more theoretically inclined sociologists would claim books and more editorially open journals. But pluralism and polyvocality, championed by liberals and postmodernists respectively, do not solve the problem of scientism's hegemony, its dominance of a discipline that reproduces itself by what it practices in the realm of the journals, graduate education, the world of grants. The fact that leading research departments of sociology would not tenure or even hire a person who had not published in the *ASR, AJS* (American Journal of Sociology) and *Social Forces* blocks public sociology, no matter how fondly a few might remember Mills. Tenure and hiring practices need to change, to be sure, and sociologists should fight for that sort of change. But that change is unlikely to occur without also transforming the ways sociologists write, especially for the discipline's house organ, the *ASR*. As long as methods-driven work dominates the discipline's official journal, departments that hire and tenure the lucky few will continue to place greater value on big-three articles than on articles in *Gender & Society* and *Theory, Culture and Society.* Once in the saddle, method is very difficult to unseat as a dominant language game that defies readings. Although a tenure committee in a high-powered Midwestern research department of sociology might allow the lone theorist or qualitative sociologist to publish her dissertation as a book en route to tenure, everyone else will be expected to publish mainstream journal articles and write grant proposals. Publishing in the *ASR* will remain talismanic, only reproducing the hegemony of method, until the *ASR* changes, valorizing different sorts of sociological writing that do not substitute figure for reason.

A public sociology will use method, where necessary. It may even use quantitative methods, for example in studying structured social inequality. But its methodical moves will not gesture a figured world that it pretends only to reflect, presuppositionlessly. Method will confess its own literary and social investments, not positioning itself as the transcendental subject of idealist philosophy. Method can be defended, but only through argumentation that acknowledges its own undecidability, the circularity of its reasoning and its deferral of final solutions. A public sociology does not dwell on method but instead is preoccupied with building a democratic society, which it models in its awareness of its own fallibility, its self-translation into animating assumptions, and its engagement with pressing social problems. Public sociologists will write, review, and edit differently, attending to their work as a literary craft and not the cold product of method that freezes on the page. With this attitude, the pages of sociology will beckon readers, who need not possess credentials of higher learning.

The books that matter to me are those I read again and again, learning anew from them and noticing things about them I missed the last time. My most-thumbed book is probably Marcuse's *Eros and Civilization,* with the pages clipped and taped together, followed by O'Neill's *Making Sense Together* and *Sociology as a Skin Trade;* Mills's *Sociological Imagination;* Marx's *Economic and Philosophical Manuscripts;* the introduction and first chapter of Horkheimer and Adorno's *Dialectic of Enlightenment,* which I have finally mastered; Jacoby's *Last Intellectuals;* and Gitlin's *The Sixties: Years of Hope and Days of Rage.* On the fiction side, I reread Robert Parker's

Spenser novels! Rereading Habermas makes me cringe, although I wish I was half as erudite. I don't think I have ever read a sociological journal article more than once, and I can't remember any that moved me.

Perhaps I should end this story about stories just here, with free advice for would-be sociologists, like the young woman whose dilemma I described at the outset of this book: Try to write so that you would want to reread your own writing! Although you will learn a great deal in graduate school and in your emerging professional career, ingesting huge amounts of wisdom about theory, method, and field, try to view your graduate education as reading and writing, not as training. If you become well trained but nothing more, you may, with the right mentorship, hard work, and good fortune, carve out an estimable professional career, publishing in the leading journals and finding employment in a very good department of sociology. However, people who are well trained tend to do work that merely replicates existing work, even if they innovate at the thin margin of such literature. People who eschew the notion of training and instead treat sociology as a literary craft tend to be less well-connected to field and discipline, which costs them certain publication and employment opportunities, but they stand a better chance of making real intellectual contributions by writing what I am calling public sociology—sociology that you would want to read again and again, like a favorite novel.

Whether sociology has a place for such literary craft is an important, but not decisive, question. If you can't get your work accepted by the *ASR* or the other leading sociology journals because you violate the strictures of such writing, you can find more marginal outlets for your work, but outlets that do not force you to compromise your intellectual sensibility and literary preferences in the same way. This may mean that you won't find a tenure-track job in sociology at North Carolina or Pennsylvania. But if you publish work that other people want to reread, work that does not disclose itself fully upon first reading but, through its craft and sensibility, entices the reader back for a second, deeper, meditation upon it, you *will* find a job somewhere, especially if you bring the same excitement to your teaching as to your writing. "Somewhere" may be a small liberal arts college or a second-tier state university, off the beaten path. But living in Oberlin or Pullman has its charms, and you will be doing what you want, which is living the life of the mind and doing work that is important to you. There are many sociologists who share my view of sociology as a literary activity, to be pursued in order to make good ideas about social change accessible. You will not be alone!

9

Has Mainstream Sociology Gone Public?

Since the first edition of this book was published, U.S. sociology seems to have taken heed and gone public! The term "public sociology" is found everywhere—in the journals, in a recent American Sociological Association annual meetings theme, in ASA *Footnotes*. Does this signal real change in the discipline, away from the positivist monolith portrayed in the previous chapters and toward a more open sociology? In this new concluding chapter, I assess Michael Burawoy's impact on the discipline, the methodological inclinations of the journals since 2000, whether what has happened is mainstreaming or cooptation, the status of the public intellectual and its implications for notions and practices of disciplinarity, and finally the relevance of the 1960s for a model of public sociology. Since the first edition was published, American sociology has become increasingly torn between disciplinary insiders at the "core" of the discipline, deeply invested in scientific method, and outsiders on the periphery who favor theory and qualitative work and who question the impermeable boundaries cutting off the discipline from humanities and cultural studies (see Imber 2001). This conflict has yet to be resolved.

On the one hand, I welcome discussion of public sociology in the discipline. This helps diminish the emphasis on method that has distracted sociology since the 1970s from broad-gauged issues of practice, problems, and policy. On the other hand, I confess to a degree of cynicism when I see the American Sociological Association endorsing the brand of "public sociology" and Burawoy traveling the country promoting that brand. For reasons that I explore below, I think Burawoy's version of public sociology is problematic, essentially ceding the core of disciplinary power to the positivists who edit the journals and control the major departments. But at the same time it is no longer possible to maintain a rather monochromatic view of American sociology inasmuch as people on the periphery of the discipline reject the religion of science and have elected several renegade ASA presidents recently, signaling their dissatisfaction with positivist business as usual. I situate this book on that periphery and I hope that this second edition contributes to emerging debates about positivism and activism. I conclude this chapter by exploring the relevance of New Left sociology for what several of us are now calling a public sociology.

"PUBLIC SOCIOLOGY" AS A BRAND?

Michael Burawoy, a Berkeley sociologist, was elected ASA president for the year 2004, beginning his term as president-elect in 2003. At the time, he was chair of the Berkeley sociology department. Burawoy ran for office on the platform of supporting and promoting public sociology. This platform was published in the March 2002 ASA *Footnotes,* just before Herb Gans (2002) made a call for public sociology in the July/August 2002 *Footnotes.* Burawoy announced that the theme for the 2004 ASA convention would be "public sociologies." I first heard of all this when I received the preliminary program for the 2004 meetings and was surprised that Burawoy was using the term that is the title of this book.

Burawoy employed the term "public sociology" strategically to advance his candidacy for the ASA presidency and thrust his own department into the vanguard of a public sociology movement. That is exactly how "mainstreaming" takes place, as I have discussed in books such as *Socio(onto)logy* (Agger 1989c). For this to happen from the left is a twist on the usual mainstreaming, which takes Marxist or other renegade concepts and turns them into the currency of scientific method, thus removing their political edge.

I have it on good authority that Burawoy was a very reluctant candidate for the ASA presidency, perhaps recognizing that a leopard—and a leftist—cannot change his spots. At issue are politics and power. Burawoy, as I will develop in this chapter, embraces a Durkheimian/Parsonian conception of the sociological division of labor (his term) that compartmentalizes public sociology (and, weirdly set against it, critical sociology) and retains what he calls professional sociology (or what I term positivism). And he does this in a framework that purports to be ecumenical, allowing positivist and nonpositivist sociologies to coexist, where, in fact, positivism often swallows whole its opposition. And Burawoy even deploys some of the figuration of the positivists as he taxonomizes a sociological division of labor in, of all Parsonian ways, a two-by-table. Burawoy has a more mainstream conception of sociology than I do, even though he has been attacked from the right as overly partisan, which is rather like viewing John Kerry as a socialist. It is a misreading to suppose that all or most American sociologists are leftish in their personal political sentiments, even if they purvey the dominant positivism. More than one hundred sociologists opposed the ASA resolution against the war in Iraq, and there is even a charming Web page, called www.savesociology.com, devoted to saving sociology from the likes of me and Burawoy.

Public sociology has proven to be a surprisingly durable brand, as evidenced by the ripples, both political and intellectual, created by Burawoy and his ASA campaign. The Berkeley sociology department is not the only department to have reoriented itself around public sociology. The same thing has happened at the University of Minnesota, which has, in recent years, been a traditional positivist place. The ASA has begun to institutionalize public sociology, although not as a thoroughgoing critique of methods-driven work, of positivism by another name, but as a compartment for various Upton Sinclair-like crusades that don't deter or distract mainstreamers from logistic regression. For another interesting perspective on the unwittingly conservative effects of the concept of public sociology, see Judith Stacey's (2004) discussion of the legal role of expert sociological witnesses.

A person with my perspective should welcome this upsurge of interest in public sociology. But the story I am telling suggests that the mainstreaming of the concept of public sociology has blunted the concept's critical edge, which is the tendency of all mainstreaming and disciplining (as Foucault has shown). In particular, Burawoy's laudable attempt to introduce a critical sociology into the disciplinary mix has required him to be all things to all people in order to get elected as ASA president. This has watered down the concept that I have developed herein of a sociology that engages with large issues of the day and serves as a lever of radical social change, composing itself in accessible ways and not relying on method and technique to solve its intellectual problems. In effect, the discipline has swallowed Burawoy and his brand of public sociology much as Moby Dick swallowed Captain Ahab. This has coopted a critical concept and turned it into an advertising slogan demonstrating the diversity and "relevance" of the discipline. The discipline *has* become more diverse and politically relevant since I published the first edition, but this has not been a smooth and consensual process. There is mounting conflict over method, power, and control between the positivist core and the politically-oriented periphery (who may embrace empiricism but not positivism—a reflection theory of knowledge that pretends that the Knower can transcend time and space, an Einsteinian impossibility).

Burawoy distinguishes between two types of public sociology: traditional and organic. By "traditional" I think he means the type of big-picture theorizing promulgated by public intellectuals in Russell Jacoby's sense—Jean-Paul Sartre, Susan Sontag, Lewis Mumford, C. Wright Mills. By "organic" I think he means that public sociologists would fasten onto existing social movements and offer them guidance, much in the fashion of Antonio Gramsci's organic intellectual.

I am not opposed to any of this. Burawoy inserts sociology into the political fray, which is exactly what I am trying to do. To a positivist, our positions, for what they are worth, are nearly identical—and nonsociological. But we have our differences. With Derrida and the Frankfurt School, I notice that all intellectual work is always already political; positivism is the most political stance of all where it pretends to be purely objective. This is precisely the argument about positivism made by Max Horkheimer and Theodor W. Adorno (1972) in their *Dialectic of Enlightenment*. I am also more interested than Burawoy seems to be in the literary gestures of positivism that conspire against a politicized, public sociology. These gestures, as I have traced them in this book, replace the author and her argument with the gestural flourishes of a methods-driven science, which seem to displace the author, burying her in the appendix, perhaps, or in acknowledgments. Burawoy does not draw from postmodernism, as I do here, in reading science politically.

But our most important difference is that Burawoy believes more than I do in the possibilities of professional sociology. Burawoy is a reluctant insider. His Berkeley department has reoriented itself around public sociology and temporarily housed the new ASA journal *Contexts*, which supposedly publishes public sociology. He was elected ASA president. His election probably validated him, demonstrating to him that he belongs, and that disciplinary sociology is worth belonging to. We all seek recognition. And building bridges between the core and periphery is not necessarily a bad thing, especially if it transforms core sociology.

At stake is what it means to do sociology, what I am calling public sociology. In my preceding chapter, I discuss what it takes for a sociology to be considered public. A sociology is public if it embraces Marx's eleventh thesis on Feuerbach, which merges theory and practice, and if it recognizes that method doesn't solve all intellectual problems but is merely one form of rhetoric (discourse) among many. A public sociology must want to change the world, and it must recognize that it is already changing the world by intervening in it. Finally, a public sociology addresses itself to various publics, to which it doesn't condescend but seeks to mobilize.

My argument in the preceding chapters is that the politics and power positions of positivism—a way of writing science and social science—are imbedded in the literary gestures on the journal page. Of course, as I have acknowledged, positivism is doctrine, too: it claims that the world can be known objectively, without bias or distortion; the world can be captured on the lens and page of science; the knower can stand outside of the world; the language of science, especially mathematics, can be clear and unambiguous; nature and social nature are governed by laws. But, since the 1970s, American sociology has shifted its positivism from doctrine to discourse. After all, the busy scribes writing for the leading journals—and for tenure and reputation—are impatient with all doctrines, whether of the Vienna Circle or Frankfurt School. Theirs is a positivism in practice, a discourse, the way that science rests on the journal page, squeezing out prose in favor of figure and gesture.

This gestural positivism is deeply political for what its "subtext" implies—notably, the silent contention that history is frozen and that changes can only be made at the margin. I have been advancing this reading of our American discipline (but much less so the disciplines found in Canada, the United Kingdom, Europe, Australia, and New Zealand) since the late 1980s, when I put Derrida to work in reading science, and blended him with the neo-Marxist concerns of Frankfurt. Burawoy ignores this subtext; perhaps he isn't in the business, as most sociologists aren't, of attending to such subterranean matters. His taxonomy of sociologies—professional, critical, policy, public—ignores these issues because I don't think that he understands science and sociology as disciplining language games through which power is transacted. Although the term postmodern crops up in his work, he does not offer a discourse-theoretic version of a critical sociology of sociology, which prevents him from recognizing that positivism is predatory and will never allow his version of public sociology to go forward. Fourfold tables always collapse because one quadrant becomes dominant and disciplines the others.

Perhaps in spite of his transforming intentions, Burawoy offers a mainstream version of public sociology. He reaches out to positivists in a spirit of ecumenism. But sharks swim in the mainstream and gobble up small fry like us. He Parsonianizes public sociology, offering a sociological division of labor. There are four equally legitimate sociologies. It is clear that Burawoy (Burawoy et al. 2004) views my and Russell Jacoby's critiques of professional academia and its discourses as going overboard ("utter contempt for the discipline"), abandoning much mainstream empirical work unnecessarily. My view is that Burawoy has cleverly crafted a coalition of methodologies and epistemologies in order to entrench himself as a compromise candidate equally acceptable to the methodological and political right and left. He is the Hubert Humphrey of contemporary American sociology and, like Humphrey, his is a voice of reaction, even though he postures as progressive. I am drawing on three published pieces by Burawoy, found in *Social Forces* (Burawoy 2004a), *Social Problems* (Burawoy 2004b) and the *American Sociological Review* (Burawoy 2005), all mainstream publication outlets. It is notable that the mainstream profession, including the ASA and some of the leading journals, have already devoted considerable attention to public sociology, making a Frankfurt-oriented Derridean like me instantly suspicious about what is going on.

Burawoy's 2004 ASA presidential address has been published as an *ASR* article, as is the custom for ASA presidents. Form and content both deserve notice because they blur to the point of near identity. Burawoy offers eleven theses on public sociology, repeating Marx and Engels' trope in their eleven theses on Feuerbach, the last one of which urges the merging of theory and practice. Even Burawoy's title is evocative—"For Public Sociology"—recalling Althusser's essays collected as *For Marx*. Not allowing the reader to miss the significance of these portentous allusions, Burawoy begins his piece with an epigram from Walter Benjamin's own theses. The piece that follows is framed as an important theoretical contribution, rivaling Marx, Althusser, and Benjamin.

But in his first footnote, Burawoy adds a touch of Hollywood. We can have access to what he calls "the live version" of the paper delivered at the 2004 ASA convention, now available on DVD. This is an information-technologic contribution to his own cult of personality—live Burawoy, enriching the dead text before us.

Early in the paper, Burawoy situates himself as a torchbearer of the new public sociology, boasting that he has presented and debated these ideas "in over 40 venues, from community colleges to state associations to elite departments across the United States—as well as in England, Canada, Norway, Taiwan, Lebanon, and South Africa." He was well received, by his own telling, demonstrating the durability of his ideas. These travels led to symposia on public sociology, appearing in the leading journals noted above. There is now a column on public sociology in the ASA's newsletter, *Footnotes*, an ASA Web site, and other examples of the rapid institutionalization of Burawoy's version of the sociological world. As icing on the cake, the ASA convention over which Burawoy presided "broke all records for attendance and participation and did so by a considerable margin." Clearly, this was a plebiscite on Burawoy himself. Playing on Benjamin's thesis about progress,

Burawoy concludes that "[t]hese dark times have aroused our angel of history from his slumbers." The peripatetic public sociologist is nearly a world-historical figure and public sociology is a latter-day messianism.

The fact that Burawoy and recently Frances Fox Piven were elected ASA president, and before them Joe Feagin (who is an even more trenchant critic of mainstream positivism), requires explanation. Even if Burawoy's position on public sociology is, in effect, Parsonian, both differentiating critical and public sociologies and then allowing what he calls professional sociology its due, he did get elected president, running against Terry Sullivan, who is now an administrator at Michigan. Sullivan is quantitative and worked in a very traditional department at Texas, in which demographers and other quantitative people hold the power. Burawoy ran on the platform of public sociology, and, interestingly, in his 150-word statement printed in *Footnotes* Burawoy did not disclose his Parsonian taxonomy of the four types of sociology, only one of which was public. His statement makes it sound like the only kind of sociology he favors is political and engaged. And Burawoy beat Sullivan in the election.

I have already touched on this issue in addressing Feagin's positioning within American sociology in a chapter of my *Postponing the Postmodern* (2002), in which I argue that Feagin is essentially black. (One might say that his chosen subject position is black, marginal, that of an outsider.) I might also have said that Feagin, like C. Wright Mills before him (another Texas plain Marxist), is also Irish, or, exactly, Irish on the inside (as Tom Hayden [2001] characterizes himself in his intriguing book of that title). The fact that Feagin and now Burawoy and Piven were elected tells us that the discipline is fragmented, containing its center and its periphery, or rather many peripheries occupied by nonpositivist sociologists who are women, minorities, young, gay and lesbian, theoretically oriented, political, ex-Students for a Democratic Society (SDS), and so on.

The majority, or at least plurality, of American sociologists, coalescing into a voting bloc and perhaps even an intellectual bloc, elect the Feagins, Pivens, and Burawoys over the Sullivans. This is certainly a step in the right direction. But the dominant midwestern-empiricist departments and journals are still controlled by positivists, who would disqualify nonpositivist sociologies as illegitimate. And even the Burawoys concede far too much to the mainstreamers, as we can see in his 2x2 table that allows the positivists a central position. They do this because they think they need to build coalitions and because they don't fully understand what went wrong with the Enlightenment, which, in the guise of scientific method and mathematics, behaves like a dictator, as Horkheimer and Adorno argued in *Dialectic of Enlightenment*.

Addressing the changing demography of U.S. sociology, in which the occupants of the periphery now outnumber members of the positivist core, Joe Feagin made this observation:

A great many of the American Sociological Association voters in elections now are younger sociologists, such as grad students and junior faculty, many of them still idealistic in their general views (though pressed by their seniors to be good positivists to make tenure and promotion). And they have played a key role recently in voting in several nonmainstream folks as president. . . . Indeed, a substantial majority of ASA members now are younger white men, women, and people of color. That is one major reason I beat out the mainstream candidates and why Burawoy and Piven won. The old-guard professors who still run many major departments often get outvoted in ASA matters by those they pressure or control in the tenure process! Many young people go into sociology mostly to change the world, but the older, disproportionately white and male positivist guard too often tries to beat that out of them as they become senior grad students and young faculty. Thus, many younger faculty live schizoid lives, wanting or trying to be progressive but forced to sell-out to get their degrees or tenure. . . . The times are changing demographically in the sociological professoriate, but the old guard is still trying to impose the outdated past on a rapidly changing present. (private correspondence)

At issue, now as before, is the politics of epistemology, method, and writing. This is the heart of the matter—how the words and figures lie on the page and seek to convert their contingent meanings into a metaphysic of subordination by eliciting their enactment. In a famous example, Parsons (1951) in his writings about the sexual division of labor would have men and women choose gendered—masculine and feminine—roles and thus reproduce the world he pretends only to describe. Burawoy opposes untoward inequalities of wealth, power, gender, and color, as he should, but he believes that he can do this within the orbit and ambit of what he calls professional sociology. He doesn't appear to appreciate that the mainstreamers don't want him to be ASA president, nor do they want their departments to turn to the left (or become partisan in any way). They want power and control of the discipline and method, as the prophets of the Enlightenment have since the seventeenth century.

COOPTATION OR CONTESTED TERRAIN?

Has the discipline really changed since Burawoy? If one examines the leading journals and departments, the answer is no. If one examines the theoretical, qualitative, and interdisciplinary periphery the answer might be yes, gradually. There is certainly mounting conflict over the method and meaning of sociology. Public sociology is a misleading brand reflecting Burawoy's ambitions for the discipline and not a genuine intellectual shift. His is not a "real" public sociology committed to the eleventh thesis, nonmethods driven intellectual work, and writing for a broad public. Burawoy favors professional sociology over the role of the public intellectual, sketched by Jacoby, Edward Said, Cornel West, Christopher Lasch, Barbara Ehrenreich. Although his politics are leftish, they are ensconced within the standard disciplinary division of labor according to which many crunch numbers, others secure policy-driven grants, still others teach and write theory, and others address and engage with broad publics (including students). This division of labor doesn't work because, as I have been saying, the professionals—or positivists, as I prefer—hold the real power as gatekeepers of the journals and the graduate programs. Indeed, Burawoy's election as ASA president is a prefect example of what Marcuse (Wolff, Moore, Marcuse 1969) called repressive tolerance or what Piccone (1975) and Luke (1975) termed "artificial negativity," involving both cooptation and the simulation of difference.

A review of the leading American sociology journals since 2000 reveals little change from the three previous decades. Method is still in the saddle. Articles are dominated by method and its figural gestures; prose, and especially theory, is displaced and minimized. The same people, from the same dominant departments, control the journals and publish there. I have heard no anecdotes to the effect that the Ohio State, Wisconsin, or Penn State departments are now less stringent about their requirements for tenure—articles published in the big-three journals, grants, team research, a neglect of book writing.

My claim that the methodological center still holds is contested by Jerry Jacobs, current *ASR* editor. In a 2005 piece titled "Multiple Methods in *ASR*" (Jacobs 2005), Jacobs argues that 25 percent of the papers he has accepted for publication since his editorship began in 2003 have used what he calls "multiple methodologies." At face value, this could be taken to mean papers that use both qualitative and quantitative methods. That might well signal a disciplinary reorientation of a significant kind. However, Jacobs admits that he is counting articles as bi-methodological if they use two different types of quantitative methods, hardly what one might construe as methodological diversification in the discipline. Now Jacobs is somewhat unusual by mainstream/*ASR* standards in that he has made a genuine effort to reorient the discipline's leading journal by opening it to heterodox voices and intellectual styles. Perhaps authors of my ilk simply don't submit their work to *ASR*, believing that this would be an exercise in futility.

Although supporters of public sociology hope that *Contexts*, now housed at New York University, an exemplar of public sociology, is changing things, it is not yet clear that *Contexts* is much different from other mainstream journals except in the accessibility of its presentations. Do *Contexts* articles "count" for tenure? Are they read by people beyond the narrow confines of academic sociology? Although Burawoy has traveled widely in spreading the word about his new agenda for the discipline, he has not convinced the discipline's power brokers to rethink their epistemological and methodological commitments.

There are two issues here. First, as I have been saying, the power holders (professionals, to him) aren't going to relinquish power to advocacy and activist sociologists. Second, the problem with the discipline isn't professionalism but positivism. Although these are related, they are not the same. A professional belongs to a guild, has credentials, and provides services of sorts. A positivist describes the world in order to freeze it, choking off history. In spite of Burawoy's critique, my work here doesn't exude utter contempt for disciplinary professionalism. I simply oppose positivism as the monolithic and conservative posture that it is, burying the author underneath the gestures of method and making the merger of theory and practice impossible.

The guild of what he calls professional sociology is a closed shop, even though seeming outsiders like Burawoy get elected. Many sociologists don't accept the positivist rules of the game, but they are relatively powerless to change things because they aren't in the major departments and don't control the major journals. They can vote for ASA elected officials, though, and in this case they preferred Burawoy's seeming merger of theory and practice (public sociology) over Terry Sullivan's straight demography and obeisance to method.

This makes it all the more unfortunate that Burawoy's public sociology has turned out to be merely an occupant of a Parsonian cell. Burawoy nowhere tells us how we can distinguish among the four types of legitimate sociology: professional, policy, critical, and public. I can't imagine how a public sociology, in the sense of a practice-oriented and nonmethods driven approach composed in nonspecialist terms, would not also be a "critical" sociology. Even Burawoy's distinction between traditional and organic versions of public sociology doesn't explain this adequately, where by traditional he means Jacoby and me and by organic he perhaps means the kind of material published in *Contexts*.

Frankfurt theorists have always understood the positivist version of "enlightenment" to involve a secret authoritarianism, according to which the only legitimate knowledge is mathematical and disengaged from history and politics. Knowing (e.g., science) reflected an inert object world, whether of nature or society. Although knowledge could gain power over the object, expressed in the various technologies of Fordism and post-Fordism, the object—here, capitalism—cannot be fundamentally transformed given that society is located in what Kant called the realm of necessity, not also the realm of freedom. Science is a kind of "identity theory," Adorno's term for knowledge that perfectly captures (identifies with) the object. In my terms, it involves a scientific text or page that represents nature or social nature by replacing prose with figure, an insight I draw from Derrida who enriches the Frankfurt-oriented critique of science with insights about how positivists actually produce their discourse (also see Knorr-Cetina's [1981, 1999] work on the conversion of laboratory work into texts within epistemic cultures).

Marcuse in *One-Dimensional Man* (1964) understands that post–World War II capitalism must produce the images of tolerance, openness, pluralism—difference, to use a French theoretic term. It closes the universe of discourse by appearing to remain open to many discourses and political valences. It does this for reasons of what Habermas (1975), drawing from Weber, terms legitimacy. Indeed, one of the central legitimation crises in late capitalism is a rule-bound ritualism within organizations (see Whyte Jr. 1956) that militates against creativity and innovation. This hyper-conformity both blocks innovation (in product lines) and gives the lie to the thesis of an open political system in which real debate actually occurs.

And so, by the late twentieth and early twenty-first centuries, capitalism produces the simulation not only of openness but of actual rebellion and critique. The appearance of opposition conceals the reality that the major American political parties are essentially the same, especially in this era of neoliberalism in which liberal and labor parties since Ronald Reagan and Margaret Thatcher have moved to the right. Adorno, Horkheimer, and Marcuse all understood that the ideology of late capitalism is no longer a set of falsifiable claims about the nature of social reality but positivism itself, a mode of consciousness (Marcuse's one-dimensional thinking) that is preoccupied with everyday appearances and eschews theoretical thinking, which would lead to normative critiques of society. Ideology today involves an intellectual laziness that eschews books, disdains mandarin culture in favor of reality television shows and promotes a culture of celebrity gossip—a state of ideological affairs that Kellner (1995) appropriately terms media culture.

In this context, Burawoy's disciplinary critique is a moment of artificial negativity; it does not go to the heart of the matter—the language game of positivism, which extends beyond the journals and afflicts everyday life itself, a "damaged" life according to Adorno—but remains on the surface of things. My critique is not utterly contemptuous of the discipline but a recognition that disciplinary power, and discipline generally, is a literary practice, process, and product involving social amnesia (Jacoby 1975) and the decline of discourse (Agger 1990). The politics of mainstream sociology lies between the lines of articles and monographs, in the intended but silent subtexts of their pages. Positivist discourse is secret writing, silent argument—for one state of affairs over another. It argues for the present as a plenitude of social being. Most notable about the prevailing text of science, including mainstream sociology, is that it displaces the author, argument, prose, and passion into the margins. These constitute an invisible but imagined presence, bedeviling the reader with unacknowledged perspective and position. Am I alone in turning to the acknowledgments and preface first, and the body of the text last, in search of the heartbeat of authorial agency?

Most notable about *ASR* articles since I published the first edition of *Public Sociology*, in addition to their incessant figuration and methods-driven quality, is how aimless they are. One is no more likely today than between 1970 and 2000 to pick up an issue of the journal for a coherent read. The articles continue to be written for publication, not to be read. Narrativity is nearly totally absent. Instead, we are treated to the leaden images of science that compel no one. As I have been arguing throughout this book, the articles conceal the authorial perspective from which their topics were originally of interest.

Equally apparent is that the articles, despite their claims to constitute normal, accumulating science, are disconnected from "literature." They don't add to existing knowledge and neither do they call forth new researches. Coupled with their lack of narrative and literary purpose, this isolation from other texts and context makes them appear anomic, without foundation. Journal science experiences and exhibits this alienation, which makes even a perusal of the table of contents of each journal number depressing. Unless one knows the author(s) or happens to plow the same narrow field in one's own research, there is no reason to read further, except perhaps to sample the article abstracts and perhaps read through (now, scroll down) the pages of text in sheer wonderment at the thick figural displays that become prose because they marginalize prose, the subtext of method becoming a main text in its own right.

A fully—one might say methodologically—adequate test of the possible "Burawoy effect" (has Michael Burawoy really made a difference in reorienting the discipline of sociology?) will await another five or ten years. It is not enough to notice increasing attention in official ASA publications and on its Web site to "public sociology." That brand is easily exploited to demonstrate the artificial negativity I discussed above. The real test of the Burawoy effect is to notice that the leading journals, and the graduate programs from which they spring, have fundamentally changed their approaches, both literary and substantive, to the writing, organizing, publishing, and teaching of sociology. These will probably only change by virtue of conflict between sociological core and periphery over method. I am not holding my breath because the science model has considerable momentum. In how many introductory sociology classes are students *not* taught that sociology is a science? As well, the left rump (plurality? majority?) in U.S. sociology has not yet developed a compelling model of the relationship between theory and practice. As I argue below, this model could be found forty years ago in the praxis of 1960s sociological activists.

The election of a Feagin, Piven, or Burawoy may be quite misleading as a barometer of the mainstream discipline, even as it is telling. It tells us that people on the fringes, in liberal arts college and utilitarian universities that don't offer the doctorate in sociology and among younger faculty, women faculty, and faculty of color, aren't working on the science model, or at least they don't embrace it even if they must purvey it to get tenure. Theory and critique have undergone a diaspora, flowing to the periphery of the discipline and across disciplinary boundaries to humanities departments and interdisciplinary programs such as women's studies, cultural studies, and queer studies. As the core discipline of U.S. sociology remains a positivist monolith, exciting critical sociologies and protosociologies that cross disciplinary boundaries are being developed. This is why ASA journals are edited and controlled by positivists, while recent ASA presidents have been renegades dedicated to a quite different discipline.

Such elections mislead us that most sociologists in Ph.D.-granting departments are now heeding the eleventh thesis, abandoning method as their central focus, imbedding theory into the practice of research, and refuting the pre-Kuhnian model of a cumulative body of knowledge. This is not happening both because the center holds and because there are few good models of a genuinely public sociology in a national intellectual context in which Marx is not studied seriously, or the Frankfurt School, or French theory, or cultural studies. These sources have been demonized by positivists and compartmentalized by nonpositivists such as Burawoy, who restricts such sources to a single cell within his 2x2 table intended to make peace with the positivists.

The brand "public sociology" has been so successful because it changes very little. It is easy for the leading departments and journals to mouth the adjective *public* instead of the more politically incisive adjectives *radical* or *critical*. I drew the title of this book from Jacoby's Frankfurt-inspired discussion of the role of intellectuals in the public sphere, not anticipating that the term "public sociology" could be readily mainstreamed. Indeed, Burawoy distinguishes between public and critical sociology precisely in order to depoliticize public sociology, which one would have thought impossible. The ASA's public sociology is certainly not the public sociology espoused in this book, especially where Burawoy and the mainstreamers who embrace his usage of the term imagine sociology to engage with various "publics," neglecting the deeper textual/political/disciplinary analysis I have performed in this book. A positivist/private sociology resides in between the lines and figures on the journal page, in graduate school curricula, in the informal networks operating at the sociological conventions. It is a site—many sites—of power, possessing what Foucault considered a microphysics in order to avoid detection. As I have said often in my work, this type of positivist sociology is secret writing in which the author and her politics are buried deep beneath the footnotes and methodological appendices.

THE PROVENANCE OF THE PUBLIC INTELLECTUAL AND ITS IMPLICATIONS FOR DISCIPLINARY WORK

Let me return to the work of Russell Jacoby, for whom Burawoy reserves considerable wrath. Burawoy knows, because he has told me, that Jacoby is central to this whole question of public sociology. Burawoy and I formulated versions of public sociology a decade after Jacoby published *Last Intellectuals: American Culture in the Age of Academe* (1987), an argument that itself grew out of the Frankfurt School (Habermas 1989), the 1960s, and Jacoby's own academic and personal biography. I have been writing along the same lines since the late 1980s, especially in my work on the decline of discourse, which, it could be said, supports Jacoby's arguments about the demise of the public intellectual with insights from French theories of discourse, notably by Derrida and Foucault.

In 1989 I published *Fast Capitalism* (Agger 1989a), my position statement on the third generation of the Frankfurt School, to which I, Doug Kellner, Tim Luke, Mark Poster, and Jacoby belong. Critical theory's first generation includes Adorno, Horkheimer, and Marcuse, and the second generation was dominated by Jürgen Habermas. My argument in *Fast Capitalism* is that we not only have experienced the decline of public intellectuals but also the decline of the book itself, which has now been immersed in the quotidian cultures of everyday life in which people browse but don't ponder. I published a sequel to *Fast Capitalism*, in light of the Internet, which has only accelerated the decline of discourse. That sequel, *Speeding Up Fast Capitalism* (Agger 2004), addresses the decline of discourse's acceleration, to which the antidote remains writings and postings by public intellectuals, people who read and write slowly and broadly and seek the merger of theory and practice, especially in these dangerous times.

As I have argued, sociology played a major role in 1960s campus activism. Less than a year after I started college as an undergraduate in 1969, the Kent State killings brought U.S. higher education to a halt, as students struck in sympathy. For those of us in college at the time, there was no question that college was "relevant," relevant to the turmoil and tumult of the times. I did not envisage an academic career somehow separate from New Left political projects; critique and enlightenment went hand in hand with the exegesis and mastery of important texts, such as those of Hegel, Marx, Sartre, Merleau-Ponty, Camus, Beauvoir, Malcolm X, Fanon, and many others.

We may have been naïve about the bureaucratic university, already critiqued in Mills' *The Sociological Imagination*. Yet our naivety was toughened by our political experience, which, by the time I graduated with an undergraduate degree in 1972, had exposed us to Nixon, Westmoreland, Hoover, and the Chicago police. The bureaucratic university seemed like small potatoes compared to the organized state repression of white and black activists.

There are important parallels between now and then: Iraq is Vietnam; Bush Jr. is Nixon; Homeland Security is the FBI's COINTELPRO. Those were dangerous times, too. A difference is that there is no draft today, diminishing student activism. When I was in high school, the New Left was relatively vital, whereas when I finished college, Weatherman had gone underground and the right was firmly in control.

Once the 1960s were over, leftist students chose either careers in academia or freelancing. Some dropped out of academia altogether. Academic careerists had to learn jargon in order to publish lest they (we!) perish. Independent scholars and cultural creators, such as Jacoby, were adrift in the vast cultural marketplace that was increasingly hostile to small presses and lonely scholars. Two forces converged to split New Left theory and practice: the right ascended with Nixon's counterrevolution, and the post-1960s university confronted tight budgets and moved toward a model of state-sponsored funded research. Few universities needed critical theorists, let alone radical gadflies. As I have suggested in this book, sociology, which had been highly activist during the Vietnam era, followed suit, promoting grant-worthy empiricism. By the 1980s, the few former sixties activists who survived the transformation of academic life into a business—indeed, into a corporation—were the few (like me) who lucked into tenure. We became tenured radicals—arguably an oxymoron.

As I noted earlier, the critique of academia was received with defensiveness by tenured radicals who didn't doubt their own importance. Jacoby was accused of glorifying earlier eras such as the 1950s in which public intellectuals like sociology's own C. Wright Mills cast long shadows on the intellectual landscape. To be sure, as Jacoby himself readily admits, the decline of public intellectuals is a gradual and nuanced process; like the dinosaur, their disappearance was not immediate and in some quarters is slowly being reversed—as the example of his own work demonstrates. The left itself is not immune to criticism. It is difficult for outsiders to get published in "public" liberal/left outlets such as *The Nation*, which are controlled by a New York City elite who write short sentences and don't traffic in theoretical concepts. At play here is hierarchy—the distinction between those on the inside, who hold power, and those on the outside. And so we need to attend not only to the public/private distinction in assessing the relevance or obscurantism of intellectual work, but also the extent to which publishing outlets, whether *ASR* or *The Nation*, open themselves to authors outside their circles.

Jacoby has been persuasive, even if many dispute the sweeping resolve and tone of his analysis. Many believe that academic work has become too narrow and self-referential. Hence, they reasonably call for a public sociology. However, I contend that Jacoby's critique, although not explicitly grounded in Foucault's critique of the "disciplining" power of academic disciplines, implies a critique of disciplinarity that Burawoy largely ignores. Public intellectuals are, almost by definition, pan-disciplinary, crossing disciplines and working on their borders as well as margins. Jacoby holds a doctorate in history but writes social theory. My doctorate is in political economy. I have worked in departments of sociology, political science, comparative literature, and humanities. Most scholars who do critical theory work within multiple disciplines and across them.

Certain faculty members have singular and strong disciplinary identities, while others have multiple and diffuse identities. Although there is certainly room for both types in the academy and larger world of letters, critical scholars in the early twenty-first century tend to be of the second type. Indeed, it is the ability to move across and around disciplines that enables such scholars to paint the big picture and perform as public intellectuals. Such scholars are also uncomfortable with the particular methodological and cultural strictures of single disciplines, which they experience as restricting their intellectual curiosity and creativity.

Burawoy's construction of public sociology appeals to those whose sociological identities are strong and singular. His version of the sociological division of labor contains no cells or spaces for meta- or protosociologies of the kind that we find in other social sciences and even in the humanities. Theoretically-oriented scholars in English departments these days do protosociology; indeed, as I just commented, theory has been dispersed into the humanities, both into singular disciplines such as English and into interdisciplinary sites such as cultural studies, women's studies, queer studies, and postcolonial studies. Hostility to theory is far weaker in these humanities and interdisciplinary sites because faculty in these areas did not turn their back on the engagements of the 1960s, as many sociologists did. Sociologists, as I have argued throughout this book, turned away from the 1960s, politics, and theory, and toward quantitative method, as a way of shoring up their discipline's eroding legitimacy beginning in the 1970s, somehow ashamed of their and their colleagues' erstwhile activism.

At stake, then, is what it means to do sociology. I contend that sociologies are found in all sorts of places: in disciplines, in between disciplines, and outside of the academy proper. John O'Neill (1972, 1974), blending critical theory and ethnomethodology, argues that sociology is a lived practice involving theorizing, empathy, and struggle. Burawoy cannot believe that most versions of sociology are restricted to what is published in the journals and presented at the official meetings. This would confine us to a version of discipline that, almost by definition, cannot go public in the sense of addressing large and interrelated interdisciplinary problems. By his own account, he feels strongly that we must reserve a role for what he terms professional sociologists, the kind of people who promote and practice science, have paid-up memberships in the American Sociological Association, attend the annual meetings and vote in the elections for Association officers.

I wouldn't quarrel with this if I saw significant evidence that professional sociologists did research and writing that transcended method and engaged politics and struggle. All I have to go on is what I find in the journals, the programs of the national and regional meetings, and graduate school curricula. No matter how vigorously Burawoy promotes the brand of public sociology—albeit perhaps unintentionally emptied of the politicizing meanings attached to it by Jacoby, me, and others—most empirical sociology today remains disconnected, methods-driven, and self-referential. As I contend, it is written for publication, not to be read. It conceals its authorship underneath the heavy apparatus of method, but it is secret writing. This book has been a deconstructive reading of such secret writing, not intended with utter contempt, as Burawoy maintains, but out of a belief that sociology is worth doing as long as it comes clean about its own literary, political nature. There are many natures, many ways of writing about the self's inherence in society and history. Each such version changes the author and the world, the more so the more that sociological writers pretend to be copying the truth of the world onto their pages, without mediation. A public sociology begins by acknowledging that writing is practice; the text of analysis and argument inserts itself in the world from which it tries to gain a heuristic distance in order to appreciate the interdependence (some might say dialectic) of subjects and objects.

One could conduct a piece of ethnographic research to assess the increasing conflict between positivist core and theoretical periphery within American sociology. In the book display at the annual meetings of the ASA, one will find publishers such as Routledge, Blackwell, Paradigm, Rowman & Littlefield, and university presses with lengthy lists of books in critical theory, cultural studies, media studies, feminist studies, and queer studies. The journals publish the positivist work, while scholars on the fringes of the discipline write, read, and adopt these heterodox books, which frequently sell in the many thousands. (For instance, Doug Kellner's *Media Culture* has sold over 100,000 copies.) The reading and writing habits of sociologists diverge as sharply as their methods and politics.

Jean-Paul Sartre and the existentialists recognized that existence precedes essence, by which they mean that knowing, writing, and teaching are always grounded in the everyday contexts of experience and practice. I came to the realization that sociology is secret writing when I observed a number-crunching colleague at a former snowbound university holding his keyboard on his lap, feet up for comfort, and pounding away as he composed his articles for tenure. He was productive, according to the usual indicators of mainstream articles and grants. I stuck my head in the door and told him that he was a writer! He responded, "Nope, I'm just doing science!" Perhaps he believed that using SPSSX removed his authorial perspective and transported him out of the land of the literary. Years later we don't talk to each other, having disagreed about the direction of our department, which we both left in the meantime. What really separated us, though, was the essentially philosophical question of what it means to hold your keyboard in your lap while you type your stuff, your sociology. That remains the question before us.

THE SIXTIES AT FORTY: A MODEL FOR A
TWENTY-FIRST CENTURY PUBLIC SOCIOLOGY

Jacoby's critique of disciplinary academics stalls because he does not situate his analysis of the decline of discourse in sufficiently structural terms. True, he identifies the causes of academic obscurantism and the eclipse of independent intellectuals: the decline of urban bohemia and bookstores, a corporate media culture, the academization of intellectual work, and, finally, the authorial failure of nerve. But he does not reflect sufficiently on the relationship between intellectuals and social movements in recent American history. This prevents him from noticing that we already have an excellent model of public intellectuality, indeed a model taken from a period in which Jacoby and I and many other 1960s people came of age politically and entered academic life. I am speaking especially of the early 1960s, when college students and young faculty, inspired by the work of C. Wright Mills, started a powerful social movement that won civil rights for blacks and other minorities, toppled the Johnson presidency, and hastened the end of the Vietnam war.

Tom Hayden, Richard Flacks, and Todd Gitlin, two of whom are official sociologists—Flacks at UC–Santa Barbara and Gitlin at Columbia—worked within the structure of the early Students for a Democratic Society to reformulate traditional goals of socialism as "participatory democracy," ushering in a "new" left that could speak to Americans. This New Left avoided the sectarian and exegetical hair-splitting of the old left and of European socialists and Marxists without abandoning goals of humane social change taken by Mills from early Marx. Hayden drafted the 1962 Port Huron Statement of SDS that was debated, revised, and ratified at an early-summer meeting of young SDSers, many of whom were from the University of Michigan, at a UAW camp on the shores of Lake Huron in Michigan. Hayden was inspired by Mills's call for the articulation of private troubles and public issues and wrote a thesis on Mills, recently issued in book form (Hayden 2006). Of particular importance in the Port Huron Statement was the section on "values," which the SDS campers urged Hayden to move forward in his original document in order to highlight the potential impact of participatory democracy on the everyday lives of students, their parents, minorities, even citizens of the Soviet Union.

This Mills-era intellectual and political work was "public sociology" in the best sense of the term. It dealt with large issues of social and political concern. It was composed accessibly, but without sacrificing nuance and complexity. It had action implications as well as policy recommendations. This work flowed from the passionate pens of young Americans concerned with facilitating civil rights in the South and ameliorating economic inequalities in northern cities (primarily through ERAP [Economic Research and Action Project], an excellent example of organic intellectuality dealing with poor urban dwellers' real problems of living). The SDS-era public sociologies of Hayden, Flacks, Gitlin, and Paul Potter tried to "name" the system of national and international oppression, inviting young American radicals to rethink and reformulate—without recanting—traditional goals of democratic socialists. These young thinkers and activists well understood that the name of this system was capitalism, but they tried to formulate "capitalism" in terms that would resonate with Americans in struggle at the time.

The social movements of the 1960s changed the world, but they also were defeated by a Nixon-era counterrevolution that saw the police murder of Black Panther Fred Hampton, organized repression of leftists, and the degeneration of Port Huron idealism into the adventurism of the Weather Underground (see Varon 2004). With President Nixon, American political discourse and practice was shifted to the right, occasioning an eventual neoliberalism that reframed the Democratic Party as a centrist party equally supportive of business and the middle class. This neoliberalism resulted most recently in John Kerry's stunning defeat by George Bush Jr., whose agenda combines xenophobia, isolationism, military adventurism, and procorporate mendacity and greed. Kerry lost because the Democratic Party has become so indistinct from its Republican opposition that millions of traditional Democratic voters and supporters simply stayed home, allowing Bush to achieve a narrow victory (see Varon 2005).

As I have discussed in this book, sociologists reacted to the 1960s and to their own activism during that era with a sustained retrenchment that sought to relegitimize sociology with academic administrators, foundations, and tuition payers. Thus, during the 1970s, the major journals and graduate departments moved sharply in the direction of a highly quantitative methods-driven approach to sociological writing and graduate training. The positivist domination of the leading publication outlets, the graduate programs, hiring, and ASA Council stems from this move—begun during the 1970s and beyond—to transform sociology into a high-science discipline and one oriented to pragmatic engineering (see Turner 1998). As I have argued throughout this book, this retrenchment, which responded to the demise of the 1960s, cost sociology a purchase on public and political issues.

We need to return to the 1960s not only for good ideas, such as participatory democracy and ERAP, but for an exemplar of an engaged "public" sociology that translated Mills and other radical sociologies into an action plan, one so efficacious that it mobilized millions of young Americans and brought the war effort to an eventual halt (see Wells 1994 and 2005). Perhaps the best way to reverse disciplinary positivism is to return to the intellectual and political influences, such as Mills, Hayden, and early Marx, which provoked the sweeping movement activism that eventually became the target of state repression and led mainstream sociologists to recant their earlier engagements and enthusiasms. Sociological positivism emerged from sociology's own rightward shift that began after the Chicago Democratic Convention, Hampton's murder, Days of Rage, Kent State and Jackson State, and the unraveling of SDS. A revitalized public sociology would reach back into the dusty archives of SDS and other movement resources for energy and examples of political and intellectual engagement that would be most appropriate to these 1960s-like times of Bush/Rove, the unwinnable war in Iraq, domestic repression, and sexual-political attacks on women's reproductive rights and on gays and lesbians.

Anecdote: I recently showed Michael Moore's *Fahrenheit 9/11* and *The Weather Underground* to my undergraduate class. I was surprised that they hated Moore's treatment and loved the documentary about Weatherman. They felt that Moore was didactic and one-sided, but they loved the Bonnie and Clyde resonance of the attractive, kick-ass protagonists of the Days of Rage. They didn't see the parallels or connection between the 1960s and the present. Sociology majors then expected sociology to explain the world to us and offered solutions. Now my students experience their sociology training as largely a matter of surmounting the high hurdles of the methodology and statistics courses. The discipline doesn't speak to them anymore. A public sociology today needs to help young people read the world in some depth and complexity, especially using theory, and it needs to give young people a stake in the world. This is exactly what Hayden intended more than forty years ago, when he encrypted a critical and public sociology in the pages of Port Huron.

Image: Frances Fox Piven is a young faculty member at Columbia. The year is 1968, and SDS's action faction, led by Mark Rudd, has taken over several administrative buildings in the university, protesting the university's plan to build a gymnasium on public property adjoining Harlem. She is being assisted by Hayden as she climbs through a window to join the student protest and occupation of university buildings. (Her daughter is also perched in the windowsill, which opens into the math building.) Today, Piven is 2007 ASA president. She doesn't turn her back on the 1960s and one hopes that she will appreciate the sixties at forty as a critical intellectual and political resource today, as she steers ASA away from the religion of science and toward the type of public engagement that she, Rudd, Hayden, and the other Columbia activists demonstrated nearly four decades ago. With the Bush gang in the White House, with an ascendant New Wrong that has mobilized evangelical citizens from middle America, with the quagmires of Iraq and Afghanistan, with a naked corporate agenda among the executive committee of the bourgeoisie and with global inequalities that fester and become malignant, there is no reason why young and older Americans cannot mobilize around images of participatory democracy (perhaps now with a cyber component) and social justice. A public sociology can provide analysis and energy for this incipient movement, much as it did during the 1960s, when Paul Potter of SDS urged people at a major 1965 demonstration in Washington, D.C. to "name" and analyze the system that oppresses them. No less is needed today.

Metaphor: Piven climbing into the Columbia building, to occupy it in solidarity with the students. Today, Piven seeks to occupy the house of sociology and to transform it. Hayden assisted her in 1968 and he can do so again if we take from him, Flacks, Mills, early Marx, and the civil rights movement an agenda for the next Left.

It is perhaps too early to tell whether American sociology, which is an increasingly contested terrain, will allow the Pivens and Feagins to take the discipline back to a New Left model of engagement or whether the power brokers who dominate the official discipline and control the leading departments will keep method in the saddle. In the short run, I believe that method will dominate, but over time I think this may change, as younger scholars learn from their mentors who were active during the 1960s that a radical sociology can once again contribute to ongoing social movements designed to enhance social justice and redistribute power and wealth. Part of this will depend on whether the 1960s people in the discipline (think of Flacks, Lemert, Aronowitz) can tell persuasive stories about the exciting days when students and young faculty strategized to end the war and win civil rights. Time it was! The kids who led the movement over forty years ago have something to teach the kids today about the power of imagination and analysis to change the world. Young people can use sociology as a vehicle only if sociologists rethink their relationship to politics and the public sphere, using method where necessary but not allowing themselves to be used by it. A good beginning for all of us, as we confront intellectual and political quandaries, is to ask What Would Mills Do? And he might have asked What Would Early Marx Do?

Appendix

Articles in the Sample

FULL CITATIONS FOR THE FIGURES IN THE TEXT

Figure 3.1 Morris, Martina, Annette D. Bernhardt, and Mark S. Handcock. 1994. "Economic Inequality: New Methods for New Trends." *American Sociological Review* 59:211.

Figure 3.2 Sweeney, Megan M. 1997. "Remarriage of Women and Men after Divorce: The Role of Socioeconomic Prospects." *Journal of Family Issues* 18:479.

Figure 3.3 Cherlin, Andrew J., P. Lindsay Chase-Lansdale, and Christine McRae. 1998. "Effects of Parental Divorce on Mental Health Throughout the Life Course." *American Sociological Review* 63:239.

Figure 3.4 Treas, Judith. 1993. "Money in the Bank: Transaction Costs and the Economic Organization of Marriage." *American Sociological Review* 58:723.

Figure 3.5 Nielsen, François. 1994. "Income Inequality and Industrial Development: Dualism Revisited." *American Sociological Review* 59:657.

Figure 3.6 Mark, Noah. 1998. "Beyond Individual Differences: Social Differentiation from First Principles." *American Sociological Review* 63:309.

Figure 3.7 Webster, Jr., Murray, and Stuart J. Hysom. 1998. "Creating Status Characteristics." *American Sociological Review* 63:351.

Figure 3.8 Orloff, Ann Shola. 1993. "Gender and the Social Rights of Citizenship: The Comparative Analysis of Gender Relations and Welfare States." *American Sociological Review* 58:303.

Figure 3.9 Sanchez, Laura, and Emily W. Kane. 1996. "Women's and Men's Constructions of Perceptions of Housework Fairness." *Journal of Family Issues* 17:359.

Figure 3.10 MacDermid, Shelley M., and Margaret L. Williams. 1997. "A Within-Industry Comparison of Employed Mothers' Experiences in Small and Large Workplaces." *Journal of Family Issues* 18:546.

Figure 3.11 Somers, Margaret R. 1993. "Citizenship and the Place of the Public Sphere: Law, Community, and Political Culture in the Transition to Democracy." *American Sociological Review* 58:595.

Figure 3.12 Turner, R. Jay, Blair Wheaton, and Donald A. Lloyd. 1995. "The Epidemiology of Social Stress." *American Sociological Review* 60:104.

Figure 3.13 Berger, Joseph, Cecilia L. Ridgeway, M. Hamit Fisek, and Robert Z. Norman. 1998. "The Legitimation and Delegitimation of Power and Prestige Orders." *American Sociological Review* 63:379.

Figure 3.14 Kiser, Edgar, and Joachim Schneider. 1994. "Bureaucracy and Efficiency: An Analysis of Taxation in Early Modern Prussia." *American Sociological Review* 59:187.

Figure 3.15 Somers, Margaret R. 1993. "Citizenship and the Place of the Public Sphere: Law, Community, and Political Culture in the Transition to Democracy." *American Sociological Review* 58:591.

Figure 3.16 Treas, Judith. 1993. "Money in the Bank: Transaction Costs and the Economic Organization of Marriage." *American Sociological Review* 58:723.

Figure 3.17 Misra, Joya, and Alexander Hicks. 1994. "Catholicism and Unionization in Affluent Postwar Democracies: Catholicism, Culture, Party, and Unionization." *American Sociological Review* 59:304.

Figure 3.18 Firebaugh, Glenn, and Frank D. Beck. 1994. "Does Economic Growth Benefit the Masses? Growth, Dependence, and Welfare in the Third World." *American Sociological Review* 59:632.

Figure 3.19 Nielsen, François. 1994. "Income Inequality and Industrial Development: Dualism Revisited." *American Sociological Review* 59:656.

Figure 3.20 Boyd, Elizabeth A. 1998. "Bureaucratic Authority in the 'Company of Equals': The Interactional Management of Medical Peer Review." *American Sociological Review* 63:201.

Figure 3.21 Webster, Jr., Murray, and Stuart J. Hysom. 1998. "Creating Status Characteristics." *American Sociological Review* 63:352.

Figure 3.22 Somers, Margaret R. 1993. "Citizenship and the Place of the Public Sphere: Law, Community, and Political Culture in the Transition to Democracy." *American Sociological Review* 58:587.

Figure 3.23 Sanchez, Laura, and Emily W. Kane. 1996. "Women's and Men's Constructions of Perceptions of Housework Fairness." *Journal of Family Issues* 17:360.

Figure 3.24 Heckathorn, Douglas D. 1993. "Collective Action and Group Heterogeneity: Voluntary Provision versus Selective Incentives." *American Sociological Review* 58:330.

Figure 3.25 Qian, Zhenchao, and Samuel H. Preston. 1993. "Changes in American Marriage, 1972 to 1987: Availability and Forces of Attraction by Age and Education." *American Sociological Review* 58:483–84.

Figure 3.26 Boswell, Terry, and William J. Dixon. 1993. "Marx's Theory of Rebellion: A Cross-National Analysis of Class Exploitation, Economic Development, and Violent Revolt." *American Sociological Review* 58:682–83.

Figure 3.27 Long, Scott J., Paul D. Allison, and Robert McGinnis. 1993. "Rank Advancement in Academic Careers: Sex Differences and the Effects of Productivity." *American Sociological Review* 58:705.

Figure 3.28 Kiser, Edgar, and Joachim Schneider. 1994. "Bureaucracy and Efficiency: An Analysis of Taxation in Early Modern Prussia." *American Sociological Review* 59:189.

Figure 3.29 Morris, Martina, Annette D. Bernhardt, and Mark S. Handcock. 1994. "Economic Inequality: New Methods for New Trends." *American Sociological Review* 59:206.

Figure 3.30 Amato, Paul R., and Alan Booth. 1995. "Changes in Gender Role Attitudes and Perceived Marital Quality." *American Sociological Review* 60:59.

Figure 3.31 Duncan, Greg J., W. Jean Yeung, Jeanne Brooks-Gunn, and Judith R. Smith. 1998. "How Much Does Childhood Poverty Affect the Life Chances of Children?" *American Sociological Review* 63:406.

Figure 3.32 Spenner, Kenneth I., Olga O. Suhomlinova, Sten A. Thore, Kenneth C. Land, and Derek C. Jones. 1998. "Strong Legacies and Weak Markets: Bulgarian State-Owned Enterprises During Early Transition." *American Sociological Review* 63:611–12.

Figure 3.33 Sanchez, Laura, and Emily W. Kane. 1996. "Women's and Men's Constructions of Perceptions of Housework Fairness." *Journal of Family Issues* 17:359.

Figure 3.34 Moaddel, Mansoor. 1994. "Political Conflict in the World Economy: A Cross-National Analysis of Modernization and World-System Theories." *American Sociological Review* 59:277.

Figure 3.35 Long, Scott J., Paul D. Allison and Robert McGinnis. 1993. "Rank Advancement in Academic Careers: Sex Differences and the Effects of Productivity." *American Sociological Review* 58:705.

Figure 3.36 Kiser, Edgar, and Joachim Schneider. 1994. "Bureaucracy and Efficiency: An Analysis of Taxation in Early Modern Prussia." *American Sociological Review* 59:187.

Figure 3.37 Prechel, Harland. 1994. "Economic Crisis and the Centralization of Control over the Managerial Process: Corporate Restructuring and Neo-Fordist Decision-Making." *American Sociological Review* 59:723–24.

Figure 3.38 Sanchez, Laura, and Emily W. Kane. 1996. "Women's and Men's Constructions of Perceptions of Housework Fairness." *Journal of Family Issues* 17:367.

Figure 3.39 Heckathorn, Douglas D. 1993. "Collective Action and Group Heterogeneity: Voluntary Provision versus Selective Incentives." *American Sociological Review* 58:329.

Figure 3.40 Somers, Margaret R. 1993. "Citizenship and the Place of the Public Sphere: Law, Community, and Political Culture in the Transition to Democracy." *American Sociological Review* 58:588.

Figure 3.41 Morris, Aldon D. 1993. "Birmingham Confrontation Reconsidered: An Analysis of the Dynamics and Tactics of Mobilization." *American Sociological Review* 58:622.

Figure 3.42 Stolzenberg, Ross M., Mary Blair-Loy, and Linda J. Waite. 1995. "Religious Participation in Early Adulthood: Age and Family Life Cycle Effects on Church Membership." *American Sociological Review* 60:84.

Figure 3.43 Turner, R. Jay, Blair Wheaton, and Donald A. Lloyd. 1995. "The Epidemiology of Social Stress." *American Sociological Review* 60:104.

Figure 3.44 Mark, Noah. 1998. "Beyond Individual Differences: Social Differentiation from First Principles." *American Sociological Review* 63:309.

Figure 3.45 MacDermid, Shelley M., and Margaret L. Williams. 1997. "A Within-Industry Comparison of Employed Mothers' Experiences in Small and Large Workplaces." *Journal of Family Issues* 18:545.

Figure 3.46 Martin, Karin A. 1998. "Becoming a Gendered Body: Practices of Preschools." *American Sociological Review* 63:494.

Figure 3.47 Misra, Joya, and Alexander Hicks. 1994. "Catholicism and Unionization in Affluent Postwar Democracies: Catholicism, Culture, Party, and Unionization." *American Sociological Review* 59:309.

Figure 3.48 Baker, Wayne E., Robert R. Faulkner, and Gene A. Fisher. 1998. "Hazards of the Market: The Continuity and Dissolution of Interorganizational Market Relationships." *American Sociological Review* 63:154.

Figure 3.49 Mark, Noah. 1998. "Beyond Individual Differences: Social Differentiation from First Principles." *American Sociological Review* 63:315.

Figure 4.1 Somers, Margaret R. 1993. "Citizenship and the Place of the Public Sphere: Law, Community, and Political Culture in the Transition to Democracy." *American Sociological Review* 58:593.

Figure 4.2 Somers, Margaret R. 1993. "Citizenship and the Place of the Public Sphere:

Law, Community, and Political Culture in the Transition to Democracy." *American Sociological Review* 58:599.

Figure 4.3 Boyd, Elizabeth A. 1998. "Bureaucratic Authority in the 'Company of Equals': The Interactional Management of Medical Peer Review." *American Sociological Review* 63:206–7.

Figure 4.4 Firebaugh, Glenn, and Frank D. Beck. 1994. "Does Economic Growth Benefit the Masses? Growth, Dependence, and Welfare in the Third World." *American Sociological Review* 59:648.

Figure 4.5 Qian, Zhenchao, and Samuel H. Preston. 1993. "Changes in American Marriage, 1972 to 1987: Availability and Forces of Attraction by Age and Education." *American Sociological Review* 58:488–89.

Figure 4.6 Qian, Zhenchao, and Samuel H. Preston. 1993. "Changes in American Marriage, 1972 to 1987: Availability and Forces of Attraction by Age and Education." *American Sociological Review* 58:489.

Figure 4.7 Long, Scott J., Paul D. Allison, and Robert McGinnis. 1993. "Rank Advancement in Academic Careers: Sex Differences and the Effects of Productivity." *American Sociological Review* 58:705–7.

Figure 4.8 Moaddel, Mansoor. 1994. "Political Conflict in the World Economy: A Cross-National Analysis of Modernization and World-System Theories." *American Sociological Review* 59:287.

Figure 4.9 Stolzenberg, Ross M., Mary Blair-Loy, and Linda J. Waite. 1995. "Religious Participation in Early Adulthood: Age and Family Life Cycle Effects on Church Membership." *American Sociological Review* 60:89.

Figure 4.10 Heckathorn, Douglas D. 1993. "Collective Action and Group Heterogeneity: Voluntary Provision versus Selective Incentives." *American Sociological Review* 58:336.

Figure 4.11 Qian, Zhenchao, and Samuel H. Preston. 1993. "Changes in American Marriage, 1972 to 1987: Availability and Forces of Attraction by Age and Education." *American Sociological Review* 58:484–85.

Figure 4.12 Misra, Joya, and Alexander Hicks. 1994. "Catholicism and Unionization in Affluent Postwar Democracies: Catholicism, Culture, Party, and Unionization." *American Sociological Review* 59:313–14.

Figure 4.13 Firebaugh, Glenn, and Frank D. Beck. 1994. "Does Economic Growth Benefit the Masses? Growth, Dependence, and Welfare in the Third World." *American Sociological Review* 59:636–37.

Figure 4.14 Long, Scott J., Paul D. Allison, and Robert McGinnis. 1993. "Rank Advancement in Academic Careers: Sex Differences and the Effects of Productivity." *American Sociological Review* 58:716–717.

Figure 4.15 Stolzenberg, Ross M., Mary Blair-Loy, and Linda J. Waite. 1995. "Religious Participation in Early Adulthood: Age and Family Life Cycle Effects on Church Membership." *American Sociological Review* 60:92–93.

Figure 4.16 Smits, Jeroen, Wout Ultee, and Jan Lammers. 1998. "Educational Homogamy in 65 Countries: An Explanation of Differences in Openness Using Country-Level Explanatory Variables." *American Sociological Review* 63:275–79.

Figure 4.17 Heckathorn, Douglas D. 1993. "Collective Action and Group Heterogeneity: Voluntary Provision versus Selective Incentives." *American Sociological Review* 58:339.

Figure 4.18 Stolzenberg, Ross M., Mary Blair-Loy, and Linda J. Waite. 1995. "Religious

1998. "How Much Does Childhood Poverty Affect the Life Chances of Children?" *American Sociological Review* 63:411.

Figure 5.13 Jang, Sung Joon, and Terence P. Thornberry. 1998. "Self-Esteem, Delinquent Peers, and Delinquency: A Test of the Self-Enhancement Thesis." *American Sociological Review* 63:595.

Figure 5.14 Spenner, Kenneth I., Olga O. Suhomlinova, Sten A. Thore, Kenneth C. Land, and Derek C. Jones. 1998. "Strong Legacies and Weak Markets: Bulgarian State-Owned Enterprises During Early Transition." *American Sociological Review* 63:613.

Figure 5.15 Moaddel, Mansoor. 1994. "Political Conflict in the World Economy: A Cross-National Analysis of Modernization and World-System Theories." *American Sociological Review* 59:286.

Figure 5.16 Nielsen, François. 1994. "Income Inequality and Industrial Development: Dualism Revisited." *American Sociological Review* 59:658.

Figure 5.17 Smits, Jeroen, Wout Ultee, and Jan Lammers. 1998. "Educational Homogamy in 65 Countries: An Explanation of Differences in Openness Using Country-Level Explanatory Variables." *American Sociological Review* 63:270–71.

Figure 5.18 Orloff, Ann Shola. 1993. "Gender and the Social Rights of Citizenship: The Comparative Analysis of Gender Relations and Welfare States." *American Sociological Review* 58:303.

Figure 5.19 Somers, Margaret R. 1993. "Citizenship and the Place of the Public Sphere: Law, Community, and Political Culture in the Transition to Democracy." *American Sociological Review* 58:587.

Figure 5.20 Baker, Wayne E., Robert R. Faulkner, and Gene A. Fisher. 1998. "Hazards of the Market: The Continuity and Dissolution of Interorganizational Market Relationships." *American Sociological Review* 63:147.

Figure 5.21 MacDermid, Shelley M., and Margaret L. Williams. 1997. "A Within-Industry Comparison of Employed Mothers' Experiences in Small and Large Workplaces." *Journal of Family Issues* 18:545.

Figure 5.22 Treas, Judith. 1993. "Money in the Bank: Transaction Costs and the Economic Organization of Marriage." *American Sociological Review* 58:587.

Figure 5.23 Smits, Jeroen, Wout Ultee, and Jan Lammers. 1998. "Educational Homogamy in 65 Countries: An Explanation of Differences in Openness Using Country-Level Explanatory Variables." *American Sociological Review* 63:264.

Figure 5.24 Taylor, Marylee C. 1998. "How White Attitudes Vary with the Racial Composition of Local Populations: Numbers Count." *American Sociological Review* 63:587.

Figure 5.25 MacDermid, Shelley M., and Margaret L. Williams. 1997. "A Within-Industry Comparison of Employed Mothers' Experiences in Small and Large Workplaces." *Journal of Family Issues* 18:545.

Figure 5.26 Morris, Aldon D. 1993. "Birmingham Confrontation Reconsidered: An Analysis of the Dynamics and Tactics of Mobilization." *American Sociological Review* 58:633.

Figure 5.27 Boswell, Terry, and William J. Dixon. 1993. "Marx's Theory of Rebellion: A Cross-National Analysis of Class Exploitation, Economic Development, and Violent Revolt." *American Sociological Review* 58:697.

Figure 5.28 Kiser, Edgar, and Joachim Schneider. 1994. "Bureaucracy and Efficiency: An Analysis of Taxation in Early Modern Prussia." *American Sociological Review* 59:187.

Figure 5.29 Stolzenberg, Ross M., Mary Blair-Loy, and Linda J. Waite. 1995. "Religious

Participation in Early Adulthood: Age and Family Life Cycle Effects on Church Membership." *American Sociological Review* 60:84.

Figure 5.30 Baker, Wayne E., Robert R. Faulkner, and Gene A. Fisher. 1998. "Hazards of the Market: The Continuity and Dissolution of Interorganizational Market Relationships." *American Sociological Review* 63:149–50.

Figure 5.31 Smits, Jeroen, Wout Ultee, and Jan Lammers. 1998. "Educational Homogamy in 65 Countries: An Explanation of Differences in Openness Using Country-Level Explanatory Variables." *American Sociological Review* 63:264.

Figure 5.32 Mark, Noah. 1998. "Beyond Individual Differences: Social Differentiation from First Principles." *American Sociological Review* 63:309–10.

Figure 5.33 Ridgeway, Cecilia L., Elizabeth Heger Boyle, Kathy J. Kuipers, and Dawn T. Robinson. 1998. "How Do Status Beliefs Develop? The Role of Resources and Interactional Experience." *American Sociological Review* 63:331.

Figure 5.34 Webster, Jr., Murray, and Stuart J. Hysom. 1998. "Creating Status Characteristics." *American Sociological Review* 63:352.

Figure 5.35 Berger, Joseph, Cecilia L. Ridgeway, M. Hamit Fisek, and Robert Z. Norman. 1998. "The Legitimation and Delegitimation of Power and Prestige Orders." *American Sociological Review* 63:382.

Figure 7.1 Bowers, Raymond V. 1938. "Differential Intensity of Intra-Societal Diffusion." *American Sociological Review* 3:22.

Figure 7.2 Popenoe, Paul. 1938. "A Study of 738 Elopements." *American Sociological Review* 3:48.

Figure 7.3 Schuessler, Karl. F. 1948. "Social Background and Musical Taste." *American Sociological Review* 13:335.

Figure 7.4 Mangus, A.R. 1948. "Personality Adjustment of Rural and Urban Children." *American Sociological Review* 13:569.

Figure 7.5 McGinnis, Robert. 1958. "Randomization and Inference in Sociological Research." *American Sociological Review* 23:409.

Figure 7.6 Gibbs, Jack P., and Kingsley Davis. 1958. "Conventional Versus Metropolitan Data in the International Study of Urbanization." *American Sociological Review* 23:507.

Figure 7.7 Bloombaum, Milton. 1968. "The Conditions Underlying Race Riots as Portrayed by Multidimensional Scalogram Analysis: A Reanalysis of Lieberson and Silverman's Data." *American Sociological Review* 33:81.

Figure 7.8 Rubin, Zick. 1968. "Do American Women Marry Up?" *American Sociological Review* 33:755.

Figure 7.9 Armer, Michael, and Larry Isaac. 1978. "Determinants and Behavioral Consequences of Psychological Modernity: Empirical Evidence from Costa Rica." *American Sociological Review* 43:319.

Figure 7.10 Armer, Michael, and Larry Isaac. 1978. "Determinants and Behavioral Consequences of Psychological Modernity: Empirical Evidence from Costa Rica." *American Sociological Review* 43:322–23.

Figure 7.11 Armer, Michael, and Larry Isaac. 1978. "Determinants and Behavioral Consequences of Psychological Modernity: Empirical Evidence from Costa Rica." *American Sociological Review* 43:327.

Figure 7.12 Halaby, Charles N. 1988. "Action and Information in the Job Mobility Process: The Search Decision." *American Sociological Review* 53:15.

Figure 7.13 Markovsky, Barry, David Willer, and Travis Patton. 1988. "Power Relations in Exchange Networks." *American Sociological Review* 53:229.

FULL CITATIONS FOR OTHER ARTICLES
INCLUDED IN THE SAMPLE

Alexander, Jeffrey C. 1978. "Formal and Substantive Voluntarism in the Work of Talcott Parsons: A Theoretical and Ideological Reinterpretation." *American Sociological Review* 43:177–98.

Clark, Carroll D., and Noel P. Gist. 1938. "Intelligence as a Factor in Occupational Choice." *American Sociological Review* 3:683–694.

Ellis, Albert. 1948. "The Value of Marriage Prediction Tests." *American Sociological Review* 13:710–18.

Harrist, Amanda W., and Ricardo C. Ainslie. 1998. "Marital Discord and Child Behavior Problems: Parent-Child Relationship Quality and Child Interpersonal Awareness as Mediators." *Journal of Family Issues* 19:140–63.

Kanter, Rosabeth Moss. 1968. "Commitment and Social Organization: A Study of Commitment Mechanisms in Utopian Communities." *American Sociological Review* 33:499–517.

Knoke, David. 1988. "Incentives in Collective Action Organizations." *American Sociological Review* 53:311–29.

LaPiere, Richard T. 1938. "The Sociological Significance of Measurable Attitudes." *American Sociological Review* 3:175–82.

Lenski, Gerhard E. 1958. "Trends in Inter-Generational Occupational Mobility in the United States." *American Sociological Review* 23:514–23.

Merton, Robert K. 1948. "The Bearing of Empirical Research upon the Development of Social Theory." *American Sociological Review* 13:505–15.

Westoff, Charles F., Philip C. Sagi, and E. Lowell Kelly. 1958. "Fertility Through Twenty Years of Marriage: A Study in Predictive Possibilities." *American Sociological Review* 23:549–56.

Bibliography

Adorno, Theodor W. 1945. "A Social Critique of Radio Music." *Kenyon Review* 9:208–17.
———. 1954. "How to Look at Television." *Quarterly of Film, Radio and Television* 3:213–35.
———. 1973. *Negative Dialectics.* New York: Seabury.
———. 1974a. *Minima Moralia: Reflections from Damaged Life.* London: New Left Books.
———. 1974b. "The Stars Down to Earth: *The Los Angeles Times* Astrology Column: A Study in Secondary Superstition." *Telos* 19:13–90.
———. 1984. *Aesthetic Theory.* Translated by Christian Lenhardt. London: Routledge and Kegan Paul.
———. 1997. *Aesthetic Theory.* Translated by Robert Hullot-Kentor. Minneapolis: University of Minnesota Press.
———, Else Frenkel-Brunswik, Daniel Levinson, and R.N. Sanford. 1950. *The Authoritarian Personality.* New York: Harper & Row.
Agger, Ben. 1976. "Marcuse and Habermas on New Science." *Polity* 9:151–81.
———. 1979. *Western Marxism: An Introduction.* Santa Monica, CA: Goodyear.
———. 1989a. *Fast Capitalism: A Critical Theory of Significance.* Urbana: University of Illinois Press.
———. 1989b. *Reading Science: A Literary, Political and Sociological Analysis.* Dix Hills, NY: General Hall.
———. 1989c. *Socio(onto)logy: A Disciplinary Reading.* Urbana: University of Illinois Press.
———. 1990. *The Decline of Discourse: Reading, Writing and Resistance in Postmodern Capitalism.* London: Falmer.
———. 1992. *The Discourse of Domination: From the Frankfurt School to Postmodernism.* Evanston, IL: Northwestern University Press.
———. 1994. "Derrida for Sociology?" *American Sociological Review* 59:501–5.
———. 2002. *Postponing the Postmodern: Sociological Practices, Selves and Theories.* Boulder: Rowman & Littlefield.
———. 2004. *Speeding Up Fast Capitalism.* Boulder: Paradigm.
———. 2006. "Euros to America: The Disciplining, Deconstruction and Diaspora of American Social Theory," pp. 361–71 in Gerard Delanty, *The Handbook of Contemporary European Social Theory.* New York: Routledge.
———. Forthcoming. *Self and Cybersociety,* Cambridge: Blackwell.

Alexander, Jeffrey C. 1982. *Theoretical Logic in Sociology.* Volumes 1–4. Berkeley: University of California Press.

Althusser, Louis. 1970. *For Marx.* London: Allen Lane.

Bakhtin, Mikhail. 1978. *The Formal Method in Literary Scholarship: A Critical Introduction to Sociological Poetics.* Baltimore: Johns Hopkins University Press.

———. 1994. *The Bakhtin Reader.* Edited by Pam Morris. London: E. Arnold.

Barthes, Roland. 1975. *The Pleasure of the Text.* New York: Hill and Wang.

Baudrillard, Jean. 1983. *Simulations.* New York: Semiotext(e).

Becker, Howard. 1986. *Writing for Social Scientists: How to Start and Finish Your Thesis, Book, or Article.* Chicago: University of Chicago Press.

Bellah, Robert N., Richard Madsen, William M. Sullivan, Ann Swidler, and Steven M. Tipton. 1985. *Habits of the Heart: Individualism and Commitment in American Life.* New York: Harper & Row.

Berger, Peter. 1963. *Invitation to Sociology.* Garden City, NY: Doubleday.

Berger, Peter L., and Thomas Luckmann. 1967. *The Social Construction of Reality: A Treatise in the Sociology of Knowledge.* Garden City, NY: Anchor.

Blau, Peter, and Otis Dudley Duncan. 1967. *The American Occupational Structure.* New York: Wiley.

Bourdieu, Pierre. 1984. *Distinction: A Social Critique of the Judgment of Taste.* Cambridge, MA: Harvard University Press.

———. 1988. *Homo Academicus.* Stanford, CA: Stanford University Press.

Brodkey, Linda. 1987. *Academic Writing as Social Practice.* Philadelphia: Temple University Press.

Burawoy, Michael. 2004a. "Manifesto for Public Sociologies." *Social Forces* 51, 1:124–30 (within Burawoy et al. [2004]).

———. 2004b. "Public Sociologies: Contradictions, Dilemmas, and Possibilities." *Social Forces* 82, 4:1603–18.

———. 2005. "For Public Sociology." *American Sociological Review* 70:4–28.

Burawoy, Michael et al. 2004. "Public Sociologies: A Symposium from Boston College." *Social Problems* 51, 1:103–30.

Caesar, Terry. 1992. *Conspiring with Forms: Life in Academic Texts.* Athens: University of Georgia Press.

Coleman, James S. 1990. *Foundations of Social Theory.* Cambridge, MA: Harvard University Press.

Colletti, Lucio. 1973. *Marxism and Hegel.* London: New Left Books.

Covey, Steven. 1990. *The 7 Habits of Highly Effective People.* New York: Simon and Schuster.

Cronin, Blaise. 1984. *The Citation Process: The Role and Significance of Citations in Scientific Communication.* London: Taylor Graham.

Culler, Jonathan. 1982. *On Deconstruction: Theory and Criticism after Structuralism.* Ithaca, NY: Cornell University Press.

Davis, Kingsley, and Wilbert Moore. 1945. "Some Principles of Stratification." *American Sociological Review* 10, 2:242–49.

Denzin, Norman. 1992. *Symbolic Interactionism and Cultural Studies.* New York: Blackwell.

Derrida, Jacques. 1976. *Of Grammatology.* Baltimore: Johns Hopkins University Press.

———. 1978. *Writing and Difference.* Chicago: University of Chicago Press.

Durkheim, Emile. 1950. *Rules of Sociological Method.* Glencoe, IL: Free Press.

Eagleton, Terry. 1983. *Literary Theory: An Introduction*. Minneapolis: University of Minnesota Press.

England, Paula, and George Farkas. 1986. *Households, Employment and Gender: A Social, Economic and Demographic View*. New York: Aldine.

Feagin, Joe, and Herman Vera. 1995. *White Racism: The Basics*. New York: Routledge.

Fekete, John. 1978. *The Critical Twilight: Explorations in the Ideology of Anglo-American Literary Theory from Eliot to McLuhan*. London: Routledge and Kegan Paul.

Feyerabend, Paul. 1975. *Against Method: Outline of an Anarchistic Theory of Knowledge*. London: New Left Books.

Fish, Stanley. 1989. *Doing What Comes Naturally: Change, Rhetoric and the Practice of Theory in Literary and Legal Studies*. Durham, NC: Duke University Press.

———. 1995. *Professional Correctness: Literary Studies and Political Change*. New York: Clarendon Press.

Foucault, Michel. 1977. *Discipline and Punish*. New York: Pantheon.

Frankfurt Institute for Social Research. 1972. *Aspects of Sociology*. Boston: Beacon.

Friedrichs, Robert. 1970. *A Sociology of Sociology*. New York: Free Press.

Gans, Herbert. 2002. "More of Us Should Become Public Sociologists." *Footnotes* July/August, 30:10.

Garfinkel, Harold. 1967. *Studies in Ethnomethodology*. Englewood Cliffs, NJ: Prentice-Hall.

Gates, Bill. 1995. *The Road Ahead*. New York: Viking.

Gitlin, Todd. 1980. *The Whole World is Watching: Mass Media in the Making and Unmaking of the New Left*. Berkeley: University of California Press.

———. 1987. *The Sixties: Years of Hope, Days of Rage*. New York: Bantam.

Gouldner, Alvin W. 1970. *The Coming Crisis of Western Sociology*. New York: Basic.

Graff, Gerald. 1992. *Beyond the Culture Wars: How Teaching the Conflicts Can Revitalize American Education*. New York: Norton.

Grafton, Anthony. 1999. *The Footnote: A Curious History*. Cambridge, MA: Harvard University Press.

Grossberg, Lawrence, Cary Nelson, and Paula A. Treichler, Editors. 1992. *Cultural Studies*. New York: Routledge.

Habermas, Jurgen. 1971. *Knowledge and Human Interests*. Boston: Beacon.

———. 1975. *Legitimation Crisis*. Boston: Beacon.

———. 1984. *The Theory of Communicative Action*. Volume 1. Boston: Beacon.

———. 1987. *The Theory of Communicative Action*. Volume 2. Boston: Beacon.

Habermas, Jurgen. 1989. *The Structural Transformation of the Public Sphere*. Cambridge: MIT Press.

———. 1996. *Between Facts and Norms*. Cambridge, MA: MIT Press.

Hayden, Tom. 1988. *Reunion: A Memoir*. New York: Random House.

———. 2001. *Irish on the Inside*. London: Verso.

Hechter, Michael. 1987. *Principles of Group Solidarity*. Berkeley: University of California Press.

Hegel, G.W.F. 1967. *The Phenomenology of Mind*. New York: Harper & Row.

Heidegger, Martin. 1962. *Being and Time*. New York: Harper & Row.

Hochschild, Arlie. 1989. *The Second Shift: Working Parents and the Revolution at Home*. New York: Viking.

Horkheimer, Max, and Theodor W. Adorno. 1972. *Dialectic of Enlightenment*. New York: Herder and Herder.

Imber, Jonathan. 2001. Review of Agger's *Public Sociology*. *Social Forces* 80, 1:353–54.

Jacobs, Jerry. 2005. "Multiple Methods in *ASR*." *Footnotes*. December 2005. www2.asanet .org/footnotes/dec05/.

Jacoby, Russell. 1975. *Social Amnesia: A Critique of Conformist Psychology from Adler to Laing*. Boston: Beacon.

———. 1976. "A Falling Rate of Intelligence?" *Telos* 27:141–46.

———. 1981. *Dialectic of Defeat: Contours of Western Marxism*. New York: Cambridge University Press.

———. 1987. *The Last Intellectuals: American Culture in the Age of Academe*. New York: Basic.

———. 1999. *The End of Utopia: Politics and Culture in an Age of Apathy*. New York: Basic.

Jameson, Fredric. 1981. *The Political Unconscious: Narrative as a Socially Symbolic Act*. Ithaca, NY: Cornell University Press.

———. 1984. "Postmodernism, or, the Cultural Logic of Late Capitalism." *New Left Review* 146:53–93.

———. 1991. *Postmodernism, or, the Cultural Logic of Late Capitalism*. Durham, NC: Duke University Press.

Jay, Martin. 1973. *The Dialectical Imagination*. Boston: Little, Brown.

Kann, Mark E. 1982. *The American Left: Failures and Fortunes*. New York: Praeger.

Kellner, Douglas. 1995. *Media Culture: Cultural Studies, Identity and Politics between the Modern and the Postmodern*. New York: Routledge.

———. 1997. "Intellectuals, the New Public Spheres and Technopolitics." *New Political Science*:169–88.

Kiser, Ed, and Joachim Schneider. 1994. "Bureaucracy and Efficiency: An Analysis of Taxation in Early Modern Prussia." *American Sociological Review* 59:187–204.

Klein, Julie. 1990. *Interdisciplinarity: History, Theory and Practice*. Detroit, MI: Wayne State University Press.

Knorr-Cetina, Karin. 1981. *The Manufacture of Knowledge: An Essay on the Constructivist and Contextual Nature of Science*. New York: Pergamon.

———. 1999. *Epistemic Cultures*. Cambridge: Harvard University Press.

Kuhn, Thomas. 1970. *The Structure of Scientific Revolutions*. 2nd edition. Chicago: University of Chicago Press.

Lasch, Christopher. 1979. *The Culture of Narcissism: American Life in an Age of Diminishing Expectations*. New York: Norton.

Laumann, Edward O., John H. Gagnon, Robert T. Michael, and Stuart Michaels. 1994. *The Social Organization of Sexuality*. Chicago: University of Chicago Press.

Leiss, William. 1973. *The Domination of Nature*. New York: Braziller.

Lemert, Charles. Editor. 1993. *Social Theory: The Multicultural and Classic Readings*. Boulder: Westview.

———. 1997. *Social Things: An Introduction to the Sociological Life*. Lanham, MD: Rowman & Littlefield.

Lenski, Gerhard. 1966. *Power and Privilege: A Theory of Social Stratification*. New York: McGraw-Hill.

Lewis, Lionel S. 1998. *Scaling the Ivory Tower: Merit and its Limits in Academic Careers*. 2nd edition. New Brunswick: Transaction.

Lichtheim, George. 1961. *Marxism: An Historical and Critical Study*. London: Routledge and Kegan Paul.

Lukacs, Georg. 1971. *History and Class Consciousness*. London: Merlin.

Luke, Timothy W. 1975. "Culture and Politics in the Age of Artificial Negativity." *Telos* 35:55–72.

———. 1998. "Discourse and Discipline in the Digital Domain: The Political Economy of the Virtual University." *Virtual Technologies and Tertiary Education*. Edited by Michael Peters and Peter Roberts. Palmerston North: Dunmore Press.

Lyotard, Jean-Francois. 1984. *The Postmodern Condition: A Report on Knowledge*. Minneapolis: University of Minnesota Press.

Mannheim, Karl. 1936. *Ideology and Utopia: An Introduction to the Sociology of Knowledge*. New York: Harcourt, Brace and Company.

Marcuse, Herbert. 1955. *Eros and Civilization*. New York: Vintage.

———. 1960. *Reason and Revolution: Hegel and the Rise of Social Theory*. Boston: Beacon.

———. 1964. *One-Dimensional Man*. Boston: Beacon.

———. 1968. "Industrialization and Capitalism in the Work of Max Weber." In *Negations*. Boston: Beacon.

———. 1969. *An Essay on Liberation*. Boston: Beacon.

Marx, Karl. 1964. *Early Writings*. Edited by Tom Bottomore. New York: McGraw-Hill.

———. 1967. *Capital: A Critique of Political Economy*. New York: International Publishers.

Merleau-Ponty, Maurice. 1964a. *Sense and Non-Sense*. Evanston, IL: Northwestern University Press.

———. 1964b. *Signs*. Evanston, IL: Northwestern University Press.

Merton, Robert. 1996. *On Social Structure and Science*. Chicago: University of Chicago Press.

Michael, Robert T., John H. Gagnon, Edward O. Laumann, and Gina Kolata. 1994. *Sex in America: A Definitive Survey*. Boston: Little, Brown.

Mills, C. Wright. 1951. *White Collar: The American Middle Classes*. New York: Oxford University Press.

———. 1956. *The Power Elite*. New York: Oxford University Press.

———. 1959. *The Sociological Imagination*. New York: Oxford University Press.

Mulkay, Michael. 1979. *Science and the Sociology of Knowledge*. London: Allen and Unwin.

———. 1985. *The Word and the World: Explorations in the Form of Sociological Analysis*. Winchester, UK: Allen and Unwin.

Natanson, Maurice. 1970. *The Journeying Self: A Study in Philosophy and Social Role*. Reading, MA: Addison-Wesley.

O'Neill, John. 1972. *Sociology as a Skin Trade: Essays in Reflexive Sociology*. New York: Harper & Row.

———. 1974. *Making Sense Together: An Introduction to Wild Sociology*. New York: Harper and Row.

Paci, Enzo. 1972. *The Function of the Sciences and the Meaning of Man*. Evanston, IL: Northwestern University Press.

Parsons, Talcott. 1937. *The Structure of Social Action*. Glencoe, IL: Free Press.

———. 1951. *The Social System*. Glencoe, IL: Free Press.

Piccone, Paul. 1971. "Phenomenological Marxism." *Telos* 9:3–31.

———. 1975. "The Crisis of One-Dimensionality." *Telos* 35:43–54.

———. 1983. *Italian Marxism*. Berkeley: University of California Press.

Poster, Mark. 1975. *Existential Marxism in Postwar France: From Sartre to Althusser*. Princeton, NJ: Princeton University Press.

———. 1990. *The Mode of Information: Poststructuralism and Social Context*. Chicago: University of Chicago Press.

Richardson, Laurel. 1990. *Writing Strategies: Reaching Diverse Audiences.* Newbury Park, CA: Sage.

Ritzer, George. 1975. *Sociology: A Multiple Paradigm Science.* Boston: Allyn and Bacon.

Robertson, Roland. 1992. *Globalization: Social Theory and Global Culture.* Newbury Park, CA: Sage.

Rorty, Richard. 1979. *Philosophy and the Mirror of Nature.* Princeton, NJ: Princeton University Press.

Ross, Andrew. 1989. *No Respect: Intellectuals and Popular Culture.* New York: Routledge.

Ryan, Michael. 1982. *Marxism and Deconstruction.* Baltimore: Johns Hopkins University Press.

Ryan, William. 1971. *Blaming the Victim.* New York: Pantheon.

Sartre, Jean-Paul. 1956. *Being and Nothingness.* New York: Philosophical Library.

Schutz, Alfred. 1967. *The Phenomenology of the Social World.* Evanston, IL: Northwestern University Press.

Seidman, Steven, Editor. 1996. *Queer Theory/Sociology.* Cambridge: Blackwell.

Sennett, Richard. 1977. *Fall of Public Man.* New York: Knopf.

Sjoberg, Gideon, and Ted R. Vaughan. 1993. "The Bureaucratization of Sociology: Its Impact on Theory and Research," in *A Critique of Contemporary American Sociology.* Edited by Ted R. Vaughan, Gideon Sjoberg, and Larry T. Reynolds. Dix Hills, NY: General Hall.

Smith, Adam. 1937[1776]. *An Inquiry into the Nature and Causes of the Wealth of Nations.* New York: Modern Library.

Smith, Dorothy. 1987. *The Everyday World as Problematic: A Feminist Sociology.* Boston: Northeastern University Press.

Spielberg, Herbert. 1982. *The Phenomenological Movement.* 3rd edition. The Hague: Nijhoff.

Stacey, Judith. 2004. "Marital Suitors Court Social Science Spin-sters: The Unwittingly Conservative Effects of Public Sociology." *Social Problems* 51, 1:131–45.

Sykes, Charles J. 1990. *Profscam: Professors and the Demise of Higher Education.* New York: St. Martin's.

Turner, Jonathan. 1998. "Must Sociological Theory and Practice be so Far Apart?: A Polemical Answer." *Sociological Perspectives* 41:243–58.

———. 1999. "The Case for Sociology as an Engineering Discipline." Paper presented at American Sociological Annual meetings, Chicago, Illinois, August.

Turner, Stephen P., and Jonathan H. Turner. 1990. *The Impossible Science: An Institutional Analysis of American Sociology.* Newbury Park, CA: Sage.

Varon, Jeremy. 2004. *Bringing the War Home: The Weather Underground, the Red Army Faction and Revolutionary Violence in the Sixties and Seventies.* Berkeley: University of California Press.

———. 2005. "Killing the Field of Dreams: George W. Bush, Empire and the Politics of Misrecognition." *Fast Capitalism* 1.2. www.fastcapitalism.com.

Watkins, Evan. 1989. *Work Time: English Departments and the Circulation of Cultural Value.* Palo Alto, CA: Stanford University Press.

Wells, Tom. 1994. *The War Within: America's Battle over Vietnam.* Berkeley: University of California Press.

———. 2005. "Two Wars, Two Movements: Iraq in Light of Vietnam." *Fast Capitalism.* 1.2. www.fastcapitalism.com.

Whyte, William H. Jr., 1957. *The Organization Man*. Garden City, NY: Anchor.

Wilson, William Julius. 1987. *The Truly Disadvantaged: The Inner City, the Underclass and Public Policy*. Chicago: University of Chicago Press.

Wittgenstein, Ludwig. 1976. *Philosophical Investigations*. Oxford: Blackwell.

———. 1986. *The Blue and Brown Notebooks*. New York: HarperCollins.

Wolff, Robert Paul, Barrington Moore, Jr., and Herbert Marcuse. 1969. *A Critique of Pure Tolerance*. Boston: Beacon.

Index

About the Author

Ben Agger is professor of sociology and humanities and is director of the Center for Theory at the University of Texas at Arlington.